What Ministi
Christian Leaders ᴀʀᴇ ᴊᴀʏɪɴɢ . . .

"The missionary statesman Jordan Grooms once said, 'If God calls you to be a missionary, don't stoop to be a king.' In the almost 30 years I have known Bo Barredo, his passion and commitment to serve native church leaders around the world have not diminished. Our organization, Asia Harvest, has been honored to partner with ANM, and together we support over 600 indigenous missionaries among unreached people groups in Asia.

"The Apostle Peter exhorted us, 'Each of you should use whatever gift you have received to serve others, as faithful stewards of God's grace in its various forms' (1 Peter 4:10 NIV). Many mission groups start by serving those on the mission field, but sometimes the roles become corrupted, and the indigenous churches end up serving the vision of the mission organization. Not so with Bo and ANM. Over the years they have not operated with any hidden agenda, but have lovingly come alongside native leaders, through good times and difficult, and encouraged them to keep going forward for the kingdom of God.

"Bo and Marlou have been on an adventure with the Lord Jesus. They serve as a shining example of God's grace and love, which any young person starting out in their service for the Lord would do well to emulate."

—**PAUL HATTAWAY**, International Director/Founder, Asia Harvest, and author of *An Asian Harvest* and *The Heavenly Man: The Remarkable True Story of Chinese Christian Brother Yun*

"Reading the story of Bo and Marlou fills my heart with joy. I'm captivated by their compelling story of faith and determination that led to a fruitful and God-honoring global ministry. And I know it will have the same effect for anyone who reads the book. They have the gift of casting their vision so clearly that others like us have the opportunity to move the vision from 'their heart' to something tangible and concrete. At times I'm brought to tears because their story seems familiar with ours and with many others, as the heart of their story is all about being chosen and following the call."

—**ANNE BEILER**, Founder, Auntie Anne's Pretzels,
and author of *A Twist of Faith* and *Overcome and Lead*

"This book by Bo and Marlou Barredo offers a beautiful sampling of how our gracious Heavenly Father creates his fruitfulness even through imperfect believers. I praise the Lord for this touching account of the courage and dedication of ordinary people who have done great things for God. These small stories within his grand, magnificent story will inspire us all to greater love, faith, obedience, and sacrifice."

—**RON TILLETT**, Founder, Living Water Trust

"When we look back at the history of the indigenous mission movement, one of the most important milestones we can observe in the last thirty years was the pivot made by Bo Barredo to a more positive approach. Rather than view indigenous missions as a replacement for the traditional approach, Bo helped the church see indigenous missionaries as our allies in the common vision we share to reach all nations with the Gospel. This pivot happened at a crucial time and made the movement more relatable and acceptable to a broader scope of churches and believers in the West."

—**DAVID BOGOSIAN**, President and CEO,
Christian Aid Mission

"At first glance, *My Love Story with the God of Missions* is the remarkable success story of Benjamin (Bo) Barredo, a poor Filipino child who rose to a position of international recognition and influence. But one does not have to read very far before realizing that the book is much more—it is a 'God story'! Step by step, the book traces how the one true God of the Universe chose a young boy who sold boiled bananas in the street to help feed his family, gave him a heart of compassion and love for the downtrodden, developed and equipped him through life experiences, instilled in him an unshakeable faith, and used him to co-found and lead a major international missions organization that has assisted 13,500 indigenous missionaries in reaching thousands of hopelessly lost people with the saving Gospel of Jesus Christ. It is a story of how that which is humanly impossible is successfully accomplished through the actions of our sovereign God.

"For those who think they know Bo, the book will enlighten you even more about the heart and soul of this selfless man who seeks only to allow God to work through him. For others, you will be amazed to see how God works through the most unlikely people to accomplish his great purpose. There is no ending to this God story, as those who have accepted the Lordship of Jesus Christ and placed their faith in him can testify. As true believers, we will join with Bo throughout eternity in the presence of God, finally able to worship him in spirit and in truth."

—**TERRY L. FUTRELL**, Author of *Coal Dust: Growing up in Southern Appalachia* and *101: The Men of Company H, 3rd Regiment East Tennessee Infantry*

"It would be improper to speak about my friend Bo Barredo without using the Bible as a reference. If there is one verse that could sum up Bo's life and calling, it is Isaiah 43:4: 'Because you are precious in my eyes, and honored, and I love you, I give men in return for you, peoples in exchange for your life.'

"I met Bo about twenty years ago at a house meeting where he spoke. I was struck by the depth of sincerity and intimacy he reflected. No doubt, he had exchanged his life for the one Jesus offered him. Ten years later I joined the ANM staff and served under Bo's leadership, where I learned much from his interaction with people of all sorts. Through his example, ANM became a place where visitors felt welcomed, and staff encouraged. Our purpose and prophetic calling always took center stage.

"The impact of Bo's leadership flowed out of his love for Jesus. It became a ripple effect that will persist into eternity, as many sons and daughters are still being brought to glory around the globe.

"I endorse this book because Bo made the right investment. His life of service to Jesus the Messiah has borne much fruit, extending deep into the nations where countless families have been saved and set free, because God keeps His promises."

—**PAUL ROBBINS**, Director, Comfort My People, and author of *The Milkman Story* and *Inappropriate*

"There are times when you meet someone you would really like to work with, but you must release the person to God and trust that you will be reconnected if God wills. This was my situation with Bo Barredo. When he first came into my office at Christian Aid Mission in Charlottesville, Virginia, in August 1986, my heart immediately liked him, but he was uncertain about his path, and I encouraged him to continue his search for God's place. It turned out that God led Bo to Christian Aid, and I had the privilege of working with him from the fall of 1986 to the fall of 1992. In October 1992, we co-founded Advancing Native Missions (ANM) and worked together there until December 2019.

"Much of this book chronicles these thrilling years, during which the Lord Jesus allowed us to touch many nations and peoples for his name. Through our labors together, by the grace of God, untold numbers of native mission leaders and their co-workers have been directly and indirectly impacted by the resources of God's people in North America that we were privileged to steward. I prayerfully believe that we have just seen a tiny fraction of how the Lord of the Harvest will use our joint labors to impact the Kingdom, and I trust that God will use this book as a fruitful instrument in this process."

—**CARL A. GORDON**, President, 24:14 World

"This exciting book testifies to what God can do with just one life when it is committed to the lordship of Christ, dedicated to spreading the gospel, and determined to love well at all times. No human eye can see the full ripple effect of the events recorded in these pages, but I have every confidence that our Heavenly Father, who alone knows the whole story of the life and accomplishments of Bo Barredo, is very pleased.

"In 1991, Bo and his wife, Marlou, left elite professional positions and financial security in their native Philippines and moved by faith with their children to America. The early years were filled with financial and other struggles, but the entire family was 'all in' trusting God. As Bo championed the 'new thing' that God was doing in indigenous missions, tensions developed with some who were strongly committed to 'traditional' approaches to missions. Instead of perpetuating division in the Body of Christ, Bo drew a circle of love and fellowship that included all who sought to win souls for Jesus Christ. The ministry known as Advancing Native Missions that he, Carl Gordon, and a handful of others launched in 1992 is the result, and it has succeeded beyond human expectations. The amazing story is captured wonderfully in the book you hold in your hands. I believe your spirit will be uplifted and your faith strengthened as you read it. Praise the Lord!"

—**GEORGE AINSWORTH**, Executive Vice President
for International Operations, Advancing Native Missions,
and author of *Helping Christians Understand Islam*

Love and blessings,

Bo and Marlou

1 John 4:16-17

MY LOVE STORY

WITH THE

GOD OF MISSIONS

JEREMIAH
9:23-24

Thus says the Lord:
"Let not the wise man glory in his wisdom,
Let not the mighty man glory in his might,
Nor let the rich man glory in his riches;
But let him who glories glory in this,
That he understands and knows Me,
That I am the Lord, exercising lovingkindness,
judgment, and righteousness in the earth.
For in these I delight," says the Lord.

MY LOVE STORY WITH THE GOD OF MISSIONS

BO BARREDO
with Marlou Barredo
and Michael Dowling

WOOL STREET PUBLISHING
Madison, Tennessee

WOOL STREET PUBLISHING
130 Vandiver Drive
Madison, TN 37115

Scripture taken from the New King James Version®. Copyright © 1982 by Thomas Nelson. Used by permission. All rights reserved.

Scripture quotations marked (NLT) are taken from the Holy Bible, New Living Translation (italics), copyright © 1996, 2004, 2015 by Tyndale House Foundation. Used by permission of Tyndale House Publishers, Carol Stream, Illinois 60188. All rights reserved.

Scripture quotations marked (NIV) are taken from the Holy Bible, New International Version®, NIV®. Copyright © 1973, 1978, 1984, 2011 by Biblica, Inc.™ Used by permission of Zondervan. All rights reserved worldwide. *www.zondervan.com* The "NIV" and "New International Version" are trademarks registered in the United States Patent and Trademark Office by Biblica, Inc.™

Scripture quotations marked (ESV) are from The ESV® Bible (The Holy Bible, English Standard Version®), copyright © 2001 by Crossway, a publishing ministry of Good News Publishers. Used by permission. All rights reserved.

ISBN 978-0-9792325-6-5 print
ISBN 978-0-9792325-7-2 ebook

Book design by: TLC Book Design, *TLCBookDesign.com*
Cover: Tamara Dever; Interior: Erin Stark

Interior Photographs by Bo and Marlou Barredo, unless otherwise noted.

Printed in the United States of America

This book is dedicated
in loving tribute to:

The God of Missions, who declares,
"I have loved you with an everlasting love;
Therefore with lovingkindness I have drawn you."
Jeremiah 31:3

**Our faithful supporters and friends,
our co-workers, and the missionaries we serve:**
Into their stories and the stories of everyone who loves
and trusts in him, the God of Missions has written
his love story that never ends.

Maria Lourdes Carisma-Barredo, to whom God has gifted
"the incorruptible beauty of a gentle and quiet spirit,
which is very precious in the sight of God."
1 Peter 3:4

Our beloved children: Benjamin III, David, Felisa, and Jacob;
Their respective spouses: Tanya, Jennifer, Andrew, and Kristen;
And their precious children, our grandchildren:
Luke, Halle, Jessica, David, Eric, Georgia, Darcy,
Jude, Isaiah, and Ruth.

My beloved fathers: Pastor Benjamin G. Barredo,
who prepared me for the vision;
Dr. Robert V. Finley, who showed me the vision.

My other spiritual fathers, mothers, brothers, and sisters
who have come along by my side to help me work out that vision.

Our precious co-founders: Carl and Minda Gordon.

Our supporting co-founders:
Ron Tillett, Graham Stewart, and Philip Zodhiates.

LUKE
17:10

"When you have done all those things
which you are commanded, say,
'We are unprofitable servants.
We have done what was our duty to do.'"

ACKNOWLEDGMENTS

I wish to express my deepest gratitude to the God of Missions.

For my lovely wife, Marlou, and her vital contributions to this project. Every step of the way she supported me by collaborating on ideas, writing significant parts of the book, filtering information for accuracy, expertly typing the extensive drafts, and—most of all—serving as my primary encourager and chief prayer warrior.

For a special gift that comes by name—Michael James Dowling, whose editorial skills and writing are done with love, integrity, and God-delighting finesse; and for his wife, Sarah, our lovely cheerleader and a gifted, award-winning artist and illustrator with the courage and fire of a truth-speaker. Michael is an award-winning author, ghostwriter, and editor, with more than two dozen books to his credit. He and Sarah have created, among others, *Frog's Rainy-Day Story and Other Fables*, a children's picture book of eight thought-provoking fables for the entire family that teach a biblical worldview to the next generation.

For the skills and support of Tamara Dever and her multi-awarded team of Erin Stark and others at TLC Book Design, who did such an outstanding job of designing the cover and laying out the interior of this book. They are wholeheartedly committed to two pursuits: God and excellence.

For the kindness and graciousness of my close friend Pastor Clay Sterrett, a much-loved person in the community and the author of numerous books.

For the help of Michael and Lara, Ron and Pam, John and Elizabeth, Roger and Debbie, and Graham and Carol in making this book a reality.

For the encouragement and affirmations of Ken and Dolores Detweiler, Tom and Becky Borck, Tilahun Goshu and Meseret Workelul, Karen Thomas, Morris and Sue Worley, and Bong and Eimee De Guzman.

For the faithful caring of:

Dr. Harold Bare, VA	Pastor Jerry Steele, VA
Pastor Lindsay Ellis, VA	Pastor Sonny Vitaliz, VA
Pastor Lee Hess, VA	Dr. Ed Hampton, MD
Pastor Mark Clendenen, NV	Pastor Bryan Wyldes, IA
Pastors Fred and Beverly Brown, MN	Pastor Rod Hackett, AZ
Pastor Gideon Gaitano, PA	Pastor Bob Gayanilo, NJ
Pastor Ken Demeter, AZ	Pastor Nathan Lozada, MD
Pastor Ross Reider, PA	Pastor Glenn Steiner, OH
Pastor Eric Bautista, FL	Pastor Abraham Biangco, VA
Pastor Paul Ignacio, Philippines	Pastor Fred Virtucio, VA
Pastor Ernie De Vega, VA	Pastor Mariano Gabor, MD
Pastor Archie Agngarayngay, IL	Dr. Austin Spruill

For the love and encouragement of my younger brother, Pastor Ben M. Barredo, and my sisters, Gigi, Joy, and Joji.

For the gracious support of my sister-in-law, Dr. Maria Belen O. Carisma.

For the early assistance of our daughter, Felisa, who joyfully read my initial iPhone-typed drafts, and the early editing assistance of our sons, Benjie, David, and Jim.

For the expert proofreading of the final manuscript by our son-in-law, Andrew Needham, and by Misti Moyer.

For the professional services of Sharon Castlen of Integrated Book Marketing, who orchestrated the printing of this book.

CONTENTS

Note from the Editor

As Bo and I were working together on this book with the helpful assistance of his lovely wife, Marlou, he frequently would say to me, "Michael, do you think what I am doing is okay? I don't want to focus on myself. I'm doing this to honor the request of my children and grandchildren. I only want to bring glory to my Heavenly Father, the God of Missions, whom I love. This is his story. The true heroes are the indigenous missionaries and their families who are sacrificing to take God's love to unreached peoples. My story, to the extent that I have one, is written in the lives of those whom God has graciously allowed me to love and serve."

To his humble queries I would consistently reply, "Bo, I think your story will be a blessing to many. It needs to be shared with a wide audience. The way you have lived your life will encourage others to walk more closely with God as a loving Heavenly Father. People will be inspired to pray with increased honesty and faith, and they'll gain a greater appreciation for the importance of sacrifice. I believe your book will encourage fathers to better love their wives, and it will motivate parents to disciple their children with greater devotion. Leaders will learn helpful principles of leadership and the value of prioritizing people. All who read this book will be inspired to put their trust in Jesus Christ, listen for the Holy Spirit, and walk humbly with their God."

Many of Bo's close friends and associates voiced similar encouragements, and we can all be thankful that he listened. We hold in our hands the fruit of his faithfulness.

Even though Bo, as much as any man I know, does not seek or desire praise for himself, readers will notice that in these pages he is showered with considerable honor. This should encourage us all. When we submit our lives to God, God promises to accomplish marvelous things through us, and these accomplishments naturally result in praise. Jesus said, "If anyone serves Me, him My Father will honor" (John 12:26). But when the person honored is a humble servant of God—and I firmly believe Bo belongs in this category—the honor is directed to God. As the Apostle Paul said, "They glorified God in me" (Galatians 1:24).

Bo and I first met in 1991, not long after he came to America. I was on the staff of Trinity Presbyterian Church in Charlottesville at the time, and I felt privileged to have him speak in the adult fellowship I led on Sunday mornings. My wife, Sarah, and I also were pleased to have Bo and Marlou as guests for a Bible study in our home. However, even though Sarah and I have supported ANM since its founding, Bo and I never got to really know each other until we began working together on this book. Since then, we have become like brothers. I am far from alone in viewing Bo in this way. Being a friend who sticks closer than a brother (Proverbs 18:24) is one of his many admirable qualities.

While working on this book, tears would often come to my eyes. That's not because this story is sad, even though reading about the sacrifices made by indigenous missionaries can break one's heart. Rather, my tears were tears of joy, as the lives and events chronicled in these pages opened my heart to the heart of God.

MICHAEL DOWLING
Madison, Tennessee

FOREWORD

In late fall of 1988, my wife, Carol, and I received a call from Carl Gordon with a last-minute request to have a Philippine missionary speak at our Bible study. I was a bit put out, but we agreed to have him come. The man who arrived at our meeting, Bo Barredo, was not the "missionary" that I was envisioning. He was at least an inch taller than I, and there was an unusual grace and authority about him.

Perhaps the twenty of us who were present started off listening "politely" (as we Christians do), but to a person, we were wondering what this man and his story had to do with us. At least, that was what I was thinking. After all, I had just postponed whatever inconsequential Bible teaching I was doing at the time to "accommodate" this brother.

Bo shared about his background, his heritage from godly parents, and how his father had given up his profession as a lawyer to become an evangelist. He spoke about accepting the calling of Jesus Christ to cast aside the safety and prestige of his career in the Philippine government to seek out, encourage, and equip native missionaries by pleading their cases before churches and donors in America. He described the stresses that his wife, Marlou, and their children in Manila were enduring as they grappled with the sometimes-frightening realities of his new vocation as a missionary. Mostly, however, he told us about the grueling work that native missionaries were doing in the Philippines, and the often-treacherous circumstances under which they labored to spread the Gospel. He told us how a small provision for their basic sustenance and the most basic tools (a small canoe here, a bicycle there) could release these economically poor missionaries to bring in a much greater harvest for our Lord.

An "Uh-Oh" Moment

I have experienced many "aha" moments, when understanding dawned on me in an area where there had been none. What occurred in me as Bo spoke to us that night was an "uh-oh" moment! It was as though the tectonic plates of my soul shifted. The model of his life and the urgency of his message totally debased my myopic view of what God could do with one person who was sold out for him. Bo's short time with us created a desperation in me. It wasn't about "stepping up my game" as a Christian. I was not even in the game. And, apparently, I did not even know where the game was in my own walk with Jesus. I came to the realization that I was largely ignorant of how God's Spirit was moving throughout the world. Everything I thought I knew about world missions and about God's calling for his people to evangelize the world was shaken.

I was not the only one in the room so profoundly affected, though it seemed to be the men who were most deeply moved. Many of us were openly in tears as Bo shared. Frankly, all of us were catapulted into the sudden, inexorable conclusion that the most important contest of the ages, the one for the evangelization of every tribe and people group in the world, was occurring not *only* in the big cities, in the bright lights, and in the big churches. This stranger's words and presentation left no doubt that God's heart breaks for his servants in the forgotten places, the dark places, and the remote places where only indigenous missionaries ever go, or ever have gone, to preach the Gospel.

I had no context to assimilate the urgency of Bo's message: that my Heavenly Father yearns for, dotes on, and works powerfully through his servants—the native missionaries, pastors, and leaders who have been all but forgotten by his church. The paradox that Bo presented was cruel, stark, and, for me, inescapable: native missionaries are the apples of God's eye. Yet most of the first-world church fails to see them. It is often native missionaries who labor in the worst circumstances, but with the greatest success. They are, and will be, integral in reaching every village, every people group, with the Good News of Jesus Christ.

John Wesley once said, "The last part of a man to be converted is his pocketbook." Well, Carol and I had our checkbook converted that night! Within a week, we appeared at the office of Carl Gordon, a pioneer in the movement known as "native missions," asking for his suggestions about indigenous Gospel organizations and workers that we could support. We immediately added these names to the list of excellent western missionaries we were already helping. That was all we knew to do. After that, the desperation that Bo's visit had put in our hearts—to be part of what God was doing throughout the world—abated somewhat. I thought that was the end of the matter.

Doggedly Pursued

Actually, it was only the beginning. Over the next two years, I would learn something else about Bo Barredo. He sees God's people uniquely, and his stubborn love is not just relegated to missionaries. He almost never forgets a face (or for that matter, a name), and he doggedly pursues everyone the Father shows him, always calling out his or her highest purpose in the kingdom of God. After spending this one evening in our home, Bo regularly wrote to me from the Philippines, reminding me that he was grateful for our family and his time with us. For twenty-four months I avoided responding, wondering why this servant of God would have any interest in me. The truth is that he eventually prevailed in my life. He drew me into serving native missionaries in many places and for many years.

For seven years I had the privilege of sitting immediately next to him in the offices of Advancing Native Missions. Nearly every day, I asked the Lord why he would allow someone like me to have a mentor and a friend like Bo Barredo. I still ask that question!

During all this time, I observed Bo's overwhelming generosity in every situation, and I witnessed his stubborn love for his family, co-workers, friends, and the next person he would meet. I know how he and his lovely wife, Marlou, have extended sacrificial and unswerving service to our brothers and sisters in Christ who bring the Gospel to unreached people around the world. I saw how the needs of God's "native missionaries" always burden him. He carries that same burden for his friends and donors, as well.

It has been nearly thirty-four years since Bo Barredo shared God's Word in that Bible study, and much has changed. With Marlou at his side, Bo now advocates for native missionaries in nations around the world. Their service for the Lord is indeed global. Advancing Native Missions has grown from a small office with one typewriter and four unpaid workers into a well-staffed, robust ministry serving indigenous missionaries in just about every region on the planet.

One thing has not changed for me, however. Bo Barredo is my closest friend, the exemplar of everything I know about serving God, and the most loving person I have ever known. To be mentioned, even in a footnote, in his and Marlou's book is an honor and a privilege for which I consider myself completely unworthy.

GRAHAM STEWART
Member, Advancing Native Missions Board of Directors
Charlottesville, Virginia

Prologue

At the start of 2010, Bo and Marlou Barredo took a month-long mission trip to the Philippines. One of their primary purposes was to encourage pastors and their wives who were engaged in the challenging work of reaching the Waray-Waray people on Samar Island, one of the nation's least-evangelized people groups.

Accompanying Bo and Marlou were Dan Reichard and Jerry Harding of ANM, and Pastor Mike Curry, founder and president of Light Ministries in Arkansas, an ANM friend. I am including two days from the journal that Mike kept as the prologue for this book because they excellently capture the work of ANM, the gifts God has given Bo, and the dedication of the missionaries ANM serves. Even more important, they are a powerful testimony to the greatness of God.

—EDITOR

DAY 1
Out of Their Poverty

This morning we start with a time of testimony, as we usually do each session. There is no hesitation or reluctance in these people to share both the blessings of God and the needs of their lives. Just when I think I cannot stand any more blessing, I see Brother Bo get up and make his way to the front. I don't know what he is going to do, since he is not scheduled to speak.

Bo is an encourager and a giver—a lover of God and his servants. He walks over behind one of the pastors and his wife and gently puts his arms around their skinny shoulders. He then proceeds to tell us about them:

This couple ministers in a village a few hours' journey from here. It is a very poor village, and their church is quite small. The village has only 150 families in it. This pastor and his wife have four children. Their oldest son, since age twelve, has played the drums during their worship at church. He is now seventeen. His drum set is made from plastic bottles that he fills with water to provide the different pitches for the sounds. His cymbals are the lids from his mother's cooking pots and even the lid from the slop jar in the bedroom used for evening bathroom relief when the family does not want to walk outside. Imagine that . . . Pots and pans and toilet items being used for worship in the house of God! I think God would have us take an offering right now and buy this pastor's son a set of drums.

Immediately, I think, "It is a good thing that we Americans are here. There is not enough money in this entire congregation of poor missionary pastors to buy a set of drums."

After Bo prays, a wire basket is placed on a chair in front of the pastor and his wife, and the invitation is given to come and give. I try to step forward with my offering (actually, it is money that my generous supporters have sent with me), and I am nearly trampled by all the pastors and wives who are literally running up to the front to drop their gifts into the basket. There are laughs, high fives (in pure Filipino form), and hugs all around. I have NEVER seen people have so much fun giving an offering.

Finally, I manage to make it up to the basket, and I drop my offering in. On the way back to my seat, I lean over and whisper in Brother Bo's ear, "Whatever the shortage is, I will make it up. I want this young man to be encouraged, and I want this to be a testimony to his village."

When the church secretary returns with the envelope of counted pesos and the announcement is made, I'm embarrassed! Poor? Hardly! These people may only make five or six dollars per week; they may live in a one-room hut on the backside of an island whose name I can't even pronounce; and they may have more rotten teeth than good ones. But when the total of the offering is announced, there is more than enough to buy the finest set of drums in this city! The place literally erupts in applause and shouts of hallelujah! They all have just been part of a miracle.

I listen as other pastors and their wives share about how they also have been praying for drums and musical instruments. Nevertheless, they are thrilled that on this day God's blessing has come to this one pastor and his family. There is no envy or resentment—just pure joy. If God loves a "hilarious" giver, he certainly loves this place and these people!

DAY 2
The Loaves and Fishes, Philippine Version

Just when I think I've seen it all, God absolutely amazes me! I sit in complete awe at one of the most dramatic displays of the Word of God coming alive I have ever seen.

God has moved in power for over two days, and this is our final session with this wonderful group of pastors and their wives. The worship has touched heaven, and at times it has sounded as if it has originated there. Yesterday (as I have already written), God displayed his giving heart as a poor mountain pastor and his wife received the fulfillment of years of prayer—a new set of drums for their worship team at home. So, this morning, when Bo Barredo calls the pastor and his wife forward (the ones who had received the drums), I think, "Okay, he is going to use them as another object lesson for the group."

This was the understatement of the year! As Bo stands there with his arms lovingly draped around the tiny Filipino couple's shoulders, I can't believe the words that are coming forth in that deep baritone voice. "Pastor," Bo says, "yesterday God blessed you with the gift of this set of new drums that you have been praying for over many years. This was a gift that you never truly believed you would see this week. Is that true?" The pastor nods affirmatively.

Bo continues, "I want to ask you a question, pastor. If God spoke to you and asked you to give those new drums to another pastor here and his church, would you do it?"

The pastor looks surprised. I think, well, this is a great illustration. Of course, the pastor will answer, "Yes, if that is God's will, I would give them." Then, we will all say amen, applaud, and get to the point of the sermon.

From One to Another

"Okay, pastor," Bo says, "I want you to pray with your wife and ask God which pastor is to receive those new drums you were given yesterday. Then, I want you to walk over to that pastor, put your hands on his shoulders, and bring him back here to the front of the auditorium with you."

The eyes of the pastor's wife immediately fill with tears; a look of disbelief sweeps over her face. These drums were a direct answer to years of her prayers. HER SON IS THE DRUMMER IN THEIR CHURCH WORSHIP BAND. He has been praying for drums for years while playing each Sunday on his set of plastic jugs and pots and pans. NOW, GOD IS GOING TO TAKE THE DRUMS AWAY BEFORE THEIR SON EVEN GETS TO SEE HIS REFLECTION IN THE SHINE OF THEIR NEW FINISH!

The pastor bows his head and begins to pray, lips trembling. It doesn't take him long to decide which pastor deserves the drums. He looks up from his praying, drops his wife's hand, and leaving her standing at the front of the auditorium, walks straight over to where another pastor is seated. He puts his hands on this pastor's shoulders, has him stand up, and walks him up to the front of the auditorium.

In a moment, ownership of the drums is transferred from one pastor to another. The first pastor who has been praying for these drums and had originally been given them owns them no longer.

Bo now moves to this new pastor and his wife who have just taken possession of the drums. "Have you been praying for drums for your church?" he asks.

"Yes, for many months we have been begging God for instruments for our worship," the pastor answers.

"Then, these drums are truly an answer to prayer and a gift from God to you," he says. "Let us all rejoice with this couple over God's provision for them and their church." Obediently, we all applaud, but halfheartedly. The first pastor (the former recipient of the drums) stands motionless as his wife weeps. The new owners are smiling in disbelief at God's provision.

But Bo is Not Done

He turns to the new owner of the drums and his wife. "Pastor, you never dreamed you would be leaving here with the provision of a new set of drums for your church, did you?"

The pastor nods affirmatively.

"And you would never be able to afford instruments such as these on your own, would you?"

Again, the pastor nods.

"Pastor," Bo continues, "I want you to pray with your wife about which pastor God would have you give this new gift of drums away to today."

There is now so much tension in the air that it can be tasted. Even I am not sure where this is going. The pastor and his wife pray while the first pastor and his wife try to hide their tears and disbelief.

After this second couple has finished praying, the pastor makes his way into the congregation and places his hands on the shoulders of the pastor he believes should receive God's provision. By this time, it is hard for any of us to know how to react. A third pastor and his church have been greatly blessed at the great expense of two other pastors.

Over a span of some twenty minutes, Bo repeats this scenario three times. Now there are four pastors and their wives standing at the front of the auditorium, and there is only one set of drums that cannot be shared. One set of drums, and four needs. None of us knows how to respond.

Before Bo began to serve God full time, he was a brilliant attorney in the Philippines. His presentation skills and dramatic pauses would have made the most capable of trial lawyers jealous. Now, even I am saying to myself, "Lord, this is no longer funny. You need to call off the dogs. This illustration has gone far enough!"

An Invasion of Grace and Mercy

Bo stands in front of the four couples with his back to the congregation. "Just as God asked Abraham for his only son, and he held nothing back, I asked you for your newest and most precious possession today, and you held nothing back." Bo then asks each pastor and his wife to share what happened in their minds and hearts as they prayed about who would receive the gift that they thought was meant for them. As each testimony is shared, every person in the room becomes poignantly aware of what God has done through his gift that cost him so dearly. Through the drama of the drums, we experience afresh the reality of God's sacrifice.

Then comes the invasion of grace and mercy. Standing at the front of the room facing these four pastors and their wives, Bo says, "I want you all to look at me." All four of the pastors and their wives fix their eyes on the man who represents their spiritual authority and the covering through which much of their personal and church support has flowed from the US.

Bo walks up to one pastor and his wife. Calling them by name, he says, "You have a new set of drums!" He walks up to the next pastor and his wife and says, "You have a new set of drums, in Jesus' name!" And to the third pastor and his wife, "You have a new set of drums!" Finally, he approaches the couple with whom this drama of giving and receiving started: "You have your set of drums back, in Jesus' name!"

The room is electric! There is shouting, lifted hands, and deafening applause. What was an unbelievable gift yesterday of one set of drums has now multiplied into four gifts. It's a Philippine version of the loaves and fishes. Wow!

Tired Feet Are Refreshed

Bo then beckons for a pastor and his wife who are seated with the congregation to come up to the front. After explaining to the assembly that they serve in the mountains, he asks them to tell everyone what they have been praying for.

"To take the Gospel to an unreached people in another village, we need to cross a river," the pastor explains. "But our outreach angers some of the unbelievers in our community. Each time we want to cross the river, they hide the only boat. We have been praying for a small, motorized wooden boat so we can reach these peoples for the Lord."

Bo looks at the couple and says, "In Jesus' name, you have your own motorboat. No more depending on rented motorboats."

The place is now wild with worship! There is an aroma in the air; it smells like Jesus. There is a thickness in the air; it feels like a fresh dew of faith has just fallen on us all. We have not heard another sermon. WE HAVE SEEN ONE!!

The theme of the conference was "Refreshing Tired Feet." Tired feet have been refreshed. Fresh faith has shod them.

MATTHEW
24:14

"And this gospel of the kingdom
will be preached in all the world
as a witness to all the nations,
and then the end will come."

INTRODUCTION

'This humble work was written, in fear and trembling, as a way of giving thanks, praise, and glory to God, "who works in you both to will and to do for His good pleasure" (Philippans 2:13). It is to give witness to the truth that the God who calls men to know, love, and serve him is a living God. It is to testify to the sheer joy of the blessings of obedience, particularly in the preparation, training, and actual process that come about in responding to the call and working toward the goal—in this case, Matthew 24:14: "'And this Gospel of the kingdom will be preached in all the world as a witness to all the nations, and then the end will come.'"

Oswald Chambers, in his devotional *My Utmost for His Highest*, said, "What we call the process, God calls the end . . . It is the process, not the end, which is glorifying to God . . . What men call training and preparation, God calls the end . . . if we realize that obedience is the end, then each moment as it comes is precious."

This book gives an account of the gracious, timely, and merciful workings of the Almighty God in my life and in the lives of my loved ones, co-workers, friends, and supporters, as well as the native missionaries we serve. It is in the process that we experience and savor the sweetness of God's presence, love, mercies, providence, care, encouragement, comfort, miracles, vindication, and, most of all, growth in grace as we fellowship in his sufferings.

I was hesitant about writing a book despite the strong suggestions of well-meaning friends who had heard some of our "God stories" in my preaching and sharing. But on my sixty-seventh birthday, when all our children and older grandchildren graciously shared their thoughts and feelings about me, I was deeply moved when our oldest granddaughter, Halle, then fifteen years old, choking back her tears, shared how our commitment to our faith and our obedience had deeply touched her:

> One of the best qualities that you have is your commitment, and not just commitment to people, but commitment to your faith and pursuing whatever God wants you to pursue, whether you know what it is or don't know what it is, even if it means moving your entire family out of the country you've always lived in and going to a brand-new place without really knowing what's in store. I think that is something that's really inspiring me and that I always try to keep in mind—like, even if I don't know what else is going to happen, stick with it.

It is my prayer that this book would help build the faith not only of young people like Halle, but of everyone who is a God-seeker.

Lastly, I pray that this book will help heighten a believer's awareness of God's call to prayer for missions, missionary service, and resource mobilization in order to hasten world evangelization. And, "When you have done all those things which you are commanded, say, 'We are unprofitable servants. We have done what was our duty to do'" (Luke 17:10).

BO BARREDO
Crozet, Virginia

IN THE BEGINNING

If somebody asked me when my love story with the God of Missions began, my answer would be in the month of July 1901 in the Bay of San Francisco, United States of America. A vessel in port at that time named the USAT Thomas was about to voyage to the Philippines with six hundred passengers aboard. The passengers were from forty-three states, and they included graduates of 193 colleges and universities like Harvard, Cornell, Yale, and many of the other best American institutions of learning. They were the best of the best, the cream of the crop of American youth.

These passengers became known as the Thomasites, after the name of the ship. They were sent by the US Philippine Commission to enhance education in the Philippines, and they became the first American teachers and missionaries to the natives. In the ensuing years, some of them found their way to Negros Island, one of the 7,641 islands of the Philippines. The native Filipinos learned from them about this new religion, where there is eternal life in the name of the Son of God, Jesus Christ. Their message: "For God so loved the world that He gave His only begotten Son, that whoever believes in Him should not perish but have everlasting life" (John 3:16).

Two of those on Negros Island who came to faith in Christ because of the ministry of the Thomasites were my grandparents, Cresenciano and Felicidad Barredo. Here is how my father, Dr. Benjamin G. Barredo, shared the story in his book, *Why I Love America: Profiles of an Outsider Looking In*:

> The first American missionaries arrived in the Philippines in the year 1900 and immediately began preaching the Gospel.

1

Among their first converts were my father and mother. I sometimes shudder to think where I would be today, were it not for those American missionaries who chose to leave their homeland and their loved ones to carry the Gospel to my country; those who carried the good news which pointed my father and mother to the foot of "the cross of Christ."

According to folklore, those early American missionaries were described as the sweetest, kindest, most tender, loving people the Filipinos had ever met. They lived what they preached. Through their faithful efforts, many Christian schools were established now standing as universities, monuments to their work.

When my mother was still alive, she would tell me stories of those early American immigrants. She recounted how American missionaries and teachers would visit her and her friends while they were playing in the public square. My mother said that although the Americans appeared kind, she and her friends were fearful they were like former colonizers, the Spaniards. So, every time these Americans would come, she and her friends would run in different directions until one day when these Americans came, they were accompanied by American soldiers with rifles! Frightened, she and her friends scampered in different directions only to find the American missionaries, teachers and soldiers chasing after them. Since the soldiers could obviously take bigger steps and could run faster, my mother and her friends were seized by the wrist and forcibly made to go with them.

At this point in her story, my mother had tears in her eyes, and she asked me, "Do you know where these Americans took us, son?" With eyes of wonder at her story, I questioned, "Where, Mother?" With a voice of love and gratitude, sobbing, she quietly said, "Those Americans forced us to go back with them and brought us to school to be educated! Where can you find people in the world like that?"

My grandparents were a hardworking couple who sold cooking pots in the public market for their livelihood right up until the time of their deaths in the 1970s and 1980s. Their friends and neighbors knew them as faithful Sunday school teachers.

The Place of My Birth

The town of La Castellana on the island of Negros was the place of my birth. La Castellana was taken to mean "place of the Spanish people," as many landed families living there were of Spanish descent. The town is located near the foot of a dormant volcano named Mount Kanlaon. As I have said, my father was Benjamin Barredo, and my mother's maiden name was Marietta Mijares. They had married just after graduating from high school, when Father was eighteen and Mother was only seventeen. Because I was the first son, they named me Benjamin Jr. However, growing up I was called Bo by my loved ones and closest friends.

My parents had a difficult start in their married life. Father wanted to go to college and law school, but he didn't have money for that, so he worked odd jobs. One of those jobs was as an attendant at a gas station owned by his older brother, José, and another was as a part-time security guard in a sugar mill. When I was six years old and my younger brother, Ken, was five, we helped our family by selling boiled bananas in the streets of our city. Later, I worked with Mother selling bars of sweet sticky rice cakes wrapped in banana leaves in the public market for nickels and dimes. That is how we helped support our family so my father could finish law school and take the bar review.

Because of lack of finances, our meals were very simple. When we could not afford a good meal, my mother would buy one egg, usually a cracked one to save money, and she would pour it into a large bowl of rice. Then she would mix that together with salt, and we would eat it. When there was no money for an egg, she would boil rice and mix in two or three tablespoons of sugar and sometimes some salt. That's how we survived as a young, poor family.

Fascinated by Joseph

When I was six, God started to work in my life and in my heart. Every night my mother would tell us Bible stories by the light of a kerosene lamp, which was simply an empty milk can that we filled with kerosene with a piece of cloth as a wick. The Bible story that moved me most was about Joseph and his brothers. Even today, I can recall hearing about how Joseph's father loved him so much that he gave him a coat of many colors. That's how I felt about my father. I knew that he loved me, so I related to this story.

I was fascinated by the dream of Joseph in which the sun, moon, and stars bowed before him. These turned out to be his father, mother, and brothers. In my young mind I said, "Could I be that? Could I be that?" I was fascinated with how Joseph helped his brothers despite the terrible things they had done to him. Because of jealousy they had dropped him in a pit and plotted to kill him, but they instead sold him to a caravan of traders that took him to Egypt. There he was sold into slavery. Even though he served his master faithfully, he was falsely accused and put into prison. I cried for Joseph, and I loved the way he later treated his brothers. Instead of hating them for their evil, he showed them kindness.

I put that story in the back of my mind for a year or two, but when I was ten years old, a friend of our family gave us an illustrated Bible with selected stories in it. One of the highlighted stories was of Joseph and his brothers. Now, instead of simply hearing the story, I could read it and see the illustrations. For the next few years, until about age thirteen, I read that story every week. Each time I read it, I cried, because now I could understand what it meant to have a loving heart and a forgiving heart. I could see how powerful God is with a person whose heart is right before him.

For the eyes of the Lord run to and fro throughout the whole earth,
to shew himself strong in the behalf of them whose heart
is perfect toward him.

2 CHRONICLES 16:9, KJV

I didn't realize it at the time, but that story penetrated to the core of my being. It impacted my young mind as a teenager and inspired me to be a blessing to many, starting with my own brothers and sisters. I wanted to be a giving person, I wanted to be a forgiving person, and I wanted to be a blessing to the poor. I remember lying in bed by myself and crying each time I read about Joseph and his brothers. Even today, when I read the story of Joseph, I vividly remember Mother telling it to us by the flickering light of a kerosene lamp.

In My Father's Arms

Our old house was satisfactory, but the area we lived in was pretty much a slum. Dogs roamed the streets, and in the Philippines at that time, it was assumed that every dog had rabies because the disease was rampant. No tests for rabies were available, and when our neighbor's dog bit me when I was eight years old, my parents decided I should have the prescribed treatment of twenty-five injections, each taken every day for twenty-five days. If you missed one injection, you had to start all over again. Imagine how hard it is for an eight-year-old boy to be injected once a day for twenty-five days!

I obediently took the first few injections because I was afraid of displeasing my parents. My mother or father would take me to the nurse in the neighborhood, who lived quite a distance from our house, and I would get my injection. Then one day, I said to myself, "No more needle! No more needle!" I hid from my mother and from everyone else all day. I didn't understand that the injections were meant to save my life, or that I would have to start all over if I missed one injection. My young mind only understood that the needle was painful.

When night came, I was so happy that I had survived the day without being injected. But that night, I could not sleep because I was thinking about how my father would be coming home soon. Sometimes he would come in late at night because of his work. I thought, when he comes home, I will pretend that I am asleep, and maybe he will let me get by this day without my injection.

When I heard my father come home, I pretended I was sleeping. He came into our room, and I heard him say to my mother, "Did Bo get his injection today?"

"No, we didn't find him the whole day. He was out, and when he finally came home, it was late."

I was sure my father was going to spank me or at least scold me, but he did neither. I heard him lift my mosquito net. Then I felt his arms under me as he gently picked me up, brought me to his chest, and carried me outside into the cold, dark night. In the Philippines at that time, there were no streetlights. It was almost midnight, and all the people in our neighborhood were already sleeping. My father had to hurry to get to the nurse before midnight, because otherwise I would miss a day and must restart the series of injections. As he walked me to the house of the nurse, the neighborhood dogs were barking. It could have been a scary night for a young boy, but I had no fear. I was in my father's arms.

A Man of Strength

I could smell my father; it was the smell of a man. I could feel his strength; I could feel his warmth, his love, his concern. I could feel the security and the safety of his arms. Instead of being scared about the needle or the night, I savored being in the arms of my father. When the nurse rose from her sleep and injected me, it was nothing for me. I was looking forward to being walked back to our house safe and secure in my father's arms. I grew up knowing what it's like to be loved by my father. That helped me understand later what it is like to be loved by my Heavenly Father.

At the age of nine, I started attending the adult senior Sunday school class in our church, which my grandfather taught. I loved sitting and listening to him, even though everyone else was old. I deeply loved my grandfather, but the most powerful man in the world to me was my father. He was Mr. Superman. In his presence, I had no fear or concern in my heart. I was secure. From an early age, the presence of my father gave me a sense of security and love that wiped away all fears. I adored my father with my whole heart. Because my grandparents were among the first converts to the new religion of eternal life in Christ Jesus, my father was born into a Christian family. He was an eloquent and powerful speaker by the time he was in high school, and he became a Sunday school teacher for high school students.

My father enrolled in law school, but he had a difficult time because he had to earn money as a security guard and a gas station attendant, and those jobs took virtually all his time. He couldn't afford to buy law books, so he asked the dean if he could study for his exams in the law library. The dean agreed, so my father brought a kerosene lamp, mosquito net, and straw mat to the library. He studied there and slept on the floor. This was how he passed the exams in law school.

After completing college and law school, my father's next hurdle was to pass the bar exam. The bar exam in the Philippines is widely regarded as one of the most difficult examinations in the entire world. Failure is not an option. To prepare for this exam, law school graduates take a six-month intensive course called the bar review, which is conducted only in Manila. Father did not have the money to travel to Manila from our home in Bacolod City on Negros Island, stay in a boarding house, and take the bar review class.

My father's older brother said, "Ben, I have a fish trap offshore. Lord willing, if a school of fish goes into my fish trap, I will have some money so you can go to Manila to take your bar review." My father and his brother waited and waited and prayed and prayed. Time was running out because the bar review was about to start. Then, suddenly, a school of fish entered that fish trap, and my father's brother said, "Here's the money, go to Manila." That was a joyous day for my father. He took the first available ship to Manila. The bar review had already started, but he was able to catch up with the class and take the course.

There were five kids (all boys) in our family at this time, so Father had left some of the fish trap money with Mother for the family's needs for the next couple of weeks. He was not able to take enough money with him to last the entire six months of law review, so he began earning money by tutoring other people who were studying for the bar exam. He was a skilled speaker of English, and he would go to the other boarding houses where the people taking the bar review were staying and offer to give lectures on criminal law, which was one of the eight major subjects of the bar exam. He intentionally made himself available at all hours, and many invited him to dine with them or to stay as an overnight guest in their house or boarding house. By receiving free meals and lodging in this way, he was able to make it through the law review and pass the bar.

Supporting the Family

To support our family in Father's absence, Mother and I continued to sell sweet sticky rice in the public market, especially to market stall owners. They would take the rice and tell us to come back at the closing of the day when they would already have made some sales. It was during this time that I had acute appendicitis and had to undergo an appendectomy at the local public hospital. Not even two weeks after my discharge from the hospital, I was back helping Mother.

One day, she was not feeling well, and she asked me to go to the market to collect from those who had bought sticky rice. It was a five-kilometer walk each way. It was almost dark as I made my way home. About halfway to our home, four street kids, a little older than I, ganged up on me without any provocation. They probably thought I was their age because I was tall and lanky. Still weak from my surgery, I tried to defend myself. I also tried to hold on tightly to the coins I had in my pocket. They were for our dinner that night and for breakfast the next day.

As the blows came, my emotional pain was more than my physical pain. My young mind was whirling with questions: "Why are they doing this to me? What have I done?" It was my first experience with the pangs of self-pity. But it also brought home very early to my young mind and heart the pain and anguish experienced by the

downtrodden, the oppressed, and the fatherless. Some people took compassion on me and
led me home. When Mother saw me with my
bloodied face and lumps, she screamed. It was
a mother's cry.

It was my first experience with the pangs of self-pity. But it also brought home very early to my young mind and heart the pain and anguish expe-rienced by the downtrodden, the oppressed, and the fatherless.

After Father returned home and began practicing law, my mother went to college. That
was a courageous thing to do because she was
in her early thirties and the oldest student in
the entire school. After earning her bachelor's
degree, she went on to earn a master's degree
in education and became a teacher. Gradually
our family's economic condition improved. My
four brothers—Ken, Ike, Tim, and Benjie—and
my three sisters—Gigi, Joy, and Joji—and I
were very close. It was a wonderful time for our
family. Along with a number of other families
in our country's growing middle class, we had
a new large house and a brand-new family station wagon. What's
more, Father topped the election for city councilors by a landslide!

In a testimony he wrote in much later years, my father shared the
following about himself:

*I was what may be considered a self-made man, somebody who rose
from the ranks through sheer dint of hard work. My wife, Marietta
Mijares from La Castellana, Negros Occidental, whom I married
when I was eighteen and she was seventeen, came from a well-to-do
family. Her family owned a sizeable piece of property consisting of
agricultural land planted sugarcane and rice, but their wealth did
not interest me. I virtually worked my way through college, and
when I became a lawyer, I sent my wife to school . . . and later on
produced several lawyers in my family; my oldest son, Ben, Jr., his
wife, Marlou, my second son, Kenneth, and my third son, Ike. We
were becoming very prosperous.*

The Lord Comes into My Heart

One night, my father took my mother, my brothers, and me to hear an African American evangelist at the Sea Wall, which is an extension of the public plaza on the shore of our city. As he preached the Gospel, I began to tremble. My heart had been prepared because I had been in my grandfather's Sunday school class. I had heard about the great evangelist Billy Graham, and about the prolific inventor R. G. LeTourneau, who gave God 90 percent of his profits from his highly successful business ventures and retained only 10 percent.

I was only thirteen, and I felt too awkward and embarrassed at first to do anything. But my heart trembled even more as the choir powerfully sang—

Have Thine own way, Lord! Have Thine own way!
Thou art the Potter, I am the clay.
Mold me and make me after Thy will,
While I am waiting, yielded and still.

Suddenly I found the courage to go up to the front. Even then, however, I tried to hide myself among the adults. But when I accepted the evangelist's invitation to receive Christ, I was filled with happiness. Of course, my father and my mother also were very happy, but the happiest person was my grandfather. He was ecstatic!

Later, when I was baptized in the baptistry of the Bacolod Evangelical Church, the biggest evangelical church at the time in my city of half a million, my grandfather autographed his best Sunday school lesson book and gave it to me. I am so sad that it got misplaced over the years. I took my newfound faith seriously as a young man and began attending church and Sunday school classes more regularly.

Over time, my father became a famous criminal defense lawyer. His clients were usually the defendants, or the accused, and often they were poor. In small towns in the Philippines, especially in those days, there were no amusement centers. When people heard that

Ben Barredo was going to argue a case at the Municipal Hall, they would pack the courtroom to watch him. This pleased my father because he loved to play to the crowd.

Bo, 14, with his parents and brothers Kenneth, Ike, Timberlane, and Benjie and sisters, Gigi, Joy, and Joji.

Proud of My Father

Starting when I was about twelve, Father would take me, along with my younger brothers Ken and Ike, to watch him argue a case. He would load us in the vehicle, and on the way to the courthouse, he would tell us what the trial was about. During the trial, I marveled at how Father presented his arguments, cross-examined witnesses, and retorted the accusations of opposing attorneys. In my young mind, I was so proud of his eloquence, quick intellect, and heart for the poor. Watching my father fight for disadvantaged people inspired my younger brothers and me. It laid the foundation for the last thirty-five years of my life, during which I have been privileged by God to champion the cause of Christ and advocate for native missionaries.

My father was an extraordinarily generous man. He taught us all that the best life is a life lived for others. He was so generous, in fact, that my mother always kept a pair of his trousers and two of his shirts hidden under a mattress. She knew that if somebody asked Father for clothing, he would give away even his last garment. If somebody asked him for rice, even the last handful of rice our family had, my father would give it away. That is how generous he was. When our relatives who were poor came to visit, he would rush to meet them at the gate and hand them some money, so they would not feel embarrassed.

Remembering the Poor

My father would say, "Son, remember this as you grow up. If somebody in need asks you for money, do not respond only with words because words are cheap. And do not give only money; money alone is vulgar. The poor will accept the money because they need it, but their spirits are killed. Give money with words. Charity without love kills." At another time, he emphasized to us the importance of saying thank you. He said, "Gratefulness that is not expressed is ungratefulness implied."

One day when my father was at his law office and my mother was at the college teaching, I happened to notice some books in their bedroom. One of them, a book of poems, captured my attention. As I began reading one of the poems, titled "The Man with the Hoe," tears formed in my eyes. I decided to memorize the lines. When my father arrived home from work that day, I said, "Father, I have a surprise for you."

"What is it, son?" he replied.

"Listen," I said. Then, with trembling voice, I recited the following poem, stumbling on some lines:

Bowed by the weight of centuries he leans
Upon his hoe and gazes on the ground,
The emptiness of ages in his face,
And on his back the burden of the world.
Who made him dead to rapture and despair,
A thing that grieves not and that never hopes,
Stolid and stunned, a brother to the ox?
Who loosened and let down this brutal jaw?
Whose was the hand that slanted back this brow?
Whose breath blew out the light within this brain?
Is this the Thing the Lord God made and gave
To have dominion over sea and land;
To trace the stars and search the heavens for power;
To feel the passion of Eternity?
Is this the Dream He dreamed who shaped the suns
And marked their ways upon the ancient deep?
Down all the stretch of Hell to its last gulf
There is no shape more terrible than this—
More tongued with censure of the world's blind greed—
More filled with signs and portents for the soul—
More fraught with danger to the universe.

What gulfs between him and the seraphim!
Slave of the wheel of labor, what to him
Are Plato and the swing of Pleiades?
What the long reaches of the peaks of song,
The rift of dawn, the reddening of the rose?
Through this dread shape the suffering ages look;
Time's tragedy is in that aching stoop;
Through this dread shape humanity betrayed,
Plundered, profaned and disinherited,
Cries protest to the Judges of the World,
A protest that is also prophecy.

O masters, lords and rulers in all lands,
is this the handiwork you give to God,
This monstrous thing distorted and soul-quenched?
How will you ever straighten up this shape;
Touch it again with immortality;
Give back the upward looking and the light;
Rebuild in it the music and the dream;
Make right the immemorial infamies,
Perfidious wrongs, immedicable woes?

O masters, lords and rulers in all lands,
How will the Future reckon with this Man?
How answer his brute question in that hour
When whirlwinds of rebellion shake the world?
How will it be with kingdoms and with kings—
With those who shaped him to the thing he is—
When this dumb Terror shall reply to God
After the silence of the centuries?

This happened when I was sixteen years old, and I can remember many lines of that poem even today. Whenever I recite it, I get energized and teary-eyed about remembering the poor. Edwin Markham, an American poet, wrote this poem after seeing the famous painting *Man with a Hoe* by Jean-Francois Millet. The poem was published in 1899, when workers in the United States were badly exploited.

I related to this because we had the same type of situation in our country. Negros Island is known as the sugar bowl of the Philippines because sugarcane thrives in the volcanic soil of the island. Wealthy landowners planted sugarcane on plantation fields called *haciendas*. Growing sugarcane was backbreaking, oppressive work. Workers had to labor in the hot sun all day, weeding and fertilizing the fields and cutting the sugarcane by hand. Nobody wanted to do this work, so landowners imported migrant workers, called "sacadas," from other islands. Sacadas were the poorest of the poor.

Many of the landowners exploited the sacadas by paying meager wages. Then they exploited them again by selling provisions to them from their plantation store at inflated prices. Everything a worker earned often would go straight to the store, so the worker would never even get the money. Many workers would go into debt to the store, so they would essentially become slaves to the landowner.

This issue was on my heart when I began representing native missionaries. In the early years of my missions service, native missionaries were viewed as third-class missionaries because most of them were poor and ill-equipped. But they were very faithful and fruitful for the Lord's service, and my heart was with them. I have loved representing them and championing and advocating for them, all during the past thirty-five years. What a joy it is to serve them! My love for the poor was inspired by my father.

Access to My Father

When I became a teenager, every now and then my father would say to my younger brother and me, "Bo and Ken, I'm a very busy man. I am practicing law, and I am also a government official. But this is what I'd like you to know. When you need me for anything, find me, and I will be there for you. If you call me and somebody says, 'I'm sorry, your father is talking to a client,' or 'Your father is speaking to some people,' this is what I want you to tell that person, whether it is a man, a woman, my secretary, or somebody else. I want you to say, 'My father said that whenever I call, he will come to the phone. Please tell him I am calling.'"

In all my life, my father never failed to do just as he had promised. He was always there when I needed him, no matter how trivial my request. If I called him and said, "Father, I'm in school now, and I left my books on top of the refrigerator," he would say, "Wait there." Then he would leave his workplace, go home, get my books, and deliver them to me at school. I felt like the most loved child in the world. It seemed to me that my father, the most important person in all the world to me, was at my beck and call. Because my father gave me the privilege of access to him, I have been blessed through-out my life to know that I have access to my Heavenly Father. From my relationship with my father, it was a smooth transition to my relationship with my Heavenly Father.

College Years

After I finished elementary school, high school, and one year of college, I headed off to La Salle College in Bacolod City. The school was founded by Christian brothers from America who traced their spiritual roots to St. John Baptist de La Salle, a Frenchman who had a heart for the education of children of the poor, and in pursuit of this vision, the school offered scholarships to bright children from poor families and to students who had graduated with hon-ors. To fund these scholarships and finance operations, the school also accepted children from wealthy, tuition-paying families. Over time, La Salle became known as an academically excellent school for the elite, because most of the rich families on the island sent their children there. I was one of the honor students who benefited from an academic scholarship. I am so thankful for my excellent La Salle education.

In elementary school and high school, I had always taken pride in being at the top of my class. Every graduation year, I was the class valedictorian. Somehow God has given me the gift of being good with people, and in high school, I also was class president, captain of the basketball team, and commander of the cadet corps. When I transferred to La Salle in September 1968 as a sophomore, I was immediately elected to the student council by a landslide, even though I was a brand-new student. As a result, I developed sort of an inner confidence built on pride. This was not a good thing, and fortunately, God soon went to work on it.

At La Salle, something different began to happen. In most of my classes, when the professors called out the results of the examina-tions, I was always at the top in terms of the scores. The instructor might call out, "Araneta—86, Valero—87, Lozada—91." And then he would say, "Barredo—93." I would think, "Oh, I got the highest." But in my economics and political science classes at La Salle, I started hearing another name called after mine. The instructor would say, ". . . and Carisma—97."

Carisma? Who is this Carisma? No matter what I did, she would always get a higher score. If I got a 98, I would feel sure I was the highest. Then the instructor would call out, "Carisma—100." I learned that Carisma was one of my lady classmates who sat at the back of the room. She was regal, dignified, and quiet—very, very quiet. But when she spoke, everybody listened.

One day in an economics class, we were assigned a certain subject for study, so I went to the library to borrow the book. There was only one book available, and it had been given out by the school librarian, Mr. Bonifacio. I was a bit perturbed, because there was only one book, and it should not have been given out. When I asked him who had it, he said that same name: Carisma. From the smile on his face, I could tell that he favored this student. I checked into things a bit more, and I learned that Miss Carisma's first name was Marlou. I will let her tell this next part of the story.

MARLOU

Meeting the Showoff

Bo and I were classmates in our political science and economics classes, but we had not been introduced to each other. Both of us had just transferred to La Salle from other schools, and he was a year behind me. I was quite reserved, while he was tall and well-dressed. He always raised his hand whenever our professors asked us questions. He struck me as very smart and competitive. It was only later that I came to know him to be a gentleman and a very engaging person, and one who feels things deeply.

One day, while walking on our college campus with my close friend, Terry, I noticed Bo standing tall in a circle of giggling and

Marlou's parents, her brother Alfredo, and her sister Belen. Marlou is the girl on the left. After this photograph was taken, a second brother, Ramon, was born.

laughing young coeds who were apparently listening to his animated storytelling. Having been brought up in a conservative home, I was somewhat turned off by the scene. "Do you see that new transferee?" I asked Terry. "He looks so self-absorbed!" Surprised by my reaction, she just gave me a seemingly knowing smile.

When another classmate of ours invited me to a soirée in his home hosted by his younger sister, Terry boldly approached Bo and, despite my vehement protestations, asked him if he would like to be my blind date to the event. To my great relief, coupled with a tinge of embarrassment, Bo declined!

Subsequently, I came to know the reason. When Bo had gone to the library to borrow an economics book for our class assignment, he learned that the only copy had been loaned out to a student. He didn't like it when our librarian, Mr. Bonifacio, told him, "It's with Miss Carisma." I was a favorite of this librarian.

Not long after that, the La Salle College student council hosted a major fundraising event at our school stadium. The popular American pop singer and teen idol Frankie Avalon was the guest performer. My younger sister Belen, now a cardiologist/electrophysiologist, was excited about attending with me. Tickets were expensive, so we settled for less costly seats in the bleachers. From where we sat, we could see the people who had more expensive seats up front near the stage. As we waited for the show to start, I noticed Bo sitting in the front row. I said to myself, "Look at that showoff! Who does he think he is?" I pointed him out to Belen.

After the event, my sister and I waited outside for our family car to pick us up. I stood near a lamp post and watched the people as they exited the stadium. Bo has said that what happened next was one of the most beautiful moments he has ever experienced. I'll let him tell this next part of our story.

The Girl I'm Going to Marry

I had come to the fundraising event with my second brother, Ike. As he and I were exiting through the stadium door, I suddenly stopped in my tracks. My eyes fixated on a young lady with fair skin, dark almond eyes, and long, silky black hair. She was standing beside a lamp post, and her beautiful face was illumined by the white light that shone down from above. I recognized her as Miss Carisma.

I had seen Marlou before, of course, but in this moment, it was as if I saw her for the first time. I was seeing her not only through my eyes but also through my heart. I knew without a doubt that I was seeing someone who possessed purity, integrity, chastity, strength in frailness, depth of character, inner and outer beauty, and the utter loveliness of simplicity. Transfixed, I said, "Wow, what is this? What is this?"

Marlou, 7, miniature piano recital, March 23, 1957, Holy Infant Academy, Tacloban City.

A beautiful wave of well-being rose within me. The sensation was far more powerful and more sacred than what some have called "love at first sight." It was an ecstatic experience unlike anything I had previously experienced. I felt as if I were looking through the eyes of someone else. Over the span of years, I have come to believe that the someone else was the Lord Jesus. I pulled myself together enough to say to her, "Inday, may salakyan ka?" ("Miss, do you have a ride?" The word Inday is an endearing form of address to a female in our language.)

"Yes, our family car is picking us up," she replied with a smile that conveyed a bit of surprise. I wanted only to look at her and remain with her, but Ike's gentle tap on my shoulder brought me out of my stupor. I limply bade her good night.

Frankie Avalon's exciting performance was no longer on my mind. As we drove home in silence, my younger brother thoughtfully remained silent and allowed me to contemplate and savor what had just transpired. When we reached home, I turned to him and said, "Ike, did you see that girl under the lamp post outside the stadium?"

"Yes, Manong [older brother]. Who is she?"

"That's the girl I'm going to marry!" I said these words emphatically in faith from my heart with clarity of conviction. When I heard myself speak them, the same sense of well-being again rose within me. I didn't say these words in a jesting or superficial way. I meant it when I said to him, "That's the girl I'm going to marry." I was only eighteen years old at the time.

I came to respect Maria Lourdes Carisma as the brightest student on the campus. I learned that, like me, she had been the class valedictorian all the way through elementary school and high school. I viewed her as a competitor in academics, and that caused me to up my game. She unknowingly raised my standards.

During the rest of our college years, Marlou and I became partners in school activities as well as classmates. When she was invited to be editor of the school magazine, she asked me if I would be her managing editor before she accepted the position. She reciprocated by graciously typing all my school papers. These were some of my happiest years as a young man. It was wonderful being with Marlou, not only as my college sweetheart but as my co-worker in the magazine and as one of my co-leaders in school. Although we didn't realize it at the time, God was preparing us to work side-by-side in the coming years as missionaries.

Mixed Feelings at Graduation

At our graduation in April 1970, La Salle recognized three historic firsts that took place that year. For one thing, it was the first year that ladies graduated from the school. Prior to 1967, the school had admitted only men. Marlou was in the first class of female graduates. Another historic first was the conferment of a summa cum laude award. Because the school's American teachers had incredibly high standards, they had never awarded a higher academic distinction than magna cum laude. Maria Lourdes Carisma was the first summa cum laude graduate in the school's history. The third historic first was the appointment of a female editor of the college publication. That person also was Marlou.

On graduation day, I was happy that my girlfriend was the class valedictorian, but at the same time, I was a little bit sad that I had come in only second. As we waited for the awards to be announced, I thought, "She gets gold for being number one in academics and summa cum laude, but I get only silver for coming in second place and earning magna cum laude." I felt a little better when they called

21

BENJAMIN M. BARREDO, JR.
Bachelor of Arts
Social Science
English
Magna Cum Laude
Student Leader of the Year

MARIA LOURDES O. CARISMA
Bachelor of Arts
Social Science
English
SUMMA CUM LAUDE
Special Award, Journalism
Excellence in English Awarder, 4
Corps Sponsor 3
Secretary, Student Council
Editor In Chief, Spectrum 4

La Salle College 1970

me up to the stage and gave me a gold medal for Excellence in Leadership. Then Marlou was called up and given a gold medal for Excellence in Journalism for her service as the editor-in-chief of the school publication. At the end of the day, Marlou earned two golds, and I earned only one gold and a silver.

Who Is the Smartest?

Many years later, our children found these medals. They asked me, "Papa, why did Mama have two golds, and you had only one gold and one silver?"

I said with a smile, "Because your mama is more intelligent than I am. Mama is way more intelligent than Papa."

My statement apparently defined Marlou and me to all our children, because a few years later, when our two youngest children, Felisa and Jim, were in second and first grade, respectively, I overheard them talking while at home. Marlou was at work, and the children didn't know I was in the next room. I overheard Jim say, "My homework is very hard, and I need Mama or Papa to help me."

Felisa replied, "If it's very hard, you don't need Papa. You must ask Mama if it's very hard, because she is much smarter." I just smiled and kept quiet, remembering another thing Father taught me and my brothers: "The way a father can make the children happy is to love their mother."

"The way a father can make the children happy is to love their mother."

When our sons became adults, I was so blessed by something that was said by our second son, David, who today serves as a district judge in the sixteenth Judicial District of Virginia. He said in an interview, "Our family was not neglected; family was a priority. At times, we had little money coming in, or Dad would give our money away to a needy missionary, but we never felt hungry or deprived. When there were little resources, we saw the Lord provide! Our father modeled God's love in the way he treated our mother."

I had always wanted my father to be proud of me, so prior to the graduation ceremony, I said to him in jest, "Father, I worked hard as always so you could pin the gold medal on me as valedictorian. But I am sorry that in April, when you come to my graduation from college, your son will not receive the gold medal. I achieved only second place and magna cum laude. For the first time in La Salle College's existence, a classmate will be awarded valedictorian and summa cum laude. And it's a girl."

My father, also in a jesting way, said, "Son, you must learn that if you cannot beat them, you should join them." I am an obedient son, and eventually, I did propose to Marlou. But for the next two years after graduation, she and I sort of went our separate ways. She began studying for an MBA at the Asian Institute of Management in Makati, which is considered the Wall Street of the Philippines, and I went to law school at a university in Bacolod.

A Wake-Up Call

While in law school, I joined my dad in the real estate business, specializing in low-cost housing. I also was an adjunct professor of political science at the local college. In fact, my class was the most popular on campus. Available registrations for it were always over-subscribed. With the money that flowed in from the real estate business, along with financial assistance from my father, I bought a slightly used, dark green VW Karmann Ghia with a white convert-ible top. In my early twenties, I felt on top of the world cruising around town in that tiny sports car.

Marlou and I seldom saw each other, even though we were still very much in love and best friends. Before our relationship could progress, however, God had some work to do on my maturity. He did this in a dramatic way in late January 1972.

I had just picked up my younger sister, Gigi, at her school, and as I was taking her home, we were hit by a speeding sugarcane truck. The impact of the collision was so severe that it completely crushed the front of our car and dislodged the entire windshield, throwing it into our back seat. How it missed the two of us is beyond expla-nation. It was truly a miracle that neither of us was killed, but we walked away from that accident without a scratch. I took this inci-dent as a serious wake-up call from God. I felt strongly that he was saying, "Stop this foolishness and take your relationship with Mar-lou more seriously."

After a few days, I flew to Manila and waited for Marlou after school. When she came out, she rejoiced that I had not suffered any injuries. Seeing Marlou's beautiful smiling face in the flood of sun-shine on that bright February day caused my mind and heart to race back to that ecstatic moment when I had experienced the epiphany, "That's the girl I'm going to marry!"

I took Marlou to a classy restaurant close to her school. A sense of love, peace, and joy strengthened my deep resolve to marry her. I knew without a doubt that she was not simply someone I could

24

live with; she was someone I could not live without. I asked for her hand in marriage, and she joyfully accepted. For this, I have been forever thankful to God.

It took me a few more months to ask Marlou's parents for their permission to marry their daughter. I think I was nervous about what they would say because of their strong commitment to Catholicism. When I finally did get up the nerve to approach them, their only requirement was that we get married in the Catholic Church. Her mother was the most insistent one.

My dad was the chairman of the board of elders of the biggest evangelical church in Bacolod City. Nevertheless, when I told him about Marlou's parents' precondition for our marriage, he soberly said, "If you truly love her, go ahead. You have our blessing." Two years after graduating from college and four years after meeting each other, Marlou and I were engaged to be married.

ISAIAH 55:12

"For you shall go out with joy,
And be led out with peace;
The mountains and the hills Shall break forth
into singing before you, And all the trees
of the field shall clap their hands."

BECOMING ONE

Our wedding on June 17, 1972, held at the La Salle College Chapel with school chaplain Father Sebastian Van der Hoorn officiating, was a popular affair. Marlou's father was a lawyer and a high-ranking government official in our province. My family also was quite well known because my father was a successful criminal defense lawyer, as well as a popular Bacolod City public official and politician. Among the sponsors of our wedding were the governor

(above)
Bo & Marlou with ladies chosen to stand as their godmothers at their wedding.

(right)
Marlou's beloved father walking her down the aisle to give her away to Bo.

OUR WEDDING
June 17, 1972
La Salle College Chapel
with school chaplain
Father Sebastian
Van der Hoorn officiating.

of the province and the mayor of our city. Several judges and lawyers also attended. It was a big, beautiful, wonderful event. I felt so happy and blessed to be married to Marlou. There was so much love and mutual respect between us. From a practical standpoint, we were poised to be successful because of our education. More than a year after our wedding, the Lord blessed us with our firstborn. We named him Benjamin III. Marlou went back to teaching and helped support our family, while I continued my law studies.

In 1974, tragedy struck when my mother was diagnosed with cancer. The doctors said her chances of survival were only 5 to 10 percent. Father was almost inconsolable. It seemed to him to be so unfair. From a difficult start and through great sacrifices, he was now a prominent lawyer, and she was a successful college professor. Why was God now threatening to rob them of the fruits of their hard work? How could a supposedly just God be so unjust? Father revered my mother as an extraordinarily godly person. Why could he not die in her place? Life seemed to be more painful and cruel than he had ever imagined. He lost the ability to pray, and he even contemplated suicide.

In 1973, the Church of the Nazarene started a pioneering work in Iloilo City. A missionary of the denomination named Flora Wilson came to visit my father with Pastor Jerry Tingson and his wife, Ely. They surprised him by saying they had been praying for him, and Father agreed to attend the church service the following Sunday. Through a powerful message, God convicted my father of his sinful, self-centered attitude, and on October 16, 1975, he repented and rededicated his life to Jesus as his Lord and Savior. Relinquishing the fate of his ailing wife to God, he prayed, "Lord, your will be done, but if you heal my wife, I will leave my law practice and politics and serve you full-time in the ministry for as long as I live."

Passings

In late October 1975, as I was finishing my review for the bar exam in Manila, my father came to see me personally to inform me that the doctors gave Mother only a short time to live, and that she wanted to see me before she died. What a tragedy! My mother was only forty-five years old, a much-loved teacher, and a devoted mother of eight children, with the three youngest girls still living at home.

What was I to do? The bar exam was to be administered in just a few days, and I wanted to see my mother before she passed. This was painful for our entire family, and it was especially painful for me. At night, after reading my books, I would drop to the floor and cry like a baby, "Mama! Mama! Please wait for me! Wait for me!" My heart and my attention were divided between longing to go home to see my mother and preparing for the exam.

The review course for the bar exam had been conducted during the previous five months. Now it was November, and for the next four weeks, we were scheduled to take two exams every Sunday, one in the morning and one in the afternoon. The first exam was political law, and the pressure was enormous. All of us taking the exam had spent thousands of hours studying and thousands of pesos on tuition, travel, and lodging. We all realized that the odds of passing the exam were only about 20 to 30 percent. I could look around at the ten or so bar examinees staying in my boarding house and know that only two or three of us were going to pass. That meant that even after four years of college, four years of law school, and five months of law review, there would be seven or eight of us who would not pass and would not get to practice law. There is a terrible aspect of the Asian culture, which exists also in the Philippines, that has to do with suffering shame over losing face. This added to the pressure because the names of bar examinees are published in the national newspapers before the exam. Every person in the villages, towns, or cities knows who is taking the exam. When the results are published, there is terrible loss of face for the seven or eight out of ten who do not pass. Many disillusioned young men and women are unable to live properly after failing to pass the bar. I was under much pressure.

Rising Tensions

The pressure became even more intense when one of the ten or so bar examinees living with me in the boarding house betrayed me. All of us in this boarding house had been classmates and friends in law school. This betrayal came out of the blue and was totally unwarranted. But since the exam was only a month away, this was not the time to try to straighten things out. Correcting the situation probably would not have been possible in any event.

The days at the boarding house were filled with tension. One dark, cold evening, while walking back from the review center to our boarding house, I felt so forlorn and alone. I missed Marlou and two-year-old Benjamin terribly, and I was upset about my friend's betrayal. I suddenly found myself calling out to God, "Father, I'm so lonely and despondent. Are you there? Please let your presence be known, as I need assurance." Like an answer, the leaves on the trees on my left began shaking with no breeze or wind. It was almost like the sound of hands clapping. At this same time, I received counsel in my heart—a settled peace—to say goodbye to my other friends and get a room by myself in another boarding house closer to the review center. With this realization, a flash of joy went through my spirit.

> *"For you shall go out with joy, And be led out with peace;*
> *The mountains and the hills Shall break forth into singing before you,*
> *And all the trees of the field shall clap their hands."*
>
> ISAIAH 55:12

This problem with my classmate turned out to be a blessing in disguise. I realized after I relocated that I had not been taking the review for the exam seriously enough. As I have said, we were all good friends, and we would go out in the evenings, gallivanting from one pub to another. After I moved into an apartment by myself, I focused more intently on my studies. In between my reading of law books, I read my Bible and memorized verses together with statutory provisions. My Scripture readings imbued me with hope and strength to make it through each day. In retrospect, God used this unpleasant episode for my good. Years later, on one of my mission trips as a missionary, I saw my friend who had betrayed me outside a restaurant, and we forgave each other.

Because of my mother's rapidly declining health and this friend's betrayal, the pressure on me kept rising each day. I cried out to God, "Heavenly Father, you know I am not fully focused. And you know that on average only two or three out of ten pass the bar in the Philippines. Please give me your help." The verse that primarily encouraged me each day was Psalm 17:8: "Keep me as the apple of Your eye; hide me under the shadow of Your wings." I took it to heart.

Taking the Exam

On the first day of our exam, our room proctor said, "Everybody, before we start the exam, I will give you a few minutes to go to the bathroom. Then come back, and we will start the exam for political law." More than three thousand of us were taking the exam.

Judges 6:37–40 describes how Gideon placed a fleece before the Lord when he wanted to know if God was going to save Israel. I was so nervous and distraught that I felt compelled to do the same. I prayed, "Lord, you must show me evidence that you are with me. Please, Lord, I need to hear from you, or I won't be able to pass this bar in my present physical, mental, and emotional condition."

I then opened a one thousand page review book on political law that I had brought with me and began thumbing through it. I turned to one page and then to another without reading either. When I turned to the third page, for some reason I took time to read it. It was a question about the 1973 Philippine Constitution. After I had read the question and the answer, I closed the book and went to the bathroom.

As soon as I returned to my seat in the exam room, the proctor said, "Put all books and other items under your desk." He then passed out the bar examination booklets. The first question was about the 1973 Constitution! I prayed, "Lord, thank you for giving me hope! I will pass this bar. Thank you for showing your hand to me. Oh, Lord, thank you! Thank you, Lord!" I was crying, and I was giving thanks to the Lord.

The passing score was 75. I passed the 1975 bar exam with a score of 82.25 and made it home in time to see Mother just before she went into a coma. Thanks be to God!

Deep Grief

Mother died of cancer on December 12, 1975. A few days earlier, we saw Father lift her up tenderly from her sick bed and carry her outside to the white Mercedes. She was practically skin and bones and only semi-conscious. He drove her around to her favorite spots in the city for one last goodbye.

We all were in deep grief over the loss of this godly, tall, beautiful, and wonderful person, my beloved mother. We buried her just a few days before Christmas. I had never known real sadness until that day. When Christmas Day came, we all avoided looking into each other's eyes. To this day, the coming of Christmas brings back a spirit of melancholia to all of us children, because we remember exactly what happened in that season in 1975. Whenever I feel the brisk air of winter, it reminds me of the cool air that also comes to the Philippines at that time of year. It brings back memories of the most dramatic turning point in the history of our family.

Newfound Joy

But joy also comes when this December memory flashes back because this sad event helped to transform my father's life and, with it, the lives of all his children. Father shared that the passing of my mother left an emptiness that could never be filled, but at the same time, he was consoled with the knowledge that she was in heaven and that he would someday see her again. Father gradually abandoned his law practice and toured the country giving talks at conferences and churches about his newfound joy in Christ. It turned out that his three teenage daughters who were still living at home, my sisters Gigi, Joy, and Joji (Bong), had voices that blended beautifully. They accompanied him on these trips and sang Gospel songs.

Later, a family friend, Dr. Greg Tingson, who was regarded as the Philippine Billy Graham, noticed that Father's messages were affecting many people. He suggested to Father that he study at the Haggai International Institute for Advanced Leadership Training in Singapore. It was there that Father felt God's call to full-time ministry. When he returned to the Philippines, he turned over to all eight of us children whatever material wealth he had.

In July 1978, Father accepted an invitation to speak at the International Layman's Conference in San Diego, California, where he enjoyed meeting and sharing the platform with Chuck Colson. A month after returning to the Philippines, he received invitations to speak in Orlando, Florida, and Chicago, Illinois. While in Chicago, he met a lady lawyer named Cora Sevillo, whom he had known twenty years before in Bacolod City. She was far from being a Christian, but over time she began reading the Bible that my father gave her and asking him questions. Eventually, she put her faith in Jesus, and she and my father were married in Chicago on February 10, 1979.

New Vocations

Father first studied at Northern Baptist Seminary in Lombard, Illinois, and then at Moody Bible Institute in Chicago. After that, he pastored a Filipino group in Chicago. In July 1983, he felt led by the Lord to return to the Philippines with Cora as a missionary to his own people. In the years that followed, to use his own words, he became "a country preacher, a sinner saved by grace; a nobody telling everybody about Somebody who can save anybody."

In the first three years of my father's ministry, God by his grace brought more than fifty thousand souls to faith in Christ. Witnessing this powerful work of God motivated two of my younger brothers, Tim and Benjie, and my youngest sister, Bong, to join the Lord's service full-time.

Upon passing the Philippine Bar in 1975, I joined our family law firm. After two years of practicing law, I joined the leadership team of the mayor of our city as secretary to the city council. Working with a staff of twenty employees between the executive department (office of the mayor) and the legislative department (the city council with twelve councilors), I gained deep knowledge and understanding of how a medium-sized city was run. I was twenty-seven years old. Marlou taught at La Salle College and later worked in city hall. My office was on the third floor, while hers was on the fourth.

In 1977, Marlou and I were blessed with the birth of our second child, David. We were so happy. At the same time, however, we both sensed that something was missing in our marriage. For some reason, I felt a discordant note was keeping us from bonding in a truly deep and intimate way. Our principal problem seemed to be that we were not of one accord in our spiritual life. "Can two walk together, unless they are agreed?" (Amos 3:3).

Marlou will tell the next part of our story.

MARLOU

Seismic Shifts

I was born into a Roman Catholic family and raised in that faith. All throughout my life I had attended Catholic schools. I thought that salvation was being a member of the Catholic Church because that was what I was taught from kindergarten through college.

As Bo has said, my parents' precondition for our marriage, which my mother especially held, was that the ceremony take place in the Catholic Church. So we were married in the chapel of La Salle College, which is a Catholic school. For the next six years of our marriage, I was virtually the spiritual head of our family. We attended a Catholic church, we had images in our home that were given to us by my mother, and Bo went along with all of this. Although we were on the road to success by the world's standards, there was a lack of deeper peace and mutual understanding in our relationship.

That changed dramatically in September 1978 when Bo went into the hospital for what was supposed to be a minor surgery to correct a hernia problem. He expected to be in the hospital for only two or three days at most. But on the second day, after his operation, he began to hemorrhage from the medical procedure. The medical interns and nurses could not stop the bleeding, and while waiting for the doctor to arrive, Bo lost so much blood that he went into cardiac arrest. I was at the foot of his hospital bed silently but fervently praying. Bo's younger brother, Ken, and his wife, Jocelyn, also were there and praying.

I wanted to say something or do something, but I was frozen. Fear gripped my heart. I frantically stared at Bo's motionless body in the hospital bed. I felt as if my world was falling apart. My whole being was drowning, slipping away. Was this truly happening? Was I about to lose my husband, my love, my life?

"Bo, for God's sake, breathe! Please breathe!" Ken screamed. But Bo did not respond.

The doctor rushed in. He leaned over Bo's limp body and frantically pumped his chest with his hands. But still there was no response.

"God, please don't let him die!" pleaded Ken's wife, Jocelyn, through tears.

I cried out to God, silently and from deep within, "Dear God, if you will keep Bo alive, I will do anything for you! Anything! Anything! Please God, please!"

Suddenly, Bo's body moved. His chest began to heave. He was breathing! He was breathing!

The doctor removed his hands from Bo's chest, stepped back from the bed, and slumped exhausted in a nearby chair. My brain struggled to digest what had happened. Gradually, it registered that the God of Heaven had answered my prayer. Joy inexpressible flooded my heart! My whole being erupted in silent praise. "I have not lost him! I have not lost him!"

Ken and Jocelyn began rubbing Bo's feet, uttering prayers of thanksgiving to God with tears. Nurses placed needles and bags for a blood transfusion. Gradually, Bo regained consciousness.

Recovery and Renewal

The doctor said he needed to keep Bo in the hospital three more days for observation. The three days turned into three weeks. I was thankful that Bong, Bo's younger sister, volunteered to keep me company. She sang Christian hymns that enriched our spirits. One of my favorites was "Living for Jesus." Her prayers gave me comfort and strength.

One morning, Bo called me to his bedside. "You know," he said softly, "for the past six years you have been leading our family's spiritual life. I have been fine with that, but I have been strongly reminded recently that God decrees that the husband be the spiritual head. I would like to obey the Lord and take on that responsibility. Are you willing to let me do that?"

I answered without hesitation, "Yes, of course. I know you to be a good man, and I know you won't lead our family astray. How do we start?"

Bo asked me to get the Gideon Bible that was in the room. When I handed it to him, he declared, "We will start with this." He opened it to the book of Psalms and read the first three verses of Chapter 1:

Blessed is the man
Who walks not in the counsel of the ungodly,
Nor stands in the path of sinners,
Nor sits in the seat of the scornful;
But his delight is in the law of the LORD,
And in His law he meditates day and night.
He shall be like a tree
Planted by the rivers of water,

That brings forth its fruit in its season,
Whose leaf also shall not wither;
And whatever he does shall prosper.

When he had finished reading, Bo closed the Bible and looked at me. "Today, I claim this Scripture."

Suddenly, a joy-laced quietness settled in my heart. An overwhelming peace came upon me. Ever since that day, the Lord has proven that he is true to his Word. Whatever venture in life, whatever undertaking or project that Bo, by God's grace, has put his hand to, God has prospered to his glory!

After Bo was discharged from the hospital, when he had regained his strength, we went to Sunday worship at the Nazarene Church in Bacolod. We picked this church because it met in a building owned by Bo's father. During the service, the pastor asked, "Who among you would like to receive the Lord Jesus into your heart as Lord and Savior?"

By this time, I had come to realize that salvation only comes by faith in the Lord Jesus Christ. Having been convicted by the Lord that I needed Jesus as my Savior, I lost no time in going forward and praying with the pastor the sinner's prayer to receive Jesus Christ into my heart as Savior of my soul and Lord of my life.

That was in 1978, and ever since then, I have found extraordinary excitement in seeking and knowing more about my Lord Jesus Christ. After the first taste of the goodness of the Lord, I have desired more and more. I have fed on his Word, cherished his teachings, savored his truths, and claimed his promises. While singing hymns and worship songs, I understand what Charles Spurgeon meant when he said, "To know Christ is to have real life and true joy!" I truly became the new person the apostle Paul told the church at Corinth about when he said, "Therefore, if anyone is in Christ, he is a new creation; old things have passed away; behold, all things have become new" (2 Corinthians 5:17).

Bo is my first and last sweetheart, the only man in this life I have ever loved or will ever love. But the Lord Jesus is truly my first love. I never knew the unfathomable depth of true love until the Lord Jesus resided in my heart. His love has shaped our marriage, our family life, and all my relationships in a way I could have never previously imagined. I am confident that no person or circumstance can ever take away the joy in the Lord that I experience every day. I look forward to each tomorrow with blessed expectation.

I once thought that my religion and my good works would get me to heaven. Now, as the Lord provides the opportunity, I humbly share with loved ones and friends the words of Jesus recorded in John 14:6: "I am the way, the truth, and the life. No one comes to the Father except through Me." Together with Bo, I find myself loving God's people, especially those who serve him and those who are poor and needy. I am always seeking, by God's grace, to make my life, attitudes, ways, and thoughts more pleasing to God.

In 1979, the year after I accepted Christ as my savior, Bo took a new job working with the national government. We moved to Metro Manila, a metropolitan area of almost fifteen million people. Benjamin was now six years old, and David was two. We began going to church every Sunday, first to a Nazarene church and later to a Baptist church. I would hold Benjamin's hand, and Bo would carry David in his arms.

It was at the Baptist church, a few years later, that I went forward to receive water baptism. Although I had been baptized as an infant in the Catholic Church, I wanted to be baptized as a child of God. Afterwards, I excitedly told Bo, "It is so wonderful to be born again! You should have told me about this years ago!" We just laughed because we both knew he had tried.

After I became a Christian, the discordant notes disappeared. From that point on, there was so much joy and happiness in our marriage.

A Father's Love for His Son

When we moved to the city of Manila to work in the national government, we had to start afresh. The cost of living was high, and our life was difficult. It became even more difficult when Benjamin, who was seven years old at the time, contracted a serious infection in both ears. "This infection could move to his brain, and he could possibly die of meningitis," the doctor warned. He strongly recommended surgery.

We went home to our rented apartment and studied our finances. The operation would be costly, and we had nothing because we were just starting. Bo took Benjamin to our room and tearfully pleaded with the prayer, "Lord, Father God, I come to you in the name of Jesus. I know how much you love me. That's the way I love my son. This is my firstborn. He is only seven years old, and you have already graciously given me twenty-nine years of life. Father, my wife and I don't have money for the operation he needs, and there is a chance he might die of meningitis of the brain. Would you kindly take my life and whatever years I have ahead of me, would you kindly give them to him? Take my life, please, and whatever years you have for me. I'd like you to continue his life with these years."

Hearing Bo's heart-wrenching plea caused me to suddenly burst into tears! I didn't know what to think. Of course, I didn't want to lose Bo, and I also didn't want to lose Benjamin. So I prayed and just trusted that God would do what was good. A few days later, the Lord miraculously provided for Benjamin's surgery. How thankful and relieved we were!

The lesson that our children have learned from this is that their father would give his life for them. They might disagree with us at times, and we might make mistakes, but the bottom line is that we will not withhold anything good from them. Bo has said to our children, "If you need a heart, I will give my heart for you. If you need a kidney, I will give my kidney for you. That is how much your father loves you." He means this, and the children feel secure in their father's love.

As time went on, Bo and I were able to earn more money, and our standard of living improved. In 1982, God blessed us with the birth of our third child, Felisa, and in 1983, we were blessed with our fourth child, Jim. We regularly went to church, and we were a very happy, contented family. I will let Bo continue from here.

Building a Family Heritage

I have always intentionally tried to do things that demonstrate my love to our children and draw them closer. For example, when our two youngest children, Felisa and Jim, were about five and four, I would arrive at home and say, "Hey, I am going to pick up your mother in her office. Come with me."

The drive to the bank where Marlou worked took almost an hour. As the two kids sat in the back seat, I would say, "Let's have a song." I would start to sing, "Every day with Jesus . . ." Then I would stop, and they would sing from the back, "Is sweeter than the day before." Then I would sing, "Every day with Jesus . . ." Then they would sing, "I love him more and more." Then I would sing, "Jesus saves and keeps me . . ." Then they would continue, "And he's the one I'm waiting for." So back and forth like this we sang this and other songs. We had such fun and joy during the drive to the bank. They are grown now, and they still remember these times.

Often, I would offer to take our two oldest boys, Benjamin and David, to school. For example, when David went, he would sit beside me, and I would say, "David, let's pray to the Lord back and forth, okay? We'll thank the Lord for everything. Just short prayers of thanks to God." We would pray for thirty to forty-five minutes. I might say, "Lord, thank you for the beautiful day today. David, it's your turn." And David would pray something, and we would go back and forth. I always tried to use moments like these to build their faith and to develop a heart of gratefulness.

When the kids were younger, we read stories from an illustrated Bible. We would assign the reading to one of us. After reading the story, everyone present would get to sign the page. Signing a story makes a child age seven or eleven feel great. Nobody wanted to miss our family devotions because they were exciting. But if someone was absent—sometimes Benjamin would be working in a Chinese restaurant to help support our family, or I would be traveling in Asia—the person doing the reading would note who was absent on the page that was read. Going over that Bible now and reading the notes and seeing the children's signatures bring a mixture of nostalgia and joy.

When the kids became older, we graduated from the illustrated Bible to more serious books, such as a devotional by Charles Spurgeon. I would read a sentence with some word or words omitted, and the children would immediately fill in the blanks. For example, if a sentence read, "The Lord has greatly used you, dearest friends, in bringing about this new well," I might say, "The Lord has greatly used you, dearest blank, in bringing about this new blank." The kids would then compete to be the first to fill in the missing words. After the excitement of reading, we would get on our knees and pray together. Our children are grown now, and they look back on these times with great fondness. These devotionals have become part of our family heritage. God has honored these investments of time in our children with fruits.[1]

Marlou and I also agreed that whenever we find either one of us alone with our children, we should take that as an opportunity to share with them the good about the parent who is absent. Our children found it fascinating whenever I would tell them the things I love about their mother. The same happened when Marlou shared

---

[1] There is a card that I received on Father's Day in 2018 from our youngest son, Jim, that I cherish as a reflection of Jesus' abiding love in our relationship with all our children through the years:

Dear Papa, Happy Father's Day, Pa! Other terms that have come to mind are: love, time, encouragement, patience, and, above all—an example of what it means to be a God-fearing father and husband. Your impact on my life cannot be quantified or adequately captured by words, but I am eternally grateful for you, Papa. I will always cherish our times of reflection, laughter, joy, prayer, and bonding, and hope that my son and I can have the same loving relationship you and I have. I'm looking forward to more time with you in the years to come, Pa! Love, Jim

her thoughts about me. We wanted them to see that when God is in the center, there is such a thing as a happy marriage.

I will let Marlou tell the next part of our story.

MARLOU

A Heart for the Poor

Bo always has had a special heart for the poor and downtrodden, especially pastors and their families. As we walked together in one faith, loving the Lord Jesus, I observed that he was very intentional about putting his love for them into action.

One day, I called his office to inquire why his pay slips frequently had just a few pesos in them. His secretary did not know whether to sound happy or sad in giving her reply. "Ma'am, on some mornings when Mr. Barredo arrives very early in the office, he sees more than twenty janitors sitting around waiting for all the offices to open. They would greet him good morning, and he in turn would ask them whether they had eaten breakfast that morning. They would drop their heads and not say anything. Then Mr. Barredo would say, 'Please go to the cafeteria and order yourselves breakfast and tell the cashier to charge it to my salary.' His paycheck is smaller because of all the deductions." I just smiled because I am of one heart with my beloved husband.

Bo would frequently extend the love of God to local pastors. For example, he helped a young pastor and his wife who were new in the community organize an event they called "Saturday Breakfast with Us." On occasional Saturday mornings, this husband and wife would invite different couples from the community to have breakfast with them, highlighted with a time of friendly conversation and prayers. Bo insisted that the breakfasts be elegant, and he gifted the pastor and his wife with attractive plates and silverware, white linen table-cloths, and other nice accoutrements. He also provided funds in advance for delicious breakfast food. This simple strategy promoted the growth of their work and was received with much appreciation by their neighbors.

Often at Christmas, we found ourselves with extra resources because government employees received a bonus that amounted to a thirteenth-month salary. We would ask an older pastor to use this money to buy sacks of rice and distribute them to poorer pastors he knew. He was instructed to tell them it was a gift from the Lord and not to divulge our names. The beautiful stories that this older pastor related to us about the gratefulness of the pastors who received these gifts warmed our hearts.

A *barong tagalog* is an elegant shirt worn by Filipino men. Pastors in the Philippines like to wear this traditional garment when preaching, and Bo noticed that the barongs of many pastors had become threadbare. He bought new material for barongs and arranged for these to be anonymously given to them with the instructions, "Bring your barong material to Bachelor's Tailoring in Cubao and tell them it's a gift from a couple who love the Lord. They will tailor your barong for free, as the fees are already paid." Again, the stories of expressed surprise and gratitude to the Lord filled our hearts with much joy!

One day, we heard about some discord in one of the leading evangelical churches in the city regarding the retention of their pastor. Bo knocked on the door of the parsonage and introduced himself. He told the pastor that he came just to encourage him and his wife. He invited the pastor and his young family out for dinner. Later, while being driven home, the pastor profusely thanked Bo for his much-needed and timely encouragement. Later, we helped the pastor start a new church across the city.

A Multi-Millionaire

One day in 1984, when we attended a Sunday morning service at a growing church housed in a simple wood and bamboo structure, it rained so hard that the thatched roof started to leak. Several churchgoers, including Bo, got wet. After the pastor had delivered the message, prior to the closing prayer, Bo raised his hand and respectfully asked permission to speak. The pastor invited him to come up front.

"I know I'm not in any leadership position in the church," Bo began, "but as your brother in the Lord, please allow me to humbly challenge all of us in this congregation to exercise our faith by passing a resolution approving a church building program before we are dismissed today."

The church was stunned. Nevertheless, they continued to give Bo their attention, as they had the utmost respect for him and recognized his sincerity. Bo continued, "And today, if you decide how much the church building project will cost, my family, just for starters and by faith, will commit five percent of the total amount, no matter how much."

The pastor and all the members were so inspired by my husband's boldness that they unanimously passed a resolution approving by faith a considerable amount for the project. The pastor's closing prayer was Spirit-filled!

Driving home, Bo and I were quiet. After a while, I turned to him and softly inquired, "*Palangga, sa diin kita makuha sang kuwarta nga aton gin-promisa?*" (Sweetheart, where shall we get the amount we promised?) My beloved husband fought back tears and tenderly answered without looking at me, "We will pray and try to raise it . . . and if need be, we will borrow against my salary." Then he took a deep breath and added, "And if we need to borrow, we will just have to eat less."

Moments later, Bo began striking the steering wheel of our Volkswagen Beetle with his hand. Then he burst into tears and cried, "Lord, if you make me a multi-millionaire, your people will not go hungry!"

"Hush, Palangga, don't play God," I consoled him, patting his right shoulder. Looking back, after years of missionary service, I realize I wasn't the only one that day who heard the tearful cry of Bo's heart. We know now that the God of Missions already had a plan for Bo to be a conduit for many millions of dollars to be given to native pastors and missionaries. He already had a plan for the two of us to be his servants to his poorer servants around the world who are preaching the Gospel, especially to those who are preaching to the unreached.

> *He who planted the ear, shall He not hear?*
> *He who formed the eye, shall He not see?*
>
> PSALM 94:9

Bo will now continue our story.

Letting Go of the World

In 1984, God graciously continued to bless our lives. Marlou and I were filled with joy. We were eager to help those who were serving God. She worked at the Central Bank of the Philippines, the nation's monetary authority. At the age of thirty-four, she was promoted to assistant director.

In my seven years with the national government, starting as a senior staff member at the Office of the Secretary, I was promoted four times to different capacities in areas such as administration, organizational leadership, strategy development, security monitoring systems, banking, policy formulation, troubleshooting, and lecturing. My titles advanced from chief of staff of the commissioner to chief of civil security, then to assistant corporate auditor of the Philippine National Bank, and finally to assistant secretary of the Commission on Audit, one of the three constitutional commissions of the Philippine government. For my co-leadership of the Policy Study Group, a think tank of the Commission composed of a dozen of the Commission's brightest lawyers and accountants, I received the coveted State Audit Award, which was given annually to only one person or team among the Commission's almost fifteen thousand workers.

A few weeks after receiving this award, however, I started feeling restless. I was now thirty-four years old, and I had reached the apex of relative success for a public servant of my age. I appreciated how my salary allowed me to help servants of the Lord, but I was restless.

About this time, my father, who had left lawyering to serve the Lord as a missionary-evangelist, said to me with much earnestness, "Son, this restlessness is from the Lord. You have a call upon your life to serve him." He continued saying this to me until finally I told Marlou and my stepmom, Mommy Cora, "Please tell Papa Ben that I am not called to the ministry. My calling is to continue supporting those who are in the ministry."

My heart was telling me that God was calling me to serve him, but my mind was in denial because I was enjoying the fruits of success . . .

Father consistently responded, "Son, God does not need your money or your influence. He needs you!" I would gently shake my head in disagreement. I didn't know it at the time, but there was a reason why I got so upset when my father brought up the issue of calling. My heart was telling me that God was calling me to serve him, but my mind was in denial because I was enjoying the fruits of success in government. I was in my comfort zone, so to speak.

Convicted by God

Two years later, in 1986, a people's revolution arose against President Ferdinand Marcos. The Philippine government was in turmoil, and I saw this turmoil as an opportunity to take a much-needed rest, so I requested a two-month leave of absence. Marlou agreed with me that the best place for me to find rest was with my parents in Bacolod City.

I retreated to my father's house, which was quite large. A church pastored by my father of about forty to sixty attendees met every Sunday on the first floor. On the second Sunday of my two-month leave of absence, a young evangelist from America was invited by my father to occupy the pulpit. As this evangelist passionately preached the Gospel, a spark was rekindled within me. I already loved Jesus

"Lord, you know I am a lawyer, so I will decline to answer this question on the grounds that I may incriminate myself."

Christ—I truly loved the Lord so much—but I was trying to temper my commitment. I just wanted to love him; I didn't want to devote my life to serving him.

After the sermon, we were directed to open our hymnals to a certain page. As I sang the hymn on the left-hand page with the other worshippers, my bleary gaze for some reason was drawn to the page on the right. To the best of my recollection, the first line of that hymn read something like, "Did Jesus give all his best to you?"

I stopped singing and thought about how to answer this question. Then I smiled and quietly said, "Yes, Lord, you have given all your best to me. You have given me the best wife in the world, the best father in the world, the best job in the world . . . and many other bests. Thank you, Lord Jesus." I resumed singing the hymn by reading from the page on the left.

A few seconds later, my eyes were once more drawn back to the right-hand page. The second line of the hymn read something like, "Are you satisfied with Jesus?" I immediately replied in earnest, "Yes, Lord Jesus, I am very satisfied with you. Thank you, Lord Jesus."

By this time, I was beginning to feel a bit uneasy, but I forced myself to resume singing with the congregation. The words on the left-hand page for some reason were again blurry to my eyes, so I took another glance at the page on the right. The third line read something like, "Did you give all your best to Jesus?"

This caused my mind to reflect on my accomplishments and successes as a young leader up to that point. As I quickly reviewed my life, I felt convicted by God, gently but firmly. There was no place to hide. All my best efforts and accomplishments had not been done for the Lord Jesus, but for myself!

In a childish effort to avoid God's convicting questions, I tried to inject some lightheartedness into the dialogue. I said, "Lord, you know I am a lawyer, so I will decline to answer this question on the grounds that I may incriminate myself." Then, I resumed singing with the congregation from the left-hand page of the hymnal. But my attempt to parry God's inquiry with a flippant answer didn't work. After a few moments, a disquiet in my spirit caused my eyes once more to focus on the right page. The next line read, "Is Jesus satisfied with you?"

Upon reading these words, tears began to sear my eyes. I knew the answer, and it broke my heart. I hurried out of the church after the service and looked for my father. He took one look at me and knew something had happened. After he had led me to a corner of the yard where we could be alone, the words came rushing out of my mouth. "Papa, I want to seek God's will in my life. Where do I start?"

A New Direction

"Son, let's drive to the nearest telegraph office and wire your immediate irrevocable resignation to your office," Father answered. "Then, you can travel with us to the US and study for the ministry at Moody Bible Institute, just as Benjie, Bong, and I did."

"Papa, I will gladly submit my resignation. But please let me first call Marlou. She needs to agree."

At the telegraph station, I placed a long-distance call to our home in Manila. Marlou was so happy to hear my voice, and as always, I was happy to hear hers. "Palangga," I said, "I am calling to tell you that I am seeking God's will in my life. I am here in a telegraph office with Papa, and I'm about to send my irrevocable resignation to my office. What do you think?"

Unexpected news of this magnitude typically is followed by several moments of silence, as the listening party processes the information. But Marlou's response was immediate: "Praise the Lord! It's about time!"

To say I was encouraged would be a huge understatement. With a smile on my lips, I replied, "Sweetheart, thank you for your joyful answer. But don't forget that we will be losing more than half our monthly income, since I earn more than you."

"But you were the one who shared with me, 'Seek ye first the kingdom of God, and his righteousness; and all these things shall be added unto you!'" she replied. Her faith-filled response was a delightful gift from heaven! I was smiling, and in my mind's eye, I could see her beaming countenance on the other end of the line.

I sent the wire to my government office with equal measure of faith and joy. In the Philippine summer of 1986, my intense quest for professional success came to an end. I threw myself and my family's tomorrows completely at the mercy of the Lord Jesus.[2]

---

[2] Years after Marlou and I began serving the Lord, I found a copy of the Baptist hymnal we had been using when I saw those lines that affected me so profoundly. The nearest thing to the actual hymn was "Satisfied with Jesus" on page 436, a right-hand page. The words are shown below. Tears came to my eyes as I read stanzas three and four:

I am satisfied with Jesus,
He has done so much for me:
He has suffered to redeem me,
He has died to set me free.

He is with me in my trials,
Best of friends of all is He;
I can always count on Jesus,
Can He always count on me?

I can hear the voice of Jesus,
Calling out so pleadingly,
"Go and win the lost and straying;"
Is He satisfied with me?

When my work on earth is ended,
And I cross the mystic sea,
Oh, that I could hear Him saying,
"I am satisfied with thee."

Refrain:
I am satisfied, I am satisfied,
I am satisfied with Jesus,
But the question comes to me,
As I think of Calvary,
Is my Master satisfied with me?

You will find your niche

In July 1986, I found myself seated in a taxi with Father and Mommy Cora. The three of us were about to depart for the airport, where we would board a plane for what would be my first trip to the United States. As the taxi was about to drive us away, I took one last look at my precious family. My four children—Benjamin, age twelve; David, age nine; Felisa, age four; and Jim, age two—were all waving to me with expressions of love mingled with sadness that touched my heart. But it was Marlou's lovely countenance that the Lord engraved in the deepest recesses of my heart and memory. Her face reflected a sweet blend of tenderness and faith, of melancholy and hope. As my mind grasped the reality that I was about to be separated for an indefinite period from the woman I so deeply loved, and that I was going to a foreign land where my fate was uncertain, a rush of anguish and panic attempted to rise within.

One of the most important qualities a person can possess is commitment. I am talking not just about commitment to people, although that is important, but commitment to live out one's faith. This kind of commitment demands a high price. A cost must be paid to pursue God's will. Sometimes that cost is separating from family and going to a strange land. Other times, it might mean moving your entire family out of the country where you have always lived without knowing what lies ahead. In my life, this was such a time. I was tempted to fling open the door of the cab and run back to Marlou's waiting arms. After the Lord, she is my greatest and most cherished treasure. Thankfully, God gave me the courage and strength in this moment to stay the course and pursue what I believed to be his will for my life, even though it was heart-wrenching to leave my cherished wife and the mother of my children.

Let me have Marlou share here how she felt that day when I left on my first trip to the US.

MARLOU

Saying Goodbye

As I waved goodbye to Bo while he was boarding the taxi to take him to the airport for his flight to the United States, I was holding back a rush of emotions. First, I was very happy for Bo that somehow his restlessness would find its answer in the US. Knowing Bo, I realized that unless I released him to seek what he was looking for, there would be no peaceful days ahead for us. Early in our marriage, we defined love as one's consistent seeking of the other's happiness.

Second, I was driving away thoughts of the horror stories I had heard about Filipino husbands or wives who would go overseas seeking jobs and never return to their families! Third, I was trying not to entertain the logistics of taking care of our home, our four young children, and my full-time job. Trying to hold back the tears was futile.

It may sound corny to some people, but Bo and I, aside from loving the singing of hymns and worship songs, also enjoy clean love songs. One of our favorites is a heart song composed by Michel Legrand for the French musical *The Umbrellas of Cherbourg*. We had sung it to each other many times when we were together, and it reminded us of our promise to wait for each other if we were ever far apart. It begins, "If it takes forever, I will wait for you; For a thousand summers, I will wait for you." As Bo departed, I fervently hoped he would remember these words. I knew I would.

Arriving in the New Land

When we arrived in the bustling city of Chicago, the change from the damp rainy season of the Philippines to the warmth of summer elevated my spirits. It was marvelous to behold "America," the land of the people my grandparents had so revered and spoken so highly about until their last days, even though they were never able to visit the country. My father, of course, had not only been to America; he even had expressed his high regard for the country and its people by writing a book, *Why I Love America*. In fact, he loved America so much that he memorized long lines of the Declaration of Independence.

Even today, I get goose bumps recalling how my father publicly in his speaking tours in America would with fervor and eloquence recite in a captivating, oratorical style the first stirring lines:

When in the Course of human events, it becomes necessary for one people to dissolve the political bands which have connected them with another, and to assume among the powers of the earth, the separate and equal station to which the Laws of Nature and of Nature's God entitle them, a decent respect to the opinions of mankind requires that they should declare the causes which impel them to the separation.

Then, in a rising crescendo with flaring nostrils and an emotionally charged voice, he would continue:

We hold these truths to be self-evident, that all men are created equal, that they are endowed by their Creator with certain unalienable Rights, that among these are Life, Liberty and the pursuit of Happiness. That to secure these rights, Governments are instituted among Men, deriving their just powers from the consent of the governed. That whenever any Form of Government becomes destructive of these ends, it is the Right of the People to alter or to abolish it, and to institute new Government, laying its foundation on such principles and organizing its powers in such form, as to them shall seem most likely to effect their Safety and Happiness.

Father once confessed to us that in 1957, when he did not know the answer to one of the questions on the political law portion of the bar exam, he wrote the Declaration of Independence verbatim up to the line that ends, " . . . to effect their Safety and Happiness." It was not the right answer to the question, but the examiner must have been impressed because Father received a high grade on the exam.

The deeply rooted love that my grandparents and father had for America had given me a high and warm esteem for the country and its people even before I set foot on American soil. On top of this, I had been positively influenced by my American professors and the evangelists and pastors I had met through my parents in their ministry in the Philippines.

My father's undying love for America could be found immediately in the introduction of his book, *Why I Love America*. He wrote:

My oldest son, Bo Barredo, President of Advancing Native Missions in Charlottesville, Virginia, knows of my undying love for America . . . Since gratitude unexpressed is ingratitude implied, I share my simple, often crude, and naive memoirs, written in behalf of a grateful people that serve as a sacred token of expressed gratitude and thanks to a loving, caring, compassionate and unselfish American people . . .

For several years and on several occasions, whenever I have been invited to speak in American churches, I have quoted the Preamble to America's Declaration of Independence from memory, as well as the Gettysburg Address when appropriate.

It seemed a normal reaction for Americans present in the services to stand amazed at hearing a brown-skinned, flat-nosed foreigner from 10,000 miles away recite patriotic documents from the foundations of their own country by memory, when, in fact, the majority of Americans themselves do not know what these documents say, nor do they remember the price that was paid for these words to be penned. Many attending later asked why I quoted these famous declarations of freedom, and my response would invariably be, "Are you familiar with the song, 'Love Letters in the Sand'?" The last stanza of the song begins, "I memorize every line, I kiss the name that you sign . . ."

When you love someone or an ideal, you want to know all there is to know about that object of affection. I love America as much as I love my own country. I love the Country, her history, her people and the principles she was founded upon. No country's history can so easily move me to tears or touch my innermost being as greatly as the history of America and the feats of her remarkable, historical people.

I felt overwhelmingly blessed as I took my first few steps on American soil. A sense of something new and wonderful welled up within me. I had not the slightest idea about what this new thing might be. I only knew that etched deeply in my heart was a vision of my Heavenly Father seated at one end of the table, while I was seated at the opposite end. I then said to him, "I am seeking your will in my life. Please take me seriously; please, Heavenly Father."

The Search Begins

We stayed in the apartment of my youngest sister, Joji. Just as most everyone knows me as Bo instead of by my legal first name, Benjamin, one and all know my sister Joji as Bong. She was studying at Moody Bible Institute and working there as one of the secretaries of the faculty.

The next two days for me were very, very lonely. I missed the Philippines, and I especially missed Marlou and our four children. On my third morning, I felt so miserable that I could not continue sleeping, so I rose shortly before sunrise, put on some shorts and a T-shirt and my pair of sneakers, and went for a walk. Not far from Bong's apartment, there was a baseball park. Nobody was there, so I went inside and sat on one of the bleachers.

"Father, I am so lonely," I said with tears. "I feel so lonely. I miss Marlou, and I miss the children. I don't have a job, and I don't have

"Would you kindly let me know you are here? Please let me know that you are with me, that you are listening to me."

papers to stay here. I'm not even sure I want to go to Moody Bible Institute. Father, I feel so lonely. I am seeking your will in my life, but I am a total stranger in this new land. Would you kindly let me know you are here? Please let me know that you are with me, that you are listening to me."

Suddenly, a thought impressed itself on my mind. It was so clear that it felt as if my lips were uttering the words: "It is just a matter of time. You will find your niche in the work of the kingdom."

Emboldened by this encouragement, I exclaimed, "Father, if you are here, would you kindly let me know?" An instant later, a gentle breeze brushed my cheek. "That is your Heavenly Father kissing you," my mind informed me. I touched my face where the breeze had kissed me; a sense of peace settled in my heart and spirit. "Father, thank you for your assurance." This breeze had a special meaning for me because my siblings and I grew up being kissed by Father, either on the top or the side of our heads.

Hope filled me that day. God cured my loneliness by giving me hope. Hope came because God made his presence known by kissing me through the breeze. Hope also came because I heard from God in my heart that I had a niche to occupy in the work of his kingdom. So I eagerly looked forward to what was next.

During the following days and weeks, Father and Mommy Cora took me to various meetings and churches. They introduced me to numerous people, many of whom were their friends and ministry supporters. The Filipino community of believers was very gracious and generous to us.

I was especially inspired by the gentleness, love, and humility of a Filipino pastor named Dr. Archie Agngarayngay. Dr. Archie pastored a growing Filipino American church while also serving as a much-loved medical practitioner. One of his patients who had passed away had left him a million dollars in appreciation for his loving and vigilant care.[3]

One day, Father took me to Moody Bible Institute, where he had studied back in the late seventies. I was excited about visiting Moody because I expected to gain some clarity there about God's next steps for my life. During the visit, I learned exciting things about evangelist Dwight L. Moody, the founder of the school. I also heard wonderful stories about some of the esteemed graduates of Moody Bible Institute. Father showed me all around, including the classrooms where he had studied and the restrooms he had cleaned when he worked part-time on the janitorial staff to help pay for his schooling.

After we had taken in all the sights, I was quite perplexed because I sensed no excitement in my spirit. It had been a blessing to see the school's facilities and an even greater blessing to hear many "Moody God-stories." But I did not resonate with any of it. No inner messages of any kind, either negative or positive, stirred my soul. On our way home and during the days that followed, Father said nothing about our visit. Two of his most precious gifts from the Lord were wisdom and discernment. I didn't know it at the time, but he discerned after our visit that God had not called me to enroll at Moody, at least not yet, and he wisely refrained from trying to influence me. He was just as eager as I was to find the path the Lord had prepared for me.

---

[3] When I later became a full-time missionary, whenever I spoke in churches or met people, I would pray, among other things, this prayer: "Dear Father, in Jesus' name, as I speak before this church (or person/s), please set not my heart and my eyes on things which are not, but only on things which are." For me, things which are not are recognition and money, while the things which are include recommitment of lives, saving of souls, and loving favor. These are worth more than silver and gold. Dr. Archie invited me several times to preach at his church. The church he pastored, Family Worship Center, has supported Advancing Native Missions for many years.

A Fateful Trip

In early August, Brother Elias Ramos, a Filipino missionary who was a long-time friend of my parents, drove Father, Mommy Cora, and me from Chicago to Maryland and Pennsylvania. Father was scheduled to speak at some churches in these states. On our way, they decided to stop and see some friends at Christian Aid Mission in Charlottesville, Virginia. Little did I know that this stop would turn out to be one of the pivotal intersections in my life journey.

Charlottesville is a charming town that has been recognized as one of the ten best places to live in America. It is the birthplace and former home of Thomas Jefferson, the main author of the Declaration of Independence and the third president of the United States, and the home of the top-flight University of Virginia, which Jefferson founded. Charlottesville also is where the ministry Christian Aid Mission has its headquarters.

Father and Mommy Cora explained to me that one of the friends we would be seeing at Christian Aid Mission was Carl Gordon. I was informed that he headed the Overseas Department and was married to a very smart Filipina. They also told me that the other friend we were to see was Ruth Shank, who handled all Christian Aid's communications with missionaries around the world.

While Father and Mommy Cora visited with Carl, I waited in the living room of the mission's guest house. A short time later, a lady with a warm smile entered the room. "Are you Bo, Ben's son?" she asked.

I stood and nodded respectfully. "Yes, Ma'am, I am."

"I am Ruth Shank, and I am your father's friend," she said, motioning for me to sit down. "I have heard many good things about you from your father. I understand you are planning to enter the ministry, and that you came to the US to go to a seminary." With a sparkling personality and smiling, open face, she impressed me as the type of person everyone would like to have as his mother or favorite teacher.

"Yes, Miss Ruth," I answered somewhat shyly. "I'm seeking God's will in my life, and my father said that seminary should be the first step." As we talked, I could never have foreseen that this lovely lady would someday "adopt" me as one of her two sons and become both a mother and a mentor to me and Marlou![4]

Ruth began shaking her head. "I agree with your father that seminary or Bible school training is important. I have that background, and so does my husband. But you know, Bo, there are certain people in the world that God has selected and already prepared for his use. These people should not go to seminary." She paused and looked directly at me. "And I believe you are one of them."

---

[4] I am humbled and honored that Ruth Shank later mentioned our relationship in her popular book, *God Recycles Broken Dreams*. Here is what she said:

"My Virginia state license tag bears the message, 'BST4LST,' which expresses my true hopes and dreams. And truly the Lord has been fulfilling those dreams in remarkable ways . . .. In conclusion, allow me to brag on God's marvelous recycling process by sharing a poem He gave to me in 1988.

My Two Sons

In the year of 1951
A precious son was born to me;
But without life or breath—
What a tragedy!

For many years the Lord had promised
Sons would come from afar;
I'd often wonder and ponder—
Even bringing daughters on their arms.
He also promised I'd look and be radiant,
My heart would throb and swell with joy
Because of the riches brought my way
From nations of their employ.

These treasures of God
Arrived one by one;
First, Bo Barredo from the Philippines,
Then P.R. Misra of India—
two wonderful sons!

How can I fully describe
These precious sons—Bo and P.R.?
It would require volumes
To tell of their work, both here and afar.

Bo, a brilliant attorney,
But also a humble servant of the Lord;
A model gentleman, compassionate and kind
Always ready to assimilate and practice the Word.

P.R., so articulate and poised.
Full of enthusiasm and fun;
Yet takes seriously God's assignments
God's love has planted you there
Never to depart.

And I'm reminded once again
That God never deals in less;
Instead of one son I had hoped for
With two I have been blessed.

Meeting Carl Gordon

I was taken aback and somewhat offended. Was she saying that I was not qualified to go to seminary and serve the Lord? This was how I interpreted her statement because I was immature in terms of missionary service. But I kept quiet and refrained from asking her why she made this statement. Just then, our Filipino missionary friend, Brother Elias, entered the room and informed me that Carl Gordon wanted to meet me. I excused myself and went looking for Carl's office.

Within fifteen minutes of entering Carl's office, I knew I was in the presence of a genuinely sincere man of God. He talked at length with tears about the need to love and support native missionaries who are declaring the Good News in many parts of the world. Our conversation was exciting and passionate.

When Carl asked me for my thoughts, I said, "This is all new to me and a bit difficult to grasp, but maybe I have some understanding about the mission of Christian Aid because my wife and I help the poorer pastors in my country. We have provided them with preaching shirts, for example, and we have given sacks of rice to poorer families. This is what I know about loving God's servants."

As we were parting, Carl said, "Brother, if you do not find God's will for your life in Chicago or elsewhere, would you come back again so we can talk some more? We will send you tickets so you can travel here." I learned later that Carl had interviewed hundreds of missionaries and had never said or offered anything like this.

I nodded and respectfully thanked him. On the way back to the car, Brother Elias appeared to be excited. "Bo, what did Carl say to you? He has considerable influence here at Christian Aid."

I replied in jest, "Nothing much, Brother Elias, except that he offered me the job of vice president." We both laughed. I didn't take my time with Carl very seriously from a personal standpoint because Christian Aid was not in my thinking. Little did I know that when ANM started in 1992, I would be vice president and Carl would be president.

Meeting Dr. Finley

Before Brother Elias and I reached the car, word came to us that Dr. Bob Finley, the founder and president of Christian Aid, had invited us to stay for lunch. When we entered the dining area of the ministry's guest house, I noticed that our seats at the long dinner table had already been assigned. Dr. Finley sat at the head of the table, and I was seated at the other end opposite him. My parents and Brother Elias sat on Dr. Finley's left, and an older missionary couple visiting from India sat on his right. After Dr. Finley prayed, he presided over our conversation.

What an honor this was! As a young evangelist in the late 1940s, Dr. Finley had preached with Dr. Billy Graham at Youth for Christ rallies. He also had traveled to China and South Korea as a missionary with Bob Pierce, the amazing Christian who went on to found World Vision and Samaritan's Purse. A tall and very dignified-looking man, Dr. Finley spoke with authority and projected an aura of commanding strength. I have a high respect and a healthy fondness for father figures, borne mainly in my family upbringing and my deep love for my Heavenly Father and his only begotten Son, the Lord Jesus. I immediately became fascinated by this unique man of God.

During the meal, I remained quiet, but I noticed that Dr. Finley kept glancing in my direction. Suddenly, he looked straight at me and bellowed, "Young man, do you know what 'grace' is?"

This caught me totally by surprise. My legal training had taught me not to risk an argument with an expert witness, and Dr. Finley certainly fit that description. He was very knowledgeable on matters of theology and Christian doctrine, and his elegant demeanor commanded respect. I hesitated to respond, so I politely shook my head.

Dr. Finley then began to expound with authority on the meaning of grace. "The word for grace in the Greek language is charisma . . .," he began.

When he said these words, like a schoolboy who has just remembered the correct answer to a teacher's query, I quickly raised my hand. "Excuse me, Dr. Finley. I may not know 'grace,' but I know 'Carisma' well."

A puzzled look came over Dr. Finley's face. For a moment, he was speechless. The Indian couple appeared equally perplexed. Out of the corner of my eye, I noticed that Father and Mommy Cora were smiling. They seemed to know where this was heading.

"You see, sir," I continued, "my wife's name before we were married was Maria Lourdes Carisma. And in college, our American professors liked her family name so much they called her Carisma. So I really know Carisma. In fact, I live with Carisma, and I love Carisma!"

Dr. Finley had a reputation for possessing a photographic memory. This later worked to my advantage, because he never forgot this answer nor the one who gave it. Our stimulating and respectful dinner-table interaction was the beginning of my relationship with this remarkable man, whom I consider to be one of the greatest missionaries of the twentieth century. He was my beloved spiritual father and mentor. Through the years, our relationship involved love, joy, separation, pain, and sweet reconciliation.[5]

---

[5] The visit Marlou and I had with Dr. Finley at a hospice in March 2019 is fresh in my memory. He appeared happy to see us even though his first words to us were, "I am dying." We stood on each side of his bed and gently held his hands and prayed for him. As we were leaving and saying our goodbyes, I said to him, "I love you." His response I will never forget. He said, "I love you, Bo." Cynthia, his wife, heard it and said afterward, "I have not heard him say those words openly to anyone." I was not surprised. He was a father to me. And I was a son to him. He left me a great legacy: his God-given vision.

This expression of love culminated in my delivering a eulogy with a tearful and grateful heart during his April 6, 2019, memorial service, thirty-three years after our first meeting in August 1986. I have included this eulogy at the end of this chapter because I made him a promise that in the subsequent years I will have people remember him as one of the greatest missionaries of the twentieth century.

Dr. Finley has been called the "father of the global indigenous missionary movement." A couple of months after he died, it was a great honor for me to be one of the first two people to receive the Dr. Robert V. Finley Leadership Award in global evangelization through indigenous missions. In the presentation at a COSIM (Coalition on Support for Indigenous Missions) conference in Charlottesville, David Bogosian, President and CEO of Christian Aid Mission, deeply honored me with the following words:

Visiting with Dr. Hampton

One of our stops on this trip was at Emmanuel Baptist Temple in Hagerstown, Maryland. The pastor, Dr. Ed Hampton, is another spiritual father God has given me. He has the scrutinizing and discerning demeanor of a sitting judge when he looks you in the eye, but his loving, fatherly ways make one want to adopt him as a father. A much-loved pastor and founder of the church and a much-respected figure in the Christian community, he is also adored by his wife and four daughters. He came to me and said, "Your father is going to speak in the worship service, and I would like you to speak in Sunday school."

"I'm not a missionary or a pastor," I respectfully protested. I was thirty-six years old, and although I had spoken publicly during my student days and government service, I had never spoken in a church. I felt very inadequate.

"Just share your testimony, Bo," he insisted.

I trusted that God was the one calling me to do this. So I stood that morning before the Sunday school class and shared from my heart about my heritage, the heritage of those who fear God's name, the first American missionaries, my grandparents, what happened in the revolution against Marcos, and other things. I say this in humility, because all glory belongs to God, but the people were transfixed. Afterwards, I was so nervous that I retreated immediately to the bathroom because I felt like vomiting. Years later, as a missionary speaker, I found out that such accompanying nervousness was borne not out of fear of man but out of a godly and holy

---

"When we look back at the history of the indigenous mission movement, one of the most important milestones we can observe in the last thirty years was the pivot made by Bo Barredo to a more positive approach. Rather than view indigenous missions as a replacement for the traditional approach, Bo helped the church see them as our allies in the common vision we share to reach all nations with the Gospel. This pivot happened at a crucial time and made the movement more relatable and acceptable to a broader scope of churches and believers in the West."

fear of speaking about the creator of the heavens and the earth, the God of the Universe.

Dr. Hampton followed me and said, "Bo, you are a great communicator—an excellent communicator! You are like your dad."

In retrospect, I can see that God was preparing me for such a time as this. As a student leader and activist, as well as in my job with the government in Manila, I was considered a very good speaker. I didn't know then that God would allow me to use this gift in missions work. This was my first exposure to the American church. Dr. Hampton cured my nervousness with his fatherly encouragement. In the ensuing years, he would become one of the most beloved spiritual fathers the God of Missions would bring into my life.

More than thirty years later, Dr. Hampton and I are still in communication. I love him, and he loves me. When we began our US missionary work at Christian Aid, he sent us a new desktop computer. Later, when we started Advancing Native Missions, Dr. Hampton sent Marlou and me a brand-new laptop to replace the office computer we were using, which we had retrieved from the dumpster and cleaned of nicotine stains.

Another Separation

After we had returned to Chicago, my father said, "Son, your mommy and I are going back to the Philippines. Would you like to go back with us and pursue God's will for your life in the Philippines, or would you like to stay here in the United States?"

I said, "Father, I came here to seek God's will in my life, and I believe I can find it here. I'd like to stay."

My father felt sad about leaving me in Chicago, and I felt sad about staying in America without him. But he respected my decision, and I was convinced that I was obeying God's will. Father and Mommy Cora left me in the care of their friend, Brother Elias. He would go around to different churches speaking and advocating for needy pastors and missionaries in the Philippines. He would raise money and send it to them so they could buy books, equipment, and other things they needed in the work of the Gospel.

"I came here to seek God's will in my life, and I believe I can find it here. I'd like to stay."

For the next two months, after my father and stepmother returned to the Philippines, I traveled with this missionary. I didn't realize until later that God was letting me experience what is known as missions advocacy. My Heavenly Father was sort of saying, "See, this is how this advocacy works." I accompanied and assisted this man somewhat like Timothy accompanied and assisted the Apostle Paul. The two of us would go to churches where he would speak and show slides of missionaries and pastors in the Philippines. He would explain how much money they needed and how they planned to use it, whether it was needed for evangelism, orphans, food, Bibles, bicycles, medicines, or something else. Sometimes I would help him box books and hymnals for shipment.

Brother Elias was an excellent Bible teacher and preacher. I learned many things from him. At a church retreat somewhere in Lynchburg, he gave the devotional from 2 Samuel 24:24 where King David refused to accept Araunah's offer to give him for free all the things he needed to present as burnt offerings to the Lord. King David's words of refusal powerfully impacted my whole being. These words also helped define my life's calling. "Then the king said to Araunah, 'No, but I will surely buy it from you for a price; nor will I offer burnt offerings to the LORD my God with that which costs me nothing.'"

He had a good heart, and he was sincere and effective, but I soon realized that he needed to do a better job of balancing the needs of his family and the needs of those he served. He had married an American lady, and they had three children. One day, when we returned to his home from a trip, the house was empty. His wife and three young children had left him. He broke down and cried, and I cried with him.[6]

Later, when I became a missionary myself, I learned that you must seek a balance between loving and serving God and loving and serving your precious family. We are called to serve God with all our heart, and at the same time, we are called to love, provide for, and spend time with our spouse and children. Because I had previously worked with teams, I also saw his need for a supporting team and a working board of accountability. I experienced the joy of serving God's people with this missionary, and I saw firsthand that sometimes ministry entails tears and pain. With him, I learned my first lessons in missions advocacy.

---

[6] Years after we parted ways, Brother Elias remarried and had children. He gradually left the ministry and concentrated on caring and providing for his new family. In 2015, I received a call from Florida. It was his wife. She was requesting me to come and speak at the memorial service of her husband. Speaking at Brother Elias's memorial service, which his three children from his first marriage attended, I affirmed to his now grown-up children how great a man and how selfless a servant of God their father was. I also shared with them their father's deep love and affection for them. They were greatly encouraged and thankful to hear the beautiful things said about their dad.

My Eulogy to Dr. Robert V. Finley

ONE OF THE GREATEST MISSIONARIES
OF THE TWENTIETH CENTURY

At his memorial service at
Trinity Presbyterian Church on April 6, 2019

I stand here today for two reasons, among others:

First, to publicly say thank you to the Lord for the life and ministry of Dr. Robert Finley—knowing that gratefulness unexpressed is ungratefulness implied.

Second, to proclaim Dr. Finley's legacy. By the grace of God, he is one of the greatest missionaries of the twentieth century. His is the distinct honor as "the father of indigenous missions."

My association with Dr. Finley is defined two-fold: First, by a mentor-and-protégé relationship, and second, by a father-and-son relationship. I've known him close-up for thirty-three years—first, as a focused visionary, and second, as a fiery advocate.

As a visionary, Dr. Finley left years ago the safe confines of traditional missions to pursue his vision. In his own words thirty years ago, he said, "Our Lord and Savior said that His Gospel would be preached in all the world for a witness unto all nations, and then He will come again (Matthew 24:14). We seek to determine by what means the unfinished task can most effectively be accomplished."

He boldly announced: "In most mission field countries, up to 90 percent of the missionary work being done is carried out by indigenous, rather than foreign, missionary agencies." Standing his ground against the well-entrenched multi-billion-dollar traditional foreign missionary programs, Dr. Finley found himself excoriated and even slandered for many years. He was bruised, wounded, and badly beaten.

But the God of Abraham, Isaac, and Jacob is not only a God of Reward but also a God who vindicates. As Dr. Finley pioneered this new and radical paradigm in missions—that of supporting indigenous missionaries to establish a witness in every nation, tribe, and language group—the numbers of unreached peoples have also radically decreased. George Ainsworth, one of my major mentors since Christian Aid days, has assembled the following amazing figures about global missions development that vindicate God's faithful and courageous servant, Dr. Finley:

> *From the Resurrection until 1980, only about 4,000 of the world's 16,000 people groups distinguished by language and culture responded to the Gospel. But since 1980, another 6,000+ nations started to say 'YES' to Jesus—meaning they now have self-sustaining missionary movements! The conclusion: If 6,000 nations can be reached in thirty-five years, the remaining 6,000 nations can be reached in less time, thanks to the growing world missions force of native missionaries!*

Dr. Finley closed his eyes with the knowledge that his God has vindicated him. Psalm 37:5–6 illustrates this. "Commit your way to the LORD; trust in him and he will do this: He will make your righteous reward shine like the dawn, your vindication like the noonday sun" (NIV).

Dr. Finley's vindication is no ordinary vindication. It's a divine vindication called an "internal vindication," "a vindication like that of the Lord Jesus," a vindication in the spirit (1 Tim 3:16). Dr. R. T. Kendall, author of fifty books and the former pastor of Westminster Chapel, says, "This means you are conscious of God's approval, that He is pleased with you. And if you have that, you are in the best possible state!"

Dr. Finley was not only a visionary, he also was gifted by the Lord as an ardent advocate. He raised massive resources for indigenous missions. Advocacy is the superstructure of ministries like Christian Aid. There was no one like him. He knew how to work out his vision by being the intercessor, interpleader, spokesman, and champion of high-quality but ill-equipped and poorer indigenous missionaries. The following words are from one of his declarations as a fiery advocate in 1986:

> Unbelievable, incredible, miraculous, unimaginable! That's what people are saying about church growth in poorer countries—often where Western missionaries have labored for years with little fruit. The missionaries responsible for such explosive growth of evangelical Christianity in these places are native to the land in which they're working.
>
> These workers go through severe and intense difficulties. They're caught in the middle of war, are subject to intense persecution and beatings. They climb mountains and cross jungles, deserts and rivers to reach the unreached. What's more, very often they don't know where their next meal is coming from! As you read of the difficulties these missionaries face for the sake of our Lord Jesus, please consider your own sacrifice for the kingdom of God.

For me, Dr. Finley was not only a visionary and an advocate, but he was also a great missions mentor. He had no parallel. Starting in 1986, when he mentored me in regard to the vision of indigenous missions, by the grace of God he was delighted to find out that:

First, God has equipped me with a passionate heart for the downtrodden and the underdog.

Second, speaking of indigenous missionaries, I am one! I don't only have the skin color, I also have the accent. And I have the heart of an indigenous missionary!

When Dr. Finley started mentoring me in advocacy, he was pleased to find out that as a trained and experienced lawyer, I was a spokesman, a champion, an interpleader for someone or for a cause. There was just one major problem. I was empowered by the Lord to make a case for indigenous missionaries in churches and in missions conferences, but I didn't "throw and pull in the net," so to speak. In short, I did not ask for missions offerings—I had a mental block. I was shy, if not reticent. I came from a family who gave and found it difficult to receive.

In 1988, Dr. Finley, in one of those mentoring times we had, opened the Bible to me and read and expounded Philippians 4:15–17, which says, "Now you Philippians know also that in the beginning of the Gospel, when I departed from Macedonia, no church shared with me concerning giving and receiving but you only. For even in Thessalonica you sent aid once and again for my necessities. Not that I seek the gift, but I seek the fruit that abounds to your account"—meaning that I am doing you a favor that you are giving because your giving has heavenly reverberations which produce fruit for your account in the heavenly journals.

With Dr. Finley's exposition of Philippians 4:15–17, I felt released from my bondage primarily of pride and temerity. I have been on fire since that time in advocating for our brothers and sisters laboring in the frontiers of world evangelization! What's the proof? Boasting in the Lord, the proof is a very fruitful ANM, a ministry that the Lord birthed in me and my wife Marlou, together with my brother Carl Gordon and his wife, Minda, in October 1992.

One of my bittersweet memories is the day in September of 1992 when I said goodbye to my spiritual father to start a new well for missions. It pained him to see me go. On my last day at Christian Aid, he called me to his office and just like a loving father to a son, he held my hands in his and said, "Please don't go. Stay with me. Stay with us." I was adamant to go as I saw in my mind long lines of native missionaries still waiting in line for Bibles, bicycles, shoes, monthly support in order to be more fruitful in the sharing of the Gospel. I told him I had to go.

In pain, I heard my father's words, "You are a prodigal son." I received the word "prodigal" with grace as I knew it came from pain. But I held on to the word "son" as I knew it came from a father's heart. My last words to him were, "Dr. Finley, I love you." He did not respond. I prayed that the Lord would vindicate me before my spiritual father's eyes.

In 2007, at my invitation and the invitation of my co-founder, Carl Gordon, Dr. Finley came with Cynthia to ANM and addressed our staff. I wanted our ANM family to meet "the father of indigenous missions" and know the heritage of ANM. After I had introduced Dr. Finley to the entire staff, he made his way with some difficulty to the head of our long conference table. After taking a seat. he looked around at the seventy pairs of eyes fastened on him. I could picture angels jostling to hear what this great servant of the Lord had to say.

Dr. Finley took a deep breath and said, "This is a blessed day." I clung to those sweet words. I took it that my spiritual father now realized that ANM was also part of the Lord's fruit from his life, ministry, and sacrifices.

On March 11, 2019, Marlou and I visited Dr. Finley at the hospice. Cynthia gladly received us, and we stayed for almost an hour. Dr. Finley weakly told us, "Pray for me. I am dying." At the time of our goodbye, I edged up to the side of his head and repeated the last words I had spoken to him when I said goodbye to him in September 1992: "Dr. Finley, I love you."

My father, Dr. Finley, this time had a response. In a crystal-clear voice heard by both Cynthia and Marlou—I know heaven heard it, too—he said, "I love you, Bo . . ." And he went back to sleep.

That, beloved friends, is my precious legacy from Dr. Bob Finley, my spiritual father and one of the greatest missionaries of the twentieth century—a legacy I will carry in gratefulness for the rest of my life.

PROVERBS 19:21

There are many plans in a man's heart,
Nevertheless, the LORD's counsel—
that will stand.

FINDING GOD'S WILL

One day in early September 1986, Brother Elias learned about the First Filipino Baptist Church that was being started in Virginia Beach, so we decided to go there to see if this new congregation would like to provide support to ministries in the Philippines. The engine on his rusty old car had caught fire, and we didn't have money for bus fare, so Brother Elias and I went to a local church and asked for help. It felt to me like we were begging; I was so embarrassed that I wanted to hide under the table because I wasn't accustomed to asking for money for myself. Nevertheless, we received enough money to take a bus to Virginia Beach.

When we arrived, Pastor Carlos Vidal, the Filipino missionary leading the church plant, met us and took us to his home. The entire congregation of the First Filipino Baptist Church numbered not more than fifteen people. I ended up joining the church, and they adopted me as one of their own. They were my first group of fellow Christians in the United States.

I developed a strong friendship with almost every one of the worshippers. In fact, one beautiful and godly couple still sends me a box of chocolates with an enclosed fifty-dollar check every Christmas! In the succeeding years, under the able leadership of Pastor Paul Ignacio and later under the dynamic leadership of Pastor Sonny Vitaliz, First Filipino Baptist Church became a sending church for Marlou and me. Today it is called International Christian Church and has almost four hundred members from many different countries, many of whom are our very close friends and supporters. What a blessing this church and its pastors have been to us!

When Advancing Native Missions started in October 1992, First Filipino Baptist Church was one of the first churches I visited. I explained how our family was stepping out in faith and shared ANM's vision and mission with my brothers and sisters. At the end of my message, as I stood in front of the congregation trying hard to blink my tears away, almost all of them came up one by one to me and lovingly placed in my hands and in my pockets their love offerings for the new ministry. Through such a spontaneous show of love and support, I could feel God lovingly confirming his approval of my decision to "dig a new well" for his native workers serving him across the globe. This church has a big heart for missions and, with its dynamic pastors and lay leaders, has hosted various ANM missions conferences. It has supported and continues to support several ANM ministry partners and missionaries.

Beset by Doubts

Even though I now had a home church, I was beset by doubts. Daily I cried out to God, "Lord, did you really call me? Did you really call me? I don't see any place for me in the ministry." One day, Pastor Vidal said to Brother Elias and me, "Today there is a meeting of many pastors from this area. There will be a free lunch afterward. Would the two of you like to come with me?"

The opportunity to save money with a free lunch attracted us, so we accompanied Pastor Vidal to the meeting. About forty American pastors were there. As various reports and other matters were being discussed, self-pity began to envelop me. In desperation, I cried out to the Lord, "Father, what am I doing here? My life has no direction. I don't even belong in this place. I am not a participant; I am just a spectator. I am just here for a free meal." I had trouble staying in my seat, so I got up and headed for the restroom.

On the way, I noticed an empty classroom with a Bible on one of the desks. I ignored it and proceeded to the restroom. As I passed that classroom on the way back, I felt strongly prompted to go inside. I went in, opened the Bible, and read a portion of Scripture.

I don't remember what I read, but after I had finished reading this passage, a sensation welled up within me that caused my body to become warm and tremble. I left the room feeling rather strange and returned to the meeting.

Just as I had retaken my seat in the conference room, the chairman presiding over the meeting said, "We will close our session now unless somebody has something else to say. Would anybody like to say something?" "

Surprising Boldness

For some reason, I found myself raising my hand. I don't know why I was so bold. We were just guests of Pastor Vidal, and we had simply come to get a free lunch. But whatever had caused me to tremble was also causing me to raise my hand. Brother Elias looked at me wide-eyed with an expression on his face that said, "What are you doing? This is not the place to raise your hand to say something. The men in this meeting are important pastors of big churches." He looked like he wanted to push my hand down.

The chairman gave me a puzzled look. He had no idea who this stranger was or why he was raising his hand to speak. I said, "Sir, my name is Bo Barredo. My parents are missionaries in the Philippines. If you will give me five minutes, I will share something about what God has done in my life."

Surprised by my boldness, the chairman said, "Okay, yes, come up and share." I stepped up to the front of the room and began to share about how my love story with the Lord, with the creator of the heavens and the earth, started in the Bay of San Francisco in July 1901 aboard the United States vessel the USAT Thomas. I explained how the six hundred passengers on that ship, who became known as the Thomasites, were among the first Protestant missionaries of the Lord to the Philippines. God gave me these words, and I shared from my heart.

I do not mean to boast when I say this, because this was clearly a work of God, but the audience seemed captivated. They sat on the edge of their seats as I testified about how my grandparents were faithful Sunday school teachers who died poor in worldly goods but rich in the Lord. It was a powerful experience for everyone, including me. In fact, I was unaware of myself.

Suddenly, out of the corner of my eye, I noticed that the chairman was pointing at his watch to signal that I was taking up too much time. This snapped me out of my "daze," so to speak, and I began to feel embarrassed. I said, "I am sorry; I took too much of your time. Thank you so much." However, as I turned to go back to my seat with my head hung down, something unexpected happened. Many of the pastors who had been listening to me came up and began crowding around. Several of them asked, "Can you come speak in my church next Sunday?" Others said, "How can we help you?"

I was totally surprised. All I could say was, "Please talk to Brother Elias, the friend I came with." As Brother Elias excitedly fielded questions about our goals and circumstances, he happened to mention that we were in need of a car. One pastor said, "I have two cars; one is a station wagon, and the other is a sedan. Just choose." Brother Elias chose the beautiful, slightly used, white Buick station wagon.

A Glimpse of the Future

This was the first time I had spoken at a public gathering of pastors and missionaries. Looking back, I believe that because nothing was happening in my life, God used this experience to say to me, "You don't know yet what I have prepared for you to do, but I'm going to give you a glimpse of it so you will know you are still in my will." He filled me with his Spirit and gave me the courage to be shameless. By his grace, I was shameless enough to raise my hand and speak in a meeting where I didn't even belong. In his love, he affirmed once again that I was in his will.

Some days later, when Brother Elias and I needed another place to stay, God led us to a small church in Portsmouth, Virginia. It was a poor church, and the pastor allowed us to stay in his modest parsonage. How wonderful to benefit from God's provision through the kindness and generosity of his people. But we were hungry because we had no provisions.

Brother Elias knew a Christian brother who belonged to Calvary Baptist Church in Virginia Beach, and this brother invited us to participate in the church's Wednesday evening service. When we arrived, the pastor of the church said to Brother Elias, "Why don't you share something in the service?" He then turned to me and said, "You also should share something."

After Brother Elias shared for five minutes, he said to those in the service, "My brother in the Lord, Bo, is seeking God's will in his life. I'd like him to come up and share." That morning God had placed strongly on my heart Psalm 30:4–5. I began,

> Sing praise to the LORD, you saints of His,
> And give thanks at the remembrance of His holy name.
> For His anger is but for a moment,
> His favor is for life;
> Weeping may endure for a night,
> But joy comes in the morning.

Then I shared my testimony. When I finished, the church was hushed. Moments later, people began lining up to speak with Brother Elias and me. The pastor said to the congregation, "Let us minister to our visitors." As we stood in front of the congregation, people filed by and put checks and cash into our hands; some even kissed us.

We left the church rejoicing that God once again had provided for us. I said, "Lord, thank you! Thank you, Lord, that in my dryness of spirit, you again affirmed that you are calling me. Father, you have affirmed that I am in the center of your will. But what is your will? I still don't know what it is."

Fighting Discouragement

With the money that God provided, we bought some canned goods, bread, and other kinds of food. Brother Elias said to me, "Bo, why don't you buy something that will help you remember the giving of this church?" I went to Sears and bought my first camera, so I could record my travels in the United States. I didn't realize it at the time, but later, I used this camera to photograph the workings of the Lord among his missionaries and pastors in the Philippines. Some of the photographs I took with that small camera appeared in Christian Aid's *Missions* magazine. Two even appeared on the front cover. I had started teaching myself how to take good photographs by reviewing numerous issues of *National Geographic* and seriously studying the excellent photos and their composition, captivating moments, color, and distance from the subject.

Despite these affirmations that the Lord so graciously had provided, by October discouragement was again trying to grab me by the neck. I found myself thinking, "I still haven't found God's will in my life. I need to return to the Philippines." I called my sister Bong in Chicago and told her that I planned to fly back to the Philippines but that I'd like to see her first. She said, "Yes, yes, please come."

While in Chicago with Bong, I called Marlou in Manila and told her that I was planning to come home. After a brief silence, she asked, "Have you found God's will in your life?"

"I am sorry, my darling, but I have not," I replied. "But I am going to come home and set up my own private law practice, specializing in religious arbitration."

Marlou asked what I meant by that, and I explained, "My law office is going to cater to churches that have problems from within. I would like to offer my services to arbitrate their issues. You are aware that serving as a peacemaker is one of my gifts. Even the university professors and other professionals in our condominium building have asked me to help them settle disputes. I believe God can use me to do this between and within churches."

After Marlou had listened, she said, "I love you so much, and I want you to come back home because our children and I deeply miss you. Life is not the same without you." She paused, then continued, "But I don't want you to come back home before you have found

God's will in your life. I know you, and if you come back home without finding God's will, you will be greatly disturbed and restless. Please continue to seek God's will in your new life."

Choosing God

I promised to pray about it. Around midnight, as I was lying on the bed and looking up at the ceiling, with many things swirling in my mind, I could not focus on what to do next. In my mind, going home was my plan B. I was not aware that in the kingdom of God, there are no plan Bs. In the midst of these aimlessly swirling thoughts, I found myself praying in a crescendo the following words: "Heavenly Father, in Jesus' name, I'd like you to know these following words. Please listen to me. I hope you hear me. I choose you, Father. Do you hear me? I choose you. I choose you, Father. I choose you. I choose your plans for me. I choose your will for me. Please, Father, hear me. I choose you. I make this decision. I choose you. I choose your heart. I choose your plans."

After I prayed, my mind slowly became quiet, and I slept. I didn't know it at the time, but this was my midnight cry, so to speak. It was a tremendously important moment in my life.

There are many plans in a man's heart,
Nevertheless the LORD's counsel—that will stand.
PROVERBS 19:21

When I awoke the next morning, an impression was in my heart. I suddenly remembered what Carl Gordon at Christian Aid had said. He had said that if I didn't find God's will in my life, call him, and he would send tickets for me to come to Charlottesville, Virginia, so we could have another talk. When God has a plan for us, he does not forget it. He is faithful. I know that now.

I picked up the phone and dialed the number Carl had given me. A lady answered, and I said, "This is Bo Barredo. I'd like to speak with Carl Gordon, please."

"I am sorry," she said, "but Carl is not here. He went out fishing. It's his vacation day."

My spirit sank. I thought I was being obedient to the Lord, and now I was feeling disillusioned and depressed. I thanked the lady and started to hang up the phone. Suddenly, the voice on the other end said, "What is your name again?"

"It's Bo Barredo," I answered.

"Oh, Bo, this is Ruth Shank. I am sorry that Carl is not here. But hold on; I'd like you to speak to Dr. Finley."

Wow! She was about to connect me with the big man himself! I felt intimidated. I started to say, "No, no, don't bother. That's okay." But before I could say this, a man's voice said, "This is Bob Finley. What can we do for you?"

"Sir, if you remember me, my name is Bo Barredo," I answered. "I was there a couple of months ago. I am seeking God's will in my life, and I haven't found it. If I come to Christian Aid, would you have a place for me?"

Dr. Finley was known to be a very decisive man. He said, "Why don't you cash your plane tickets and buy a train ticket from Chicago? Then come here to Christian Aid. We will see what God has for you." It was apparent that he remembered me! I suspected it was because of our unforgettable exchange on the Greek word *charisma*.

"Oh, thank you so much, sir! Thank you so much!" I borrowed some money from Bong, went to Union Station in Chicago, and bought a ticket to Charlottesville, the headquarters of Christian Aid.

Encouragement on the Train

On October 17, 1986, I departed Chicago. This was the first time I had ever ridden on a train. As we passed through Pennsylvania and parts of West Virginia, the yellow, gold, green, red, and maroon leaves were so beautiful. The magnificent fall flowers and foliage filled my heart with a peace that was beyond understanding. I cried out to God, "Lord, I believe I am in your will. I don't know what it looks like, but I believe I am in your will!" And then I said, "But Lord, I miss Marlou. I miss Marlou and the children."

As I was crying out to God in this way, something astounding happened. A familiar song came over the speakers in my railroad car. It began, "If it takes forever, I will wait for you. For a thousand summers, I will wait for you."

This was the exact song that Marlou and I considered to be "our song"! How remarkable that the God of the Universe, just when I needed encouragement, would care so much for me that he would have this special song played at this exact time on this specific train. He seemed to be saying to me, "Marlou is well; your children are well. They all love you, and they are waiting for you. I am sending this to encourage you." I interpreted this as God's presence with me because he did not want me to be despondent.

All I Have to Offer

When I arrived in Charlottesville, I called Christian Aid, and they sent a young missionary to pick me up. On the way to Christian Aid's headquarters, this missionary asked, "Bo, what are your plans?"

"I have no plans," I answered. "I will take each day as it comes." I settled into the guest house of Christian Aid.

The next morning, Dr. Finley invited me to have breakfast with him in the kitchen. As he cooked, I sat on a chair by the small dining table nearby. After he had finished frying our eggs and placed them on our plates, he turned and addressed me directly: "Young man, you came here seeking God's will in your life. What could you do for us?"

I was tongue-tied. I didn't know what to say. In my former life, I was a trained lawyer. I had commanded lawyers and accountants. I was a specialist in group dynamics and policy formulation. I had crafted strategies and all those things. I felt that at that point in my life, I had already accomplished much. But when Dr. Finley asked me what I could do for Christian Aid, I realized I was a nobody. Yes, I was a nobody who had nothing to offer the Lord. What can any of us offer the God who made the heavens and the earth? I have nothing to offer the Lord except this life that he has given me.

As Dr. Finley stood there waiting for my response, I silently prayed, "Lord, teach me how to answer this gentleman." Suddenly, I found myself standing up. I gently took the frying pan from his hand, picked up a soap rag from the sink, and began slowly washing the frying pan. All during this time, Dr. Finley was silent. Then I turned to him and clearly said, "Dr. Finley, for starters, I know how to wash frying pans." Then I burst into tears!

In this moment, I realized a great truth: nobody can work for the God who made the heavens and the earth unless he humbles himself. He must first be broken. This is the initial requirement in serving the Lord. In my legal language, such is a *requisite sine qua non*, something that is a must, something that is indispensable. When you are broken, God can use you because he is the one who can put you back together. He is the one who can shape and mold you to fulfill your divinely ordained purposes in your generation. I realized that I had nothing to offer to Dr. Finley except what little service I could.

Starting as Nothing

Dr. Finley was somewhat taken aback by my answer, but he let it be. He said, "Well, you can act as a volunteer here." So I gladly volunteered with Christian Aid. I picked up the trash, I washed the dishes, I mowed the grass. This is how I started my service to the Lord. I was nothing. My law degree didn't matter. My accomplishments didn't matter. The papers I had written didn't matter. God wanted me first to be broken.

As I was mowing the grass one day, Carl Gordon started a conversation with me. He said, "Bo, tomorrow we will have our usual staff meeting. Would you kindly come and tell us how you would visit the ministries in the Philippines, if you were asked to do it?" I said, "Yes, I will be happy to do that."

The next day in the staff meeting, I used a large map of the Philippines and explained how I would travel to the various parts of the country to visit the different groups that Christian Aid supported. This kind of investigative work was familiar to me, because one of my specialties when I worked for the Philippine government was setting up monitoring systems to ensure that the government workers in our department didn't engage in graft and corruption. As the Auditor General's troubleshooter, I had been one of the most well-traveled officers in our department. I was familiar with the different islands and different key locations, and my presentation was well-received.

When you are broken, God can use you because he is the one who can put you back together. He is the one who can shape and mold you to fulfill your divinely ordained purposes in your generation.

A short time later, I was assigned to the printing department in the basement to help operate the folding machine. My supervisor was a kind-hearted man by the name of Merrill Histand. Around this time, representatives from Christian Aid returned from an international missions conference in Amsterdam organized by the Billy Graham Evangelistic Association. Information they had collected about many native missionary leaders around the world needed to be put into Christian Aid's computer, and I was one of those given the assignment. I didn't know how to type, so I pecked at the keyboard with two fingers. By the end of the first day, my head was bursting, and my eyes felt crossed.

Night Studies

One day Carl Gordon said to me, "If we send you back to the Philippines, would you be able to check out ministries to see whether they are doing a good work for the Lord? At the same time, you could keep your eyes open for other new ministries that are effective at bringing souls into the kingdom."

"I would love to do that," I excitedly said. "May I start by studying the missionary files?"

Carl said yes, so every night around 6:30 or 7:00, I would sit down on the floor of Carl's office and read missionary files. As I read these missionary reports and took notes, I laughed, cried, agonized, prayed, and rejoiced. I had so much love and compassion for these missionaries; I just wanted to serve them. I said, "Lord, these are the kind of people I'd like to serve. Would you allow me to serve them, Lord? Would you please allow me to serve them?" Every night I had this experience, and every night the God of Missions made me feel his presence.

My natural and deep interest in people caused me to observe the members of the staff. I grew to admire George Ainsworth for his brilliant mind as he performed his work in donor relations. Philip Zodhiates, Christian Aid's director for communications, earned my admiration for his gift for ministry development. The editor of the magazine, John Lindner, struck me as one who would not settle for less than excellence in his line of work. And the gentleness of my printing shop boss, Merrill Histand, I will always remember.

One day, Ruth Shank and I found out that we both had the same birthday, January 23. We had similar personality traits, and she had lost her first baby, who had been born almost the same year as I. We happily adopted each other as mother and son. Oh, how I loved my Mom Ruth! I also came to dearly love her beloved daughter, Beverly, as my very own sister. I didn't realize then that all of these people I admired would years later be working side by side with Carl and me at ANM. George Ainsworth became our first chairman of the board and later was our regional director for Europe. Philip Zodhiates succeeded George as the chairman of the board; John Lindner became the editor of ANM's magazine; and Merrill Histand became our supply officer.

During the day, I worked in the Christian Aid office, and late at night after going over the missionary files in the office, I studied God's Word in solitude in my room at the Christian Aid guest house.

As I read and studied the Scriptures, God's Word came alive in my heart as never before. I was especially stirred by Genesis 28:10–21, which describes how when Jacob left his father's house to flee from his brother Esau, he found himself one night in a deserted place, and there he dreamed of a stairway reaching up to heaven with angels ascending and descending on it. This passage strongly resonated in my heart and spirit because I, too, had left my own country, which at that time was beset by political upheavals, and had embarked on a journey. I highlighted in my Bible verses 20–21 as my own words and prayer:

> Then Jacob made a vow, saying, "If God will be with me,
> and keep me in this way that I am going, and give me bread
> to eat and clothing to put on, so that I come back to my
> father's house in peace, then the LORD shall be my God."
>
> GENESIS 28:20-21

Ready

One day in mid-November, as the cold December winds were starting, Carl Gordon came to me and said, "Are you ready to go home to the Philippines?" His question was like a very early, eagerly awaited Christmas gift!

"I am ready, sir," I answered with unrestrained joy.

I could hardly wait for the day when I would be flying home. I would daydream each day about tightly hugging Marlou and all the children when I would meet them at the Manila International Airport. I had prepared some plans about where I would go to visit the ministries scattered among the islands, and I also was looking forward to times of sweet fellowship and prayers with missionaries and pastors and their families. The opportunity to write stories about God's missionaries on the mission field and take photos of their work gave me tremendous excitement.

On December 2, 1986, Carl met me at the guest house and drove me to the airport for my flight to the Philippines. Accompanying us was a fine-looking, well-dressed young gentleman sporting a bright smile. I was impressed by the way he held himself. Carl said, "Bo, I'd like you to meet Brother P. R. Misra. He may soon be joining Christian Aid and doing the same work as you."

I warmly shook P. R.'s hand, not knowing that we would have the blessing of working together at Christian Aid until 1992. I was so happy when he joined us at ANM in 1994. I love P. R. like my own younger brother. I call him by his childhood nickname, Neenu. He is a great ambassador-advocate for God's people. It was my honor to recommend him to the ANM board in 2017 to lead ANM's international operations with Oliver Asher as president.

With excitement and joy, I boarded my flight to my native land.

MISSIONARY TO THE PHILIPPINES

Aboard Japan Airlines on the first leg of my flight to the Philippines, dressed in a suit and tie, I felt like I was floating in the clouds that dotted the skies outside the plane. A short layover in Tokyo added to the excitement. I would soon be home!

On the way to board my connecting flight on Philippine Airlines, I happened to notice through a huge glass window the image emblazoned on the tail of our white aircraft sported the golden rays of a sun bursting forth through red, white, and blue triangles. These were the colors of the Philippine flag! My heart leapt with love for my native land. Memories came flooding back of my schoolboy days when every morning during the flag ceremony I would sing with fervor the following lines:

> *Land of the morning,*
> *Child of the sun returning,*
> *With fervor burning,*
> *Thee do our souls adore.*
>
> *Land dear and holy,*
> *Cradle of noble heroes,*
> *Ne'er shall invaders*
> *Trample thy sacred shores.*
>
> *Ever within thy skies and through thy clouds*
> *And o'er thy hills and sea,*
> *Do we behold the radiance, feel and throb,*
> *Of glorious liberty.*

Thy banner dear to all our hearts,
Its sun and stars alight,
O never shall its shining field
Be dimmed by tyrants' might!

Beautiful land of love, O land of light,
In thine embrace 'tis rapture to lie,
But it is glory ever, when thou art wronged,
For us, thy sons to suffer and die.

When our plane hit the ground in Manila, I joined other passengers in spontaneous and resounding applause that went on and on. It was as if we all were exclaiming, "We are home! We are home! At last, we are home!"

As I made my way into the terminal, my heart sank. Marlou and the children were nowhere in sight. After waiting for quite a while, I became beset with worry and a longing to get home. Flagging a taxicab, I loaded my weighty suitcases filled with clothes, gifts, and old issues of *National Geographic*. How wonderful it felt to give the driver my home address!

When I arrived home, Felisa and little Jim greeted me with excited hugs and jumps of joy. They were so happy to see me! Our household helpers informed me that Marlou, Benjie, and David had taken the public bus to the airport to meet me. When they returned home, I learned that because of heavy traffic and the need to make two bus transfers, they had arrived at the airport after I had left.

We all were so happy and utterly relieved to be together again as a family. All of us still remember that homecoming with such fondness, even details such as the fragrant scent that permeated our home that day. The source of the aroma was the Aqua Velva men's cologne that I was wearing, something new I had acquired in the US. After enjoying a feast prepared by the family in honor of the occasion, we all peacefully slept that night with joy in our hearts.

A Dangerous Assignment

After a short time at home with the family, I went into the field on behalf of Christian Aid. My assignment in the Philippines was dangerous. The communist insurgency was winning the war in the countryside, and my work took me to remote mountain villages where the New People's Army (NPA) sought to kill military and police forces. These communist guerrillas also targeted pastors and evangelists. We were a threat to them because when the young people in the villages became believers, they no longer wanted to be recruited as guerrillas. Also, when members of the insurgency became born-again Christians, they turned away from communism and stopped fighting. The Philippine government noticed this and wanted to use Christian ministries as a tool for fighting the insurgency. This angered the insurgency leaders even more, so I was placed in a very hazardous situation.

For my own protection, I was given the alias Rey Siervo. Rey means king, and Siervo means servant. So my name meant "Servant of the King." I posed as a reporter, and I wrote stories and reports under this name.

My mission field was the entire Philippines, with a total land area of about 120,000 square miles. The nation's 7,641 islands, if combined into one land mass, would be about the size of New Mexico. The nation's approximately 110 million people speak more than 140 different languages and dialects. At this time, Christian Aid assisted some thirty Philippine missions agencies, with many missionaries and pastors scattered on many islands.

God Will Make It Up to You

One of the first families I visited gave me insight into how selfless and faithful native missionaries are in serving the Lord. Nemuel and Ruth Palma were pastors of a church in Manila that was close to Smoky Mountain, which was a huge mound of trash about sixty feet high. It was called Smoky Mountain because it burned all day long. The poorest of the poor lived on the mountain and scavenged throughout the day for things to eat, even half-eaten hamburgers and other leftover food that restaurants had thrown away. They shook the food to get the ants, fungi, mold, and maggots off, and then they heated it without the benefit of cooking oil to try to kill some of the germs. Because of this shaking, the food was called *pagpag*, which in the native language means "to shake." The trash also included things thrown away by hospitals.

A nearby shallow creek caught like a basin the dark and foul-smelling liquid-like materials that leached from the terrible mountain of trash. People who lived on the mountain, especially women and children, waded through this almost-black, stinking water looking for things to salvage and sell. They washed sheets of discarded plastic in the foul water and recycled them for small amounts of money. This mountain was like hell on earth, "where 'Their worm does not die And the fire is not quenched,'" (Mark 9:48).

Carl Gordon had visited Smoky Mountain on one of his trips. When he noticed a little boy walking on the mound of trash wearing a torn shirt and pants covered with grime, something about the boy reminded Carl of his only child, Nathaniel. His heart broke, and he investigated further. After learning that Nemuel and Ruth Palma had a modest Christian outreach among the hundreds of people living on the mountain, Carl visited the couple and said to them, "If we can find friends who will provide you with some help every month, would you be able to expand your work witnessing to the people on this dump?" The Palmas responded excitedly that they could.

When I visited the couple at their church outside Smoky Mountain, I immediately fell in love with them. They had a great burden for the poor garbage scavengers who lived at the peak of the garbage dump and around its peripheries. On subsequent visits, I discussed with Nemuel and Ruth how we might help with their plans to plant a church at the top of the dump.

I was deeply moved by their commitment to the spreading of the Gospel regardless of the personal cost. They had the option of staying where they were and pastoring a growing church that had working members able to support them. Yet they could not bear to see the poorest of the poor living in the dump and dying without knowing that they could be rich in Christ! After days of prayers and preparations, Nemuel and Ruth endured the hostility of church members who resented their departure and moved to the peak of the dump.

In the subsequent years, God led me to churches and people in the US who were moved to support the work of this couple. Through the help of Heinz Fussel, a filmmaker from Indiana, a special video was made of Nemuel and Ruth's work on Smoky Mountain. I wrote the script from my heart. The response to the powerfully moving video was tremendous! In the process of visiting and helping the Palmas, I developed bronchitis that took six months to heal. As an amusing sidenote, every time I came home from the dump, Marlou would hand me a large towel outside the door of our home, and I would have to strip off my clothes so they could be washed immediately!

The Angels Were Crying

When I visited the garbage dump early one morning, I saw a little boy around six years old eating scraps for breakfast out of a fresh pile of garbage. He was nibbling on whatever bits of dirty meat he could find on leftover chicken bones. He was clearly hungry, and the grime on his face could not hide the tears in his eyes. I took a photograph of him, and as I did, I saw in my heart that this boy was surrounded by angels. The angels also were crying as they looked upon this boy eating garbage for breakfast. In my heart, I heard these angels say, "Hush, little boy, hush. We will make it up to you when you get to heaven. We will make it up to you when you get to heaven."

This is when God impressed upon my heart the principle that missionaries and believers who suffer for Christ will be paid back someday. God is going to more than make it up to them while they are here in this world, and even more so when they get to heaven. This is one of the principles that I keep in mind as my wife and our children make sacrifices, which we especially had to do during the initial years of struggle with ANM. I say to them, "Don't worry. Let us give away and not lay claims to these things. God is going to more than make it up to us, because he would never be a debtor to anyone. He is going to more than make it up to us."

This is why, when Marlou and I and our four children arrived in the US in 1991, we made a commitment before the Lord to have neither savings in the bank nor a special retirement plan. Somehow, God has always provided for us. We left father, mother, homes, properties, friendships, jobs, and all those things. But after we arrived in America, God more than made it up to us. He gave us fathers, mothers, brothers, sisters, godly friends, and the material things we needed. We don't have resources for ourselves, but we have resources from generous friends for God's servants in many parts of the world. God raised our children and their families to love him and reverently fear him. For us, that is success.

Ruth Labors On

In the early days of ANM, Nemuel and Ruth were two of the first people we helped. Many families of scavengers have come to the Lord through the ministry of this precious and sacrificing couple. Nemuel Palma passed away in 2020, but Ruth has continued the ministry. In an interview, Ruth was asked what she thought of her place of ministry. "It is heaven," she answered. And then with a joyful smile, she added, "Yes, this is where God is."

Today, Ruth battles respiratory diseases, takes maintenance medicine for her heart, and suffers from intermittent pain in her right arm and shoulder. Due to an accident that occurred when a large truck crushed the small vehicle in which she was riding, her right arm is immobilized and attached to her shoulder by metal screws. Yet, Ruth faithfully labors on in service to the Lord. "I am rich with physical pain," she says, "but the more sufferings I have been through, the stronger I have become spiritually."

With the help of some pastors and elders from her church, Ruth operates a kindergarten school ministry called the Lighthouse. Smoky Mountain no longer exists, but the Lighthouse ministers to the children of the poor families who live in government-built tenement housing on the former garbage dump.

In the following slightly edited email sent in August 2021, Ruth talks about her years in ministry and provides a brief update:

Beloved Brethren – ANM staff, Supporters and Prayer Partners, Greetings in Jesus' wonderful, glorious Name LORD JESUS CHRIST GOD. By His intercessory intervention as always even when I was survivor of that Don Juan tragedy in April 1980[7]. Only God intervened that we got saved every time challenges come. For without Him I could do nothing. We, in the church, Grace Christian Church of Smoky Mt., of whom our beloved [brother] in faith Brother Bo Barredo, a great ambassador of Christ, came and established it with my late husband. We decided to do full time in Smoky Mt. and decided to resign at Balut First Baptist Church outside Smoky Mt.

The church felt insulted and offended why we loved more [the people] of Smoky Mt. than them. So, I knew that they won't financially support us. But me and my husband had no idea where to get

---

[7] In her reference to the MV Don Juan, Ruth is recalling an incident that occurred on April 22, 1980, when she was returning by boat from Manila to her home island. She was about to be married, and she had her bridal gown with her. She was a third-class passenger, which meant that her berth was beneath the waterline of the ship.

En route, her ship collided with an oil tanker. As the ship was rapidly sinking and many third-class passengers were perishing, Ruth began praying aloud and jumping as high as she could to reach a porthole. She later reported that a big hand suddenly slid through that porthole, and she found herself being pulled out of the ship. She ended up in the water.

While struggling to keep herself afloat, Ruth heard an elderly woman desperately calling out to the patron saint of her town, "San Joaquin! San Joaquin! Save me!" Ruth forgot about her own safety and began shouting to the woman, "No, Ma'am! No, Ma'am, it's Jesus! It's Jesus!" Ruth could not remember how she was able to reach the lady, or how they survived. Perhaps they held on to a piece of wood or to life jackets that were thrown to them. But before the night was over, the woman received Christ through Ruth's bold witness!

even a single centavo. Then Brother Bo Barredo came on time. We were in tears of joy. In 1987 Grace Christian Church was born with organized deacons and elders. When our church was demolished on November 27, 1995 (the government closed the dump to construct tenement buildings), we continued in a different open space . . . We transferred only last year 2020 the finishing touches of church building was finished and Pastor [Nemuel] preached there every Sunday until last Oct. 18, 2020. Then on Oct. 23, 2020, he went home to heaven. We didn't stop even in pandemic time . . . by His power and mercy.

Now, here is my ministry update/report: (1) four Pastors have regular support and partners up to the present, (2) four Missionaries and Staff of Lighthouse Christian Ministry, (3) Part-time Elders voluntarily doing evangelism . . . Since 2015 my heart enlargement getting bigger. I have maintenance for pain. Am ready to go and follow Pastor Nemuel, but His will be done. Please don't forget us. Prayers and financial support for Jesus very sake because we are in the end times of the Last Days.

—Ruth M. Palma

A letter like the one above from Sister Palma brings tears to my eyes. As I have traveled around the globe, I have come to realize that the poorest person in the world is not the person who eats only one meal a day or earns only one dollar a day. The poorest person in the world, I believe, is the one who has never heard that the Son of God came and died for him, so that he who is condemned to eternal damnation could have eternal life in Christ Jesus, the Son of God.

Fishers of Men

In 1988, just a year or two after I began serving the Lord as a missionary, I went to see a faithful and fruitful missionary couple named Ben and Nene Singcol, who lived near the seashore on the remote island of Biliran. This couple allowed me to see firsthand the high return on investment that results from investing in selfless and sacrificing native missionaries.

When I arrived, the children said their parents were away preaching the Gospel in coastal villages. They invited me to come into their house and wait for their parents to return. The home was a mere shanty with a dirt floor and thatched roof. I waited for many hours, but Ben and Nene did not come. At the invitation of the children, I spent the night in their home sleeping on the only bed they had. It was made of bamboo.

The next morning around sunrise, Ben and Nene arrived home. They were so happy that I had come to visit. I said, "Thank you for having me as your guest, but why didn't you come home last night?"

"Because people are hungry for the Lord," they answered. "We preach the Word of God in a coastal village called Tuktok, and after we preach and share about the Gospel of the Lord Jesus Christ, the people insist that we keep talking. They say, 'Tell us more; tell us more.' So we stay there for a long time, and then we go to another village, and the same thing happens. People are hungry to hear about Jesus Christ."

"How do you get to these villages?" I asked them.

"We use a boat," Ben answered. "It is faster to travel with a boat."

Paddles for the Boat

I asked them if they would kindly show me their boat. They took me to the shore and showed me a small skiff. It was so narrow that I would have had trouble sitting in it. Then I noticed that the boat had many holes that Ben had tried to patch with pieces of glued plywood. It broke my heart to see this shabby vessel. I said, "Pastor Ben, your boat is so old; the wood is rotting, and it is full of holes. Aren't you afraid it might sink?" I tried to suppress my sadness and say this in a lighthearted manner.

"Brother Bo, it is not even our boat," Pastor Ben replied. "We do not have enough money to own a boat. The people who live in the villages where we minister earn their living fishing. They are very poor. When we pass the offering plate in our church here, they don't look at me because they are so embarrassed about having nothing to give. Each Sunday we only collect about twenty or forty pesos (about one or two US dollars). It has been our dream to have our own boat, but God has not yet supplied us with one."

I asked Pastor Ben how much a new wooden boat would cost. He answered eight hundred pesos, which at that time was about forty American dollars. I went behind a coconut tree and counted my money. I had a little over eight hundred pesos. This happened to be my birthday, January 23, 1988, so as a gift to the Lord I went back and said, "Pastor Ben and Sister Nene Singcol, I have good news for you. I have here in my pocket eight hundred pesos. Here it is. Go and buy yourself a new wooden boat for you to use to spread the Gospel."

Pastor Ben dropped to his knees and began praising the Lord, but his wife seemed unable to respond. "Sister Nene," I said, "why don't you receive this money immediately?" She made some motions with her hands, as if to say she needed to get something that would help me understand. Then she ran to the house and returned with two wooden paddles.

"Several weeks ago," she said to me, "I reminded my husband that we had dreamed and prayed about a new boat for many years. I felt that if we show God that we had faith, then he would answer our prayer. I suggested that we demonstrate our faith to God by making paddles for the boat he was going to provide. Ben agreed, and he cut down two trees for us to use. Just last week, when we finished carving these paddles, we raised them toward heaven and said, 'Lord, here now are the paddles. Please send us the boat.' Today, through you, God has sent us the boat." As she said these words, she and Ben began to cry. I cried with them.

Two Years Later

Two years later, I again had an opportunity to visit Ben and Nene Singcol. I was so very happy when they told me how the boat had enabled them to plant three more churches in the coastal villages and do a few other outreaches. How wonderful to see how God multiplies little gifts that are placed in the hands of faithful native missionaries! It would have taken thousands of dollars for somebody from America to go to this remote island and accomplish what this native missionary couple had been able to do with forty dollars. What's more, a missionary from America would have needed to learn the language and how to live within the economic and cultural circumstances of a foreign community. Native missionaries do not need to learn these things.

In 1993, while I was preaching at a church in the US, God put it in my heart to ask for funds for a wooden boat with a motor. I don't know why I asked for this; it was just an act of faith. The pastor invited the congregation to contribute toward this need, and almost $2,000 was collected. On my third visit with Pastor Ben and Sister Nene, I had this money with me. I said to the couple, "How is your wooden boat?"

"Oh, it is wonderful," they replied.

"And have you planted more churches?"

"Yes," Pastor Ben answered. "But Brother Bo, I'd like to tell you a funny story. My wife wants me to conserve my energy when we go in the boat because I must preach the Gospel. So she insists on doing the paddling, but when she does, she vomits blood because she has tuberculosis."

"We will give you money so she can be treated," I promised. "But there is nothing funny about that."

"Oh, thank you for helping us get medical treatment for my wife, Brother Bo!" exclaimed Ben. "God is good! And now, I want to tell you the funny part. One day, as I was paddling to give Nene a rest, I started making a loud 'putt, putt, putt' sound with my mouth. She asked me why I was making this strange sound, and I said, 'I am making the sound of a motor. Do you remember when we made the paddles in faith, and God answered our prayer for a new boat? In faith, I am now asking God for a boat with a motor, so you won't have to paddle.' She laughed and told me not to make that sound because people might say we're crazy. I said, 'Let them say we're crazy. I'm going to show the Lord what we need. Putt! Putt! Putt!' That's the funny story."

Faith Honored Again

"Pastor Ben," I said, taking a deep breath, "today, again, God is going to honor your faith. I'd like you to buy a new and bigger boat with a motor." I handed him the $2,000. He was speechless!

This is how God honors the faith of his people. When we act on our faith in humility and put legs and arms and even sounds to it, God is faithful to provide. It was inspiring to me to see how native missionaries put their commitment to the spreading of the Gospel and serving the Lord far above everything else, sometimes at great sacrifice to their families.

The leadership of the ministry to which Ben and Nene belong credits them with planting a total of fourteen churches. Neither Ben nor Nene has finished high school. Yet not only the poor, but also the highly educated, receive Christ through their witness and teaching.

Now when they saw the boldness of Peter and John,
and perceived that they were uneducated and untrained men,
they marveled. And they realized that they had been with Jesus.

ACTS 4:13

A Secondhand Bicycle

On one of my excursions, I had an opportunity to meet with graduates of a Bible school who had become pastors and church planters. The school had kindly asked these young pastors to travel at considerable inconvenience to meet with me. I interviewed several of them, hoping to collect some powerful testimonies that we could feature in Christian Aid's magazine. While conducting these interviews, I noticed that one young pastor looked very tired. His name was Julito.

"Tell me about yourself, Julito," I said to him. "Why do you look so tired?"

"I woke up very early this morning because I heard you were coming, and I did not want to miss seeing you," he explained. "But my wife asked me to come back as soon as possible to help her with our baby. We were both up most of last night because our baby would not stop crying. My wife tries to give her milk, but there is not much milk in her breasts because we have not eaten well. I didn't have money to take a bus here, so I walked several hours. That is why I am tired."

My heart was melting. "Thank you for coming," I said. "Now, tell me, what is your greatest need?" I expected he would say, "Please give me money for a bus ride back to my village, or please give me money to buy milk for my baby." But he didn't ask for anything like this. He said, "Brother Bo, this is what I have been praying for a few years now. I am asking the Lord to provide me a secondhand bicycle so I can cover more villages."

This melted my heart even more! When I shared this story in a church in the US, a widow came forward to give money for that bicycle. With that bicycle, Julito covered more villages and started more outreaches. I lost contact with him after that, but a few years later, I learned that a team we were sending to the Philippines planned to visit his ministry. "Please take this fifteen hundred dollars and buy Pastor Julito a new motorbike," I said to the team leader.

When the team returned, I learned that Julito had been planning to leave the ministry due to discouragement. He was exhausted from trying to do the Lord's work in the face of continual hardship and meager resources. This gift of a new motorbike changed his mind! It was like handing someone the key to a new Cadillac!

During my trips, in addition to meeting with pastors and missionaries, I visited well-organized organizations and groups that are faithful and fruitful in the Lord's service. All met the standards and guidelines of ministry partnership that I had designed at Christian Aid before I left for home in 1986. One of these is the Translators

Association of the Philippines. They do literacy work, language learning, and translation of the Bible for people groups who do not have the Bible in their native tongue. This organization is staffed with highly educated leadership and staff missionaries who produce quality work for the body of Christ.

A Perfect Heart Toward Him

As I mentioned in Chapter 2, Ruth Shank, who handled all Christian Aid's communication with missionaries around the world, had lost her first child, a boy, at childbirth. Later she had a beautiful daughter named Beverly, whom she very much loved, but she never forgot about that son she did not get to raise. We were very fond of each other, and as time went on, she began to consider me her son, and I called her Mom Ruth. You might say that we "adopted" each other. When I would go back to the United States to visit Christian Aid, everybody would know me as Ruth's son, and they would know Ruth as my mother.[8]

It just so happens that Mom Ruth and I were born on the same day, January 23. Every year on our birthday, she had a habit of giving me a check for thirty dollars. Whenever I received a personal gift, especially a gift of money, I waited to hear from God about how I should use the gift because I did not feel worthy to spend it. Second Samuel 23:15–17 tells us about a time when David felt a similar way. While he was hiding with his fighters in a stronghold, and the Philistines had their garrison at Bethlehem, David said longingly, "Oh, that some-

---

[8] In 1988, Ruth remarried, and her name became Ruth Shira. I was honored in 2013 when she asked me to write an endorsement for the back cover of her autobiography, *God Recycles Broken Dreams: An Intimate Look at My Down-to-Earth Heavenly Father's Care.* Below is what I wrote as president and CEO of Advancing Native Missions:

> "Refusing, with her child-like faith, to allow her life to be defined by broken dreams, the author, Ruth Shira, found a loving God who more than made it up to her. By extending this God-given, resilient strength to many young and struggling native missionaries around the world, she gave rise to hundreds of sons and daughters among the nations, all who lovingly call her 'Mom Ruth.' How do I know this? I am one of them."

one would give me water to drink from the well of Bethlehem that is by the gate!" Upon hearing this, three mighty men in his army went to Bethlehem, broke through the Philistine battle lines at great risk, and brought water from that well to David. David poured the water on the ground and did not drink it, because he did not consider himself worthy of their courageous deed. This is how I feel when I receive a gift of money that someone has sacrificially given.

And with my eyes, I saw the one whom God could use. It was not the swiftest; it was not the strongest; it was the one with the willing heart.

On this birthday, as was my custom, I had put Mom Ruth's thirty-dollar check in my wallet. It was with me when I returned to the Philippines. One weekday, while I was standing with a pastor outside his small church in a slum area of Bacolod, I noticed three young boys about the same age playing tag. The first boy was tall and lanky; he was the swiftest. The second boy was the biggest and clearly the strongest. But it was the third boy who caught my eye. He did not run fast because his left leg dragged behind. He was the pastor's son. He had contracted a fever as a young baby, and the nurse had hit the sciatic nerve while giving him an injection. Since that day, his leg had not functioned properly.

The pastor interrupted our conversation and said, "Boys, boys, stop playing and get Brother Bo a chair from inside the church. Put it here, so he can sit in it." Suddenly, these boys froze in their tracks. I was immediately curious to see who would follow the orders of the pastor. The fastest boy and the strongest boy did not move. The boy with the lame leg went inside the church and, dragging his leg behind him, brought the chair. "Sir, this is for you," he said, looking into my eyes. And with my eyes, I saw the one whom God could use. It was not the swiftest; it was not the strongest; it was the one with the willing heart. The boy with the lame leg forgot his infirmity and showed his love.

As this boy turned to go, I said, "Young man, stay here." I reached for my wallet and pulled out Mom Ruth's check. Thirty dollars is a fortune in Philippine pesos. "My American mother gave this to me, but I don't deserve to spend this because she's a widow. She was left by her husband. I did not know who to give this to, but today, I know that this is for you. You deserve this. Buy some new clothes or whatever you'd like to buy. God bless you." This young man is now married. He and his wife are serving as missionaries.

Through this incident and God's Word, I have learned that when God wants something done, he does not look for the most important or talented person. A PhD in theology, a law degree, or a medical degree is not important to God. Rather, he looks for someone whose heart is completely given over to him. This lesson was illustrated before my eyes on this day, and I had personally learned it also on my first day at Christian Aid, when Dr. Finley had asked me what I could do for the Lord. I realized then that all I had to offer was a heart that is completely devoted to God. God is not looking for a perfect man. He is looking for one with a perfect heart towards him.

> "For the eyes of the LORD run to and fro
> throughout the whole earth, to shew himself strong
> in the behalf of them whose heart is perfect toward him."
> 2 CHRONICLES 16:9 KJV

Representing Christian Aid in America

In 1988, while I was in the US visiting churches, I was asked to join other Christian Aid staff members for a time of corporate prayer at a Wednesday morning staff meeting. This was a serious matter because the local newspaper, the *Daily Progress*, had published a negative article about the workings of Christian Aid. It was agreed that someone should go and talk with the editors of the paper to explain our ministry, but we didn't know whom to send.

As we went on our knees, I was praying that God would send George Ainsworth or Carl Gordon. After we had prayed, the question was posed, "Whom do we send?" I was astounded when it was unanimously decided that I should go, and that Rod Montgomery, the manager of Christian Aid, should accompany me. As the most junior member of the staff, I felt inadequate for this assignment. However, it seemed clear that the Lord had spoken, and I could not refuse it.

The meeting at the *Daily Progress* went well, and a favorable article with a nice photo appeared the next day on the features page.[9] This brought me closer to Dr. Finley and to the staff.

A Trip to Iowa

In 1989, Christian Aid sent me to a church in Ottumwa, Iowa. This was my first church visit on behalf of the ministry. I met with the missions committee and excitedly told them about the ministry of David Yone Mo. The Holy Spirit filled me with passion as I told the committee about how Pastor Yone Mo ministered to lepers in Burma. He was one of my heroes. After my presentation, Pastor Tim Dobson took me to lunch while the committee discussed whether to support the ministry of Pastor Yone Mo. When we returned around 2:00 p.m., the elder overseeing the meeting announced, "We have decided that the church should support you, Brother Bo Barredo."

"Not me," I insisted. "Please support David Yone Mo. I came here to request support for him. He deserves your support. He needs that support more than I do."

"No, no, no, we will support you, Brother Bo," they answered. "We trust you. You are our first missionary." Later, I brought David Yone Mo to this church, and the people loved him so much that they also supported his work.

On to Nevada

From there, I flew to Nevada to meet with another church. Christian Aid had scheduled this visit as part of the same trip to save money.

---

[9] The article is included as Appendix A.

This was a new church composed mostly of young people, and it was growing. Jack Evans, the oldest member of the church, was also the chairman of the church's missions committee. He had been a captain of a bomber squadron in the US Army Air Corps during World War II. He had written me a letter when our family still lived in the Philippines, and he had offered to provide support to Marlou and me as missionaries. I never responded because I did not want to start the process of raising my own support. Now that we were in the United States, I had reached out to him on behalf of Christian Aid.

When I arrived, the missions committee was so excited because Jack Evans had told them about Marlou and me. Mr. Evans said to me, "Bo, during the Second World War, I was in the Philippines with my squadron of bombers. We bombed many islands, especially the ones that grew sugarcane and produced alcohol for the Japanese forces occupying the islands. What island do you come from?"

"From Negros Island, sir," I replied.

"We bombed that island, Bo," he said.

"Thank you, sir, for helping my country," I replied.

"No, no, no, no, no," he answered. "Where was your father?"

"He was working in a Japanese military camp. He was then twelve years old, and he and his older brother Jesse washed the daily laundry of the Japanese soldiers. This way they could eat. He told me that when the American bombers and fighters came, he would quickly climb a coconut tree and shout at the top of his voice, 'The Americans are coming! The Americans are coming!' He was loudly cheering for you because he saw and experienced the cruelty of the Japanese inside the camp. They were not treating them right. The little food they gave them had worms in it."

"Bo," said Captain Jack Evans, looking a bit sad, "I would like to confess something to you. Those of us who flew in the planes were young; I was just nineteen years old, and others were about the same age or maybe in their early twenties. We dropped our bombs where we were told. I could have dropped a bomb and killed your father."

Then he said, "You know, Bo, I think we're going to sponsor you at fifty dollars a month. Now, tell me about Marlou."

"Marlou comes from the island of Leyte," I said.

"We also bombed the island of Leyte," said Captain Evans. "Now, where was Marlou's father?"

"He was one of the guerrillas who met the army that landed in Leyte led by General Douglas MacArthur," I answered.

"We could have dropped bombs on Marlou's father, as well," Captain Evans said, shaking his head. "We will increase that support soon."

Showered with Love

After Captain Evans and his wife, Miss Mickie, began supporting our family, they hosted me in their home. Such a wonderful and godly couple! They gave me a private room with a nice bed, but on the first night, shunning the bed, I laid some towels from the bathroom on the floor and lay down to sleep. In the early dawn, I was awakened by the extreme cold. I looked for the thermostat but couldn't find it. Suddenly, there was a knock on my door. From the other side came Miss Mickie's sweet voice, "Bo, it's cold. We will adjust the thermostat in your room."

Before I could jump up into the bed, the door opened. Miss Mickie looked at me with wide-eyed amazement. She obviously wondered why I had been sleeping on the floor instead of on the soft mattress.

"Please excuse me," I rushed to explain, "but I am in the habit of sleeping on the floor whenever I spend the night as a guest in a home. I want to always remember that I am now a servant of the servants of the Lord. I want to keep at the forefront of my mind that I serve servants who will receive crowns in heaven that are bigger than mine and bigger than the crowns of others like me."

Miss Mickie chuckled. Then, in a rather stern tone, she said, "But not in my house, young man! We would like to honor you as our special guest and as a servant of the Lord."

At breakfast, Captain Evans also laughed about this incident. "Bo," he said, "I agree with Mickie. You must know how to receive honors."

From that time on, Captain Evans and Miss Mickie showered love on Marlou and me as if we were their own children. In later years, after we moved to Virginia, they visited us there. In the ramrod-straight Captain Jack Evans, God provided me with another father. He and Miss Mickie personally supported us until God called them home. Their oldest son, Pastor Neal Evans, and their youngest son, Marvin Evans, continue to support the work of ANM.

A Loving Heart

It was raining in Manila one morning in 1989 as I drove out of our development to take Marlou to her job at the Central Bank of the Philippines. Suddenly, through the pitter-patter of the rain on the roof of our car, I heard an audible voice. Although no one else could have heard it, in my mind it was very distinct, and I knew it was the Lord. The words I heard were, "Today, if you ask me one thing, I am going to give it to you." I needed time to think, so I turned to Marlou and said, "Marlou, I just heard from the Lord. He said that if we ask him for one thing today, he will give it to us." I included Marlou, and she also began thinking. Forty-five minutes later when we arrived at the Central Bank, I asked Marlou what she thought. She gave me an answer, but later, neither of us could recall what it was. I believe that's because the question was directed solely to me.

I dropped Marlou off and headed home. During the forty-five-minute return drive, I prayed, "Lord, what do I ask of you? Do I want to go back into government and become a commissioner?" That was a very high rank, but I felt no joy or excitement when I said this. "Would I like to become a multimillionaire, so I can help many more people?" This idea also generated no excitement within me. "Do I want a mansion so I can bring my children and all their future families there and perhaps even some relatives who are poor? Do I want fancy cars? Do I want to be governor of my province?" All during the drive home I thought about what to ask from the Lord, but nothing stirred my heart.

Finally, as I was about to enter the gates of our development, I asked the Lord, "Father God, what do you want me to ask from you and of you?" Before I could hear the answer from him, I knew exactly what I wanted. He didn't have to tell me. I said, "Lord, I want a loving heart. Without a loving heart, I am useless for your kingdom. Lord, would you kindly give me a loving heart?" When I gave this answer to the Lord, I felt so broken and began crying.

I don't know whether God has given me a loving heart, but this is what I asked of him. I asked for a loving heart from the Lord because I know that any heart that does not come from God—any heart that I might try to engender for myself—would produce only superficial love. It could even be disastrous to the building of the kingdom.

> *"The heart is deceitful above all things,*
> *and desperately wicked; who can know it?"*
> JEREMIAH 17:9

Ready To Die

My own family needed lots of faith while I was serving in my new calling as a missionary for Christian Aid. Whenever I would leave our home in Manila and go out into the remote villages in the mountains of the Philippines, I was in constant danger. During this period, it was common for guerrilla assassination teams, called "Sparrow Units," to come up behind police officers and pastors and shoot them in the head. Almost daily, reports of these murders were in the newspapers. I traveled incognito, so the villagers would not know that I was a missionary. But still it was dangerous.

Marlou and the children knew about this danger. Before I left on trips, they would gather in the living room and lay hands on me and pray for God's protection. Before one of these trips, after our family had prayed together, our daughter Felisa took my hand and led me down the stairs to the first floor of our condominium. At the time, she was about five years old. Before I opened the door to take a taxi to the airport, she turned to me and said, *"Papa, Papa, babalik ka. Papa,*

When I prayed this, peace settled in my heart; I was ready to die that day.

babalik ka. Aantayin kita." In English this means, "Father, please come back. I will wait for you."

She wasn't aware that I was going to a mountain village on Negros Island where NPA communist guerrillas were active. Only days before, they had killed five non-villagers who were making some repairs inside the village. They just didn't like their presence, so they killed them.

When I visited this village, the guerrillas were still there. But I didn't realize this until somebody said to me, "Oh, by the way, Brother Bo, there are guerrillas here, and they're asking who you are." I knew that I was in great danger because I was a stranger, and I had a big camera and tape recorders. This is the type of paraphernalia a spy might carry. I immediately got in my vehicle with my companion and some passengers who were hitchhiking with us, and we headed out of the village. By God's grace, I was able to flee the area just minutes before rebels entered the hut where I had been staying. They had been looking for me with the intention of capturing me.

While we were driving away, a voice whispered in my head, "Today, you shall die. Today, you shall die. Down the road, some guerrillas will flag down your vehicle. They will line you up in the ditch beside the road and shoot you. Today, you shall die."

Fear enveloped me. Trembling, I looked up to heaven and prayed, "Holy Father, I come before you in the name of Jesus. If you allow that I be killed today beside the road in an unknown village, would you kindly do one thing for me? Would you please send someone to tell my little girl that her father is never coming back, but that I will wait for her in heaven where I will see her again?" I said this because I could not bear the thought of closing my eyes in death knowing that my little girl would be continuing to wait for me. When I prayed this, peace settled in my heart; I was ready to die that day. But I thank God that I escaped that danger with no incident.

Heightened Danger

In 1989, Billy Graham sponsored a worldwide missions conference in Manila. It was called the Lausanne Conference, because a similar conference had been previously held in Lausanne, Switzerland, and it was attended by more than three thousand missionary leaders from around the world. Carl Gordon came from the United States, and we attended the conference together.

While the conference was in session, a leftist national newspaper reported that the Philippine government and the United States government were providing support to US-based Christian missions agencies who preached the Gospel in the villages. Christian groups were accused of using spiritual warfare as part of a low-intensity conflict strategy formulated as an anti-insurgency weapon by the US government. On the front page was an illustration of a man holding a gun and a Bible. Beside the illustration was written,

BIBLE AGAINST COMMUNISM.
US gov't uses American evangelists for
counterinsurgency operation in RP. Page 3.

On page three, one paragraph of the actual article read,

Christian Aid, one of the most active US based ministries in the Philippines, directs its new converts to go out and "win souls" among Catholics considered "antagonistic to the Gospel," the NPA members and students who might otherwise join progressive groups.

Realizing that this article identifying Christian Aid was bound to stir up the guerrillas' ire even more, Carl Gordon said to me, "Bo, your work has become more dangerous. You should take your family out of the Philippines and come to the US. You can work from Charlottesville. We will expand your work into other countries."

I said, "No, Carl, this is my mission field. This is where God has placed me. I was born here, and I'm going to help share the Good

News with my own people. I still have lots of work to do and lots of places to cover."

Carl quietly accepted my response. But afterward my father was urged by his fellow pastors to seriously warn me of the danger. I gained a greater appreciation for the seriousness of the situation when Colonel James N. Rowe was ambushed by suspected NPA guerrillas as his car was approaching a US military compound in Manila. Colonel Rowe was the chief of the Army division at the Joint United States Military Advisory Group, which provided counter-insurgency training and logistical support for the Philippine Armed Forces.

The Most Difficult Mission Field

Marlou's mother retired from her position as a teacher and school supervisor, and in 1988, she came to live with us in Manila. Marlou's father had gone to be with the Lord several years before, so at this time, her mother was a widow. Prior to his death, Marlou's father had been a successful lawyer and the provincial treasurer, which had made him the third-highest public official in the province of two million people. Both of Marlou's parents were highly educated people who commanded great respect in the community.

When I married Marlou, her mother was the only person who had strongly objected. She was not happy about her daughter marrying someone who was not a Roman Catholic. On the island of Leyte, where Marlou was raised, some of the prominent Roman Catholic families had their family names carved on their donated church pew.

A year after Marlou and I became missionaries, I tried to witness to Marlou's mom, but to no avail. So I decided to try a different approach. I deliberately started doing special things for Marlou to demonstrate my love for her. I already was in the habit of telling Marlou that I loved her, and I began doing more practical things to show my love. These acts of kindness were natural and genuine because I loved Marlou so much. There was much joy in our household as Marlou's mom saw how I cared for her beloved daughter.

One morning when I woke up, I went to the kitchen and found my mother-in-law crying. I said, "*Nanay, nganu man nga gahibi ka nga temprano pa man?*" In English that means, "Mother, why are you crying so early in the morning?"

She replied, "Son, I have been looking at you and my daughter as you live as husband and wife. All these years, I have been watching the way you and your young family live. I want that kind of life for myself and for my other children. I would like to change my religion."

I was taken aback! I said, "*Nanay*, you don't have to change your religion. All you must do is receive Christ Jesus into your heart. I will tell you how you can do this later today."

That evening, Marlou's mom sat down with Marlou and me and our four children, and she received Jesus Christ as her Lord and Savior. When we left for the US in 1991, one of our neighbors in the condominium who was a pastor did the follow-up of Nanay's newfound faith.

Eight Years Later

Eight years later, in 1999, Marlou's mom became very ill. At this time, Marlou and I and our four children were living in the United States. Marlou and I flew back to Manila with Felisa and Jim and ministered to Marlou's mom for a few weeks. As she was lying sick in the hospital, she drew strength and comfort from our singing Christian songs together. She especially loved Felisa's singing.

We praise God that Marlou's mom died as a born-again Christian a few months after we returned to the US. Sometimes when speaking to men in the churches, I say, "The hardest mission field in the world is not with the headhunters somewhere in Indonesia, or with the African people living in the bush. The hardest mission field in the world is your own mother-in-law. If you do not show genuine and sincere love to her daughter, she will never believe what you say about the love of Jesus. You cannot convince a mother-in-law of the love of Jesus unless you live an authentic believer's life in your own family."

111

Much Is Required

As I continued my ministry of visiting, checking, encouraging, and equipping the missions partners Christian Aid served, working out of my base in the Philippines, everything seemed to be flowing fruitfully and comfortably. I also had fruitful trips to the US in 1988 and 1989 to visit Christian Aid and various churches. But one day in 1990, as I was driving Marlou home after her workday at the Central Bank of the Philippines, she suddenly turned to me and said, "You know, *palangga*, to whom much is given, much is required."

Perking up, I asked Marlou what she meant. "The Lord has blessed you with so many talents," she replied. "Christian Aid is offering you a wider scope of responsibility, and yet you refuse to take it."

"I don't want to go and live in the United States," I protested. "I want to work here in the Philippines. We have a stable life here, and my ministry is fruitful." I paused for a moment. "But since you feel this way, I will ask the Lord about it."

One of the major reasons why I didn't want to go to the US was because I didn't want to have to raise support for myself and my family. I had no trouble asking for money on behalf of others, but I disliked the idea of asking for myself. Just as the apostle Paul provided for his ministry by making tents, Marlou's "tentmaking" work at the Central Bank coupled with a modest monthly stipend from Christian Aid were providing funds for our family's living expenses. If we moved to the US, how would we survive? But because I respected Marlou, I promised to pray about it.

As I continued to seriously pray about this matter without receiving clear guidance from the Lord, I decided one day to do something that many Christians, including myself, may consider rather humorous or bizarre. I decided to seek an answer for my question by opening my Bible and seeing what verse first caught my eye. I was familiar with the pitfalls of this approach. I had heard the joke about the man who randomly opened his Bible to get some direction for his life, and his eyes alighted on Matthew 27:5: "Then [Judas] .

. . departed, and went and hanged himself." Nevertheless, I opened my Bible and solemnly said, "Lord, I'm seeking an answer from you. Please allow me to do this."

A New Thing

My eyes landed on Isaiah 43:18–19. I had never encountered these verses before. It said, "Do not remember the former things, Nor consider the things of old. Behold, I will do a new thing, Now it shall spring forth; Shall you not know it? I will even make a road in the wilderness And rivers in the desert."

I prayed, "Lord, are you speaking to me? Are you telling me that you are preparing a new thing for me?" I felt in my heart that this was God's answer to my question. He was uprooting me and my family from the Philippines and moving us to the United States, where I would do a new thing by working at Christian Aid. But I was not sure, so I said to Marlou, "Marlou, I heard from the Lord that he is going to do a new thing for us, but to be more certain, I am going to place a fleece before him."

"What do you mean?" she asked.

"We will go to the American embassy. You and I have our passports with our visas, but the children do not have visas. It is well known that the American embassy never gives visas for a whole family because they know there is a greater risk they will not return. If the embassy gives us visas for the children, I will take that as a word from the Lord that we should go."

At the American embassy, as we were waiting our turn to plead our case, I happened to look over at the vice-consuls who were conducting the interviews. One of them I recognized as the same lady who had interviewed me when I had applied for a tourist visa several years before. She fit the stereotype of a stern spinster. Her hair was drawn back and tied with a rubber band; her hard face looked as if it had never cracked a smile.

On my previous visit to the embassy, when I had applied for that tourist visa, I had come dressed in my best shirt and tie. I even wore a new Rolex watch that I had bought with Marlou's permission using my accrued pay increase differentials. I was high in government at the time and relatively prosperous, and I had brought my land titles, my bank account passbook, and other things to make an impression. Even though I simply wanted a tourist visa to visit America for a short time, she denied my application.

Now here she was again. I prayed in my heart several times, fervently imploring, "Heavenly Father, Lord, I come to you in the name of Jesus, please don't assign us to her. Please don't. Please!"

An Embarrassing Miracle

When our names were called to be interviewed, as I had dreaded, we ended up with this lady. I thought, we may as well write *finis* on our plan to go to the United States. This lady will never give visas to our whole family.

Marlou and I and our two oldest children, Benjie and David, marched up and stood before the interviewing booth of this surly woman. I don't scare easily, but on this day, my knees were knocking, and my heart was racing. From the other side of the glass of the interviewing booth, her stern face glared back at me. "Who is this?" she demanded, not in words, but with an arrogant nod of her head in the direction of Marlou.

I fully intended to answer clearly and distinctly, "Ma'am, this is my wife." But I was so rattled that the words that haltingly stumbled out of my mouth were, "Ma'am, this . . . this . . . this is my . . . my husband."

Realizing my mistake, I immediately straightened up and attempted to correct myself. "I mean, this is my wife," I said with as much confidence and dignity as I could muster. But it was too late. Marlou and the children had already started laughing. They had never seen me so nervous or flustered. I was so embarrassed! Then something unbelievable happened. This stern vice-consul also started laughing. When she settled down, she asked me a few questions. Then she said, "Come back this afternoon."

"Come back this afternoon!" This meant she was going to approve our visa application! Later that afternoon, Marlou and I picked up the visas for the children. We left the embassy rejoicing. "Thank you, Lord! Thank you, Lord! Thank you, Lord! And thank you, Lord, for that vice-consul." We joyfully celebrated by eating out at the Aristocrat, a popular restaurant in Manila that specializes in fried chicken.

What did we learn from this? We learned that God can and does use anyone and anything to accomplish his will. He can even use humor, especially humor that keeps us humble. God doesn't have to arm us with land titles, bank books that record millions of pesos, or expensive jewelry. He can use even an insignificant, funny mistake to instantly change a heart. We learned that he loves to help those who seek to fulfill his purpose for their own generation.

> *"Behold, I am the LORD, the God of all flesh.*
> *Is there anything too hard for Me?"*
> JEREMIAH 32:27

1 CORINTHIANS
15:58

Therefore, my beloved brethren,
be steadfast, immovable, always abounding
in the work of the Lord, knowing that your
labor is not in vain in the Lord.

A NEW THING

After we received the visas for the children, I said to Marlou, "When we go to the United States, there can be no looking back, because he who puts his hands to the plow and looks back is not worthy. By faith, we must cut clean. We must give away or sell everything we have." She agreed.

Leaving the land of one's birth is not easy. My father was prepared, as he had already been forewarned by friends whose children had left for the US. "Ben," they had told him, "when your children go to the US with their families, be sure to accept that not one of them will ever come back."

When we said our goodbyes to our loved ones, friends, and neighbors, we were met with a mixture of joy and sadness. Our household helpers were like family to us. Typically, none left us except for some major reason, and some had been with us for up to fifteen years. When we called them together as a group and told them about our plans, they all cried. They loved our whole family, especially the children. We gave them the equivalent of six months of salaries and many of our possessions. To one we gave the color TV, to another the sewing machine, and so on. More tears were shed as we did this.

One of the biggest expenses in the US is dental care, so our whole family scheduled visits to the dentist. We sold our two cars and our condominium, and we kept only what personal possessions we could carry on the plane because we knew we were not coming back.

Arriving in a New Land

Marlou, Benjamin, David, Felisa, Jim, and I arrived at Dulles Airport outside Washington, DC, on February 27, 1991. It was in the middle of an ice storm, and the temperature was twenty-seven degrees Fahrenheit. All of us were wearing only Filipino cotton shirts. As we ventured out of the terminal into the cold, our brown skin turned blue!

Carl and Minda Gordon, Pastor Harold Bare, and Pastor Bare's youngest son, Josh, met us at the airport. They drove us to Charlottesville, and we settled into the Christian Aid guest house. We had made plans to rent a small townhouse, but we didn't yet have any furniture for it.

On our first Sunday in the US, we worshipped at Trinity Presbyterian Church. At one point during the service, at the invitation of Pastor Skip Ryan, our family sang to the congregation. As Marlou played the piano and eight-year-old Felisa's beautiful voice rose above all the others, we sang,

> *Beautiful, beautiful, Jesus is beautiful,*
> *And Jesus makes beautiful things of my life.*
> *Carefully touching me, causing my eyes to see*
> *That Jesus makes beautiful things of my life,*
> *That Jesus makes beautiful things of my life.*

According to Carl, there was not one dry eye among those present. Afterwards, an announcement was made about our need for clothes and furniture, and the church responded with overwhelming generosity. Within three days, we had enough tables, chairs, dressers, beds, blankets, pillows, kitchen utensils, dishes, and other things to furnish our townhouse. We were so touched that we have kept to this day the list with the names of the donors and what they gave. Many of these people have been our supporters for many years.

I began working with the Overseas Department as the Southeast Asia Director for Christian Aid Mission. We were so happy at Christian Aid, so very happy! Churches invited me to come and speak, and we were able to begin raising support for Christian Aid. After each outreach, I would report back to the Christian Aid staff, always giving credit to Dr. Finley. He was the first advocate for native missionaries, and I learned from him.

Ambassador for Christian Aid

On April 14, 1991, the Sunday before the world-famous annual Boston Marathon, Dr. Finley was invited to speak at the First Congregational Church in Hopkinton, Massachusetts. This was an important event because runners from around the world came to the area, and many would be attending the service. It turned out that Dr. Finley could not preach due to a prior commitment. It was decided that during our Wednesday meeting, the whole staff should go on our knees and inquire of the Lord who should be sent in Dr. Finley's place. After prayer, the staff elected to send me.

When I arrived in Hopkinton on that Sunday, the church was surrounded by vans and trucks from NBC, ABC, and other TV networks. I felt so small and terribly intimidated. The pastor of the church, Dr. Richard Germaine, and the assistant pastor, Dr. Michael Laurence, appeared nervous as I introduced myself to them. No doubt they were wondering, "Is this substitute that Dr. Finley sent going to disappoint the people from around the world who have come for this important service?" Truthfully, I was the most nervous one. As I looked with trepidation at the assembling group of TV networks, I cried out to my Heavenly Father in the name of Jesus, "Lord, how should I open my message? What do you want me to say?" I had prepared a message, but I still needed an introduction that would immediately capture the attention of the listeners and relate to the occasion, just like a lawyer who wants to persuade a jury needs a good opening for his address. I started praying for the right way to begin my talk.

That Saturday night in the home of my host, I went to the bathroom to brush my teeth, still struggling in thought and prayer about how to open my message. Suddenly, I had a strong impression in my heart: "Where was the first marathon run in the Bible for Jesus Christ?" I knew in my spirit that the Holy Spirit had given me the answer to my prayer! After scribbling some more notes that night, I went to sleep in peace.

The First Marathon for Jesus Christ

Sunday morning, when I got up to speak, I opened by boldly proclaiming Luke 2:8–16. "The greatest story ever told runs this way. 'Now there were in the same country shepherds living out in the fields, keeping watch over their flock by night. And behold, an angel of the Lord stood before them . . .'"

I paused and looked out over the congregation. Faces from many nations were gazing at me with rapt attention! I continued, "And the glory of the Lord shone around them, and they were greatly afraid. Then the angel said to them, 'Do not be afraid, for behold, I bring you good tidings of great joy which will be to all people.'" To honor the people from all over the world who were in the congregation, I made a sweeping motion with my arms and repeated the words, "All people! Yes, all people."

After a pause, I continued, "'For there is born to you this day in the city of David a Savior, who is Christ the Lord. And this will be the sign to you: You will find a Babe wrapped in swaddling cloths, lying in a manger.' And suddenly there was with the angel a multitude of the heavenly host praising God and saying: 'Glory to God in the highest, and on earth peace, goodwill toward men.' So it was, when the angels had gone away from them into heaven, that the shepherds said to one another, 'Let us now go to Bethlehem and see this thing that has come to pass, which the Lord has made known to us.'"

At this point, I picked up my Bible and read from Luke 2:16: "And they came with haste and found Mary and Joseph, and the Babe lying in a manger." After a pause, with volume and clarity I repeated, "And they came with haste . . ."

Looking out over the congregation, I continued, "The first marathon run in the Bible for the Savior happened that night. Would you say they ran fast? Of course, they did. In fact, very fast. Who would not run fast to see the face of the Savior? Who would not run fast for the joy, for the honor, for the blessing of seeing the face of the Savior? The first marathon was run for Christ that night."

As I continued to talk about our Savior, Jesus Christ, I could see that some of the athletes in the congregation had tears in their eyes. Looking back, I speculated that many of them must be true believers. Perhaps they were recalling the stirring words from the 1981 award-winning movie *Chariots of Fire*, when runner Eric Liddell said, "I believe God made me for a purpose, but he also made me fast. And when I run, I feel his pleasure." After winning the Olympic gold medal in 1924, Liddell went to China to do missionary work with his father. He died inside a Japanese camp during World War II.

After my sermon, the pastoral staff sincerely thanked me. Over the next several years, the assistant pastor, Dr. Michael Laurence, and his dear wife, Sheila, became our close friends and supporters. Dr. Laurence became the senior pastor of the church, and thirteen years after we first met on that wonderful occasion in April 1991, Marlou, Felisa, and I visited him and his beautiful and godly family in Hopkinton.

Digging a New Well

One day, Carl Gordon came to me and said he intended to leave Christian Aid. He sensed that the Lord was calling him to start a new mission, and he asked me to join him. After praying, I felt that Carl was right.

I studied the Scriptures about wells. In Genesis, we read how Abraham and Isaac needed to dig new wells to have fresh water. I felt compassion for the long lines of native missionaries waiting for a single Bible, a pair of shoes, a bicycle, thirty dollars a month to support their family, or a new roof on their church. We knew so many missionaries and pastors in need. I agreed with Carl that we should

We sensed the Lord saying to us that the brook from which we had been drinking had run dry, and it was time for us to move on.

leave Christian Aid and dig a new well that would supply more fresh water to the native missionaries who need to be equipped with better tools to more effectively and efficiently spread the Gospel in all the world.

Believing that God cloaks major moves with wise counsel and Scripture, in the first week of August 1992, about one month prior to our planned resignation from Christian Aid, Carl and I invited godly men whom we trusted to a one-day retreat in Syria, Virginia. Participating with us were George Ainsworth from Charlottesville, P. R. Misra and John Varghese from India, and Laurent Mbanda from Africa. After prayers, fellowship, and seeking God's mind, we were drawn to 1 Kings 17:1–8. In this passage, Elijah proclaims a drought, and God directs him to the Brook Cherith, where he finds fresh water to drink for a time. But after a while, the brook runs dry, and the Lord tells him to move to another place. We sensed the Lord saying to us that the brook from which we had been drinking had run dry, and it was time for us to move on.

As lawyers, both Marlou and I have a high regard for evidence. The Bible also talks about how a fact is established by two or three witnesses. It also says Jesus is our advocate, which is a way of saying that he is our attorney. He presents our case before his Heavenly Father, asking that our sins be exchanged for his righteousness, and he champions those who have not been saved. At the retreat, God had provided one piece of evidence that he was directing us to dig a new well. Carl and I waited on God for additional evidence as confirmation.

By his grace, God had this second piece of evidence waiting for us when we returned home from the retreat. It was in the form of a letter addressed to Carl from Ron Tillett. At this time, Ron and his wife, Pam, were supporters of my father's ministry. They are a godly and generous couple who are devoted to helping bring the Gospel to unreached peoples and tribes.[10] Remarkably, he had written the letter while Carl and I had been at the retreat seeking God's will. In the letter, he expressed deep concern that native missionaries were not being properly served, and he encouraged Carl to "start a new ministry to help nationals now!"

Seeking Confirmation

Carl and I immediately decided to travel to Indiana to meet with Ron and Pam. I didn't have a credit card, so Carl rented the car. We drove for fourteen straight hours, arriving in the town of Rensselaer at two o'clock in the morning. The next day, we met with Ron, Pam, and the widow of their pastor, Virginia Tobias[11]. As we told them about our plans and asked for their counsel, they said, "We believe that God has put this new ministry in your hearts. You must start a new well."

During a Wednesday staff meeting on September 23, 1992, with much emotion, Carl and I said goodbye to Dr. Finley and our brothers and sisters at Christian Aid. The entire staff was unhappy and sad about our decision. Some were crying. Dr. Finley especially was not pleased. But I strongly felt that to be in God's will, I had to say goodbye to him and to Christian Aid. Many missionaries overseas were facing great struggles and life-threatening dangers. God had brought my family and me to the US to help them, and I needed to be obedient to God's call on my life.

---

[10] Ron personifies many things that are good in a man by the grace of God! We consider him as one of ANM's co-founders.

[11] Virginia began supporting our family as soon as ANM started. She would mail a check for $100 or $150 directly to our home with a note stating, "I am not sending this to ANM as I want you to use it for your family." But I could not bring myself to cash these checks and use them for family needs. Each time a check from Virginia arrived, I would kiss the check many times with tears in my eyes, raise it toward heaven, and pray, "Dearest Lord, if this 'poor widow from Zarephath' remembers us, surely, you, our Heavenly Father, remember us and hear our cries." Then I would give the check to ANM. I felt that Virginia's check was so sacrificial that those we served deserved it more than we did. These initial years of ANM were struggling years for our family.

When the meeting was dismissed, three brothers in the Lord approached me one by one. Each tried to discourage me from starting a new ministry. One told me that only one of many new ministries survives the first year. Another shared with me not to worry about poor missionaries, that there will always be many poor native missionaries. The last one whispered to me that it would take at least five to six years for a new ministry to be on its feet.

Hearing these words of discouragement from some of our coworkers and seeing the pain on many of their faces undermined my confidence. I didn't hold these reactions against any of them because our departure was understandably disturbing to them personally and to the organization, but their emotionally charged negativity gave me pause. I went to a restroom in a corner of the building, locked the door, and went down on my knees. I prayed, "Heavenly Father, in Jesus' name, if this plan of ours is not from you, please kill me. Yes, please kill me, as I don't want to bring trouble to the work of building your kingdom." I prayed this prayer because I truly love God, and I only aim to please him and none other. After that, Carl and I went to our separate homes.

It was an extraordinarily difficult time. The following day, I stayed home as my heart was troubled and my courage was being tested. I believed what we were doing was right, but our decision to leave had hurt a number of our dearest brothers and sisters in the Lord. It also had exposed my own family to considerable risk financially, and I wondered how we would survive. I was greatly in need of encouragement.

That very day I received a letter from John Scully, a longtime and much-respected member of the staff at Christian Aid, whom I highly admired. It was such an encouragement to me that I am reprinting portions of it below:

Dear Bo:

I am not one to speak swiftly or to offer my personal counsel on the spur of the moment. Last night I thought about what you have decided to do, and I have come to this conclusion: I believe you are making the right decision, and I am 100% behind you.

The Lord knows your heart, and the Lord knows your future. You put yourself at God's mercy, and that to me is a resounding testimony of your faith in action. Very bold. Very necessary if God is to do even bigger things through you. You have been, more than most people who come through here, an example of a vessel emptied for God to fill. We have all seen how God has filled you to do his mighty works.

I believe, brother, that you will have even greater opportunities to be used, and there is no fear in my heart that you are putting yourself or your family at risk.

Now I do not have a word from the Lord here, but I am personally convinced that you need to remain in ministry for the brethren in the Philippines. I believe that you can be the most active and productive instrument of help for missionaries in your country. You can be the financial channel that they desperately need. I will commit to pray that you will continue to reach out to the churches and connect them with ministries in the Philippines.

Lord bless you and your family,

John Scully

Filled with Sadness

Even though Carl and I were confident we were doing what God wanted, I was filled with sadness. Upon waking one morning, the realization that I was no longer at Christian Aid hit me especially hard. I missed Christian Aid, and I missed Dr. Finley most of all. I loved Dr. Finley, and I knew he loved me. I owed him so much, especially for teaching me about missions and giving me the opportunity to serve God at Christian Aid. We reconciled several years later, as I have written earlier, but my departure at this time was not easy for either of us.

I also missed Cynthia Finley, Dr. Finley's wonderful wife, whom I regarded as my own sister. I began crying. I cried and cried, sobbing deeply, until I could not take it anymore. As I sought comfort from the Lord, I felt prompted to call Dr. James Taylor, the chairman of the mathematics department at the University of Virginia and the chairman of the missions committee at Trinity Presbyterian Church in Charlottesville.

I said to Dr. Taylor, "Sir, I need a father; I need a father so I can cry on his shoulder." Dr. Taylor immediately came to meet with Marlou and me in our kitchen. As I poured out my heart to him, he cried with me. Then he said, "Bo, my wife and I are going to help you. Just tell me what we can do because I believe in your call." Dr. Taylor was a great comfort to me. God has graciously blessed me with so many godly fathers. My own father was first, and then came Dr. Bob Finley, and then Dr. Ed Hampton in Hagerstown, Maryland. After that, it was Gordon Shira, chaplain of the Salvation Army in Charlottesville and my former coworker at Christian Aid. Then God brought me Captain Jack Evans, and now he was providing Dr. James Taylor. I was further comforted when Carl and some pastors who had come to know me over the years wrote gracious letters of recommendation that I could use to establish our new ministry.[12] Truly, God comforts his people!

Papa Tom and Mama Karen

When Marlou and I left Christian Aid, we had no support, and we didn't expect to receive any. Because of the circumstances, we figured people were likely questioning our decision. But God in his grace ministered to us in the midst of this trial. One day, out of the blue, we received in the mail a check for $1,200 from a couple named Tom and Karen Thomas. The accompanying letter said that when they received news that we had stepped out in faith from Christian Aid, they immediately went on their knees to pray. The Lord then laid on their hearts to send us $1,200!

---

[12] *Note from editor:* Because these testimonials proved to be vital for establishing the credibility of the new ministry, excerpts from them are included as Appendix B.

Marlou and I had never personally met Tom and Karen, but Tom had previously written us a note and enclosed a photo of the two of them. In the note, he explained that during World War II, he had been with General Douglas MacArthur's invasion forces as they landed on Leyte Island, and that in recent years, he had supported the evangelistic ministry of my father, Ben Barredo. When he learned that Ben Barredo's son was a global missionary with Christian Aid in the United States, he felt compelled to write to us.

Marlou immediately wrote back to Tom: "Sir, you landed in the Philippines in 1944 to liberate the Philippines together with the army of General MacArthur, and you landed on my island, Leyte Island. And my father was one of the guerrillas who met your force when you landed on the Red Beach in Leyte Island."

A few days later, we received another letter from Tom. "Marlou," he wrote, "I love the Filipino people because when I was on your island, I got sick. I was not wounded, but I got sick. While I was in the field hospital of the American Army, there were two or three Filipino boys who would crawl under the barbed-wire fence of the camp and bring me boiled bananas and boiled eggs. My heart was so touched by their acts of charity towards me. I truly loved them. After the war, I tried to find them, but I could not. Ever since, I have loved Filipinos. Could my wife, Karen, and I come to see you?"

Not long afterwards, Tom and Karen Thomas came from Wickenburg, Arizona, to see Marlou and me at Christian Aid in Charlottesville. There was an instant bonding. Tom seemed to be redirecting his love for these two or three World War II Filipino boys to Marlou. Over time, he and Karen became like a spiritual father and mother to us. We lovingly addressed them as Papa Tom and Mama Karen.

A Genuine Cowboy

Tom was a genuine cowboy. He had been cowboying since he was seven years old, and he could shoot a coyote with his rifle from twenty-five yards away. He showed us a state postcard that pictured a chuckwagon and cowboys sitting around the campfire. He was one of the cowboys in the photo. In the evenings, Tom also wrote poems.

Tom and Karen were members of Calvary Baptist Church in Wickenburg, and Tom served on the church's missions committee. In 1993, he invited Marlou and me to make a presentation to the committee. Ever since that time, the church has faithfully supported us.

After we started Advancing Native Missions, Tom and Karen came to visit us again. Tom owned a saddlery shop in Wyoming, where he carved saddles that sold for $1,000 and up. He said, "Bo, I'm going to donate my house and my saddlery shop to the Lord's work. It is personally financed by me, so the installments every month can now go to ANM. Could ANM use this money?" We were so touched; we thanked him profusely.

After conferring with Carl, I requested that he allow us to use his gift to pay ANM's utilities each month. For the next several years, God allowed Papa Tom to provide power, light, and water for Advancing Native Missions.

The Night Horse

On one of his visits, Papa Tom told me about the "night horse." He said,

Bo, there are two kinds of horses: day horses and night horses. Day horses are the ones the cowboys use for herding and corralling. But at night, the two or three cowboys that are assigned to ride around the camp to ensure the safety of the herd will always choose the night horse.

The night horse doesn't have to be the tallest, strongest, or handsomest. As a rule, the night horse is an old horse that is calm, sensible, reliable, surefooted, and trustworthy. Every cowboy that has ridden a night horse knows that many times his very life depended on him. A good night horse does not run away when the diamondback shakes its rattle, the lightning flashes, or the thunder roars. He stands steady all through the night waiting for instructions from its rider.

In these fast-darkening days, God is looking for men and women who will be night horses. He wants followers of Jesus who will remain trustworthy and wait for instructions from the Holy Spirit. He is looking for men and women who will persevere and not lose hope because they know that on the other side of the darkness the light of dawn will come, that joy comes with the morning."

I have always remembered what Papa Tom told me about the night horse, and I have often used this illustration in my sermons and talks in conjunction with 1 Corinthians 15:58: "Therefore, my beloved brethren, be steadfast, immovable, always abounding in the work of the Lord, knowing that your labor is not in vain in the Lord."

In early 2020, Pastor Ken Demeter and the missions committee of Calvary Baptist Church invited me to speak at the church's missions conference. An offering was collected, and God used it together with a gift from Wickenburg Bible Fellowship, a neighboring church pastored by Pastor Rod Hackett, which also supported Marlou and me, to build a new library building for a Bible school on the Philippine island of Panay. The previous libraries had thatched roofs that kept getting blown away by typhoons. Now, thanks to these two Arizona churches, this village school for missionaries has a library that weathers the storms.

Launching a New Ministry

Now that Carl and I had decided to start a new ministry, we had to pick a name. Our vision was to help indigenous missionaries, but the word "indigenous" seemed too complex. Some people even had difficulty spelling it. Carl's wife, Minda, suggested the name Advancing Native Missions. A few people we checked with thought the word "native" was downgrading, but Minda countered, "Native describes the people you are helping. They are native to the land; they know the native languages; they know the native people; they know the native culture." Carl and I said, "That's it!" We settled on the name

Advancing Native Missions, or ANM for short, and we give Minda credit for coming up with it.[13]

I proposed to Carl that we next needed to form a council of elders composed of godly people from the local area with a heart for our vision. He agreed, and the inaugural members were Pastor Harold Bare from Covenant Church, Chaplain Gordon Shira of the Salvation Army, Ruth Shank Shira, Dr. James Taylor of Trinity Presbyterian Church, Pastor George Ainsworth of Christ Community Church, and Pastor Bob French of Oakleigh Church. We also wanted to include Brother Graham Stewart, but he was in Honduras at the time. In our first meeting of the council, we posed the question, "Is starting this new ministry a righteous thing to do?" The members of the council unanimously agreed that it was.

Carl and I decided that Carl should be president, and that I would be vice president with the responsibility for organizational and ministry development because that is the gift God has given me. My responsibility was to design and develop an organizational structure for the ministry and its functionalities. Building on this foundation, I would go as an ambassador of ANM to churches in the United States to advocate on behalf of missionaries around the world. My third responsibility would be to travel around the world to identify and vet new missions groups we were considering supporting using the experience I had gained vetting people and organizations as a missionary in the Philippines. We wanted to establish relationships only with dynamic and godly ministries that operated with integrity. I would be responsible for ensuring that the vision, beliefs, and practices of all new missionary partners of ANM were in conformity with ANM's statement of faith and guidelines for financial accountability, organizational structure, and godly ministry and family relationships.

---

[13] Minda Lopez Gordon is a successful businesswoman admired and loved by many in the community and by native missionaries whom she hosts in their lovely home. Her gift of hospitality is well known. She is an articulate and effective advocate for native missionaries.

Receiving Our Vision

The next question Carl and I had to address was where to begin sharing the vision of ANM. After prayer, I felt led by the Lord to ask my friend, Rev. Gerald Ripley, pastor of Abundant Life Church in San Antonio, Texas, if Carl and I could come and share our vision with his congregation. I had spoken at this church a year before, and God had given me favor in their hearts. Since then, Pastor Ripley and I had become like brothers. He was a godly man married to a godly woman, Sharon. As a leader of the ministerial fellowship in San Antonio, he had stature in the community. His congregation of forty to fifty people met in a rented storefront. One day, as I read Zechariah 4:10, I realized why God might have stirred my heart to visit this church first. In this passage of Scripture, we are cautioned not to despise the day of small beginnings: "For who has despised the day of small things?"

Pastor Ripley was open for us to come. The problem was that neither Carl nor I had cars capable of making the 1,500-mile trip. Carl's wife, Minda, kindly loaned us her car, which unfortunately wasn't much better. On the way, we spent the night in Tupelo, Mississippi, at the home of family friends Frank and Peggy Scott. As we were about to leave the next morning, they said, "That car of yours is not reliable. Why don't you borrow our new van?"

With much rejoicing, we packed our belongings in this more reliable vehicle and headed down the Natchez Trace Parkway toward San Antonio. It was such a beautiful morning! The branches of the pine trees glistened in the sunlight, and the aroma of fresh pine wafted in through the open windows.

Because I Am Coming

Suddenly, I found myself lifting my eyes towards heaven and crying out, "Father, why are you calling my brother and me to this ministry? Why are you leading us to dig this new well? Marlou and I have no money. We have no resources. Why are you calling us?" In this moment, an impression came into my heart. The Lord said to me, "Because I am coming. Because I am coming."

Immediately, Matthew 24:14 came into my mind. It says, "And this gospel of the kingdom will be preached in all the world as a witness to all the nations, and then the end will come." I said, "Carl, we have our vision for Advancing Native Missions! It is Matthew 24:14."

Carl said, "I agree! I agree!"

While on this trip, God spoke to me further about this vision. I don't remember if these words came as a voice or as a strong impression, but the message was clear and distinct. It was based on Revelation 3:8. God was saying to Carl and me, "I will open a door for you that no man can close, provided you do three things. Number one, you must always remain humble and admit that you are but of small strength. Number two, you must walk in accordance with my Word. And number three, you must never deny my name." These are the three qualities that Jesus praised the church at Philadelphia for possessing, as recorded in Revelation 3:8.

I said, "Carl, God is telling us that he is going to open doors for us. Do you agree with this?" Carl said, "Oh, yes, yes!" And since that time, he and I have done our best to be faithful to that vision. I truly believe this was a word from the Lord. The Word of God says that the Shepherd's sheep will hear his voice, and this impression was very strong.

I also received the impression from the Lord during this trip that he was going to bless everyone who joined ANM as a staff member, prayer warrior, or donor. The basis for this promise is contained in the following words of Psalm 112:

> *Praise the LORD!*
> *Blessed is the man who fears the LORD,*
> *Who delights greatly in His commandments.*
> *His descendants will be mighty on earth;*
> *The generation of the upright will be blessed.*
> *Wealth and riches will be in his house,*
> *And his righteousness endures forever.*

Unto the upright there arises light in the darkness;
He is gracious, and full of compassion, and righteous.
A good man deals graciously and lends;
He will guide his affairs with discretion.
Surely he will never be shaken;
The righteous will be in everlasting remembrance.
He will not be afraid of evil tidings;
His heart is steadfast, trusting in the LORD.
His heart is established;
He will not be afraid,
Until he sees his desire upon his enemies.
He has dispersed abroad,
He has given to the poor;
His righteousness endures forever;
His horn will be exalted with honor.
The wicked will see it and be grieved;
He will gnash his teeth and melt away;
The desire of the wicked shall perish.

Lunch Money

We arrived at the San Antonio church on a Saturday. Pastor Ripley said, "Carl, I would like you to speak at our Sunday school tomorrow, and, Bo, I want you to deliver the message." The next day, as Carl was speaking from his heart about serving native missionaries in the Sunday school, he broke down in tears three times. I had to finish his presentation.

Afterward, I spoke in the worship service about the midnight advocate. Referring to Jesus' story in Luke 11:5–8, I talked about the man who was in need because a friend on a journey had arrived at midnight, and this man didn't have any food to give his guest. The man knocked on his neighbor's door and asked to borrow three loaves of bread, but his neighbor said, "Do not trouble me; the door is now shut, and my children are with me in bed; I cannot rise

133

and give to you." Nevertheless, the man in need persisted until his neighbor opened the door and gave him what he wanted.

I said to the congregation, "This is our ministry. We are this host. We are being visited by native missionaries, and their families are hungry, but we don't have money to give to them. They need Bibles and many other things. I am knocking on your door because you are our neighbors, and they need our help." The church gave their biggest missions offering ever. Only about forty members were present, and they gave $880.87![14]

Carl and I went back home to Charlottesville. In our hearts, we lifted that check to heaven and said, "Lord, this money is like the five barley loaves and two fish that the little boy offered to you, which you multiplied for the crowd of five thousand. Please take this 'lunch money' offered by this little church and multiply it, just as you multiplied the small offering of that little boy" (John 6:8–13).

Opening the Door

Carl and I took this modest offering and rented our first office that measured only twelve feet by fifteen feet, and we furnished it with borrowed tables and chairs. It didn't bother us that the phone had to sit on the floor because we didn't get any phone calls. The office was scheduled to open on the next day, October 20, 1992. Unfor-

---

[14] In May 2021, I received a sad phone call from Chad, Pastor Ripley's only son, that his dad was under hospice care. I said, "Tell your mom that I'm coming." I flew to San Antonio with Oliver Asher, who had not long before become the new president of Advancing Native Missions. Pastor Ripley was so happy to see me. "I didn't know that you were coming, Bo," he said. He loved me, and I loved him. While Oliver and I were alone with Pastor Ripley in his bedroom, he shared some things with us. Then I asked if he would lay hands on Oliver as the new president of ANM. He gladly did so, and a little later, we left to return to Charlottesville. About two weeks later, Pastor Ripley passed away. The family and the church appreciated our coming to see him before he died. Pastor Ripley and I were so very close. He was like a father to me. Chad has since become the pastor of Abundant Life Church.

tunately, no one was going to be there because Carl and I had a prior commitment.

A few days before our trip to San Antonio, while Carl and I were driving around Charlottesville, I had said to him "Carl, we don't have any money as we start this new ministry."

"Then we must pray for an excellent team," Carl replied.

"Let's both pray," I agreed, "but don't you close your eyes because you're driving!" So we began to pray for an excellent team. I really pleaded with my eyes towards heaven for God to give us a team. In my former professions, I had run teams and seen the importance of working with teams, and I knew we could not be successful without one.

Just prior to midnight on the day before the ANM office was due to open, I was at home reading and meditating on Psalm 119:62–63:

> *At midnight I will rise to give thanks to You,*
> *Because of Your righteous judgments.*
> *I am a companion of all who fear You,*
> *And of those who keep Your precepts.*

Suddenly, there was a knock on our apartment door.

It was Cris Paurillo, whose father, Dr. Conrado Quemada, had devoted his life to serving the Lord as a medical missionary in the Philippines. "I heard that you are starting a new work," Cris said. "I just came from the church, and the Lord has convicted me. God called my dad to be a missionary, and I am a missionary. I would like to work for you and Carl."

"I am sorry, Cris," I said, "but we don't have any resources to hire you. Go home and help your husband. He sells newspapers early in the morning to help augment your family's income. He needs your help."

"No, Brother Bo," she replied. "God called me to help you. I could be your secretary."

"Cris, we don't even have a typewriter," I protested.

Just then, Cris's husband, Allan, appeared. He had overheard our conversation. "Brother Bo, Cris is going to report tomorrow at your office, and she's bringing her own typewriter."

The next day, Cris was there to staff the ANM office for the first time. She informed us later that when she opened the door, she was overcome by the glorious presence of the God of Missions that filled the small room. She fell to her knees and began touching the walls and the doors and praying, "Lord, bring people inside here . . . and when you do, let every one of them sense your presence in a very special way."

To this day, God takes great delight in answering this humble prayer of Cris, my little sister. This was the start of Advancing Native Missions.

PLANTING THE SEEDS

We were excited that Advancing Native Missions had an office, and we were thankful that Cris Paurillo had graciously volunteered to staff it. We put her in charge of the technical support system of ANM. But at the end of the first week, Carl and I went to a corner of the office and whispered, "Where do we get the wages for Cris? Her husband is struggling with their finances, and we have no salary for her."

At this very moment, there was a knock on the door. I opened it to find Pastor Bob French of Oakleigh Christian Fellowship standing before me. We invited him in, and as we were sitting around our only desk chatting, he said nonchalantly, "Oh, by the way, brothers, a very exciting thing happened to me today. While I was walking on the road in front of the mall, I saw three green, crumpled pieces of paper being blown by the wind. I ran after them because they looked like dollars, and they turned out to be three twenty-dollar bills. I know the Lord gave these to me for some reason, but why?"

Carl and I looked at each other, and then at Pastor Bob. "Let us tell you the story of Cris Paurillo, our first volunteer." After we had told him about how Cris had come with her own typewriter, I added, "As a matter of fact, Carl and I were just wondering where we would get her first week of wages."

Pastor Bob's face became flushed. "I think this is for her." He reached in his pocket and pulled out two twenty-dollar bills. "Please forgive me; I can only give you forty dollars because I spent one of the bills."

Carl and I called Cris over, handed her the two twenty-dollar bills, and said, "Cris, this is from the hand of the Lord. Make no mistake; the Lord has provided for you in a beautiful way." Carl and I took this as a sign that God was there.

Lucille Reports to Duty

Shortly after this incident, a godly woman who had been a fellow worker with Carl and me at Christian Aid came to us and said, "I would like to work for you and Carl." The name of the woman was Lucille Lebeau. Carl and I loved and respected her. She had grown up in a Roman Catholic, French-speaking family in Massachusetts, and as a child, she had always reserved a spot on her pillow for her angel. Upon receiving Christ, she loved him with all her heart and vowed to serve him for her whole life. After completing nursing school, Lucille ministered to the outcasts in the slums in Brazil, to the mujahideen in Afghanistan, and to the poor in Haiti and Appalachia. Gifted with a lovely singing voice, she was like a modern-day Florence Nightingale.

Lucille shared that she needed at least $600 of monthly support to join ANM, so over the next few days, I telephoned and wrote letters to some of my friends. After two weeks, we had commitments for $640 a month. I called Sister Lucille and said, "We have good news: You have $640 a month of support! God was so amused about our asking for $600 a month that he added another $40. That's an amusement tax!"

Lucille was the second person to join our staff. She took charge of all ANM overseas communications and prayer times. As time went on, under my direction, she handled my speaking schedule and corresponded with churches that had invited me to speak. The positive feedback from the churches motivated her to fill every available slot in my speaking schedule. I appreciated her dedication, from which ANM greatly benefited, but this packed speaking schedule caused me to feel exhausted most of the time.

Lucille is one of the finest Christian ladies that you could ever find in your life. She's so godly, so spiritual, so prayerful. She also has the qualities of a Joan of Arc. If you get out of line spiritually, she's going to speak up. Marlou and I and our children love her so much that we made her an unofficial member of our family. Our children grew up calling her Auntie Lucille. She's a diamond of a worker, like Cris Paurillo.

Victor and Virginia Join the Team

Almost immediately, ANM became deluged with offers of support. Carl, Cris, Lucille, and I were answering phone calls and opening letters around the clock, but we had no one to process the receipts and handle the bookkeeping. That's when God brought Victor Stutzman. He was an elder in his church, Oakleigh Christian Fellowship, and one of the most beloved people in the community, a real man of integrity. Victor joined us as our treasurer.

Carl and I thanked God for answering our prayers for a team. As one of our supporters remarked, we were a motley crew, but each of us loved Jesus. We all knew without a doubt that God had called us to ANM. God delights in doing great things through ordinary people, as evidenced by the disciples of Jesus.

Late one night, as we all were working in the office, I wrote a seven-page handwritten letter to our new friend, Ron Tillett, in Indiana. I told him how we desperately needed help in our office, and I explained that we had been praying that God would send us someone wonderful like Virginia Tobias. Virginia was a pastor's widow in Ron's church who was already sacrificially sending support to ANM every month. The daughter of a pastor, she had once prayed about being a missionary.

As I had hoped, Ron made a copy of my letter and gave it to Virginia. While visiting her sister near Washington, DC, she made a trip to Charlottesville and met with Carl and me. "I would love to come here and work with you," Virginia said, "but how can I leave my ailing eighty-six-year-old mother?"

When Virginia's mother learned about my letter, she said to her daughter, "I can take care of myself; go and join ANM." Virginia Tobias became the third member of ANM's staff. She is such a godly woman. A diamond of a worker, like Cris and Lucille, she took care of writing to our friends and donors.

A Friend Who Sticks Closer Than a Brother

In 1988, while addressing audiences across the US on behalf of Christian Aid, I was invited to speak at a night meeting in Charlottesville in the home of a man named Graham Stewart. As I shared my testimony, I noticed that Graham teared up. At the end of the meeting, he laid hands on me and prayed for me. God previously had put it on my heart to remember and pursue anyone that he placed in my heart, and God placed Graham in my heart that night.

When I went back to the Philippines and ministered there, I wrote letters to Graham quite often. He never replied, but God has given me what you might call a dogged personality. If I believe God wants me to pursue a person, I will do it and not give up because this is how God pursued me.

If I believe God wants me to pursue a person, I will do it and not give up because this is how God pursued me.

A few years later, when we started ANM, Graham immediately came to help us. At first, he volunteered once a week. Then, at my request, he began coming three days a week. After a few months, I said, "Graham, could you come fully and completely?" He agreed to do this for no salary. In fact, we would sometimes co-invest in new staff and overseas projects.

Graham became a wonderful brother in Christ to me. Like Carl, he is the quintessential "friend who sticks closer than a brother." He is highly regarded by all to have the virtues of love, wisdom, generosity, and most of all, truth. He became one of the major donors to ANM. A proficient writer, he became the first editor of our magazine and ultimately our vice president of publications. He was essentially our co-founder and co-leader. Wherever I traveled, he would travel with me. We were like Paul and Barnabas. Sometimes, like Barnabas and Paul, we were iron sharpening iron. My days at ANM were more enjoyable because of working with my brothers Graham Stewart and Carl Gordon.

As Graham and I visited churches and invited people to become donors and friends of ANM, Carl supported us from the office. He was the perfectly typical selfless, hardworking servant-leader and accountant who took care of the finances and directed our growing overseas department. He was president from 1992 through 2005. I served as president after him until the end of 2017.

A Touching Tribute

On December 5, 2012, the whole ANM staff and the ANM board surprised Carl and me with an appreciation program in celebration of the mission's twentieth anniversary. The board members presented both of us with a plaque, and long-time co-worker, friend, and "baby brother" P. R. Misra, who at this time was senior vice president for International Strategic Partnerships, read the following letter of recognition:

Looking back, we are in awe at how our Lord put together two most unlikely persons from different parts of the world, so different in temperament and giftings, to fulfill His goal for the extension of His kingdom.

Our Brother Carl: what can we say about him? As we have often discussed, maybe God broke the mold after making him, because during our extensive travel around various parts of the world, Anju and I have never come across another person so humble and self-sacrificing. He has a true servant spirit, willing and ready to serve others anytime, anywhere! Sometimes it comes to a point of astonishment.

Then along came the big man from the Philippines to join hands with Brother Carl. The deep-throated man with a commanding voice—as the words come forth, the buildings shake! Born to be a leader, but at the same time very gentle, polite, loving, and, literally speaking, willing to give the shirt off his back. That is our Brother Bo.

Humanly speaking, it is most unlikely that these two unique individuals would unite to fulfill a great purpose. But as we all know,

141

what is impossible for us is absolutely possible with God. And that is what our Good Lord has accomplished. As we look back twenty years to the inception of ANM, it is not a story of "rags to riches," but instead the story of rags sanctified by God to be a blessing to millions around the world. However, the best is yet to come 'til all hear.

Do you believe these two precious brothers could have accomplished what they have done without the proper helpmates? Absolutely not! Minda, the successful lady entrepreneur, hardworking, and extremely diligent to keep her business going and yet the perfect helpmate to stand with Carl, encouraging him in every situation—physically, financially, and emotionally. She is a great hostess, entertaining guests from various parts of the world without complaint.

The beautiful, gentle, and soft-spoken Marlou—how can one describe Bo without Marlou? A lawyer by profession, highly intelligent and gifted like her husband in so many ways, she could have done anything she wanted in this land of opportunity and become successful. Yet she chose to sacrifice her career, stand by Bo, and encourage him in every way possible.

Carl and I were so touched by this tribute! We give all glory to the Lord. He is the one who has brought us this far.

Two More Diamonds

Shortly after Virginia Tobias joined us, the Lord sent us two more diamonds. The first person came as a result of a conversation I had with Graham Stewart about the vital need for someone to handle the sponsorship of missionaries, orphans, and missions projects. This was the heart of ANM's operations, and it required a super-organized person. Graham suggested Danny McAllister. In the interview, we were impressed with Danny's qualifications. When we learned that he already had a heart for ANM, we asked him to come aboard. As soon as he reported for duty, our ministry processes began to get smoother.

Later that year, when Victor Stutzman and his wife moved to Florida, we prayed for someone to take charge of our accounting and bookkeeping. Again, Graham brought in the perfect person for an interview. Her name was Marion Riley; she was a retiree from the US Navy.

I found Marion to be a very dignified person with a strong character. She deeply loved Jesus and her family. We also learned that she was a huge fan of the women's basketball team of the University of Virginia. During the interview, however, Marion seemed uneasy. She had doused herself with strong perfume, apparently hoping that it would cover the overpowering smell of cigarette smoke. But looking beyond the smoking issue and Marion's crusty exterior, Graham and I could see a dignified woman with a marshmallow heart in the right place.

Across the room, however, our "Joan of Arc," Lucille, could not hide her displeasure. She was holding her nose and fanning the air with her hand. Nevertheless, Carl, Graham, and I unanimously believed that God had sent Miss Marion to ANM, and we asked her to join us. The smell of cigarette smoke soon disappeared, and as the months and years passed, the glitter of this rough diamond of a person shone for Jesus more and more. In time, she became the sweetheart of the place. Not many people knew that on paydays she joined Graham, some board members, and me in placing funds in the pay envelopes of staff members whose support fell short of what they needed to live. In fact, sometimes she gave all her pay to cover the deficits.

Before Miss Marion's health declined and she passed away, we surprised her with a birthday gift that exceeded her dreams: a new basketball signed by Debbie Ryan, the coach of the UVA women's basketball team! Miss Marion was much loved. Her life brightened ours.

ANM's Vision and Values

One day, Carl and I felt we should document what God had placed on our hearts regarding ANM's vision and values. We already had our vision. As I have said, it was based on Matthew 24:14: "And this gospel of the kingdom will be preached in all the world as a witness to all the nations, and then the end will come."

With this vision as our foundation, we turned our attention to creating ANM's mission statement. After considerable discussion and prayer, we agreed on the following:

> *The mission of ANM is to encourage, equip, and advocate for native missionaries to hasten world evangelization.*

Next, we needed an overall strategy to achieve our vision. We agreed as a group that our main strategy would be to focus on relationships. Relationship is at the heart of God, and we felt that it should be at the heart of ANM. Among other things, relationship meant that we would value the friends that God brought to us and not seek friends simply for what they might do for us.

We then turned our attention to the ministry's values. For this task, we received excellent guidance from George Ainsworth. George is a graduate of Princeton Theological Seminary and a brilliant, sober-minded follower of Jesus. He was one of our dearest friends, and he agreed to be the first chairman of our board of directors. He served as chairman of the board for the next fifteen years, and we consider him as one of the co-founders of ANM. Our board was composed of mature Christian friends from the local area who were trustworthy and qualified to hold us accountable.

We identified four values that would guide our decisions and actions: integrity, relationship, innovation, and stewardship. These could be easily remembered by the acronym IRIS, which appropriately is part of the human eye.[15]

We completed the process of structuring the ministry by enumerating the following initial policies for day-to-day guidance:

---

[15] In 2018, we changed the four values to Christ, relationship, integrity, and stewardship (CRIS).

144

1. We will conduct the ministry with prayer. The business of ANM will always start with prayer and be covered with prayer.

2. We will love those who work with us within the ministry and those we serve outside the ministry. We will express this love to others in words and actions.

3. We will put the needs of others, especially the needs of the missionaries we serve, before our own.

4. We will close the doors of our ministry if we ever become guilty of "eating the bread" of the missionaries we serve by sending too little to them and keeping too much for ourselves.

5. We will be led by a collegial team rather than by a single individual so that no person will be tempted to become a dictator.

6. We will rejoice and consider ourselves successful when other ministries doing similar work to ANM are successful. (We chose this value to guard against envy and a spirit of competition with other ministries that may be serving the Lord even more wonderfully than ANM.)

7. We will give priority to building and preserving our relationships, especially relationships with supporters and friends of the ministry. We will truly care about people.

8. We as a staff will be held accountable to these values, and we commit with God's help to being prayerful, loving, and trustworthy.

9. We will be transparent about finances and other matters that staff and supporters deserve to know.

After documenting these policies in writing, Carl and I agreed that every year, we would seek God's Word for an umbrella passage under which we would conduct our ministry. In our first year, 1992, God put on our hearts the theme of "door." This was based on God's promise in Revelation 3:8: "I have set before you an open door, and no one can shut it; for you have a little strength, have kept My word, and have not denied My name." During this first year, we asked God to open more doors for ministry.

In 1993, the covering theme God put on our hearts came from Psalm 127:1: "Unless the LORD builds the house, They labor in vain who build it." In our third year, 1994, our covering theme was from 2 Corinthians 4:16, which speaks about our inner man being renewed day by day. In 1995, many battles were being waged against us, and our theme came from 2 Chronicles 20:15: "For the battle *is* not yours, but God's." This practice of identifying a new theme each year continues to this day.

Mike and Bill

Carl and I saw our immediate and urgent need for promoting the ministry by using brochures and other literature. We approached another beloved person in the community, Mike Erkel, a highly respected graphic artist and film producer who owns an advertising agency, Erkel Associates. He was excited to help Carl and me start the ministry, and he designed a very beautiful logo for ANM and did our other graphics works—all for free! I spent delightful days with Mike in his workplace, as I was fascinated by his use of his God-given talents.

When we heard that a serious believer by the name of Bill James owned a printing company in Lynchburg, Carl and I went to see him. We found him so very busy, but upon knowing that we are his brothers and needed printed materials in our hands to start a global ministry, he stopped in his tracks and did not even blink. "I will do it for you, all for free!" he said. How we thank the precious Bill James family and their workers at Print World! In later years, his daughter Heather and her husband, Christopher Kirk, helped in the design of a multi-awarded ANM magazine. Carl and I asked both Mike and Bill, men of godly wisdom and God-given stature, to join the ANM board. We considered it a blessed thing to hold ourselves accountable to these beloved brothers.

Mining Trash and Mining Data

In 1993, as I was sharing before a small group at a local church's annual missions conference about the ministry of Nemuel and Ruth Palma in the garbage dump of Manila, I saw a young man in the back row unashamedly crying. My heart was stirred to see the tender heart of this handsome and well-built man, who struck me as a man of men. He was obviously moved by the sacrifices of God's servants and the abject poverty of the people they ministered to.

He introduced himself to me as John Elder. I learned that he had a PhD and was suitably addressed as Dr. Elder. Over time, God allowed me to form a solid friendship with this wonderful man of God. When the time was ripe, I asked him to pray about joining the ANM board to help guide the ministry, and he graciously accepted my invitation. Later, John and his missions-hearted wife, Elizabeth, founded a successful and trusted business, Elder Research, Inc., which provides data mining and predictive analytics services to businesses.

John and Elizabeth are not infatuated with material prosperity. That's why I believe God has entrusted them with more and more riches, visible and invisible. In some of his talks before businessmen, John would share about the impact of seeing the photos of the Smoky Mountain garbage dump in Manila. As the leader of a company that mined for useful information in vast troves of data, he identified with, and was humbled by, the hundreds of scavengers who tediously mined for food and other things of use among the millions of pieces of trash on that enormous mountain. The filthy backbreaking work of those fathers was worth it, he knew, if food could be found for their children. John felt renewed conviction, as one in great comfort, to help his brothers and sisters across the world in extreme poverty. As a member of the ANM board of directors, John has helped guide the stewardship and direction of ANM for the past twenty years.

Seven Specific Things

Each Thursday morning, ANM conducted a Bible study for our team that is also an outreach to the community. As I was opening the session one Thursday, I noticed a boyish-looking visitor dressed in shorts. I thought he might be a senior student from the local high school. After the Bible study, I introduced myself to him, and to my great embarrassment, I learned that he was a doctor of internal medicine at the local Martha Jefferson Hospital!

The doctor's name was Jason Strampe, and Marlou and I became very close friends with him. His deep love for God was so inspiring that we asked him to pray about joining the ANM board. It was clear to us that God had sent him to us for this purpose.

Jason was unmarried, and the Lord strongly placed it in my heart to ask Marlou to help me organize a special lunch for him after one of our Thursday Bible studies. We invited seven couples from the ANM staff, and we seated Dr. Strampe at the head of the table. To Jason's great surprise, I said to the seated guests, "Before we pray for the food, let's ask Dr. Strampe what seven specific things he is praying for in a wife." Jason's face flushed, but when he realized the sincerity of the question, he began to enumerate the seven qualities he would like his spouse to possess. I then asked each couple to pray for one of the seven things.

A few years passed. One day, Jason came to see me in the office. Almost in tears, he handed me a card and asked me to read it. This is what it said:

I wanted to say thank you for something you may not even remember. But a few years ago, you arranged a special lunch for me at ANM with several other couples, and then you asked me to name "seven specific things you are praying for in a wife," which I did. You then had everyone agree upon those things in prayers.

The thing is that this gathering came at a low point in my life, when the only way I was able to sense love from another individual or from God was by their concern over my future spouse. I felt the love of God that day, through you. And moreover, God answered your prayer on each of the "seven specific things" and so much more when He brought Amy to me. So I just wanted to let you know that I will always remember your kindness to me on that day.

With much love in Christ—Jason Strampe

On September 29, 2018, Jason married a lovely lady named Amy, who was also a medical doctor. My friend, Pastor Todd Cothran of Crosslife Church, officiated. I did their pre-marital counseling and offered the prayer of blessing at the wedding. In February 2022, God blessed Jason and Amy with a baby boy. They named him Nathaniel, which means "gift of God." This is what Marlou had prayed over them.

A Year of Struggle

We started Advancing Native Missions on October 20, 1992. During 1993, our first full year of operation, we had many struggles with finances and other issues. I spent a great deal of time traveling and building relationships. One of my first trips took me to a church in Arizona, where in one exhausting weekend, I taught three classes and preached three times.

The Lord next opened the way for me to visit another church in a nearby state. I was so happy because I would be staying with two very close friends, Ken and Dolores Detweiler. When Dolores opened the door with Ken standing behind her, I lost it. For months, I had been trying to pretend I was strong in front of my children, my wife, and my coworkers. God used the Detweilers to comfort me and cry with me.

While driving me to the church on Sunday, Ken said, "Bo, I apologize, but I am afraid very few people will be here today. This is Memorial Day weekend, and as you know, many Americans prefer picnics to church."

I was relieved to hear this because it removed some pressure. I said, "Ken, even if just one person comes to the service, I'm more than grateful."

On this morning, about a dozen people heard one of the hardest-hitting messages I have ever preached. The title of my sermon was, "This Year, Thou Shalt Die." I spoke about the encounter between Jeremiah and the false prophet, Hananiah, as recorded in the book of Jeremiah. The people listening to me were taken aback by the strength of the message.

I concluded my sermon by sharing from Luke 13:6–9 about Jesus' parable of the barren fig tree. I read, "A certain man had a fig tree planted in his vineyard, and he came seeking fruit on it and found none. Then he said to the keeper of his vineyard, 'Look, for three years I have come seeking fruit on this fig tree and find none. Cut it down; why does it use up the ground?' But he answered and said to him, 'Sir, let it alone this year also, until I dig around it and fertilize it. And if it bears fruit, well. But if not, after that you can cut it down.'"

After sharing the parable, I asked the congregation, "How would you describe this tree? What kind of tree is this?"

One person said, "It is a useless tree." Someone else said, "It is a lazy tree." Another said, "It is an unnecessary tree," and so on like this. But one man in a colorless T-shirt, jeans, and a pair of tennis shoes raised his hand and said, "The tree defiles the land!"

I was now the one who was taken aback. A tree that "defiles the land" should not remain standing; it violates the ground. I said, "Some people in the world are like this in the vineyard of the King." Then I dismissed the congregation.

Receiving Sympathy

Suddenly, I felt so exhausted that I had to retreat to the privacy of the pastor's study. I began crying like a boy and pouring out my heart to God. "Lord, I am so tired; I am so tired! What am I doing here? You know the sacrifices that my wife and children are making. You know that our oldest son, Benjamin, is legally deaf, and we can't afford treatment for him. You know about the two holes in the soles of my shoes and my torn twenty-dollar suit that my wife bought for me at the Salvation Army."

As I poured out my heart, there was another couple with me in the room. They were sympathizing with me, and the more sympathy I received from them, the sorrier I felt for myself. I said in the presence of this couple, "Maybe I should go home. The burden is too heavy. I am almost as useless as that tree that did not bear fruit. I am not needed." A plan for taking my family back to the Philippines began to birth in my mind.

God doesn't forget his chosen servants. He strengthens them, sometimes through admonishment, and sometimes with undeserved blessings.

The names of this couple were Mr. and Mrs. Self-Pity. We read in 1 Kings 19 about how they sympathized with Elijah when he fled from Jezebel and hid in a cave. I certainly am no Elijah, but I know exactly how Elijah felt. Like him, I thought God had forgotten me and left me all alone. But God doesn't forget his chosen servants. He strengthens them, sometimes through admonishment, and sometimes with undeserved blessings. In this instance, he graciously chose the latter approach.

Suddenly, there was a knock on the door. After composing myself, I opened it to see the man I had noticed who was dressed in the colorless T-shirt, jeans, and tennis shoes. He said, "I am just visiting this church for the second time, but I heard you today, and I'd like you to know that I placed a thousand dollars in the offering plate for your ministry, Advancing Native Missions. Then, as I was about to drive away from the church, the Spirit of the Lord said to me, 'Turn back; do something more.' So I turned back, and this is for your family." He placed a folded check in my hand.

During my sermon, I had shared about a miracle that had happened to our oldest son, Benjamin. In 1990, while he was a student at the University of the Philippines in Baguio, an intensity 7.7 earthquake had hit the island of Luzon. The mountaintop where his school was located was the area hardest hit. Our family lived in Manila at the time, and we were so worried because there were reports of demolished buildings and many deaths. Marlou's mother, who lived with us, was the most distraught. She was crying, "Oh, my grandson! Oh, my grandson!"

Benjamin's Miracle

After a few hours of suspense, there was a knock on the door of our apartment. It was Benjamin! We were as joyful as the people in Mary's house when the apostle Peter knocked on their door (Acts 12:13–16). Normally, Benjamin would have gone straight to his dorm after class. He had been instructed never to spend money on a five-hour bus ride home except in an absolute emergency. But on this day, he had experienced some discomfort in his ears, so after his class that morning, he went straight to the bus station and headed home. While riding the bus, he had felt only some slight rumblings. It was only after he got home later in the evening that he learned about the earthquake.

When the earthquake struck at 4:26 p.m., Benjamin was already more than halfway home. Almost two thousand people died from the quake, and about one million people were affected by it. There were landslides on the two mountain roads coming down to Manila from the city where Benjamin's school was located. Huge boulders fell on buses and other vehicles. The school building where Benjamin had been studying collapsed, and some of his classmates died.

A Happy Man

I had told this story in my sermon, and I had mentioned that Benjamin had a problem with his ears. The man in the white shirt had remembered this, and that is why he was now giving me this check for our family. I said, "No, sir! Thank you, sir, but everything that comes to me is for the Lord."

"I have already given one thousand dollars for your ministry," he countered. "This is for your family."

I looked at the check. It was made out to me in the amount of $10,000, which is the equivalent of half a million Philippine pesos! In the Philippines, that one check would have made me a half-millionaire. This was sufficient for all our family's needs.

Suddenly, I found myself doing something I had never done before. I prostrated myself before this man, placed my two hands on his feet, and prayed a blessing over him. This is the ultimate show of gratitude in the Orient. God put this gesture on my heart because I was extremely thankful.

When Jesus healed the ten lepers (Luke 17:11–19), this is how the only one who returned to thank him expressed his gratitude. My father had taught us, "Gratefulness that is not expressed is ungratefulness implied." Therefore, I always try to express my gratefulness immediately when someone blesses me. This man took me by my shoulder and said, "No, no, no, stand up! Stand up."

I thanked him again, and he left. As I got up to preach in the second service, I was a happy man. This $10,000 would also allow Marlou to be treated by a doctor for the constant, pulsating pain in her frozen shoulders, which she had developed from doing housework. It would allow us to buy eyeglasses for Felisa, shoes for all of us, and many other things we badly needed.

Talking with Ken and Dolores

When I returned with Ken and Dolores to their house after the church services, we counted the money that had been given for ANM. It amounted to almost $5,000. "Oh, Bo, how wonderful!" Ken exclaimed. He and Dolores were so happy for me.

"Yes," I said, "but I have here another check. The giver said this one is for my family. He gave it to me in the pastor's study." When Ken and Dolores saw the four zeros, they broke down in tears because they knew our needs. However, as my friends were rejoicing, God was speaking to me.

"I am sorry, Ken and Dolores, but I cannot keep this. Do you remember the story about how King David remarked in a casual

153

manner that he longed to drink from the sweet waters at the gate to Bethlehem, and without his knowledge, three of his generals risked their lives to get him a pitcher of that water? Do you recall that when they handed the water to him, David poured it on the ground because he felt he did not deserve to drink water that his bravest men had risked their lives to bring? This is what I am feeling now. I do not deserve this; I am going to give it away." With many tears, Ken and Dolores pleaded with me to use the money for our family's needs. I agreed to pray about it.

Counseled by Carl

When I arrived back at the office in Charlottesville, I gave Carl the offerings from the two churches that amounted to more than five thousand dollars, and I gave him the ten thousand dollar check from the man in the white T-shirt.

"Wow, Bo! In my many years of missions, I have never seen two small churches contribute this much money! You were given more than fifteen thousand dollars. But I notice that this check for ten thousand dollars is made out to you."

"That's a mistake," I said. "It is for ANM."

"Wonderful, Brother!" said Carl. "This is a great start for ANM."

The next day Carl came looking for me. "I received a fax from the pastor of the church you just visited," he said. "I will read it to you. It says, 'Mr. Gordon, we have received word that when Bo was here, one of our visitors gave one thousand dollars for the ministry of ANM and ten thousand dollars for Bo's family. Please make sure the Barredo family gets the ten thousand dollars. Otherwise, we will not be able to support ANM.'" Carl looked me in the eye. "Does Marlou know about this?"

"No, sir, she doesn't have to," I politely replied.

Carl folded the ten thousand dollar check and handed it to me. "Go home; this is for your family. It's an answer to prayers."

I walked away so happy. I said to myself, "Wow! The president of ANM has just told me that I must keep the $10,000 for my family. He is the president, and I am the vice president, so I must obey.

Marlou will be able to get the physical therapy she needs; our son can immediately see a doctor about his ears; everyone in our family can get new shoes; and Felisa can get new eyeglasses."

"Do You Love Me?"

On the drive home, I was mentally going over the list of critical family needs that my colleagues at ANM had helped me compile. Marlou would surely be excited when I told her the news. But as I was about to drive past Covenant Church, where we were members, a voice spoke in my mind. It was a strong, clear voice, and I knew it was the Lord. The voice said, "Do you love me?"

I slowed down. "Yes, Lord, I love you."

Once again, the voice spoke: "Do you love me?"

"Oh, Lord, I love you so much. You know that I brought my family here because we want to serve your people."

A third time the voice came into my heart: "Do you truly love me?"

"Lord, you know that I love you!"

"Then give it away."

I wheeled into the parking lot of the church, just as Pastor Bare happened to arrive. After greeting each other in the parking area, we went inside to his office. "Pastor Bare," I began, "I have good news! Donors have given five thousand dollars for the ministry of ANM."

"Praise the Lord!" he exclaimed.

"But I have a problem," I continued. "Someone also gave ten thousand dollars for my family. The problem is that this ten thousand dollars is for the Lord's work, and my ministry will not allow me to give it away. Please help me give this money away."

After trying without success to convince me to take the check home, he reached for a pen and paper. "Where do you want it to go?"

"I want to send $3,000 to a ministry in India that badly needs financial help," I answered. "And I'd like $1,000 to go to Cris Paurillo because her first week's wages were only $40. Of course, a $1,000 tithe should go to this church, and I'd like to give Lucille Lebeau $1,000 because the $640 she receives a month is not enough. And there is a widow in the Philippines who is in need. Could we send her $300?" The widow I had in mind was Marlou's mother, Nanay.

Pastor Bare suddenly stopped writing. "Hold your horses! Your oldest son needs work on his ears. As your pastor, I'm going to put $3,000 in escrow here in the church for that purpose, and you cannot touch it."

"Well, okay," I said, "since you are making this decision as my pastor. And will you please permit my family to keep the remaining $700 because we badly need it?"

"Of course," said Pastor Bare. "In fact, we should give you even more if you want it."

Teaching Moments

That evening I gathered Marlou and our four children and told them what had happened. Everyone agreed with the decision to give the money away. We learned later that the ministry in India, Cris Paurillo, Lucille Lebeau, and Marlou's mother were greatly blessed by the timeliness of the gifts they received. And our family was blessed by the $3,000 that was set aside for Benjamin's ear care and the $700 we could use to buy new shoes and other necessities.

But perhaps the greatest blessing was what we learned about selflessness. This is the kind of teaching moment that has helped to define our family's lifestyle. Selflessness is an especially important lesson for young minds to learn.

God uses many circumstances in life to teach us. Whenever something important happens in our family, we try to use it as a learning opportunity. These precious teaching moments knit us together and help us better understand how God might be moving.

For example, when one of our children, or even Marlou or I, do something wrong or make a mistake, I gather the family that evening and say, "Somebody made a mistake today. Who is it?" The child I am referring to might say, "Papa, I already asked for forgiveness from the Lord and from you and Mama."

"Yes, wonderful!" I will reply. "Now, what is the worst thing that can happen with a mistake?"

"That we fail to learn from it!" the kids will answer, practically in unison because they have heard this question so many times.

"Yes, the worst thing is not that a mistake was made, but that we fail to learn from it." We then will talk about what God might want us to learn. Everyone, including the person who made the mistake, is invited into the discussion. The children learn that forgiveness is always available, so they are not fearful, and they do not try to hide their mistakes. This is the kind of teaching moment that has become so precious in our family.

A Family Council

One evening, while ANM was in its first year, Marlou, the four children, and I had a family council to discuss finances. Our entire family was continually sacrificing during this startup phase of the ministry, and I wanted to explain why I kept so little money for our own use.

"As you know, ANM is in a startup phase, and we need to recruit staff to work with us," I began. "But we do not have enough money to pay our staff adequate salaries, so they must raise their own support. It takes time for people to build their support base, and in the meantime, we need to help subsidize their efforts. This is one reason why I give ANM a large portion of the donations that come for our family."

The kids nodded that they understood, so I continued. "Another reason why we give away donations that come to our family is because the missionaries desperately need them. These missionaries are the reason for ANM's existence. They have God-stories about their lives and their ministries that can help ANM raise money. We can then send this money to help them. But their stories are their treasure. If we take their stories without investing in them in return, we will be using these poor missionaries instead of serving them.

"God has put it on my heart to give money away, and this honors the Lord. But there is also another practical reason. When we receive one thousand dollars, if we keep all the money for ourselves, we are promoting only one ministry: ourselves. But if we keep only one hundred dollars for our family and give one hundred dollars each to nine different missionaries around the world, we are planting nine seeds. We are building relationships with nine new ministries for ANM donors to support.

"This is how we can help hasten the growth of the ministry and help to advance Christ's kingdom. Nevertheless, I am concerned that the sacrifices I am asking our family to make are too great, so I am planning to ease the pressure by applying for a part-time job as a cashier or as a butcher assistant in a grocery store."

"No, Papa!" pleaded all four kids. "God called you to be a missionary. We will support you so you can work in the ministry full-time. Please, Papa, full-time. We will support you."

"I will postpone my college education and go to work in a Chinese restaurant," said our oldest son, Benjamin. "I can earn lots from tips."

"I will babysit for the children of pastors to earn money for our family, and I will babysit Felisa and Jim while you and Mama work," said our second son, David. Felisa was nine at this time, and Jim was eight. So the family became my supporting group.

A Stern Rebuke

When I received a donation specifically for our family, typically I would make a note telling Gordon Shira, the man who handled the receipt of donations for ANM, how to distribute the money. Pastor Shira had started several Lutheran churches in California that had grown to more than one thousand members each. He was known as the "Sock Man" there, because at night he would distribute hundreds of pairs of socks to homeless people on Skid Row in Los Angeles.

When he moved to Charlottesville, he first worked at Christian Aid, and then he volunteered at ANM. When he married Ruth Shank, whom I called Mom Ruth, I began calling him Dad. I loved him so much, and he loved me. He was a father to me. But he did not agree with the way I typically gave away money that had been donated to our family. One day, he confronted me. "Don't you know that he who does not take good care of his family is worse than an infidel!" He was a kind man, but this was a severe scolding. He had a right as my spiritual father to rebuke me, but his words did not resonate with me.

I felt that God had said to me, "If you take good care of my servants, I will take good care of your family."

I had learned that the kingdom of God is a kingdom of investment. What we plant will bear fruit. During this period, Marlou and I were planting seeds at ANM and in some ministries around the world. When we sacrifice for God, he will more than make it up to us. Self-sacrifice is participating in the sufferings of Christ. Jesus Christ, our Lord and Savior, sacrificed for us, and we should emulate him. I felt that God had said to me, "If you take good care of my servants, I will take good care of your family."

I know of many very poor native missionaries who put the needs of others before the needs of their family, not because they are not loving fathers or mothers, but because the Lord has given them a consuming passion for the people they minister to. I have the same passion. Our family gets great joy from blessing others. Self-sacrifice motivated by faith and love pleases the Lord.

I explained my views to Dad Gordon without arguing, and he still did not agree. Nevertheless, I continued to give away a large portion of our support. When someone says something that does not resonate with my spirit, I just smile because my Heavenly Father protects me.

As the one in charge of our receipting department, Dad Gordon tabulated ANM's income as it steadily increased, so that at the end of the first calendar year, which consisted only of the months of October, November, and December in 1992, we had received contributions of $55,000. Exceeding $50,000 was a wonderful blessing, because it meant that we could apply for membership in the Evangelical Council for Financial Accountability. Approval by the ECFA helps enormously in fundraising.

Helpful Recognition

I am very proud that in the year 2016, just before I voluntarily stepped down as president, ANM garnered a stellar record for financial stewardship. For example, out of the 1.5 million nonprofits it surveyed, MinistryVoice ranked ANM #92 on its list of most trusted nonprofits. We earned a five-star rating from Ministry Watch and the Platinum Seal of Transparency from GuideStar (their highest rating). Theology Degrees named ANM one of the "Top Ten Most Amazing Christian Charities."

On November 1, 2016, ANM received the following letter of commendation from Charity Navigator:

Dear Bo Barredo:

Astute donors are yearning for greater accountability, transparency, and for concrete results from us. With more than 1.5 million American charities, Charity Navigator aims to accentuate the work of efficient and transparent organizations . . . We are proud to announce Advancing Native Missions has earned our seventh consecutive 4-star rating. This is our highest possible rating, and it indicates that your organization adheres to sector best practices and executes its mission in a financially efficient way.

Attaining a 4-star rating verifies that Advancing Native Missions exceeds industry standards and outperforms most charities in your area of work. Only 3% of the charities we evaluate have received at least 7 consecutive 4-star evaluations, indicating that Advancing Native Missions outperforms most other charities in America. This exceptional designation from Charity Navigator sets Advancing Native Missions apart from its peers and demonstrates to the public its trustworthiness.

Dad Gordon faithfully served the Lord at ANM for many years. When he was ninety years old and dying, he wrote down his last wishes. Mom Ruth and her daughter, Beverly, whom I view as my sister, called me to their house and said, "Bo, these are the last wishes of your dad regarding his memorial service." They handed me a handwritten document that specified what the opening prayer should be and what hymns should be sung. Further down, I read, "The main message should be given by Bo, and tell him not to make it long." Even in his dying days, he was so funny. That's how I remember him. I loved him, and he loved me.

MARLOU

Marking the First Anniversary of ANM

On the evening of October 20, 1993, Bo gathered our family in our bedroom for a special family devotion to mark ANM's first anniversary. On our knees, we thanked God for his faithfulness over the past twelve months as we had stepped out in total faith as a family to help dig a new well, ANM. The steadfast prayers and sacrificial love gifts of our friends had raised an army of native missionaries in twenty countries that were sent out by almost fifty native missions boards to do God's work. Already this was resulting in thousands of souls being led to the Lord's feet.

We recalled with emotion how our daughter, Felisa, had asked her father when ANM had started twelve months before, "Papa, do we still get to eat? It will be winter soon." Tears came to my eyes as I recalled the words of our youngest son, Jim, who was eight at the time. He said, "Papa, my only pair of shoes has been 'smiling' for the last three months, and my socks get wet and cold. But please do not worry. These shoes can still last me for another month."

I remembered with emotion the day that Bo had bought his "new" preaching suit from a thrift store. It was a twenty dollar charcoal-gray suit with some cigarette burns on one side. He spent another ten dollars to extend the cuffs and hemline and five dollars for dry cleaning. His only pair of leather shoes had holes in both soles. But he said the suit and shoes helped him preach with a grateful heart because he knew the native missionaries for whom he was advocating were doing with much less.

One principle that Bo has always taught our family was that God will more than make it up to you when you put your own needs second to those of another. Our family has seen God demonstrate the validity of this principle time and again. At the dinner table one evening during this past year, Felisa joyfully remarked, "Papa, Mama, we are missionaries by faith, but we do not lack anything!"

Bo remarked during our devotional time that he had grown more gray hair during the past year than in all previous years. I said, "So have I." Jim had grown amazingly in physical height and a cheerful spirit during the past twelve months, and eleven-year-old Felisa was now almost as tall as I. David was a sixteen-year-old senior in public high school. As editor of the school's sixteen-page paper, he had written a strong editorial on prayer rights in public schools.

But our oldest son Benjamin was for Bo and me the most obvious indicator of the swift passage of time. That evening, he asked Bo and me if he could start bringing his girlfriend to our home the following month when he turned twenty. Before either of us could answer, David piped up, "But it would affect your grades in school." And Felisa added, "It would be costly, and you don't have money." And then Jim chimed in, "I object because you won't have time to play with us anymore." Poor Benjie turned red, scratched his head, and managed to laugh.

Just prior to this evening, we had received a call from two of our dearest family friends, Jack and Mickie Evans. They were so happy to know how much the Lord had blessed ANM during its first year. Bo told them that a bumper sticker he saw perfectly captured how this past year had felt. The bumper sticker read, "Get in. Buckle yourself. Close your mouth. And hang on."

Felisa's Dress

Marlou and I involve our children in all major decisions that affect the family. We take time to explain why we want to do certain things, and we ask what they think, especially in financial matters. We do not want them to have the impression that we love them less than the ministry, so they grow up bitter. When the decision involves money, inevitably they will say, "Oh, Papa, let's give it away! Let's give it away!" Experiencing the joy of giving and watching God provide for our family has helped to strengthen their faith and develop within them a generous spirit.

When we lived in Manila prior to moving to the US, Marlou and I gave our only daughter, Felisa, a beautiful dress to wear when she graduated from kindergarten. It was a white dress with a yellow ribbon. She was six years old, and she looked so pretty in it. After she wore this special gift at her graduation, she hung it in her closet and often admired it.

Below is a story that Felisa wrote about this incident several years later:

"Selflessness"—A Christmas Story

Here I sat on my bed, holding the old photograph, staring at a little girl of six seated on the piano bench, wearing a radiant smile. Attired in a white cotton dress with frills on the edges, she had a pretty yellow ribbon across her waistline that accentuated the glow of her childish joy. Memories rushed in.

It was my kindergarten graduation day. That morning, I woke up to find the white dress with yellow ribbon hanging on my bedroom door. It was the prettiest dress I ever had. Sporting my new dress, I proudly received my class's highest honors. That white dress, however, was also used by God to teach me my first spiritual lesson on "selflessness."

A few days later, I sat in front of our apartment playing with my doll. "Here, Millie, drink your milk," I coaxed my tiny doll as I rocked her back and forth. My Papa, a big man with a soft heart, called me. "Felisa, Felisa, please come inside."

As I sat beside him, Papa said with some hesitancy, "Sweetheart, there is a little girl who would like to borrow your new dress with the yellow ribbon." I immediately recoiled. The dress was mine and no one could take it away from me! I lowered my head as if to cry. My pouting lips showed my clear disapproval. I was ready to stomp my feet. I was an "unica hija," an only daughter.

Papa sat still for what seemed an eternity. When I raised my face, I saw something glint in both his eyes. He struggled for words. "Felisa, a father will always do his very best for his children." He paused, then continued, "Today a poor pastor came by with tears in his eyes, pleading if there was any way he could borrow a presentable dress for his little daughter to wear at her own graduation. He has no means to buy her a new one." Papa choked on his next words. "I'd like you to know that it was very difficult for him to tell me the purpose of his visit. But he swallowed his pride so that his little girl could somehow know how much he truly loves her. Sweetheart, please. . ."

I did not hear my Papa finish his plea. An overwhelming tenderness welled up inside me. Tears suddenly blinded my eyes. I no longer wanted the dress. All I wanted was for this other little girl to have it! I felt a sudden surge of love for her. Excitedly, I said, "Papa, we must make sure to place the dress in a box and wrap it! I would like her to receive it as a gift."

At such a young age, God's love (my Mama brought me to the Lord Jesus when I was five) taught me how to make an act of sacrifice for someone else. I had my first taste of one of the greatest victories in a person's life—victory over self.

I was smiling as I lowered the old photograph. I was imagining the other little girl's own smile at the very moment she beheld the white dress. Angels must have brushed their wings

Writing to the Generous Donor

Now that I had given away most of the $10,000 that the generous donor had specifically designated for my family, I faced a challenge. The donor was sure to be angry because he had given $1,000 to ANM, and he had specified that I must use the additional $10,000 for my family. I wrote him an initial letter that essentially said, "Sir, I ask your forgiveness. I wanted to obey you, but I heard from a higher source, God, that I should give away most of the exceedingly generous contribution that you gave for my family. I even disobeyed Carl Gordon, the president of ANM. He said I should use it for my family, but I had to obey the Lord. Please accept my sincere apology."

A while later, I decided to send him a follow-up letter. A slightly edited version is below:

February 8, 1994

Dear Sir,

Loving greetings, again, dearest friend and brother in the Lord.

We are busy preparing for a three-day church missions conference this week, and I will be sharing our Lord's agenda in a workshop and speak in a dinner fellowship. What a great honor to speak on our Lord's behalf and for His precious laboring but fruitful servants across the seas. Next Sunday, two days before I leave for Asia, I will be sharing God's Word in a church here in Charlottesville. I am in much trembling each time I share—just like the trembling you felt that morning when I was sharing God's Word and about my own son Benjamin during a 7.7 intensity earthquake. What a great day it was to behold my Lord's glory through you, Sir! I think of the events as just in a dream.

Sir, enclosed is a receipt for the very generous gift you gave to our family. (I cry each time I remember this goodness of our Lord through you.)

If you remember, Sir, the ANM president, Carl Gordon, gave me the $10,000 check as a way of honoring your designation. He folded it and placed it in my pocket, telling me at the same time to bring it home to my family. (They have known of it, but they have not seen it.) While driving home, many beautiful plans came to my mind. For the last seven years of my working in our Lord's Vineyard, I've never been handed this amount of money. One of our friends, Rev. and Mrs. Shira, strongly suggested that we should consider putting the check as a down payment for a bigger place in lieu of our very cramped rented apartment. (Benjamin's place to sleep for the last two years is still on a used couch that was given to us.) It was a tempting suggestion as the monthly mortgage payment would be much lower than our monthly apartment rental.

Then another brother had suggested that I would need a newer vehicle to enable me to drive to more places on behalf of native missions. This would save on plane fares and do away with the fear of car trouble in the highways. This, too, was a very justifiable suggestion. Our friends who know of our sacrifices were all "rooting" for us for the use of the generous gift. Then another brother reminded us that the $10,000 would all be used up for Benjamin's medical needs. He was right to remind me.

But then, my eyes flooded with tears when I remembered my friends who don't have a chance to come to America, or don't have church doors open for them, because God has not placed [someone like you] in their paths.

I found myself, Sir, driving straight to Covenant Church and going to see a very much respected pastor, Rev. Harold Bare. He, too, was almost teary-eyed when I handed him your check. He told me that our family needs the gift and that I should save it for rainy days. His church loves our family.

I gently told him, however, to please disburse the gift in the following way (Editor's note: Descriptions are moderately edited):

- $1,000 tithe of the Lord
- $3,000 for a ministry in India
- $1,000 for a co-worker who left her job as a nurse and is working for ANM by faith

- *$1,000 for a co-worker who is working at ANM by faith and whose parents are sick after years of medical missions in the Philippines*
- *$300 for an eighty-one-year-old widow who needs help in the Philippines*
- *$3,000 to be kept in escrow by Rev. Bare's church for Benjamin's medical needs*
- *$700 for our direct family needs*

That evening at dinner, I told the family the whole story and the disbursements I made for our Lord's glory, and I showed them our family's share of $700. All were greatly moved. They knew the moments when our Lord's tender presence permeates our being. I believe in my heart, Sir, that what happened that night after dinner will always be used by our Lord to point out to my children and wife the way to God's presence. This testimony will guide them in their dealings with other people. Thank you for affording me this unique and lasting blessing.

Thus, this is the reason why the receipt is by a church and not by the mission. But the funds were all disbursed for missions work for God's glory.

You may not know it, Sir, but you are quite well known here now in the circle of our friends. Many are praying for you and your concerns. God bless you, again and again, Sir.

Love in Jesus Christ,

Bo Barredo

II Cor 5:15

I wrote the letter by hand and included an itemized receipt from Covenant Church detailing how the $10,000 had been disbursed, but I did not mention how I had heard from the Lord because that would have been difficult to explain. I never expected to hear again from this donor.

When I told Carl about my letters, he said, "Don't tell anybody what I'm going to say, but I think he's going to send us $100,000."

"Carl, I disobeyed him, and I've just apologized to him. What makes you think he's going to send $100,000?"

"I don't know, brother; that's just how I feel."

"I WILL MORE THAN MAKE IT UP TO YOU"

One day early in 1994, when I came into the office around 11:00 a.m., everybody except Carl was in tears. No one could stop crying long enough to tell me what was wrong. Finally, Carl said, "Remember the man who gave ANM one thousand dollars? And he also gave you ten thousand dollars with strict instructions to spend it on your family, but you disregarded his instructions and gave that ten thoousand dollars away. Well, we just received this letter from him. He has sent us a check for five hundred thousand dollars with specific instructions about how it should be used."

After I had caught my breath, Carl continued, "The donor has stipulated that one hundred thousand dollars of the total amount should be used by you and your family. He has further instructed that you should use twenty thousand dollars of this one hundred thousand dollars to buy a minivan as a Christmas present for your family from the Lord. The remaining eighty thousand dollars should be deposited into a separate interest-bearing account."

Carl looked at me to make sure what he had said had sunk in. Then he continued by reading from the letter: "The balance is to be used for your ANM ministry through the Lord's guidance and your confirmation. However, I strongly urge that you follow Bo's heart. Because he has been faithful in little, the Lord has now given him much."

Lucille was bawling. She had never seen a check with five zeros! Carl folded the check and handed it to me. "Bo, I have to follow his instructions. Go home and pray about where this half a million dollars will go."

I was astounded. I stood speechless for several moments. Then Carl and I called everyone at ANM together, and we had a time of corporate prayer of thanksgiving, praise, and worship.

Carl as ANM president subsequently sent the following letter to the gentleman and his wife:

We are praising the Lord Jesus for the joy of being coworkers together with you as ANM links God's people together around the world. It is His wonderful plan that each of His children minister to one another, that there be no lack. (Acts 2:45) The Lord of the Harvest allows ANM the privilege of bringing together spiritually fruitful members of His Body who are on the frontlines of world evangelization with those praying and supporting elements of His Body in the West. All members of His Body share equally in the victories His Holy Spirit is bringing.

One of the important spiritual lessons I have learned is that we are not complete in ourselves. By this I mean that God has used your gift of $500,000 to equip, encourage, and send a small army of His people into the heart of some of the most difficult spiritual battles raging across the face of the earth. However, this gift is joined with others, such as that of Antone Marshall, an eighty-four-year-old gentleman who works and sells vegetables in Massachusetts. He faithfully sends us $10 each month. Both of you, along with many others, are strengthening men and women who are reaping a spiritual harvest for Christ Jesus.

Nothing else gives us greater joy than to strengthen and encourage His people. Needless to say, we are thankful for the blessings that the two of you have brought to the ANM family. Following your call, we came together as a staff. There was silence; then tears and praise and prayers of thanksgiving; and then cries for wisdom among the brethren, as we began to realize the weight of responsibility that this gracious gift brings.

Brother, we are all thrilled for Brother Bo with the news of the special blessing for his family. Everyone rejoiced for him, but in Bo's characteristic fashion (and the same would have happened if any of the other brethren had received such a blessing), it was his desire to share with other members of the ANM family. More than anything, we are a family of believers who seek to encourage and strengthen one another. Everyone prevailed upon Brother Bo to receive the entire amount, but he eventually convinced us that his way was best. We know that his decisions are not made before seeking the Father's heart.

Please forgive me for not being [also] able to keep my word about Bo receiving the entire blessing. You will note [on the enclosed statement showing the disposition of funds] that I am [also] a recipient of a portion of this blessing. Both Bo and Graham felt I needed to receive $1,000 a month for the next year. This will be the first financial blessing received by my family from ANM since we started the ministry in October 1992.

Again, thank you for joining us in the ministry of serving and strengthening "the Body of Christ" around the world.

Your brother in Christ,

Carl

Marlou and I assumed that ANM would follow the instructions and put the $100,000 that was designated for our family in the bank, so at home that evening, we began to pray about where the other $400,000 should go.

A Solemn Request

Suddenly, the sound of a malfunctioning car engine came from the street in front of our house. We looked out the window and saw a familiar missionary couple getting out of the car. We were friends of this couple, and when they knocked on our door, we invited them in.

"Bo, we're going overseas for quite a time," the husband said, "and we have seen how you love your children. We are wondering if we could appoint you and Marlou guardians of our two boys, in case something happens to us?"

Marlou and I agreed that we would be honored to be guardians. As we escorted the couple back to their vehicle, we noticed that the fabric on the car's ceiling was hanging down, the brakes were squeaking, and the engine barely ran. Humanly speaking, this was not a couple I would have chosen to support because they were not native missionaries, and they were not poor. But a voice in my heart said, "You were asking me where the money should go. Start with this couple." In obedience, I immediately noted in my heart to send them $5,000. In those days, that was enough for them to buy a nice used car by trading in their current one. Looking back, I believe it was a test of obedience from the Lord that I should not be a respecter of persons, but that I should just obey him as he guides and directs me.

I will be gracious to whom I will be gracious,
and I will have compassion on whom I will have compassion.
EXODUS 33:19

Light, Sword, Mobility, and Food

I spent the rest of the night developing and documenting a new project. I called it the Light, Sword, Mobility, and Food Project. "Light" referred to the purchase of Petromax lamps for missionaries. In some countries, missionaries must walk at night from one village to another, and often, they can get bitten by cobras. They can even sometimes get bitten when they go to the outhouse at night. These hurricane lamps are vital for their safety.

Earlier, I mentioned how Ben and Nene Singcol on the island of Leyte in the Philippines had carved two paddles in faith that God would provide a boat, and I described how blessed I was to be used by God to help answer their prayers. A few years after my visit with them, while Nene was walking home in the dark with Ben after a night meeting, she fell on a thorn and lost an eye. A relatively inexpensive Petromax lamp that burns kerosene or alcohol is a tremendous help in that environment, but few missionaries can afford to buy one. I estimated how much it would cost to furnish five hundred of these lamps to missionaries all over the world, and I put that dollar figure on my list. This was the "light" aspect of my project.

The "sword" part had to do with Bibles, because the Word of God is a two-edged sword. I thought how wonderful it would be if ANM could buy five thousand Bibles so missionaries could have them in their own language. I added this need to my list.

The third aspect of the project was "mobility." I suggested that ANM give several four-wheel-drive vehicles to certain fast-growing ministries, and we should give hundreds of bicycles to other groups. This would enable these servants of the Lord to reach more people with the Gospel. In some countries, automobiles and bicycles are luxuries that missionaries could never imagine owning. I identified five dynamic ministries that I felt would most benefit from a gift of mobility and rejoiced at the thought of each getting a Jeep or similar vehicle.

The "food" aspect of the project would provide thirty dollars a month to five hundred needy missionaries of at least fifty ministries in twenty countries for the purchase of food for their families. I also designated that 10 percent of the funds should be used for the whole ANM staff, and that the balance should be used for the training of native missionaries, the care of orphans, and for the benefit of five vital ministries in our local community.

The next day, I went to Carl with my list and urged him to distribute the money right away. "If we delay too long and Jesus comes back in the meantime, you and I might get a spanking!" I said with a smile.

ANM did indeed disburse these funds immediately, and there was much rejoicing around the world. Below is the introduction I wrote for our project:

The overall theme for the distribution of this particular gift is equipping God's army of native missionaries with "Light, Sword, Mobility, and Food."

The rising tide of missions means his coming is imminent! Our Lord's army is launching an offensive. And what privilege to know we are playing a part in it.

The financial support, the vehicles and bicycles, the Bibles and Christian tracts, and the hurricane lamps provide the basis for this theme. What a day of rejoicing it was for all of us at ANM when we received this generous gift from the heart of God through the hands of beloved friends!

When ANM was just starting, whenever we got a sponsorship or two for native missionaries, we rejoiced in the fact that we would be able to send another soldier to the battlefield. Then came days when five or ten missionaries would be sponsored by a family or a church. The ANM staff would clap their hands in glee that the Lord has used us to send a squad to the battle. Now, with five hundred more missionaries sponsored at one time, we are sending a battalion in the Lord's name and for His glory!

My son, David, who did army training in the summer of 1995, remarked, "Papa, when a battalion is sent to battle, it is considered a major offensive."

The rising tide of missions means his coming is imminent! Our Lord's army is launching an offensive. And what privilege to know we are playing a part in it.

God used this and similar incidents to set the standard for how ANM's workers should live. All who serve with ANM should have a lifestyle that puts others first. We especially are called to put the native missionaries we serve before ourselves. God has assured us that if we take care of his servants, he will take care of us. In fact, he promised more than that because he spoke to my heart, "I will more than make it up to you."

He has certainly done exceedingly more than I can ask or imagine with ANM, and in my own life as well, not just in material things, but in blessings of good health, a godly marriage, successful children, and much more.

The Blessings Come Back

Before I left for the office the next morning, I said to Marlou, "We have one hundred thousand dollars for us with instructions that twenty thousand dollars is for a new van. I am very grateful for this, but I'm not deserving of it. It's too much money. I heard in my heart that I must give at least half of this away. Would you agree with me?"

Marlou was silent for a while. Then she said, "I agree with you." At my request, she put this in writing.

When I got to the office, I said, "Carl, I have news. Of the eighty thousand dollars designated by the donor for our family support for the next two years, we are going to give away half. We want it used for additional help to the staff."

"The staff already has money designated," protested Carl, "and the donor who gave this money will get angry with us."

"Carl," I retorted, "our fellow workers need more help."

Over the next few days, we gave away forty thousand dollars to the staff that was originally designated to support our family for that year. What a blessing this was to many people!

After a couple of months, as I was driving to Virginia Beach to speak in a church, I heard a voice that was gentle and sweet, and I knew it was the Lord. It said, "So, you have something left for yourself. Give it away."

When I got home, I said, "Marlou, could we give more of the remaining forty thousand dollars away?" She agreed, and we gave away another twenty thousand dollars.

From the twenty thousand dollars that the donor had designated for a new van, we bought a nice, slightly used Dodge Caravan for almost twenty thousand dollars. As I showed it to Carl, I commented, "This is too beautiful for us."

Carl was a bit perturbed. Shaking his head, he said, "Give me a baseball bat; I'm going to make it ugly for you!" We both laughed.

What's the use of being respected by the whole world and not having strong relationships within your own backyard?

One evening almost a year later, Marlou and I called together our family. I said to Benjamin, "Son, you withdrew from college to help the family by working as a busboy in the Chinese restaurant. We are now going to make it up to you by enrolling you at Liberty University." He broke down in tears.

A few days later, as I was driving Benjie to Liberty in our beautiful, slightly used van, he said, "Papa, where will you get the money for my tuition?"

"That's easy," I answered. "We'll sell this van."

When I got home, I put out the word that our van was for sale. An elder at a local church, whose wife worked as a nurse at the University of Virginia Hospital, came to our house to see it. He said, "Could we buy it for fourteen thousand dollars? That is our budget for a vehicle."

"Brother, we need twelve thousand dollars to enroll our son in college. I will sell it to you for twelve thousand dollars." He wanted to pay more, but I insisted that twelve thousand dollars was the amount that God had put strongly on my heart.

His wife told some of her friends about this automobile incident, and the story spread around. This enhanced ANM's reputation in the community. I didn't do this for that purpose, but it turned out to be a wonderful blessing. For years afterward, whenever I was introduced to some people who worked at UVA University Hospital, more often than not they would say, "I heard about how you sold your van to our friends for less than they wanted to pay. ANM must be a wonderful ministry." This kind of reputation in the community is priceless, especially for a global ministry.

I have always emphasized the importance for a global ministry to have "the blessing of a good report in the community." What's the use of being respected by the whole world and not having strong relationships within your own backyard? In my native language, there is a saying, *"Nagalakat sa dalan pero wala landong."* Literally, this means, "One walks in the streets of his village, but he casts no shadow." In other words, it is possible for some people to have absolutely no impact on the place where they live. It is as if they do not exist in their own community. How sad it is when a global ministry has no ties with its "Jerusalem." That is why I included generous help for five local ministries that were vital to our community in the $400,000 project disbursement. This help was received with much rejoicing and thanksgiving by the recipient ministries.

Papa John and Miss Hazel Goodrich

During this startup period, a much-respected missionary-pastor in Minnesota was especially kind to us. His name was Pastor John Goodrich, and his wife's name was Hazel. John was a pastor to other pastors. He was also a missionary pilot, and he flew his plane between Minnesota and Canada, planting churches and ministering to pastors in both places. He had founded two major ministries: Continental Mission (1950) and World Wide Ministries (1974). Both were later based in Bemidji, Minnesota.

John was short—maybe about 5'6"—and he had a round, gentle face. He reminded me of Pope John XXIII, and I affectionately called him Papa John. His fellow pastors and friends adored him, and I loved him too. God gave me favor in this man's heart, and he introduced me to many pastors in Minnesota. As a result, ANM made many new friends.

One Sunday, Miss Hazel went with Pastor John and me to visit a church under Papa John's care. During the service, the pastor of the church took up an offering for ANM, and afterwards, he gave it to me. But as almost always happens, other members of the church also came up after the service and gave me money directly. "This is for you," they said, putting the cash and checks in my pocket. "This is for your family."

Before we left the church, as is my usual custom for accountability, I went to Miss Hazel and gave her the money that had been donated to ANM. "These are the offerings from the church," I said.

"Oh, that's a lot of money, Bo," she responded.

As Papa John drove us home, I was sitting in the front passenger seat, and Miss Hazel was in the back. Taking the additional money that had been given for our family out of my pockets, I said to Papa John, "Dad, these were given to me personally for my family, but they should go together with the offering for ANM."

Miss Hazel apparently had been watching me like a hawk, perhaps because of bad experiences in the past with some other guest speakers. She mumbled in a low voice to her husband, "John, this one is not a 'grabber.'" I simply pretended not to hear what she said. She didn't realize that I spoke English fluently and was even well acquainted with the nuances of the language.

ANM gained many friends in Minnesota because of Papa John and Miss Hazel. They loved Marlou and me, and we loved them. Whenever I visited this wonderful couple, they insisted that I stay in their home instead of in a hotel. Papa John and I had long times of prayer and fellowship. He truly treated me like his own son. It was sad for him and for me when Miss Hazel passed away in 1995.

One day in late 2001, I called Papa John and said, "Dad, you have to see the fruits of your prayers for me. I'd like you to come and visit ANM." I bought a plane ticket for Papa John and for a young man named Chris Satterlee to accompany him. Chris was the oldest son of our friends Pastor Ward and Sister Cathy Satterlee.

Even though ANM was a relatively young organization, we already had a staff of about twenty people operating out of a twenty-room office building that we had bought in Crozet, Virginia, just west of Charlottesville. The previous year we had received almost $3 million in contributions. When Papa John saw how much we had grown, he exclaimed, "I'm so glad I came! I'm so glad I came!"

"Yes, Dad," I said, "this is how God has answered your prayers."

A few years later, when I heard that Papa John's health was declining, I called a friend in Bemidji, Minnesota. "Is Dad still alive?" When I learned that he was, I immediately bought a plane ticket and went to see him. Close friends and supporters Pastor Pat Spicer and

Wolfgang Teklenburg, kindly met me. How I deeply love these precious brothers. Like me, they also loved Papa John.

Papa John was bedridden and living in a retirement home. "Papa John, I'm here," I said. "I'm Bo Barredo, your son."

His face beamed with a bright smile. "You're one of the people who made me so happy in my ministry," he said. We talked for a while, and before I left, he laid hands on me and prayed a blessing upon me.

A Visit with the Browns

Prior to flying back home, I visited Fred and Beverly Brown. Fred is the faithful pastor of New Life Christian Fellowship in Park Rapids, Minnesota. The special friendship Marlou and I have with this beloved couple dates back to 1991, when I made my first trip to Minnesota. Fred and Beverly attended a missions presentation I gave at that time, and they were so broken when they saw the photos of the ministry of Nemuel and Ruth Palma working among the garbage scavengers in the Smoky Mountain dump that they and the church Fred pastored were changed. Their hearts became bigger not just for the lost, but also for the lost who are the poorest of the poor. Beverly and the church ladies opened a very dynamic and fruitful church thrift store that ministered to the poor in the local area, in the Philippines, in Mexico, and beyond.

Below are excerpts of a letter Pastor Fred sent in 1992 to Christian Aid:

> Dear Dr. Finley,
>
> My name is Fred Brown. I am pastor of New Life Christian Fellowship in Park Rapids, Minnesota. A year ago, my wife and I had the great privilege of hearing Bo Barredo speak in a small church in a town close to us on a Sunday evening. His main topic was the Smoky Mountain Ministries in Manila, and his message broke the heart of my wife, in particular, and it challenged both of us to become involved more fully in helping native pastors and missionaries.

I must say that it has been a tremendous blessing, to us personally and to our church. We have learned more completely the joy of giving of ourselves, our talents, our time, and our resources to the work of the Lord Jesus Christ, in helping these needy believers in many parts of our world. We are a small church, but we have a big heart. It has been demonstrated many times since that initial meeting with Brother Bo, the giving heart that is a part of this church. As a pastor, I can tell you, Dr. Finley, that I have been blessed many times over to see the people of God rise up and meet needs of others, to consider others more important than themselves. So I want to personally thank you for raising up Christian Aid Mission, and specifically, men like Bo Barredo.

I have had the privilege of speaking at New Life Christian Fellowship and its church camps many times in the years that followed.

A Trip to Bemidji

A couple of years after my visit to Papa John, I received a phone call informing me that he had passed away at the age of ninety-nine. I decided to fly to Bemidji. Nobody knew I was coming, and they had not planned for me to speak. But when his friends saw me, they kindly inserted me into the program. The church was packed.

In my remarks, I said something like this:

I have a beloved father in this place, and his name is John Goodrich. He flew planes. He crossed lands in isolated places in the middle of the cold winter, but he had a very, very warm and loving heart on behalf of a Filipino like me. The ministry that I helped to found, and that he helped support, now serves about eight thousand missionaries around the world. These are his fruits. That's why I'm reporting to you. These are the fruits of John and Hazel Goodrich through my life and ministry.

Many people came up to me after the service and said, "Bo, thank you for coming. We didn't realize that John had impacted you in all those ways." His former secretary at World Wide Ministries, Linda Simonson, who also became one of our supporters, exclaimed, "Bo, what a blessing to see you here at John's funeral! To be reminded of the magnitude of ANM's work and John's role in it was an encouragement!"

I am in tears as I write these lines. I miss Papa John. During my life journey, God has truly blessed me with loving fathers.

I Will Take Care of Your Family

One of the greatest contributors to the success of a missionary is the wholehearted support of the missionary's family. It is such a blessing when all members of the family fully buy into the calling with heart, soul, and spirit. God in his great grace and mercy brought this about in our family. Marlou, Benjamin, David, Felisa, and Jim all put their hands to the plow. God promised that if we take care of his servants, he will take care of us. He repays in full. He will not be a debtor to any man.

After Marlou became a born-again follower of Jesus, her faith was an inspiration to me and our children. Many times when I awoke in the middle of the night or at dawn, I would stand by the side of the bed thanking God for her. I have seen God answer her prayers so many times because she prays from an almost-pure heart. God truly gave me a diamond for a wife!

In late 1992, I said, "Marlou, you are a summa cum laude college graduate and an accomplished attorney, and you speak perfect English. I need you to please find work outside of ANM so we can take the support that is given to us by our friends and invest it in missionaries and new staff. The people who come to work for us will raise their own support, but in the beginning, we need to give them some financial help."

"What do you mean?" she responded. "God put us together. We are co-founders of ANM."

"This is true, Marlou, but during this initial phase of ANM, I need you to work outside to help with support."

"For how long?" she asked with some sadness.

"For as long as it takes," I gently answered.

Marlou began working as a part-time bank teller, and later, she became an administrative assistant at a local bank. One day while I was driving her to work, she broke down. "Marlou, why are you crying?" I asked her.

"I am so ashamed," she answered. "I don't know how to pull together our finances. We have so little money." Suddenly, she caught herself. "Oh, Lord, please forgive me for not trusting that you will provide for us!"

As we pulled up in front of the bank, I said, "Marlou, please stay in the car and let's talk about this."

"I don't want to talk about it," she said through tears. "I'm just not able to pull our finances together. It's so tight. Lord, please forgive me for doubting you." She got out of the car and went inside, still weeping.

God Comforts

On the drive home, I thought about how much Marlou wanted to work with me at ANM. She often talked about how we came to America as missionaries together, but now that we had started ANM, she felt like an outsider. Her heart ached when she heard the wonderful stories about the missionaries ANM supported. She had agreed to work outside of ANM for a while, but it had been hard for her.

I began to pray, "Oh, good Lord, Marlou loves you. She is the hero of our family, not me. You know this, Lord. Your daughter is the hero of our family. Please honor the tears of my wife. You know how much she loves you."

When I arrived home, I remembered that on the previous day I had neglected to retrieve the mail. When I opened the mailbox, a small business envelope caught my eye. I opened it, read the contents, closed the envelope, and drove back to the bank. When I arrived, I called on the bank's intercom, "Marlou, could you please come down?"

"No, I'm busy. Besides, I don't want to talk about what happened this morning."

"Marlou, please come down. I'm going to wait for you here on the ground floor." When she appeared a few minutes later, I said, "Marlou, tell me what happened this morning."

"I feel too embarrassed to talk about it," she stammered. "I doubted the Lord for a moment, but then I caught myself, and—" I interrupted her in mid-sentence by placing the envelope in her hands. "Here, read this."

Marlou opened the envelope and began reading. Suddenly, she burst into tears. The first paragraph of the letter read as follows:

Dear Brother Bo and family,

Please find enclosed two checks for your work for the Lord. I've been wanting to do this for quite some time, but the Lord's timing is what I try to follow. One check is made out to you and is to be used for your family's personal needs only. Do not give it away. The other check is to ANM to be used only for your ministry. This you can give away as the Lord directs.

The first check, the one for our family, was in the amount of $10,000. The check for ANM to give away was for $50,000.

I will let Marlou tell you how this incident impacted her.

MARLOU

God Confirms His Love

One of the verses of Scripture that really touches my heart is Isaiah 65:24. It says, "It shall come to pass That before they call, I will answer; And while they are still speaking, I will hear." On this morning, I was having a really hard time with our finances. I repented and asked the Lord to forgive my lack of trust. Barely an hour later, he illustrated to me the truth of this passage of Scripture. The truth of his Word came to pass while I was yet asking him. He had already provided the answer, and I didn't know it.

God wanted to show me that his Word is true. It was as if he said, "Yes, this is my Word, and I'm going to show it to you today." When I opened the envelope and saw the checks and the note, I again burst into tears. But this time, the tears were of joy, astonishment, and love. My heart was crying, "Lord, you truly are alive! You are real, and you do care, and you do answer." I was awed by the awareness of the kindness of the God whom I know and serve and love and trust.

God Truly Loves Us!

I rejoiced with Marlou over this gift of God from a generous donor, but not for myself. I was happy for Marlou because this response to our needs helped her experience the love of our Heavenly Father. God didn't give us this gift simply because we had a need. He is merciful, and his mercy is wonderful. But there was an even more wonderful reason for this gift. God gave it to us because he loves us. He truly loves us! He is an adoring Father who delights in giving good gifts to his children. On this day, Marlou experienced this reality.

For several more months, Marlou continued to serve as a valued employee at the bank. Then she moved on to become the executive assistant to the president of the largest health maintenance organization in central Virginia. She served there for four years, taking minutes at meetings of the board of directors and handling other high-level responsibilities. God honored her obedience by blessing every step of her way.

Benjamin's Story

To help support our family, our oldest son, Benjamin, had interrupted his college studies and taken a job as a busboy at the local Flaming Wok restaurant, and a second job at Shoney's restaurant. Washing dishes was painful for him because he had eczema on his hands, but he faithfully reported to work, day after day, without complaining.

Marlou wrote about him to our friends in a section of our family's newsletter entitled, "Through a Mother's Eyes . . ." Below is an excerpt:

> My eldest son, eighteen-year-old Benjamin, works . . . all day. At night, to further help the family, he is working in a nearby restaurant. Often, he doesn't get home till after two in the morning.
>
> Last week, it was almost midnight when I asked Bo to drive over to the restaurant and possibly get a glimpse of our son. Bo stopped the car at the edge of the parking area, and from my seat in the car, I saw a small solitary figure through the all-glass walls. He was mopping the floor of the now-deserted dining place.
>
> Seeing my baby with his funny hat and "busboy/dishwasher" uniform, I felt a hard tug in my heart and a sudden sting in my eyes. What I saw is what every mother always sees in a son, no matter how grownup he is—her little boy. At that moment in time, I saw my young son as a little boy who is trying to help his family make both ends meet . . . a little boy who is struggling to raise some money for his education . . . a little boy who is striving to help his father buy a better and bigger used car for the family ministry.
>
> He is all these and more—because he says he believes in what we are doing for the Lord. Afterwards, Bo drove us home in silence. He understood my mother's heart.

In the mornings at breakfast, Benjamin was so happy to be able to put a large portion of his earnings from tips and wages in the family's food fund. He was fully engaged in the family ministry. He also would take Felisa and Jim to Toys "R" Us almost every payday to buy them toys. He even sent some money to his former classmates in the Philippines. And he found time to volunteer at ANM.

God Provides

As I have mentioned, Benjamin had a serious problem with his ears, and Pastor Bare had wanted to put $3,000 in escrow to cover his medical treatments. But after prayer, and with Benjie's agreement, we had given this money away to missionaries who needed it even more. After we disbursed these funds, Pastor Bare on his own initiative called Dr. Robert Cantrell, the provost for Health Services at the University of Virginia Hospital in Charlottesville. Dr. Cantrell was well known in the community, not only as a wonderful leader and an esteemed physician, but even more importantly as a firm believer in Christ Jesus our Lord. His wife, Lee Cantrell, was one of the godliest ladies one could ever meet.

Dr. Cantrell invited Benjamin and me to come in and see him. He referred us to Dr. Paul Lambert, an ENT specialist who also is a dedicated believer. Dr. Lambert informed us that Benjamin needed an artificial eardrum in his right ear.

"We may not be able to afford such an operation," I confessed. "We are missionaries, and we are poor."

Dr. Lambert was silent for a moment. Then he looked at us and said, "I love missionaries. I will help you. I will do it."

Our gracious God had opened the heavens once again! Benjamin's surgeries were successful. These procedures would have cost far more than the $3,000 Pastor Bare wanted to put in escrow, and Dr. Lambert had done them for free! Our family again saw how God repays those who trust in him. He will not be a debtor to any man.

With the help of student loans, Benjamin graduated from Liberty University with highest honors in 1998. After a few years, he went to Regent University School of Law and earned a JD degree. He married Tanya Ontiveros, a beautiful and godly young lady of character who also graduated with honors from Liberty University. She is the younger sister of Lucas, one of his closest friends at Liberty. God has blessed them with three delightful children: Luke, age twenty-one, Jessica, age seventeen, and Eric, age ten. Benjamin is a probation and parole officer in Lynchburg, Virginia, where they reside.

A year after graduating from Liberty University, Benjamin wrote the following life statement for his law school application:

A PERSONAL STATEMENT

There are three principles or mottoes in life that I adhere to.

First, "*I walk my talk.*" When there is something I believe in, I live and support it. I believe in missions—the spreading of the good news that there is a Savior—Jesus Christ. I sacrificed my schooling for a long season so I could work hard to help feed our family and thus enable Father to do missions work all over the world. In a speech about her "Unknown Heroes of Missions" delivered in a religious ceremony, Mother deeply touched everyone's hearts when she cited me as one of her heroes.

Second, "*I repay kindness and trust by becoming the very best I can be.*" My father and mother and Dr. Paul Lambert stand out among those who have accorded me kindness and trust. I was a legally handicapped person in my teens. I underwent several ear surgeries to alleviate my hearing impairment, but to no avail. Frustration, inadequacy, and near surrender marked my every struggle to better myself.

In 1993, we came to know of a special but costly surgery to implant an artificial eardrum and a middle ear bone. However, it was way beyond our means. But Dr. Lambert had compassion on me. He operated on my ears for free. I'm very thankful I regained at least a little over half of my total hearing.

Subsequently, my parents told me, "*Son, go back to college, do your best, and we will make it up to you.*" Inspired by such kindness and trust, I enrolled at Liberty University. I spread my wings, prayed a lot, and flew high. Last year, on graduation day, the school conferred on me its highest academic honors—summa cum laude [changed to magna cum laude due to a minor policy infraction].

Third, "*I am an advocate for children.*" My maternal grandfather, a lawyer and a very dignified man, was stern and authoritarian in dealing with his children. But he was tender towards his grandchildren, especially me. However, I didn't really know the depth of his love until one day when I was about three. I was limping because of a big glistening boil on my right leg. Everyone suggested that the boil should be pierced to let the pus out. Grandpa wouldn't hear of it. He sat me on his lap gently, lifted my right leg and sucked out the pus with his mouth. He spared me from pain. There wasn't a dry eye around me.

That moving experience and many more developed the love I have for little children. I coached children's teams, taught children Sunday school classes, and spoke at children's church. Children would follow me around. I felt like a Pied Piper. Once I become a lawyer, I will advocate for children in terms of their rights, protection, and care. I want to be their champion. Jesus did just that while on this earth. So did Grandfather. I could do no less.

David's Story

Our second son, David, earned money for himself and our family by babysitting the children of pastors. One Sunday when he was about sixteen years old, we were at Covenant Church and David heard Pastor Harold Bare share his disappointment over the slow progress of the church's building project. Pastor Bare had a heart for missionaries, and a larger building would allow the church to have more people, which would mean more money for missions.

On the drive home, David said, "Papa, take me to the bank. I have some savings from my babysitting and from my work at Burger King and the Rack Room Shoes that I want to give to the church."

I said to him, "I thought you were saving that money for college. Are you going to give it away to the church?"

"I trust the Lord for my future," David replied. "He will take care of my education." When we got to the bank, David withdrew his entire savings of $1,000.

"David," I said, "Scripture promises, He who honors me, him will I honor (1 Samuel 2:30). God is going to honor you, son. God is going to honor you." Pastor Bare and the church were so encouraged by David's sacrificial giving.

Around this time, Marlou and I needed to write newsletters to send to our supporters, but ANM had only one outdated computer that had been plucked from the trash. With considerable effort, we had cleaned nicotine stains out of the keyboard and fixed a few other things so we could use it for receipting donations, but it would not handle the formatting of newsletters. David, who at this time was editor of his Albemarle High School newspaper, said, "After dinner, let's go to Kinko's and rent a computer. I'll type, edit, and format your newsletter." Beginning that night, and for many months afterward, David was our newsletter editor. Our ministry truly was a family affair.

David joined the US Army Reserve, received an undergraduate degree from the University of Virginia, and in 2001, earned a law degree at Regent University in Virginia Beach. He married Jennifer Winans, a beautiful, godly, and quiet young lady of character, who had been his schoolmate at the University of Virginia. They had served together in the youth group in their church. Today, David and Jennifer have two lovely children: Halle, age nineteen, and David Morgan, age seventeen.

Judge Barredo

In 2014, the Virginia General Assembly appointed David to be a judge of the Juvenile and Domestic Relations Court. At age thirty-seven, he was one of the youngest judges in the state. Below are excerpts from his installation address before a large group of judges, lawyers, family, and friends:

> . . . *Bear with me as I attempt to convince you of what I am convinced is evident here today. In a trial, there are two types of evidence, circumstantial and direct . . . But may I present to you that I am living proof that people are placed in someone's life, not circumstantially, but directly appointed. Many of you have known*

my parents, brothers, sister, and me since that time in 1991 when we came to this great country as an immigrant missionary family from the Philippines. Having once been strangers to a foreign land, many of you welcomed us and took us in as friends, as family. It was not by chance that you were placed in my life when I was an impressionable teenager. You helped me stay on the straight and narrow path, and for that I am grateful . . . Some folks here today have been there since day one when we stepped off the plane at Dulles Airport on a frigid twenty-seven-degree night in February 1991.

Many thanks to my parents, brothers, and sister! My parents were attorneys in the Philippines. They were high-ranking government officials. When they received God's call to serve as missionaries, there was no hesitation to answer that call. They forsook everything, comfort, prestige, and professional successes, to step up and jump, as my father would say, from law to grace. They are a shining example to me of humility, grace, servant-mindedness. Though we did not have much, we lacked for nothing and had everything. There's a saying, "If you have health, you have everything." To that might I add "love." Thank you, Mama and Papa.

Speaking of love, a short twenty years ago, in my case, not so short since that represents more than half of my lifetime, and truly because it has been a wonderful journey, I met my wife Jennifer . . . She was sixteen, and I was seventeen. Again, I submit to you that it was not circumstantially that we met. I am convinced that she was directly appointed to be my better half. I am so thankful that God has blessed me with such a wonderful, sweet, caring, and beautiful wife. She worked to help put me through law school.

When I petitioned the Bar Association for their endorsement, I shared with them one of my life verses. It comes from Micah 6:8 (KJV): "He hath shewed thee, O man, what is good; and what doth the LORD require of thee, but to do justly, and to love mercy, and to walk humbly with thy God?" It is my hope that I have done these and will continue to do these as I continue my service to the citizens of this district and the great Commonwealth.

In December 2022, David will assume the office of Circuit Court Judge of the 16th Judicial District of Virginia.

Felisa's Story

Felisa has been on fire for the Lord since she was a little girl. She sings from her heart like a nightingale. When she sings, people lean forward to listen. Her voice is truly anointed. She has a gracious temperament, so Marlou and I were surprised when she came home from middle school one day and said, "I had trouble at school today. I was trying to tell the kids about Jesus, and some of them laughed at me. I told a girl named Sandra that she would go to hell if she didn't believe in Jesus, and we almost got into a fight."

I put my arm around her and said warmly, "Felisa, I am proud of you for delivering the Gospel and sharing about Jesus. But next time, do it a different way, or you really might get into trouble. I don't want to have to leave my missionary work and go back to practicing law so I can represent you." She got the message.

A few years later, when Felisa was in high school, she said to Marlou and me, "I have great news! Do you remember that in middle school, I almost got into a fight with a classmate named Sandra? Well, Sandra just called me. She said, 'Felisa, I am going to be baptized, and my pastor wants me to bring to my baptism the person who most influenced me to become a Christian. You are the one who most impacted my life. Will you come with me to my baptism?'"

College Days

When Felisa was a student at the University of Virginia, she developed a serious relationship with a fellow who was an assistant minister at a church. He seemed like a godly young man, and Marlou and I felt fine when they got engaged. But one day, I woke up with a strong foreboding about their planned marriage. I said, "Marlou, this wedding is not going to be a good thing. I need to talk with Felisa."

"What!" Marlou exclaimed. "They are already engaged. You have bought the wedding dress, and the date is set."

"No, she needs to know about this," I said. We talked some more, and Marlou agreed that I should talk with Felisa.

When Felisa and I got together, I said, "Felisa, you know how much Mama and I love you. We would give our lives for you. But I think this wedding is not a good thing." Felisa was taken aback, but she listened. Practically every day after that I would ask, "Felisa, have you changed your mind? If you change your mind, your mother and I will support you."

"Papa, what are you doing?" Felisa would say. "Mama, why is Papa doing this?" She was troubled by my questioning, but Marlou and I have open communication with our children, so our relationship remained close.

One day Felisa's fiancé called me and asked if we could meet. When we sat down together, he said, "Sir, please forgive me, but I have to break the engagement with your daughter. I am going to music school, and I will need to focus on my studies. I don't think it will work for me to start at a new school and start a marriage at the same time."

For his sake, I pretended to be sad, but I wanted to jump for joy! I almost wanted to give this fellow a million dollars. However, Felisa's heart was broken. She shed so many tears that she had difficulty seeing. At her request, I drove her to her college classes every day until she settled down. Marlou and I tried to console her and minister to her. "God must have prepared a better plan for you," we assured her. We gave the wedding dress we had bought to a second-hand store.

Next door to Felisa's house at UVA was a house for men. Felisa had become acquainted with a fellow who lived in this house by the name of Andrew Needham. When I first met Andrew, I said to Felisa, "My goodness! He reminds me of one of those beautiful Greek statues." He was a tall, handsome guy with long, curly hair and a sculpted face that made him one of the heartthrobs among the ladies on campus. He had remarkable depth of character and intelligence, but the best thing about this young man was his godliness.

"Papa, we're just good friends," Felisa assured me. Then one day she came home and said, "Mama! Papa! I am troubled. Why is it that of all the girls at school, I am the one Andrew invites to go with him to buy groceries?"

"Because he likes you," I said.

"Oh, I don't think so," she objected.

"No, no, he likes your company," echoed Marlou.

Not long after this, Felisa came to Marlou and me and said, "Andrew gave me this card. He is very creative, and he drew this. Drawing something like this must take so much patience." She handed us a beautiful little card with hundreds of people drawn on it.

"Maybe he gave this to you because he likes you," Marlou said.

"Oh, no! I don't think so," Felisa protested. But a short time later, she said, "I think Andrew likes me, and I like him, too."

Jim, the youngest in our family, overhead this exchange and piped up, "Why don't you just write him a love letter!"

"Andrew Is Going to Marry Felisa"

When Felisa and Andrew graduated in May 2006, Andrew asked Felisa to help him pack his belongings. Then he went to his parents' home in North Carolina. Felisa was hurt that Andrew had moved on to the next phase of his life without including her in his plans. She accepted a job as a teacher near Washington, DC.

One day while Marlou and I were driving home from the ANM office, I said, "Andrew is going to marry Felisa."

Startled, Marlou asked, "Where did you get that?"

"It just came to me," I answered. "But watch and see. Andrew is going to marry Felisa."

"Don't say anything to Felisa," Marlou cautioned me. "You don't want to give her false hopes."

It turned out that Marlou was the one who spilled the beans to Felisa about my comment, and Felisa immediately confronted me. "Papa, why did you say that? Do you know something?"

"All I know is that Andrew is going to marry you," I answered.

193

> *"And we know that all things work together for good to those who love God, to those who are the called according to His purpose."*
>
> ROMANS 8:28

"Papa, there is no evidence of that," said Felisa. But one day in June, while she was helping at church, she noticed a missed call on her phone. It was from Andrew. "Mama! Papa! Should I return Andrew's call? I want to do the right thing."

It so happened that Andrew called Felisa again before she had a chance to return his call. During a conversation about nothing of great importance, he rather matter-of-factly said, "I've been thinking that maybe we should bring our friendship to a higher level." It took Felisa a few moments to realize what had just happened. When it dawned on her that Andrew wanted to be special friends, she agreed.

Later that summer, Andrew and his younger brother went on a short-term mission trip to Belarus. When Felisa didn't hear from Andrew for more than a week, she began to worry that he had changed his mind. The problem turned out to be simply poor internet and wireless coverage in Belarus, and their relationship continued to progress.

After Andrew returned from Belarus, he asked if I could meet him at Panera Bread. When we sat down, he said, "Mr. Barredo, may I meet with you and Mrs. Barredo to ask for the hand of your daughter?"

"Andrew," I replied, "as my potential son-in-law, I ask only one thing. Please honor me before our family and before our friends by addressing me as Papa, and please address my wife as Mama."

"Sir, I would be very honored."

A Joy-Filled Day

On a sunny July 1, 2007, Andrew Needham and Felisa Barredo were married at the historic University of Virginia chapel. What a wonderful, joy-filled day this was! God showed once again, as he had with our older sons, Benjamin and David, that when we deny ourselves, he will more than make it up to us. Romans 8:28 says, "And we know that all things work together for good to those who love God, to those who are the called according to His purpose." This is a promise of God, and we hold onto it.

At the time of this writing, Felisa and Andrew have been married fifteen years. He is like our fourth son, and he is loved by all our children. They have two amazing children: Georgia, age ten, and Darcy, age nine. God says that if we take care of his servants, he will take care of our family. He even takes care of our family's heartaches! Andrew is the communications director of ANM. Felisa works as a teacher assistant in a local elementary school. What a blessing that they live only fifteen minutes away from us.

Jim's Story

Our youngest son, Jim, has always been such an encouragement to me. When he was about eight years old, he would say, "Papa, when you go to speak at the church today, would you take me with you to encourage you?" On the drive to the church, he would say wonderful prayers for me. Then he would sit in the front pew and listen while I preached.

When he was about sixteen, he worked at a PacSun retail store to help earn money for our family and to save some to buy a set of drums. Jim loves to play the drums. A self-taught drummer, he was with a band that won the Battle of the Bands competition held at the University of Virginia. He has also been part of several church praise and worship teams. Oh, I love that boy!

Jim's front teeth had not grown in properly. In fact, they were so crooked that he did not want to smile. As Marlou was flipping through the Yellow Pages of the phone directory one day, she happened to notice that a dental office in town offered a free consultation. Figuring we had nothing to lose, she asked me to take Jim there.

The dentist said, "I need to refer you to our orthodontist. Unfortunately, correcting his teeth will be quite expensive as it will require several surgeries."

I silently prayed, "Lord, corrective procedures would cost thousands of dollars. You know we cannot afford this. Please help us."

The next moment, the dentist leaned forward and whispered, "It's on the house, including the charges of the orthodontist."

"Excuse me, doctor?" The expression "on the house" was familiar to me, but I wanted to make sure I had not misunderstood.

"It's on the house," he said again. "The cost of the procedures will be on us. I am doing this because I know you. But don't tell anyone."

I was puzzled. "You know me? Have we met?"

"We have never met, but I have heard about you."

"Thank you so much!" I exclaimed. "Thank you so much! Thank you so much!" I didn't ask how he had heard about me. I just presumed that he was familiar with ANM because he belonged to the local Christian community.

On the drive home, Jim turned to me. "Papa, I have always heard about how these miracles happen to missionaries who serve overseas, and I have been happy when miracles have happened to the missionaries and to our family. But, Papa, today a miracle happened to me personally. I will never forget this!"

When we gathered as a family that evening, I asked, "What have we learned today? The children each answered differently in their own words, but in essence, this is what they said:

God showed his hand again today. He was there for us when we could not afford it. He has taken care of Benjamin's ears and David's college education and other needs of the family. Today, he took care of Jim's teeth. He is taking care of our family just as he promises.

Jim is like me in that he feels deeply about things. One morning while he was on his way down the stairs of our townhouse to go to Albemarle High School, Marlou and I noticed that the sound of his footsteps suddenly stopped. Then we heard feet racing back up the steps and heading toward our bedroom. In an instant, Jim appeared in our doorway. He was bawling like a child. We thought something serious had happened. He hugged both of us tightly.

"Son, what happened?" we gently asked him. "Is something wrong?"

Between sobs, he replied, "Mama and Papa, I was going down the stairs, and suddenly, I felt so much love for you, and I remembered that you're not getting any younger. And somehow, I decided to quickly turn around to tell you how much I love you. Please don't grow old on me!"

We felt so loved by our youngest son. Jim finished his business degree from the highly acclaimed McIntire School of Commerce at the University of Virginia. He later married Kristen Straw, another beautiful and godly young lady of character, and a former US Peace Corps volunteer in Ethiopia who now works as a director of program management for a global non-profit organization. Jim has spent most of his career in management consulting, and he now works in the technology sector. Jim and Kristen have three beautiful children: Jude, age six, Isaiah, age three, and Ruth, age one. They live in Washington, DC.

Jim's Fondest Memories

In 2019, Pastor Clay Sterrett, our dear friend and former ANM board member, asked Jim to jot down some thoughts about his father. What he wrote touched my heart. Marlou retrieved a copy of it from her computer. Please allow us to share this treasure with you:

> Some of my fondest memories growing up were the times I would accompany my dad to different churches as he would preach and share about his love and passion for native pastors and missionaries around the world. Oftentimes, it would just be me going with him and lending presence during what were undoubtedly some lonely and challenging times for him during those early days of ANM. This idea of loving someone by being present was something he modeled and something I aspire for in my own relationships.
>
> Even though his attention was (and is still) demanded by so many, my dad was never too busy to take my phone call, drive

me to early morning band practice, pick me up from school early for special outings, clean and detail my car, and lead our family in evening prayers and devotions. This kind of love is felt by just about anyone who meets him and often leaves an indelible mark on their lives.

As an example, I visited a new church in Crozet around two years ago, and I was approached by someone who asked if I was Bo Barredo's son. (I'm told I bear quite a striking resemblance to him.) With great delight, he went on to describe the two times he'd ever been around my dad: the first being decades before when my dad preached at a church he was attending; the second just a few months earlier during a chance encounter at the parking lot of a local grocery store.

My dad's love for people flows out of and is sustained by the love he has received from the Lord. I have witnessed firsthand numerous times when instead of responding in kind to an offense against him, my dad would humble himself and be the first to apologize for anything he may have done to cause the offense and seek reconciliation and peace. My dad is not a perfect man, but his love for God and people are truly inspiring and have proven to be a great example for me in my own spiritual journey.

BUILDING THE KINGDOM TOGETHER

ANM's structure at this point was straightforward. We had a president, Carl Gordon, and two vice presidents, Graham Stewart and me. Graham was in charge of publications, and I handled development. I had requested this assignment because of my passion and gifts for developing organizations and strategies. One of my responsibilities was to reach out to churches across America as an ambassador and preacher and as an advocate for ANM's missions partners. My other responsibility, in addition to challenging people to support missions, was to survey native missionaries and ministries around the globe to help determine which ones ANM should support.

Carl and I believed God had placed ANM's main strategy on our hearts: to build strong relationships. We felt it was of primary importance to build relationships with our missionary partners overseas, with our donors and friends in the United States, and among our coworkers at ANM. Missions is about people. The missionaries ANM serves are people; the donors and friends of ANM are people; and the staff of ANM are people. To be highly viable, a ministry must have very good mailing lists, not only in the number of names, but also in the depth of relationships.

Relationship Acquisition and Development

One day, as Carl and I were talking with fellow staff member John Bucchi about how much the three of us enjoyed our fishing jaunts, Carl said, "You know, Bo, if you have a nice fishing rod, you will catch more fish."

"You know, Bo, if you have a nice fishing rod, you will catch more fish."

This triggered a thought in my mind that should have been obvious from the beginning. I said, "Carl, we need to develop some really good rods for fishing for donors and friends to support native missionaries. A key part of our strategy needs to be relationship acquisition and development."

We started thinking about how we could improve our approach to acquiring and developing relationships. Relationship acquisition and development became such an important focus that it soon took on the acronym "RAD." Our next step was to identify and improve our fishing rods. We immediately began developing RAD teams to produce high-quality relationships that would enhance what God had called ANM to be: an advocacy ministry on behalf of native missionaries reaching the unreached.

Operation Barnabas International— "Refreshing Tired Feet"

We named the first RAD team Operation Barnabas International, or OBI. The purpose of this ministry was to encourage and exhort the hard-working field missionaries and pastors through organized conferences. We gave it the theme "Refreshing Tired Feet."

This team was initially led by John Varghese, then by Pastor Bubba Rose from North Carolina, a Billy Graham look-alike in both dignified appearance and dynamic speaking ability. Later, an equally explosive speaker and exhorter par excellence, Pastor Jerry Harding, accepted the leadership role. Their work enabled interested pastors, elders, teachers, and members of missions committees in numerous churches across America to accompany ANM staff members on short-term, overseas trips to teach and encourage missionaries. After these pastors, teachers, missions committee leaders, and others returned home, they had a fresh vision and excitement for the mission field, and they became fervent advocates and supporters for the ministries they had visited. By focusing greater attention on this OBI fishing rod, we acquired many new donors.

Building the Kingdom Together

The Lord reinforced our idea for our second fishing rod one day in 1995 when Pastor Charles Shearer and Pastor Ross Reider of New Love in Christ Church in Harrisburg, Pennsylvania, came to visit us at ANM. I had twice spoken at missions conferences at this church, and I highly respected both men. Pastor Charles, the missions pastor, was a wonderful brother in the Lord with such a passionate heart for missions that years later, I took him with me to the Philippines. The wonderfully strong senior pastor of the church, Pastor Ross, was such a humble man of God that I once told him in front of friends, "Each time I visit your church, you are either vacuuming or preaching!"

After we had prayed, Pastor Charles said, "Our church is a friend to many churches who would like to have us organize their missions conferences. Brother Bo, would you be our main speaker for all these conferences?"

I felt so humbled and broken that I trembled. "Why me?" I stammered.

"Because when you speak, people listen," he replied.

After the meeting, I asked Carl what he thought. He said, "Brother, that's a big open door for us. That's building the kingdom together. We will tell these churches that we are building the kingdom together with native missionaries."

I said, "Carl, would you say that again? Building the kingdom together? That's BKT, right?" We were outside at the time, and I happened to glance up and see a sign across the street for a Burger King. "Carl, I think what you said is from the Lord. The name for this outreach should be BKT, Building the Kingdom Together." This became our second new fishing rod.

A new member of our staff, a fine young man and elder of his church named Oliver Asher, began helping us with the BKT initiative. I joked that BKT stood for *Bo, Karl,* and *Toliver*. It wasn't terribly funny, but we got a big laugh out of it. Oliver formed BKT teams that organized and presented church missions conferences across the US. The teams included singers from ANM and overseas missionaries supported by ANM. An ANM staff member or I would be the speaker, along with one or more missionaries that we supported. The conferences typically would start on a Saturday and end on Sunday. Sometime during or after the conferences, the churches would ask for faith pledges. As a result of BKT, our mailing list grew by leaps and bounds. This initiative implanted a passion for indigenous missions in churches across America. The powerful testimonies and stories that were shared moved hearts, challenged believers, and strengthened churches.

Construction Teams International

A few years later, the real estate market crashed, and many builders and realtors needed work. I saw this as a kingdom opportunity to recruit volunteers for ANM, because builders who are Christians would rather serve others than sit around idle. As I arrived at the ANM offices one morning, I introduced myself to a man who was working as a volunteer on the construction of our new office building. His name was Mike Twitchell. "Brother Mike," I said, "would you go home today and tell your wife that I'm offering you the position of director of Construction Teams International?"

"What's that?" he asked.

"You're going to lead construction teams from ANM that will go overseas to build or repair churches, orphanages, or whatever else the ministries need," I told him. "We'll open up the opportunity to ANM staff, donors, friends, and other volunteers."

"But I'm not a carpenter or an engineer," he said. "I'm a retired insurance salesman."

I said, "Just go home and tell your wife."

When Mike told his wife, Bootsie, that he had been offered the position of director of Construction Teams International at ANM, she said, "That's what you get for having a big mouth!" This became a joke that is still passed around ANM.

Mike accepted the job offer and became one of the greatest ambassadors of ANM to the body of Christ. Everybody who came within two feet of Mike received his business card and an invitation to come overseas with him to help build or repair a church, school, or some other structure.

When Mike started working with ANM, he was almost seventy years old. In the years that followed, he led teams for construction projects in many countries around the world, always paying for his own travel. His efforts brought many new friends to ANM. Mike is one diamond of a person. His favorite destinations for construction teams are England, the Philippines, Ireland, and Ukraine. He and Bootsie also became generous donors of ANM.

MIKE

Mike's Story in His Own Words

God called me to Advancing Native Missions to help as a volunteer with buildings and grounds. That is when I met Brother Bo Barredo, co-founder of the mission. One day as we were passing in the hallway, he said, "We are going to start a new ministry here. It will be called Construction Teams Ministry International, and I want you to be the director."

This really excited me. When I told my wife, she smiled and said, "You opened your big mouth and got into trouble, didn't you?"

Being asked to be director of CTI (thank you, Brother Bo!) was truly an answer to prayer. It became a highlight of my life. I had retired from my insurance career with two life goals. One was to serve the Lord in a greater way, and the other was to travel. Through CTI, I had the privilege of leading numerous construction teams to many different countries to do ministry and projects for our overseas partners.

Brother Bo emulates the passage of Scripture that says we are to pray about everything. I made a trip with him—I think we went to New Jersey by car—and it was like a prayer meeting all the way. This inspired me to be a more faithful prayer warrior. Brother Bo sets an example for all of us to follow as servants of the Lord Jesus Christ.

Warehouse for the Nations— "Impacting Nations and the Community"

Some American believers are tentative about giving money to missions, but they are more open to giving things that can be very valuable to the people on mission fields who are very poor. One day, I suggested to Carl that we start a warehouse ministry. He liked the idea, and we decided that the first step was to build a warehouse. Building a five thousand square foot warehouse would cost $60,000, so I gave Oliver Asher a list of possible donors to contact. This initial outreach brought in $15,000. Where would we get the other $45,000? We made this a matter of prayer.

The year before, God had sent our way a talented engineer by the name of John Bucchi. John was a formidable man and a dynamic preacher, and he was good with his hands. He joined ANM full-time, by faith. In fact, he told us that, if necessary, he would sell his nice pick-up truck to support himself at ANM. He led the construction of ANM's office building and its extension. I said, "John, I would like you to consider being the director of our Warehouse for the Nations. But we don't yet have a warehouse. Could you build one?"

John accepted the challenge, and his work was so incredible that he eventually became the vice president and head of ANM's Overseas Department. John is one of our heroes at ANM, a diamond of a man appreciated by all.

We had no money to pay laborers, so Oliver Asher, Danny McAllister, Bubba Rose, and some other men at ANM worked on the warehouse as volunteers. One day, I asked John, "How long do you expect it will take to finish this warehouse?"

"Around three months," he answered.

"It seems like a few extra hands might speed things up," I suggested. "What if Carl and I pitch in? How long would it take you then?"

"About six months," he replied with a straight face. Then he burst out laughing! Anyway, I probably couldn't have helped much because I was always traveling.

A Trip to Texas

Around this time, I was invited to be the main speaker at the missions conference of Calvary Baptist Church in Longview, Texas. It was decided that Oliver Asher would accompany me, and I asked the itinerary department at ANM to buy roundtrip tickets for the two of us. ANM's policy was to purchase the cheapest tickets possible. Our trip had numerous layovers and took fourteen hours. We arrived just as the missions banquet was starting.

News about our trip generated quite a bit of amusement among some of the guests, especially with a businessman by the name of Terry McKinley. He came over and remarked, "Normally that trip would take only three or four hours. Why did your flight take so long?"

"I don't know, sir," I said, "but if we were going to Asia, we'd be in Japan by now." He laughed heartily at this. Then I said to him, "Let me tell you the real story. We have given instructions to the one in charge of the itinerary department to always purchase the cheapest tickets, and these tickets always have the most layovers and take the most time. It is tiresome for us, but I tell you, Mr. McKinley, it is worth it to save one hundred dollars, because that will furnish food for one month to a native missionary, and his family will not go hungry." I teared up when I said this, and he saw my earnestness. I believe he heard my heart.

He responded by asking about my plans for the following day. When he learned that our schedule was flexible, he said that he wanted me to come to his place of business.

A Blessed Morning

The next morning, Terry picked me up and took me immediately to his office. He sat me down opposite him and said, "Okay, tell me about your staff and your needs."

"Overseas?" I asked.

"No, no, your US staff. Give me the names of the people on your staff who need support."

"Well, there's Lucille Lebeau," I said.

He wrote a check for $3,000 and handed it to me. "That's for Lucille. Who else?"

"Danny McAllister," I said.

He wrote a check for $3,000. "Who else?"

"Cris Paurillo needs help."

He wrote a check for $3,000 and handed it to me. "Who else?"

"John Bucchi lacks support."

He made out a check for John for $3,000. By the time he was done, he had written eleven checks for $3,000 each.

I exclaimed, "Praise the Lord! Oliver and I are going to be like Santa Claus when we get home. People will be rejoicing."

"We're not done," he said. "What else do you need?"

I thought for a moment. "Well, we're building a warehouse. Some of the men on our staff have volunteered to build it. It's about half finished, and John Bucchi, the man who is overseeing the project, expects it to be completed in about three more months. Carl and I asked John how long it would take if we volunteered to help, and John said about six months!"

Terry laughed. Then he said, "Did you see the sign outside the front of my business?"

"Yes, sir. It says Curtis-McKinley Roofing and Sheet Metal Company."

"We also specialize in building steel buildings," he explained. "I'm going to send a team to Charlottesville, and they're going to help build ANM's warehouse. Now tell me, how are you and Oliver getting to the airport after you finish speaking at Calvary Baptist Church?"

"Pastor Richard Jones plans to drive us," I answered.

"Tell him I will drive you."

Blessing Upon Blessing

On the day the conference finished, Terry picked us up as he had promised. But instead of driving us to the airport, he took us to a car dealership and bought us a practically new Suburban. Oliver and I drove back to Virginia in the most expensive car I had ever driven up to that time. A few days later, five of Terry's workmen arrived at ANM's offices in a big pick-up truck with a hitched trailer. They finished the warehouse in just five days!

To add to this incredible story, as soon as the warehouse opened, we began collecting all sorts of things that missionaries and their families need on overseas mission fields. People contributed clothing, used cars, used tables, used office furniture, office supplies, vegetable seedlings, school chairs, bicycles, canned goods, medicines, Bibles, books, and lots of other things that mean so much to missionaries. We loaded these items into shipping containers and sent them to missionaries overseas.

Missionaries and their families welcomed these containers with much fanfare. They surrounded them and laid hands on them, singing songs of praise and thanksgiving. During the seventeen years of the warehouse's operation, we estimate that ANM sent more than $40 million worth of goods overseas. In 2005, John Bucchi was promoted, and John and Lynn Parker, who came to ANM that same year, took full charge of the warehouse ministry.

The Parkers were naturals for the position. John had spent most of his career in warehousing and maintaining inventory. Lynn had arranged international shipping for a freight forwarding company. They had become committed to indigenous missions when some friends at ANM had sent them a native missionary to host in their home in North Carolina.

Warehouse for the Nations spurred the growth of many of our ministry partners overseas. Williams Yindi in Tanzania is one example. He reports that when the containers arrived, it was like Christmas for the entire village. He credits these containers as a major reason for the growth of his ministry from 14 to 250 churches. One container alone allowed him to start a school that now educates 250 students each year.

Warehouse for the Nations also added names to ANM's mailing list, and it became a point of attraction to the Christian community in the Charlottesville area and beyond. Christian schools regularly scheduled student field trips to ANM to see the warehouse. Furthermore, the warehouse became a magnet that attracted believers to come and volunteer.

ANM—Like the Wheel of a Cart

Around this time, Oliver Asher oversaw all of ANM's RAD teams, and I found it exciting to observe his RAD meetings. One day, some of us began talking about how the administrative and functional structure of ANM resembled the wheel of a cart, with spokes linking the rim and the hub. We had a graphic created to depict this that we put in our lobby.

In our graphic, the center of the wheel, or hub, represented the missionaries, orphans, and missions projects we served. This was where we directed almost all our funding and resources. The rim of the wheel had two layers. The first layer represented the leadership of ANM; the second layer represented the administrative functions that held everything together.

Each of the spokes represented a different ministry, or RAD team. We had a spoke for Operation Barnabas International; another spoke represented Building the Kingdom Together; and still another stood for Warehouse for the Nations. Additional spokes represented our Healing Hands medical ministry, led by energetic volunteers Dr. Wes and Jackie Howard; our Comforting the Persecuted Church ministry, led by a deeply trustworthy brother, Jay Temple; and our Construction Teams International ministry, which we discussed above. Later in this chapter, I'll describe another important spoke, the Comfort My People ministry, which reaches out to the Jewish people.

All these ministries had leaders, but there was one spoke where God had not yet supplied the leader: our International Women's Ministries (IWM).

International Women's Ministries— "Helping Wipe Our Sisters' Tears"

When Marlou and I traveled overseas, we met many pastors and their wives who were very poor. Many were embarrassed when we would visit them because they didn't have chairs for us to sit. Sometimes the pastors' wives would not open their mouths to speak or smile because their teeth had rotted due to malnutrition and poor dental care. If I asked the wife of the pastor or missionary leader what we could pray for, we often would get no answer. However, we might learn later that her children couldn't attend school because the family had no money for tuition, or that the family had a medical bill they couldn't pay.

Marlou and I felt great compassion for these wives. Upon leaving, I would shake the hand of the pastor or ministry leader and enclose $200 or $300. He would say, "What is this, Brother Bo?" I would answer, "That's not for you. That's for your wife. Tell her to see a doctor or a dentist. Tell her to get false teeth. Use this for tuition for your children." Occasionally, Marlou would get several wives together as a group, and they would go to a department store to buy new clothes and undergarments. It was always a moving scene because most would never have been to a department store.

ANM's ministry to women started in this small, personal way through Marlou. For a long time, we looked and prayed for a lady to head this ministry. One day, she appeared. We had known her for a long time because she was the assistant minister overseeing the children's ministry of the church we attended. In fact, she had taught our own children when they were young. Her name was Autumn Graves.

Autumn was a single mother, with children at home, so the modest income she earned from working at the church was important to her. But she heard from the Lord that she should resign from this position and trust him. Marlou and I learned about her resignation when she came to see us for prayer.

"Why did you take such a risk?" we asked her. "The bank is about to foreclose on your mortgage, and you are in danger of losing your house. How are you going to pay tuition to send your children to a Christian school?"

Autumn answered simply, "I believe God clearly told me to do this, and I am just waiting on the Lord." What strong faith this woman has! She is a woman of character with a courageous heart. Marlou and I love and admire her.

I went to Carl and said, "Carl, I think God has brought somebody to head up our women's ministry."

"Does she have support?" Carl asked. This was a proper question coming from the overseer of ANM's finances. When I shook my head negatively, Carl said, "Oh, Bo, please. We don't have money. We need to wait."

I'm an attorney, and I tend to give the store away. But Carl is an accountant. His tendency is to hold onto resources and be more careful. We balance each other in a good way.

"Could This Be You?"

One day, during ANM's regular Thursday morning staff Bible study, I noticed Autumn sitting as a guest at the back of the room. I tried to avoid looking at her because I didn't want to be reminded that she was waiting there. Finally, I felt that the Holy Spirit would no longer allow me to remain silent. I said, "Mrs. Graves, could you see me after we adjourn?"

Following the meeting, I walked Autumn down the hallway and showed her the wheel with the spokes we had developed to describe ANM's operational structure. "If you look at this wheel, you will see there is a spoke for Building the Kingdom Together, a spoke for

Warehouse for the Nations, a spoke for our Healing Hands ministry, and so on. All these ministries have leaders, but there is one spoke that does not have a leader: our International Women's Ministry." I paused for a moment. Then, looking her in the eye, I asked, "Could this be you?"

"God saved that for me," she answered without hesitation.

I went to Carl and said, "We have somebody to lead our women's ministry. She doesn't have support, but just give me some time." I took a piece of bond paper and wrote something like:

Dear members of the ANM family,

We have been waiting for many, many years for God to bring someone to lead our ministry to women. This leader has finally appeared. Her name is Autumn Graves. Many of you know her. She is a single mother, and I really believe in my heart that God has called her.

This godly woman technically is a widow because she has no husband. I believe whoever supports her will be blessed by the Lord. If the Lord leads you, would you kindly commit $10 a month for her support until she gets on her feet?

Marlou and I started the ball rolling by pledging forty dollars a month. When the letter made its rounds, Cris Paurillo said, "I'm not going to give just ten dollars. I'm going to ask my husband to repair more cars so we can give twenty dollars." Fellow missionaries who had insufficient support for themselves were signing up to give ten or fifteen dollars; one even committed to give fifty dollars monthly. After the pledges were tallied, I went back to Carl and said, "I have commitments for at least two days per week of support. Is that enough for a start if we continue to look for more friends for her?"

When Carl said yes, it brought tears to my eyes. I asked Autumn to submit a plan of action for launching International Women's Ministries. She prepared an excellent plan, and then she hit the ground running. What a marvelous job she did right from the start!

Meanwhile, God honored Autumn's faith by performing miracles in her own life. Somehow, she was able to bring her house payments up to date and avoid foreclosure. She was even able to pay the tuition to send her children to a Christian school. A few years later, God sent her a godly, loving, and good-looking husband who immediately bought into her ministry.

When Marlou and I were involved in the modest beginnings of this ministry, we prayed that it would be used by God to help wipe away the tears of our sisters in many parts of the world. In 2018, with ANM's blessing, International Women's Ministry became an independent ministry, and today, Autumn's vision for the ministry is "wiping the tears of our sisters." By God's grace, Autumn and her fabulous team are doing just that in the US, Iran, Pakistan, the Philippines, Honduras, and many other places in the world. All glory belongs to God!

Below, Autumn tells her beautiful story in her own words:

AUTUMN

"He Called Me to Wipe Tears"

On April 2, 2010, the Lord told me to resign from a full-time ministry position. The difficult part was he did not tell me where I was going. I was in transition, seeking the Lord about where to go next.

I started attending a Thursday morning Bible study at Advancing Native Missions. I came burned out, feeling lost, and wondering if God had forgotten me. I sat and listened to missionaries share their stories in this weekly gathering. Their faith in the unseen was building my faith. Their trust in God's provision for everything challenged me to trust beyond what my eyes could see. I would leave the meetings filled with hope.

But fear and doubt began to creep in. I was a single mother with four mouths to feed, and my savings were dwindling fast. I asked the Lord, "Did you forget me?" I sensed his reply was, "Be still and know that I am God" (Psalm 46:10).

One Thursday morning in an ANM Bible study, when I was in the depths of despair, Bo Barredo, president of Advancing Native Missions, said he wanted to speak with me after we dismissed. He said he had been trying to avoid me, but the Lord kept pointing me out to him. There seems to be a hard season of faith-building before the Lord ushers in a new season. I didn't know it, but God was about to reveal his marvelous plan.

Bo took me down the hall to the lobby. There on the wall was a wheel with spokes in it. Each spoke of the wheel defined an area of ANM that was activated to carry out the vision of ANM. Bo explained that there was one area that had not been fully realized, and he wanted to see it actuated. He revealed to me that no one had stepped up to lead this international ministry to women.

"The Lord Was Saving That for Me."

It immediately resonated with me, and I said, "That is because the Lord was saving it for me!" With that response, Bo asked, "What would you do with International Women's Ministries?" To my delight, he asked me to prepare a proposal for International Women's Ministries.

I left ANM that day knowing that God had just called me to a new season! Within a few days, the Lord had inspired me to write a ninety-day plan of action for bringing International Women's Ministries alive. I brought the proposal back to Bo a few days later and dropped it on his desk for his review. Then I began to pray and fast for the Lord to open the door for me to join ANM.

I remember where I was standing on the day I received the call. I was visiting with my mom at her home. She had just been diagnosed with Parkinson's disease, and I was wiping her tears when my phone rang. On the other end were Bo Barredo and Oliver Asher.

Oliver explained that they believed I was the one who could take International Women's Ministries to the next level. They loved my proposal and knew it was from the Lord. However, they were concerned with my being a single mom and raising my own support.

I explained that God wrote my paycheck, and the Lord is my provider. Bo said I should come in and talk to them.

So the story goes that a single mom with four kids answered a call to global missions and to raise her own support. It was scary, and at the same time, a peace and calm rested on me because I knew that I was in the center of God's will.

However, I soon found myself downcast in my spirit because I had no idea how I would raise my own support. One day, as I was sitting in a coffee shop area in the middle of a mall contemplating my foolishness for thinking I could answer this big call with no funding, Bo and Marlou suddenly appeared. Bo came running over and said, "Sister Autumn, I have your first seed money for the ministry!" He showed me a check for $1,000 from a faithful donor to start International Women's Ministries. I cried that day and repented to the Lord for doubting. He is more than able to make a way in the wilderness and streams in the desert. Praise God!

Running My Own Organization

One day at ANM, Bo said something prophetic. He said, "Sister Autumn, you will someday run your own organization." I couldn't picture that. Little did I know, that is exactly where God was taking International Women's Ministries.

There is so much more to this story that I wish I could share. I will close with this final thought: I saw God work one miracle after another when I put my trust in him. I saw his faithfulness in action by trusting him for everything. Becoming a missionary was a faith exercise that took me to deeper wells of access in the kingdom.

Accepting the call to "wipe the tears of sisters globally" began a movement of epic proportions! Now IWM is being replicated in Pakistan, the Philippines, Honduras, Nicaragua, Guatemala, India, and the list goes on.

It all started as a dream of Bo's that sprung from the desire and compassion to care for the wives, widows, and single women on the mission field. I am thankful for Bo's belief that I could do it. I am thankful for Bo's nudges forward when things didn't seem to be working out, and I am thankful for the training I received under him to advocate for those who don't have a voice. I will continue to "wipe the tears of our sisters" until Jesus comes back to wipe away all tears.

"Comfort My People"— A Ministry to the Jewish People

Since my youth, God has given me a love for Israel. During the early days of ANM, he put it strongly on my heart to pray for the Jewish people. I said, "God, you made me fall in love with Joseph when I read his story as a boy. And you made me fall in love with David, a man after your own heart, and with Ruth and Boaz, and with so many others who loved you. I really love Israel. How can we say we are doing global missions if we do not reach out to Israel? I really would like a ministry to the Jewish people to be part of ANM. How can we do that, Lord?"

A short time later, I heard that my father and my stepmother had gone to Israel on a trip with their American friends, Gary and Michelle Engmann. They stayed with Michelle's friend, Mary, an American who was married to an Israeli named Ariel. Mary and Ariel love Jesus and share Scripture passages with people.

While staying in their home, my father had shared about Jesus as the Messiah with Ariel's father. He was about my father's age and a very traditional Jew. This brought Ariel and my father even closer together.

One day, my father said to Mary and Ariel, "I have just one wish while I am here. Could you take me to the Sea of Galilee?" They obliged, and when they arrived at the Sea of Galilee, my father cupped water from the Sea of Galilee with his hands and drank it. All who were with my father tried to dissuade him because of the risk of disease, but Father was determined. He said that drinking from the Sea of Galilee was for him the nearest thing to witnessing the miracles the Lord Jesus performed there. Learning about this made me want even more to support Israel.

To get more work done while at ANM, I usually would eat lunch alone with Marlou around 2:00 or 3:00 p.m. One afternoon, Mike Twitchell, the head of our Construction Teams International ministry, rushed into the ANM lunchroom while we were eating. "I'm sorry to disturb your lunch, Brother Bo, but I need to tell you that I'm not growing any younger. I need an assistant director to take over my place, just in case."

"Let's pray about this," I suggested. As we began to pray, an announcement on the public address system informed me that I had a phone call. It turned out that the call was from one of my closest friends, Paul Robbins. A Messianic Jew, Paul was a talented carpenter who earned his living in the local area as a craftsman. He and I had been friends for ten or more years, and he had never called me on the phone. Because of the conversation I was having with Mike, I began to suspect that God was up to something. I will let Paul tell you the rest of the story in his own words.

PAUL

The Testimony of a Jewish Carpenter

While I was in my shop working one day, I experienced a strong sensation. In retrospect, I would call it a "holy unrest." It was accompanied by a compelling urge to call Bo Barredo. I obeyed the urging and called ANM.

Bo answered the phone and politely asked if he could call me back. While waiting for his return call, I sat outside my shop and gazed at the western slope of Afton Mountain. It was spring, and the hills were just beginning to show signs of new life. I wondered why I had even called Bo. We had been friends for ten years, and I had never called him on the phone.

A few minutes later, Bo called me back. "Paul, you have been my friend for ten years, and this is the first time you have called me. This is a holy moment. Let's pray first."

I don't remember exactly how Bo prayed, but as he did, I remember looking at the mountain and thinking that he was on the other side. This would have significance in the years ahead.

"Lord, I am afraid! You have brought me a Jewish carpenter, and I don't know what to do with him."

At the close of our brief conversation, Bo invited me to visit him at ANM the following day. The next day, without really knowing why I was there, I knocked on the door of ANM's conference room. I expected to see only Bo, and I figured that he and I would have a private conversation. What a surprise to find the room full of people!

This happened to be the day the staff met for prayer, and Bo invited me to join them. After he had introduced me to everyone, he asked me to share what was on my heart and give a brief personal testimony. I don't recall what I said. I only remember that after I spoke, the group gathered around me and prayed.

Bo's booming voice still lingers in my mind: "Lord, I am afraid! You have brought me a Jewish carpenter, and I don't know what to do with him. Lord, I am afraid! You have brought me a Jewish carpenter, and I don't know what to do with him." He repeated this prayer a third time, and with each repetition, his voice seemed to become deeper and more powerful. For reasons I can't explain, tears streamed down my cheeks.

Following the group prayer time, Bo invited me into his office. After we had chatted for a while, he asked me to pray about joining ANM full-time as an associate with the Construction Teams International ministry. My wife and I talked and prayed about this intensely for a week. Then I called Bo and accepted his offer.

For the next four years, I recruited scores of Christians to help with numerous construction projects for ANM ministry partners. I was privileged to make friends with amazing believers across our nation and around the globe. One evening in the spring of 2014, Bo approached me with a question that would forever change my

God has a way of confounding the wisdom of the wise. He used another carpenter, Yeshua, to bring the greatest message ever told to the land of Israel and to the nations.

life. In a somber tone, he said, "Paul, please prayerfully consider this request. Would you be interested in beginning a ministry in Israel for ANM?"

Once again, I was stunned, but this time, I did not need time to think and pray. ANM had ministries in seventy-nine nations, and Israel was not one of them. I had longed for this to change, and I believed God did as well. I had never dreamed that I might be the one to initiate the change, but I have learned not to hesitate to do God's will. I immediately accepted Bo's offer. One of the first things he did was introduce me to Ariel and Mary.

Today, ANM's Comfort My People ministry partners with eleven ministries in Israel, and it is affiliated with several others. With each of these ministries, God has given us amazing favor to work as a family. The privilege of working in this ministry has given my wife and me joy beyond measure.

When I accepted Bo's offer to lead Comfort My People, I knew virtually nothing about starting and leading a ministry. Up to that time, I had worked only as a carpenter. But God has a way of confounding the wisdom of the wise. He used another carpenter, Yeshua, to bring the greatest message ever told to the land of Israel and to the nations. I am so thankful that, by God's grace and in reliance on the Holy Spirit, I am tasked by ANM to be an ambassador who helps to bring comfort to his chosen people.

ANM World Missions Magazine— "The Mouse Runs with the Elephants"

One of the desires of my heart was for ANM to have a magazine. Part of a nonprofit organization's good stewardship is to have a regularly published magazine. Studies show that this is one of the best-kept secrets of financially stable nonprofits, as it helps foster and nurture loyalty of donors and supporters. Publication of a magazine even just twice a year is viewed by donors and supporters as a major indicator of a ministry's reliability, consistency, stability, accountability, and longevity. One ministry attributes the bequests and legacies that it frequently receives to the regular publication of its magazine. Ministries with magazines are more likely to become beneficiaries of planned giving.

So I prayed for a gifted editor deeply committed to indigenous missions. In 2009, the Lord answered my prayer and sent an editor volunteer with exactly these qualifications. His name was John M. Lindner. John had mentored me on writing reports and stories when I served as a field missionary in the Philippines for Christian Aid from 1987 to 1991.

What a great catch God gave us in John! I love and highly respect this man and his high standards for writing. I had a favorite joke with him that started with the question, "What is the difference between a terrorist and an editor?" The answer is, "One can negotiate with a terrorist!"

In the Spring 2018 issue of *ANM World Missions*, John wrote the following:

When Advancing Native Missions co-founder and then-President (now Global Ambassador) Bo Barredo asked me in October 2009 to help ANM start a magazine, I told him I would give ANM the best missions magazine in America. Last year *ANM World Missions* took third place in the Evangelical Press Association's contest for best missions magazine. [About 160 evangelical magazines are published by the members of the Evangelical Press Association.]

So, we're not the best? Ah, consider this: The magazine that took first place was *On Mission*, produced by the Southern Baptist Convention, with a circulation of 177,000.

The second-place winner was *Co-Mission* (name since changed), produced by The Seed Company, an auxiliary of the world-famous Wycliffe Bible Translators, with a circulation five times that of ours.

So, to take third place in the company of these giants with our low-budget, then 4,000-circulation *ANM Magazine*, is a virtual coup. *I can say confidently, We are the best low-budget, low-circulation mission magazine in the Evangelical Press Association.* The mouse runs with the elephants. As far as I am concerned, mission accomplished . . .

To manage the continued production of the magazine, we have upgraded my assistant, Andrew Needham, to Managing Editor, while I will continue to be Editor. Andrew, holding a B.A. in history from the University of Virginia and an M.Div. from Duke Divinity School, has exceptional talent in the communications field, for both print and online media.

Below are just some examples of the encouraging compliments on the magazine and its accompanying gift catalog we have received from our readers:

Incredible—"Your publication is incredible. I would say that I spent more time with your publication than any other in this competition. It tells the story so very well . . . I love your publication. I think it shows cultures and Christians in crisis better than most."

—**JUDGE**, *California Evangelical Press Association*
magazine competition

Best missionary periodical—"I really love your magazine. It is the best missionary periodical I receive."

—**JO ELLEN**, *California*

Inspiring—"The magazine is beautiful and inspiring. It opens our eyes to what is happening."

—**LERMA AND RAMON**, *Florida*

Cover to cover—"My wife and I are blessed with all the articles in your magazine. We read each issue from cover to cover. Continue the good work you have for the Lord."

—**ANDY**, *Maryland*

It's a hit!—"Got your new magazine, and it's another hit. Could I get you to send me another 15 copies please to distribute at church and to my men's group? Blessings to you."

—**ALLEN**, *Minnesota*

Attractive and Informative—"I find your magazine to be very colorful, attractive, and informative. It lets you know what is going on around the world. And this helps me to pray better for our brothers and sisters overseas, especially the persecuted Christians. I would absolutely recommend this magazine to anyone."

—**BERNADETTE**, *Pennsylvania*

Compelling stories—"This is a beautiful magazine with such compelling stories to draw you in. It really helps you feel like a part of the global Kingdom work around the world!"

—**CHRISTINA**, *Virginia*

Encouraged—"I have so enjoyed your magazine. The inspiring stories in it encourage my faith."

—**WILLENE**, *California*

Christmas catalog a blessing—"Thank you for making our Christmas so special this year. We received your gift catalog and took it with us on a family retreat. It was one of our most valued projects. Using your message on the back of the catalog, we shared the mission with our kids and grandkids. Then we discussed all the gifts, letting the grandkids pick their very own gifts to send to the missionaries . . . ."

—**ALBERT AND SUSAN**, *Virginia*

Ministries appreciate ANM magazine—"I just got a copy of your winter magazine. Great joy—content and layout. You are a blessing to a lot of people!"

—**MISSIONS EXECUTIVE**, *Virginia*

Best-kept secret—"This magazine is a great way to make this 'best-kept secret called ANM' known."

—**BOB**, *Oklahoma*

Appreciate the details—"I can't tell you how much I appreciate the new *ANM World Missions* magazine! It's great to have more detail about the missions projects that ANM support . . . ."

—**GLENN**, *Arizona*

Joyfully read every word –"From the editorial to the last page, I joyfully read every word. The stories moved me to tears of gratitude for what God is doing. All those involved are to be commended for their wonderful work. May God use the magazine to bring many to the knowledge of Christ and His work."

—**PASTOR OTIS**, *Virginia*

The spirit of ANM—"As always, the magazine is not only a work of art, but a true representation of the spirit of ANM. Thank you especially for the encouraging and helpful words in the editorial."

—**DOREEN**, *Virginia*

ANM magazine's worth reading—"I get lots of magazines, but when yours arrives, I read it cover to cover. It's all about people, and it pulls you in."

—**TERRY**, *Ohio*

It gets better and better—"I think the *ANM World Missions* magazine gives us a wonderful picture of what ANM is really about. And the magazine itself—well, it just gets better and better."

—**CAROL**, *New Mexico*

We share the magazine—"We have been giving copies of *ANM* magazine to churches in our area. We pray that they take part in the global missions work of ANM."

—**WAYNE AND DRUSILLA**, *Maryland*

Beautifully done—"The Spring 2018 *ANM* Magazine is so beautifully done, as always. It is informative and interesting and outstandingly written and presented."

—**PAUL AND MARGIE**, *Virginia*

Love your magazine—"We love the photographs of the various children and adults that received something for the small gift we sent. We pray for you and for the missionaries all over the world that are giving their lives to serve God and to share the Good News of Jesus Christ with those that would otherwise never have a chance to hear of Jesus."

—**BARBARA**, *Virginia*

Enlightening magazine—"I want to compliment you on your inspirational and enlightening magazine, *ANM World Missions*. I remember so well when ANM began, and you have been in our prayers ever since."

—**JACK**, *Oregon*

Banquets and Retreats—
"Blessed to Behold the Nations Before Us!"

It is always a wonderful thing when ANM friends and donors can see and hear in person the various missionaries they faithfully read about, pray for, and support. In 1997, we organized our first ANM banquet to allow them to personally meet and encourage our missions partners. Our focus for this banquet was Elam Ministries, an exciting outreach to Iran and the Persian-speaking world. The event, held in a large local church, was graciously used by God to gain many new supporters for Elam and ANM.

Because Elam is so strategic in world missions, we held a second missions banquet in 2006 for this amazing ministry. It featured much-loved Christian recording artist Michael Card as the guest singer and attracted around five hundred guests. We had reserved the largest hotel banquet room in the region, and it was so packed that one guest, a federal judge, stood up from his seat, surveyed the crowd, and remarked to me, "Bo, this is the biggest banquet I've ever seen in this area!"

As we were planning for another banquet in 2008, the Lord used Dick Prins to challenge our faith. Dick suggested that we rent the new John Paul Jones Sports Arena at the University of Virginia, and that we prayerfully plan for one thousand guests. This thought both intimidated and excited us.

By the grace of God, we already enjoyed such goodwill and loving favor in the community and the surrounding towns that, by faith, we dared to venture into what we called "a bigger leap of faith." A dynamic team composed of the most creative minds and best "people persons" among us planned and coordinated the event. Sam Yeghnazar, the winsome and lovable leader and founder of Elam Ministries, was to be the principal speaker.

Two young and multi-gifted members of the ANM staff, Mindy Mullins (then Spurrier) and Trisha Tolar, brought in a super-talented group of students from their alma mater, Liberty University, to help us, and Dr. Wes and Jackie Howard won everyone's admiration for their success at inviting guests. On the evening of the event, the lines of guests waiting to enter the arena grew to hundreds and hundreds in length. People patiently endured the security protocols that had to be observed because of the focus on Iran.

A Large Undertaking

To say that a one thousand-guest banquet is a large undertaking is a huge understatement! But it was worth the effort, because it garnered considerable financial support for reaching Iran and beyond for Christ, and it enhanced ANM's credibility as a ministry. Bob Finley testified to the noteworthiness of the event when he asked me, "Bo, how did you and your group do it?"

The success the Lord graciously granted us with the 2008 banquet gave us the faith to start a series of annual retreats. We held the first annual retreat in 2010 at Wintergreen Resort, a beautiful mountainside retreat center just forty-five minutes west of the ANM offices. We continued to hold them every fall after that in the same spot.

For each retreat, we invite between 250 and 300 guests from all over the country and fifteen to twenty missionary leaders from the different mission fields ANM serves. Seeing and hearing these courageous and fruitful missionaries in person deeply impacts our donors and friends. They have read about these missionaries in *ANM World Missions* magazine, and they have faithfully prayed for them. After seeing them in person and hearing their stories, they return to their homes, workplaces, and (most importantly) churches as changed people stirred to help native missionaries advance global missions.

God Calls Dick Prins

The Lord placed it in my heart to ask our steadfast, prayerful, and beloved brother Dick Prins to be the chair for these annual banquets. Dick's involvement with ANM began in 2002 when he met Carl Gordon. Carl then told me about Dick, and I began to pray for him. I specifically asked God to send him to ANM because I foresaw that his healthy perspective on missions as a business would be a blessing.

In 2005, Carl and I visited Dick and his lovely wife, Dee, in their attractive home. When Dick showed us his office above their garage, and I saw the framed photos of ANM native missionaries that lined one of the walls, my heart was touched. At the end of our visit, the Holy Spirit gave me a very strong prayer for Dick and his family. As we said our goodbyes, I seriously told him, "Brother, please pray to join us, if the Lord leads you." It was one of my greatest joys when Dick came on board. He is one of the gifts God has given ANM.

My relationship with Dick over the years has been memorable in many fine ways, but I especially remember him for two things. First, when referring to how the Lord has grown ANM, I love the way he says, "This could happen to only one ministry in a million."

The second thing is how Dick resonated with the remarks I made to the team who were planning the one thousand-guest banquet. At the end of one of our meetings, I had said, "And remember, there are three purposes for this event. First, that the Lord be glorified. Second, that the Lord be glorified. And third, that the Lord be glorified!" It blessed me to observe Dick later declaring these three purposes at the end of every planning meeting he led.

The personal testimony that Dick wrote in 2012 is so moving that I am including excerpts from it below:

A Front-Row Seat in God's Unfolding Global Plan

In 2005, Carl came to my home office with Bo Barredo, ANM's other co-founder. Bo prayed with me about my family and about our future. That prayer opened my eyes to see where God was leading me. I still did not know the details, but now, I had a wonderful foretaste of His calling.

In 2007, my career was flourishing, accolades abounded, and the material rewards were great. Still, I was restless to move on. Then, in 2008, the company I worked for was sold.

Although I had the option to stay and finish my career, the sale was an answer to my prayer. God worked out a perfect transition, so I left. This probably shocked many of my business associates, but my heart had moved on to a different world.

I started part time at ANM and became a full-time volunteer staff member in 2010. I am currently accountable for US Operations, which includes advocacy and relationship management activities. As odd as it may sound, the functional aspects of my new assignment are remarkably similar to the functional aspects of my past career. The missionary enterprise is a lot like the investment management business. Also, I had been trained to seek out clients with highly scalable business models because these almost always created the highest returns on investment. I recognized early on that ANM does the same thing in its support of native missionaries.

While Western missionaries still play a significant role in God's plan for evangelism, native missionaries provide a more scalable approach to reach those who have not heard the Gospel message and are best equipped to be God's foot soldiers to meet local needs. The typical cost of supporting one Western missionary could support more than fifty native missionaries. Native missionaries are also more effective because they know the language and dialects, and they understand the culture and political environment. They get things done because they know the natives. In fact, they are natives.

I quickly found that I had much to learn about missions management. I am discovering that God still calls us and uses the talents that He has given us, but He does so for His purpose in His time and for His glory. Unlike anything I experienced in my earlier career, management at ANM begins with prayer. Then we wait and seek His will, and only then do we act, trusting in Him. Not only do we have front-row seats in God's unfolding global plan, but we have the opportunity to live out His will in our lives.

ANM Retreats

Our annual retreats at Wintergreen Resort help us raise support for native missionaries. Our *ANM World Missions* magazine, our attractive and user-friendly website, and our social media platforms also contribute in this way. But more significantly, all these supporting ministries allow us to showcase the fruitfulness, contemporary relevance, and highly strategic value of native missionaries in global missions in today's world of socioeconomic, political, cultural, and religious upheavals.

The value of ANM's annual retreats is evidenced by the following comments of attendees:

**So thankful to meet God
on the mountain this weekend!**

"Brother Bo and the ANM family, my wife and I are so thankful that we were able to meet God on the mountain this weekend through the ANM retreat. We experienced God's love in so many ways. I should have carried a box of tissue around with me as the tears constantly flowed. The stories that our dear brothers and sisters shared brought the reality of the things we read about up close and personal. We felt a kingdom connection with everyone. I hear guys saying that they love, but I felt the love flowing from so many of your staff. I came away from the retreat convinced of what Jesus' love looks like through us who follow Him—sacrificial, listens and hears, weeps, perseveres, shares, and connects with the body. I could go on and on. We met new friends and connected with others. Thank you for sharing the love of Christ for over twenty years. May God's genuine love overflow in your heart. We love you and are being taught by God to love better."

—PASTOR RON D., *North Carolina*

One of the most memorable events of my life!

"The retreat was certainly one of the most memorable events of my life and appears to be just one more step in God's transformation of me. We were promised a weekend of fellowship and refreshing, and it certainly was that, but you did not prepare me for the many tears that I would shed! The retreat was an emotional roller coaster for me. . . . I realized that I have been blessed with so much in human terms. . . . God has allowed me to see myself in the mirror that the ANM retreat provided. . . . I treasure the love that I have found in you and in so many at ANM."

—**TERRY F.**, *Tennessee*

The retreat changed us forever!

"We've been telling everybody that the retreat changed us forever. Missionaries' testimonies will forever be in our hearts. We've been sharing them with others. Music—we thought we've been lifted up to heaven! Please thank the people who funded this magnificent occasion. . . . We thank God for the opportunity of being involved in global missions through ANM. We will continually pray and support you guys."

—**NELSON AND AMY**, *Michigan*

A piece of heaven on earth!

"Thanks for inviting us to the ANM retreat at Wintergreen. What a privilege to attend! I had never stayed at Wintergreen. What accommodations! I felt like royalty. And the meals. . . . But the food and the resort pale to insignificance to the stories we heard of the Gospel being preached to all the nations. Thrilling. My tear ducts went into overdrive. . . . The weekend was a piece of heaven on earth. Truly the highlight of the year. An early Christmas gift."

—**BERT R.**, *Virginia*

An amazing event!

"We were blessed, loved, taken care of, greeted, welcomed, thought of—and this was not even about us! You all went above and beyond in creating an amazing event for people to hear the stories, learn about ANM, and get refreshed all in one weekend on top of a mountain. Every member of your staff made us feel like we were a part of y'all already. Your hearts are genuine and we could see Jesus in each of you—all weekend."

—**JUSTIN AND MICHELLE**, *Texas*

A part of something so beautiful!

"I wanted to express my gratitude for letting me be a part of something so beautiful that it made my heart stretch to popping. Being able to witness Timothy Kinyua's [Kenya] wide-eyed wonder as retreat attendees exuberantly shouted out offers of monetary assistance, or seeing humble and generous donor Sharon Tucker weep with both grief and awe, or hearing Helman Ocampo's [Colombia] almost tripping over his words as his passion came gushing forth from the depths of his soul, or witnessing Sokhon Khan [Cambodia] realize he was beloved by everyone in the room, feeling the immediate familial love with people we've never even met before, but are bonded together with Christ's glue—well, it was just too much to be all compacted into one weekend!"

—**DOREEN**, *Virginia*

The presence of God in the room overwhelmed us!

"The force of the missionaries and the presence of God in the room overwhelmed us. All our questions about supporting indigenous missionaries were answered."

—**PASTOR ANDY H.**, *Tennessee*

We stood in awe!

"The presence of God was at the center. We stood in awe, astonishment, and reverence at the powerful presence of God's Holy

Spirit. It was one of the highlights of our life, and we give our Lord all the praise and glory."

—**PASTOR YOUNIS AND SURRIYA F.,** *Georgia*

We had a five-sense experience!

"Wow! What a weekend! As I was praying this morning, I was impressed by the Lord that we had had a five-sense experience. We *heard* the Father's heart. We *saw Jesus.* We *smelled* the sweet fragrance of Christ in our midst. We *tasted* the goodness of the Lord. And the Holy Spirit *touched* us. Short of heaven, it doesn't get much better than this!"

—**DR. AUSTIN S.,** *Virginia*

A blessing to be surrounded by so many tribes and nations!

"It was our first opportunity to come to the retreat, and we are so thankful for the invitation and provision to share in such a great weekend. . . . I tell people that ANM is an organization that is easy to fall in love with, and as I looked around the room and heard from folks this weekend, I was reminded why that is. . . . What a blessing to be surrounded by so many tribes and nations represented; it really was a glimpse of heaven, a great encouragement to us since we don't have much diversity in our congregation (or county). The weekend helped put some things in perspective and served as almost a spiritual 'recalibration' of sorts for me. Driving home, I felt full and empty, perhaps more accurately, fuller and emptier; or to borrow John's words, Jesus increased, and I decreased a little more—may that filling and emptying continue as He gives days. . . ."

—**PASTOR JONATHAN F.,** *New York*

The retreat changed how I pray!

"Hearing the different missionaries tell what they go thru to preach the Gospel and how God restores them, appears to them thru dreams and visions, etc. made me cry. The retreat changed how I pray for the missionaries and advocate for their needs. Today when I went to the grocery store, I thought if I leave out a few items, I can help support a missionary."

—**ALMA R. (MISSIONS CHAIR)**, *Virginia*

Deeply touched!

"My wife and I were deeply touched by the people and stories we heard. I was impressed by the way you, Bo, and the staff at ANM invest in the lives of your missionary partners, and the passion with which you champion their cause. Your fervent and unashamed pleading on behalf of their great commission will haunt many (including me) for a long time."

—**ARUN AND ANNU P.**, *Virginia*

It was humbling!

"It was humbling to hear the missionaries say no matter how desperate their situation, they continued to focus on God and the work before them. It made our own personal struggles here seem trivial. So, during the Combined Federal Campaign at work last November, I designated my monthly donations to ANM, where I know they will be used to hasten the coming of our Lord Jesus Christ. We made sure the focus of our church is on missions. Our theme for 2016 is 'Declare His glory among the nations' (Ps. 96:3)."

—**ERNIE A. (CHURCH ADMINISTRATOR)**, *Virginia*

The afterglow is still fresh!

"Dear Brother Bo, while the afterglow is still fresh, I wanted to tell you how much Rosalind and I appreciated our inclusion as invited guests for the twentieth anniversary ANM retreat. The program was an inspiration from start to finish! *Every* speaker—not just our visiting brethren—was outstanding! I have to tell you that I spent most of those few hours at the feet of the Lord's servants with tears flowing from my eyes (and they are trying to do so again as I write), and, if it wasn't tears, there were smiles and laughter. The tears came as our brothers recounted their labors in faith for the Lord, going where others have not gone to win souls and plant churches, to love desperate women and needy children and to suffer loss for His sake. We left with an even deeper appreciation for the commitment of ANM and these precious saints to proclaim the Gospel 'til all hear.'"

—**BILL (AND ROSALIND) L. (DONOR-VOLUNTEERS)**,
Virginia

We shared and wept all the way home!

"We shared and wept all the way home. We were inspired and encouraged to behold the nations before us! You blessed and touched our lives more than you know!"

—**JOHN AND MARY H.**, *New York*

A Kind Offer

One day in 2009, Dr. Finley called from Christian Aid and invited Marlou and me to join him and his wife, Cynthia, for lunch at the Red Lobster in Charlottesville. In a cordial two-hour meeting, he brought up the idea of merging Christian Aid and ANM, and he offered me the position of president of the merged entity. We discussed the resolution he had drafted that, if I agreed, he planned to take to the Christian Aid board of directors. He then took Marlou and me on a tour of the Christian Aid offices on Fifth Street in Charlottesville, calling particular attention to the office I would occupy as president.

It remains a source of amazement even today when I think about how I had come to Dr. Finley twenty-three years before, so broken in realizing that I was a nobody and offering to wash dishes or do anything else to serve the Creator of the heavens and the earth. What an honor it was that this man I so esteemed was now asking me to head the organization he had founded and led.

I brought this matter to the Lord in prayer, and I consulted with co-leaders and several key staff and board members at ANM. After prayers and counsel, a senior member of our board, who was a friend of Dr. Finley, personally conveyed to him that a merger was not possible. On our end, there was a consensus that it would be a great challenge to merge two different organizational cultures. What's more, ANM was on a growth curve, and we felt a merger would probably slow down the work of both ministries. Some even suggested that having two viable ministries serving the brethren overseas might be more advantageous to God's kingdom.

Looking back, I realize that it was my heart's long-awaited and deep desire to again work with my spiritual father, Dr. Bob Finley. I retrieved from my file and read again the resignation paper I had given to him back in September 1992. Here is what I had written:

Dear Dr. Finley,

Most loving salutations in the most precious name of our Lord and Savior Jesus Christ.

This letter formalizes my verbal resignation and tomorrow, September 30, 1992, will be our last day at the Mission as our Lord's missionaries working through Christian Aid.

Please know that the intensity of our love and the depth of our personal respect for you, and all our co-workers as well, will not be diminished by our leaving. We will continue to uphold you to our great Lord in our prayers. We deeply appreciate what the Lord has done in our lives through you, Christian Aid, and our precious co-workers. I don't regret any of the days of the last six years that I have been with the Mission. We have very happy memories of them.

Until now, tears would come to my eyes whenever I remember the weeping of many of our co-workers when we said our goodbye last week during the staff meeting. And every day since that time I have humbly brought to the Lord your gracious request and theirs for me to reconsider. And admittedly, the stepping out in complete faith with my family brings tremors to my flesh, but I continue to rejoice in the consolation that there is a pervading and steadfast peace in my heart.

Thank you for your concern in pointing out our present home and family situation. I fully understand the specter of stepping out with our children in tow, with no house of our own, medical insurance, and living allowance. Sobbingly, Felisa asked whether we could still get to eat after leaving the Mission. I could understand my little girl's apprehension. In our country, when a family steps out "to the streets" in faith, at least the weather is constant. We are strangers in your country and fall is just beginning to usher in the cold season. Marlou, mother and human as she is, tearfully reminds me, "Bo, it will be winter soon . . ."

Before I left last Saturday for Virginia Beach to speak on behalf of Christian Aid in a three-day revival meeting, at morning break, our family had our prayers. And that morning with each one of them on his/her knees, I gave away Marlou and the children to the Lord for Him to keep, feed and protect. As for me, I again offered my life to the Lord for Him to use as He sees fit. He is our Keeper. He is our Shepherd. He takes care not only of a sheep but more so of a stranger. Even of a servant.

My plan, as the Lord allows, is to continue to be a servant-ambassador of native missionaries. I pray that I could soon join some brethren who have a great love for God's work through these poorer missionaries. We believe that you would have prayers on our behalf on this as we are not competitors but co-laborers in God's Kingdom.

Lastly, as a son to a "Tatay" (my native tongue's endearment for a beloved father), I sincerely ask you your blessings and humbly request you to rejoice with me in this act of faith of a son – all in the Lord's name and for His glory. We love you.

In His love and mercy that endures forever,

Bo Barredo

(with Marlou, Benjamin, David, Felisa and Jim-jim)

P.S. Sir, I have sought counsel from well-meaning friends, pastors, and elders on this act of faith. My own father, Rev. Ben Barredo, also gave me his blessings. He is in Chicago visiting friends and churches and will be going back to the Philippines sometime next month. He fully understands that we are throwing ourselves upon the mercy of the Lord.

Bo Barredo
Charlottesville, Virginia

With much emotion, I reread the letter he had written to me:

Dear Brother Bo:

It has been a joy to have you as a member of our staff. I have been delighted to watch you grow in the Lord and mature in your personal life. We have been pleased with your service to our Savior within the fellowship of this Mission.

We are aware of our imperfections as human begins. So, we recognize that you would not find everything within our organization to be perfect. Therefore, we naturally expect that at times you might become aware of these imperfections and call our attention to them so that we might make improvements. Thank you for the times you have done so.

Three times you have resigned, and each time I have asked you to reconsider. I would likely do so if you resigned three hundred times, because we appreciate you and want you on our staff.

However, today you told me that this time you want your resignation to be final. I cannot understand why. You are an excellent addition to our team, and we want you to remain. So again, I ask you: please reconsider.

I can find no satisfactory reason or explanation as to why you should leave at this time. The only reason you will give me is that you have peace in your heart about doing it. I realize that it is good to have peace of mind, but because of your present home and family situation it does not appear to me to be a reasonable decision. So, I urge you to remain with us as a member of the staff of Christian Aid.

But if you are absolutely convinced that you have to leave us at this time, there is nothing more I can say. I have no peace in my heart about it because I think you are making a mistake. All I can do is pray that our loving Lord will keep you in His care and continue to use for His glory.

Yours in His eternal bonds,

R. V. Finley, President

Reading these letters brought back painful memories of my leaving my own beloved father in the Philippines to follow God's call to bring my young family to the US for global missions. When I left Christian Aid to help minister to and advocate for many more missionaries waiting in long lines for someone to encourage them and to help equip them in their cause of reaching the unreached tribes and language groups for Jesus Christ, I had to leave another beloved father.

During and after this painful parting from Christian Aid, God's Word consoled my heart. Jesus promises, "And everyone who has left houses or brothers or sisters or father or mother or wife or children or lands, for My name's sake, shall receive a hundredfold, and inherit eternal life," (Matthew 19:29).

It is unclear to me whether things would have turned out differently if I had had a greater measure of faith, but I am certain that taking Dr. Finley up on this offer would have required a much greater measure of faith than I was capable of at this time. I love the way Oswald Chambers expresses the need for such a measure of faith in *My Utmost for His Highest*. In his devotional for March 28, he says, "Many of us are faithful to our ideas about Jesus Christ, but how many of us are faithful to Jesus Himself? Faithfulness to Jesus means that I must step out even when and where I can't see anything (see Matthew 14:29). But faithfulness to my own ideas means that I must first clear the way mentally. Faith, however, is not intellectual understanding; faith is a deliberate commitment to the Person of Jesus Christ, even when I can't see the way ahead."

To Reach All Nations

Later in 2009, not long after I sent the above letter to Dr. Finley, I shared the following report on the state of ANM with the ministry's friends and donors:

ANM—OUR BIRTH, VISION, AND STRATEGY TO REACH ALL NATIONS

Advancing Native Missions began eighteen years ago with a vision to reach all nations with the Gospel of Jesus Christ.

Our founding scripture: "And this gospel of the kingdom will be preached in all the world as a witness to all the nations, and then the end will come." (Matthew 24:14)

Our operating premise: The most effective and efficient way of accomplishing this goal is to support native or indigenous missionaries in reaching their own people with the Gospel.

Our Beginnings—Simple

That is a grand vision, but ANM began in a very inauspicious way. Carl Gordon and I pioneered ANM in a small, one-room office with a couple of donated desks, some borrowed chairs, and one precious volunteer who brought her own typewriter. Whenever visitors came, I would slip out to make room.

Bereft of financial resources, we fervently prayed for "an excellent team." God sent the people, each one in a unique way. We were a bunch of nobodies who loved the Lord. And we were committed and willing to serve sacrificially. One by one, the Lord added to our numbers, and a talented and capable crew developed.

Today, we have sixty US staff members and volunteers. These include fourteen former pastors, twelve schoolteachers, six engineers, three accountants, three PhDs (education, engi-neering, and theology), three nurses, two lawyers, two medical doctors, a former insurance agent, a restaurant manager, a telephone lineman, a theater costume designer, an investment banker, a former chief of staff of a US senator, a franchisee of snack foods, a dance instructor, a roofer, a pastor's widow, and now an experienced magazine editor.

We welcome people on the basis of the five Cs of leadership: Christ, Community, Character, Calling, and Competence. Carl and I have introduced and implemented a collegial type of leadership, and we work more as a family than as a business. When native missionaries and friends come to ANM, they feel right at home.

Our Focus—The 10/40 Window

As we surveyed the world at the beginning, we were drawn to the tremendous need for evangelistic outreach and church planting in the 10/40 Window. That is an artificially drawn rectangle between 10 degrees and 40 degrees latitude, stretch-ing from the west edge of Africa to the Far East.

Within that narrow strip of global real estate crossing sixty countries live 3.6 billion people. These include 95 percent of the world's 6,647 unreached people groups. It touches areas where every major non-Christian religion of the world is dom-inant—Islam, Buddhism, Hinduism, animism, and native religions, as well as atheism. It is also where 85 percent of the world's poorest of the poor live.[16]

If all nations must be reached before Christ returns, the 10/40 Window must be our focus.

---

[16] From *The Move of the Holy Spirit in the 10/40 Window* by Luis Bush and Beverly Peg-ues, YWAM Publishing 1999, page 27.

Our Method—Native Missions

And if that is our focus, unleashing the power of native missions must be the method. These men and women speak the language and understand the culture. They don't have visa restrictions, and they are willing to live—and suffer—at the same level as the people they attempt to reach.

We track unreached people groups and learn which ones are being reached—or can be reached—by ANM-served ministries. ANM directs over 70 percent of its resources to this most critical mission field.

Our Strategy—Building Relationships

To gain support, some organizations use mass mailings, ads in Christian magazines, and even television infomercials. When we began, Carl and I asked the Lord which method would be best for us. The Lord showed us that we should build relationships and pray for faithful friends.

To facilitate relationships, ANM offers people many ways to get involved: mission conferences, sponsorships, Warehouse for the Nations, mission trips (OBIs), and more. In all aspects, the *people*, not their gifts or objects, are what is important.

The Lord has greatly blessed this approach! He has brought us friends, and they in turn have brought us support. This gift of praying friends and cherished relationships helped carry ANM through recent difficult economic times.

Our Success—Thanks Be to God

To the glory of God, ANM had its most bountiful year in 2009 since its inception in 1992.[17] ANM received cash gifts of over $5 million for Christ's needy servants, plus donated goods valued at nearly $2 million, for a total of $7 million. ANM shipped

---

[17] As of the date of this writing, ANM's biggest income year was 2013, when by the grace of God, we received a little more than $16 million in contributions. Almost $8 million of this amount was in cash. Gifts-in-kind were valued at more than $8 million.

these tangible goods to five countries in nine containers and our brethren received them with great rejoicing.

A precious donor offered us a $100,000 matching gift, and our field of donors matched it completely. Half the amount went to help our staff, who serve at meager wages. The other half is being sent to native missions overseas.

Also, during 2009, ANM brought to the US about forty native missionary leaders from different countries. These anointed men and women testified in nearly three hundred churches, homes, schools, and other meeting places. God used them to spark revivals and awaken hearts for missions wherever they went!

And there's more: Gifts from ANM donors and friends in 2009 sent fourteen teams overseas. Eight "Operation Barnabas" teams taught, strengthened, and encouraged native missionaries on the field in six countries, while six ANM construction teams helped meet physical needs in three countries.

On top of this, Dr. Wes Howard led three "Hands of Healing" medical teams to areas in countries that had no medical services. Donors and friends helped ANM do all this, while at the same time supporting ministries that field more than 5,000 precious native workers and care for at least 2,500 needy children. Most of these children will become missionaries to their own people.

Our Future—Lord, Please Multiply!

The ANM leadership team has prayed and defined our five-year vision and goals through 2015.

In Isaiah 54:2, the prophet Isaiah speaking for the Lord writes, "Enlarge the place of your tent, and let them stretch out the curtains of your dwellings; Do not spare; Lengthen your cords, And strengthen your stakes."

And in Jeremiah 30:19, the prophet Jeremiah speaking for the Lord says, "Then out of them shall proceed thanksgiving And the voice of those who make merry; I will multiply them, and they shall not diminish; I will also glorify them, and they shall not be small."

These promises encourage us to expand our ministry "because we love the brethren" (1 John 3:14). We are praying that the Lord will honor our labors, enlarge the number of our friends and resources, and multiply the number of indigenous ministries that we serve. The whole ANM team is excited "like a bridegroom coming out of his chamber, and rejoices like a strong man to run its race" (Psalms 19:5).

We invite you to join our excitement and pray fervently for the fulfillment of the Great Commission. That, we believe, will hasten Christ's coming. Even so, come Lord Jesus!

Our young family
singing praise songs
at the Christian Aid
guest house shortly
after arriving in the US.
March 1991

Our family.
July 1998

Our family
in 1986.
Philippines

**Bo and
Mom Ruth Shira**

**Bo at Christian Aid
in 2007 with
Dr. Robert Finley,
Christian Aid founder
and president**

**Marlou with
Ron and
Pam Tillett**

Marlou and
Felisa with
Papa Tom
Thomas,
a real cowboy

John Goodrich
visiting ANM in 2002

Bo with
Dr. and Mrs.
Ed Hampton

The early ANM family: Cris Paurillo, George Ainsworth, Carl Gordon, Gordon and Ruth Shira, and Bo and Marlou. 1992. *Dynamics Building, Charlottesville, VA*

Cris Paurillo and Lucille Lebeau

Bo opening ANM's weekly Bible study for staff, community residents, and visiting guests. This event was always well attended. August 2015

Bo with Graham Stewart, editor of ANM magazine. 1997

Marion Riley (left) in the accounting department with Danny McAllister and Virginia Tobias. 1995

Bo with Pastor Otis Spellman

Pastor Gerald Ripley and Sister Sharon with elders of Abundant Life Church. Pastor Ripley is holding a plaque from ANM that thanks the church for giving ANM its first gift in October 1992. The amount was $880.87. September 2019. *San Antonio, TX*

One of the many
churches in the US
where Bo was invited
to come and speak
on missions.
Winnemucca, NV

Church missions conference.
Frederick, MD

Church
missions
conference,
Otterbein
Church.
Mt. Wolfe, PA

Bo beside the ANM display table at a church missions conference

Bo addressing the ANM board. 2016. Phil Zodhiates presiding. Looking at Bo is incoming Board Chair, Ellen Lemke.

Bo and the ANM leadership team. 2009. (left to right) Danny McAllister, Victor Morris, Dan Reichard, Gary Darcus, John Bucchi and P.R. Misra, (front) David Thacker, Jay Temple, Bo, Oliver Asher and Carl Gordon

Our friends George
and Cindy Bokorney
and the traditional
chocolate birthday
cake for Bo

Bo and
Marlou
with Timothy
and Yvonne
Kinyua. 2018.
Meru, Kenya

Bo and
Marlou with
Chandra and
Uria Tobing
Bali Island

John Lindner,
editor of *ANM World Missions* magazine

Bo and Marlou holding copies
of *ANM World Missions* magazine

I. Poctar (Israel), Helman and
Rosalba Ocampo (Colombia),
Paulus Wibowo (Indonesia),
Mammen and Abdul (India),
Sol Balbero and Dr. Linda
Balugo (Philippines)
John and Mary Biak
(Myanmar)

ANM Fall Retreat. October 2011.

Bo preaching, with missionary leader Williams Yindi translating. 2018. *Itigi, Tanzania*

Bo and Graham Stewart at the 100th anniversary celebration of the Methodist Church where Bo was the speaker. *Marianao, Havana, Cuba*

Bo and Marlou with Joy and Sam De Guzman, standing behind Brother Siswo and his mom. Also present are members of Brother Siswo's mission team. Inside the mission's training center. 2020. *Indonesia*

Bo visiting LRM missionary couple Ben and Nene Singcol. The boat God provided in answer to their prayers is behind them. 1994. *Leyte Island, Philippines*

Bo stands next to taxi driver Yohannas. His son and his wife are crying in joy over God's miraculous provision. 2007. *Indonesia*

With missionaries Nemuel and Ruth Palma of the Smoky Mountain dump ministry. *Philippines*

Bo with Narayan Paul visiting the Saura people. 1999. *India*

Swapon and Rachel Bose, missionaries from Bangladesh. When Bo brought them to the US, he introduced them to their long-time friends and supporters, Ken and Dolores Detweiler. 2001. *Winnemucca, NV*

Bo visiting Roger and Sylvia Elosendo in their Ati aboriginal village. 1990. *Philippines*

Bo and ANM treasurer Phil Gregoria with Prem Pradhan of Nepal in the ANM offices. 1996

Bo and ANM staff member Danny McAllister with missionary leaders David Yone Mo and Shi Sho Tun. 1997. *Myanmar*

Bo and Marlou with ANM staff members Pete and Melody Wong and the missions team of missionary leader Sokhon. Sokhon is seated holding his daughter. 2014. *Cambodia*

Children watching as ANM friends Anne and Jonas Beiler greet them by video during the dedication of the children's home that Anne and Jonas helped fund. Missionary leaders Apple and Jeph Garcia are translating. 2018. *Thailand*

At Covenant Church, VA, with Pastor Harold Bare. 2006

Bo and Marlou with Nepali missionary leaders. 2013. *Nepal*

Bo with ANM staff and visiting missionaries. 2009

ANM staff retreat. 2018. *Lynchburg, VA*

Bo and Marlou at a graduation ceremony of the Bible School of Myanmar Young Crusaders. Bo and John Lemke (far right) were the main speakers. 2015. *Myanmar*

Halle with her Papa Bo and Lola Marlou at her high school graduation in 2021. As mentioned in the introduction, God used her to inspire the writing of this book.

Bo with Tim and Virgie Prest. When told about eleven needy Burmese missionaries, Tim said, "We'll take them all!" 1995. *Nevada*

Bo and Terry McKinley in Panay Island. Terry built a swimming pool for the marginalized aboriginal Aeta children in Luzon Island. 2006. *Philippines*

ᎢHE PLANS I HAVE FOR YOU

Marlou and I had always believed it was God's plan for her to be my partner in the work with indigenous missions. But as I have said, in the early days of ANM, I asked her to postpone her dream and work for a time with a secular business to support our family. This was important for two reasons.

First, I wanted to give a significant portion of the support that donors gave to our family to the people who had committed to work on our staff. We needed to help them get on their feet while they raised their own support.

Second, I wanted to invest a considerable amount of the support our family received in our ministry partners around the world. Most of these missionaries are extremely poor in material things, but they are rich in stories of God's work in their lives and ministries. I did not want to simply take their stories and use them to raise money in the United States without giving them something in return. These missionaries are our partners, and they are God's people. What belongs to them belongs to God. Their stories about the holiness of God and the power of God in their lives are sacred things. Therefore, I had said to Marlou that we should start investing in some of these ministries now.

With trepidation and hesitancy, Marlou had said, "Yes, I will do what you ask, but for how long?"

"For as long as it takes," I had answered. When I said this, I was thinking in terms of two to three years. It turned out that Marlou had now made this great sacrifice for ten long years. I could only imagine how painful it had been for her to be away from ANM and the opportunity to minister with me in the United States for one whole decade.

An Extreme Sacrifice

The initial years of ANM demanded an extreme sacrifice from all of us. Once during this period, I travelled to Asia for forty-one days to survey new ministries that ANM could potentially support. My absence for this lengthy period, coupled with the stretching of our financial resources, put a severe strain on our family.

Marlou's first job in the United States was as a part-time teller at a bank. One afternoon, I drove Felisa and Jim to the drive-up teller window. When they saw their mother on the other side of the glass, Jim suddenly exclaimed joyfully, "Papa, that's Mama! She has a job! We'll get to eat! We'll get to eat!"

Marlou didn't know how to drive in these early days, so whenever I was away on travel, she had to depend on other people to take her shopping and to her job at the bank. Our children, especially the two younger ones, Felisa and Jim, who were only nine and eight at the time, felt more than a little insecure. "Do we get to eat, Papa?" they would ask me. "Do we get to eat?"

"Yes, we'll get to eat," I reassured them. "We are making some sacrifices so missionaries overseas can feed their families. God loves sacrifices, and he will take care of us."

Marlou works efficiently and gets along well with people, but one day out of nowhere and for no reason, a bank co-worker attacked her verbally. She cursed at Marlou loudly and publicly in front of the other employees with the obvious intention of humiliating her. It was a terrible attack that can only be explained as demonic. Marlou broke down in tears. She was so upset that her nose bled.

This verbal abuse had been going on day after day for some time, and management had been unable to address the situation. As lawyers, we knew we had grounds for a lawsuit, but instead, we prayed. It turned out that God had a better plan than legal action. He prompted management to transfer Marlou to the bank's home office, where she was given a full-time job in the administration of the bank with an increase in salary. God worked in this situation for good, as he promises.

I will let Marlou tell the rest of her story.

MARLOU

God's Purpose—To Mold My Character

When Bo and I left our first missions agency and stepped out in faith, we had four growing children, and we decided that I should find a part-time job to help put food on our dining table. God led me to a job as a part-time bank teller earning about $6.25 an hour, and we were thankful for it. God also gave me a young girl as a co-worker on the afternoon shift manning the drive-through window.

This girl was not very nice to me, and I prayed for her, but it was hard. She once asked me, somewhat sarcastically, "What are you doing working as a teller when you were trained as a lawyer?"

I answered her softly, "I left lawyering, and I am helping support my husband so he can serve full-time as a missionary to many parts of the world." I knew I had to work with this girl, and I did my best to maintain a good working relationship with her. But it seemed that she was determined to give me a hard time. Without any provocation, she would suddenly become verbally abusive and attempt to insult, demean, and humiliate me publicly. Even some of our co-workers were agitated and upset with what she was doing to me, but I responded with kindness.

One day, however, she pushed me to the limit. The severity of her abuse caused me to break down. I began sobbing deeply and sorrowfully in the presence of everybody, including my co-workers and the customers. My nose started to bleed, and self-pity overwhelmed me. It was terribly humiliating. Finally, the bank manager intervened and consoled me in the privacy of her office.

Bo was in Asia at this time, and I felt so vulnerable taking care of our home and our young family. That night before I slept, I turned over my deep pain to the Lord. I knew he would understand. He, too, underwent humiliation at the cross.

The Lord heard my prayer and turned what appeared to be adversity into an opportunity. I was relocated to the main office and given an administrative position! By the time I left my part-time job, because I had responded in love, the young teller became my friend.

Why did God allow this episode in my life? Looking back, I believe he used this season of my life to further mold my character and make me a better and stronger ambassador for Christ. He needed to refine me so I could be more useful to him in the more challenging days that lay ahead.

A "Second Honeymoon"— In a YMCA Room

In early spring of 1997, a few years after that painful incident in the bank that God turned for good, Bo surprised me with some wonderful news. He was going to take me with him on one of his overseas trips, and of all places, to London! We had wanted to travel together, but it had never been financially feasible.

Elam Ministries has its residential missionary training school on the outskirts of London. It had been Bo's desire to "capture the heart" of this fine ministry for quite some time, so he could share about its effectiveness and needs at a banquet ANM planned to host in Charlottesville later that year. He also wanted to promote the ministry in his US meetings.

God opened the door for me to go when the airlines sent Bo a special "two passengers for the price of one" offer on a trip to London. Our friends and all our co-workers at ANM enthusiastically urged him to take me with him on this missions trip, and our children lovingly said, "Papa, please take Mama with you also on a mission trip overseas. Besides, you need time for yourselves, too." One family friend gently reminded him, "Bo, you are always doing ministry here and ministry there. We want you to remember that a servant of God has also to minister to his wife."

I was deeply touched when some of ANM's ladies handed us some sacrificial gifts to enable Bo to take me out to dinner and to spend at least one night in a hotel in London. We stayed in the headquarters of Elam Ministries for the first couple of days. I reminded Bo that this was the year of our twenty-fifth wedding anniversary. He teased me that God did not open the door for me to go with him to the garbage dump in the Philippines, nor to the leper colony in Burma, nor to the Muslim sultanate of Brunei. But God opened the way for me to go with him to England!

"Bo, you are always doing ministry here and ministry there. We want you to remember that a servant of God has also to minister to his wife."

We were also hosted for two days of our stay by long-time friends and faithful supporters, Dr. James and Maureen Taylor, in their lovely home in Sevenoaks, Kent. After Dr. Taylor retired in 1996 from his position as dean of the Mathematics Department of the University of Virginia, the couple returned to their native land of England to volunteer as missionaries with China Ministries International. It was such an honor to be hosted by this dignified and very loving couple. We thoroughly enjoyed our tea times with them.

During breakfast one morning, Miss Maureen learned that we were celebrating our twenty-fifth year of marriage. When she observed Bo's rather nonchalant attitude toward anniversaries and other types of family matters, suddenly, an ominous glint came into her pretty eyes. Bo then received a blessed and vigorous exhortation from her on "a good husband's responsibilities to a dutiful wife." It was so amusing to see Bo and poor Dr. Taylor, a Cambridge PhD, sheepishly grinning like schoolboys at their corner of the breakfast table. Of course, I heartily (but discreetly) cheered while Miss Maureen admonished!

After the conversation, Dr. Taylor tiptoed upstairs. When he returned, he placed in Bo's hand some English pound notes. "Bo, take Marlou today to central London and afterwards to dinner. This is our special gift to you both on your wedding anniversary." Bo jokingly quipped that he had noticed a McDonald's somewhere.

"Not this time," Miss Maureen declared. "I'm going to ask Marlou when you come home where you took her."

"Yes, ma'am," came my husband's conciliatory reply. It was a very tender moment for me.

That day, we had a delightful time sightseeing around London. I enjoyed most of all spending time with the pigeons at Trafalgar Square. At the end of the day, Bo took me to a Chinese restaurant to celebrate.

During our last day in London, Bo joked, "Our friends at home might rebuke me if we don't spend at least one night in a hotel." It was almost dusk when we found a room to his liking in terms of price—at the YMCA in the town of Guildford, southwest of London! It was by far the best YMCA facility I'd been to, and it was within walking distance of the train station, so I assured him that it would do.

When we returned to the US, the ladies at ANM excitedly asked Bo, "What hotel did you take Marlou to?" Bo responded with only a smile. When we got home, he said, "Those sisters of ours at ANM would have stoned me if I had told them that for our second honeymoon, I took you to the YMCA and not to a hotel!"

A Transition for Marlou

Marlou is extraordinarily gifted by God. As she used her gifts in her secular jobs, her employers promoted her again and again, until one day, she found herself working as the executive assistant to the president of the largest health maintenance organization in central Virginia. I was very thankful to God for her success and her contributions to our family's finances.

But in late August 2001, as I passed by Marlou's side of the bed around 3:00 a.m. on my way to the bathroom, I noticed as she slept that her countenance looked downcast and utterly exhausted. I thought about how I had promised her mother that I would take good care of her daughter. In the Philippines, Marlou had been on track to someday become one of the top officials of the Central Bank, which is the Federal Reserve Board of the Philippines. She forsook that opportunity and all the other advantages she had in the Philippines to come to America with me in response to God's call.

I quietly cried out, "Lord, what have I done? Lord, what have I done? What have I done!"

We had left family, friends, and material things behind and started over. This had not been easy for any of us. Now, as I gazed upon Marlou's tired face, I felt that God was allowing me to see the price she had paid to support our family.

I dropped to my knees. Without disturbing Marlou's sleep, I quietly cried out, "Lord, what have I done? Lord, what have I done? What have I done!" Tears trickled down my cheeks. I was so remorseful about how I had failed to care for Marlou. In my drive to serve our missionary partners and our staff, had I neglected my beloved wife in the process? I wanted to gently caress her face just like I had done in college. But I restrained myself, worried that it might wake her.

Then, suddenly, I knew in my spirit that God was going to more than make it up to her. Carl Gordon had been saying, "When is Marlou going to report for duty here with us? We need her at ANM. She's a very good writer." But I had been replying, "She doesn't have her support, Carl. We're still using her salary to support our family so we can invest the support we receive from our friends in this ministry."

Resignation Day

Marlou had been sound asleep when I had knelt and prayed at her side, and she knew nothing about my prayer. But that very morning, no sooner had she arisen from bed when she announced, "Today, I am going to resign from my job, and I'm going to report to Advancing Native Missions to work with you."

I was shocked! She had known nothing about my prayer. Yet she was proclaiming this decision on the very day that I had prayed. But still I resisted, "Marlou, Marlou, I'm not ready yet. Give me some more time. You have no support."

"I don't care," Marlou replied. "God is going to provide for me. You're the one who has taught us that God is going to more than make it up to us."

I could not refute her statement. That morning, Marlou resigned from her position as the executive assistant to the president of the largest HMO in central Virginia. Her boss, Martha D'Erasmo, whom she greatly admired, offered her more money and tried to convince her to stay, but Marlou said that her mind was made up.

An Unusual Delivery

Around mid-afternoon on that same day, ANM received a call from one of our supporters asking for Carl and me. Because I was out of the office, Carl took the call. "I mailed five boxes to ANM's post office box," the supporter told Carl. "They are heavy. You will need to bring a couple of strong guys to pick them up."

When the boxes arrived, Carl followed the man's advice and took two men to pick them up. The donor had told Carl what the boxes contained, and Carl had wisely rented in advance three large safety deposit boxes. When Carl and his two helpers arrived at the post office, he called for an auditor to come and open the boxes.

All were awestruck when they saw the contents! The boxes contained 2,500 gold coins, each of which at current prices would have a value of more than $1,800!

The next day, Carl told me what had happened. Then he said, "Let's hire Marlou and give her a starting salary of $30,000 a year."

"No, no, Carl," I argued. "Her salary should be half of that. If you give her thirty thousand dollars, there is no sacrifice. Even though thirty thousand dollars is not a large amount, it is large enough to eliminate any sacrifice. We don't want to lose the best that God has prepared for us. My heart tells me that God has prepared the best thing for us."

"Okay, okay," Carl said, "but I hope Marlou doesn't learn that you cut her salary in half!"

I was confident that Marlou would not mind, because I was not asking her to do anything that I had not repeatedly done myself with her agreement. Over the years, the ANM board had wanted many times to increase my salary, and I had always fought with them. Carl and I had agreed at the very start of ANM that self-sacrifice is one of the best ways to show the Lord and those we serve, including the supporters of the mission, that we are sincere. God sees it and says, "I will more than make it up to you."

Marlou Joins ANM

One of the happiest days at ANM was August 31, 2001, when Marlou reported for work full-time. Her starting salary was $15,000 per year, which provided some financial help for our family so we could continue to invest the support we received from donors into ANM staff and ministry partners overseas. Everybody was excited about Marlou's arrival, especially Cris Paurillo, Lucille Lebeau, Virginia Tobias, and Dee Brookshire.

Marlou was assigned to the publications department, where she shared an office with Dee. On her first day at work, Marlou neglected to bring something to eat, and she fondly remembers how Dee invited her to come to her home for lunch. Marlou found in Dee a sweet, joy-filled, caring, helpful, faithful, and authentic friend. Whenever Marlou had concerns, Dee was quick to bring them before the throne of God in prayer. Marlou counts her friendship with Dee Brookshire as one of God's special gifts to her. For almost twenty years, the two ladies enjoyed writing stories about ANM's precious native missionary partners, until Marlou was appointed regional director for Southeast Asia covering the Philippines, Laos, Thailand, and Cambodia in February 2021.[18]

---

[18] During this time Marlou also served as my executive assistant.

Dee's Story

In addition to being a diligent worker and an excellent writer, Dee Brookshire is a woman of great fortitude and faith. Below is her ANM story in her own words:

DEE

After years of teaching elementary school and then homeschooling my own children, I found myself unable to get a job even as a teacher's aide. During my years in education, I had welcomed willing mothers any time they were available, but this was 1996, and times had changed.

I began praying in earnest about what the Lord would have me do next. At the end of three months, after hearing and reading so much about Advancing Native Missions, I was beginning to see the letters "ANM" on the backs of my eyelids! I shared about my interest in ANM with a prayer partner. When she emphatically said, "Call them!" tears began streaming down my cheeks.

Not long after that, a young man from Cuba spoke this word over me one Sunday evening in church: "You know I have called you to be my missionary. The door is open. You just need to walk through it."

The following morning, I met with an elder at my church, Graham Stewart, who was one of the early workers at ANM. I had no idea how I could possibly serve in native missions, but Graham told me that the ANM leaders had been praying for the last three months for someone to revitalize the child-sponsorship department. With my agreement, he arranged for me to meet with Bo Barredo two days later.

On Tuesday morning, I walked into the small ANM office, and I was invited to take a seat facing a semicircle of chairs in which were seated all nine members of the staff. Bo proceeded to interview me in what I have since learned is his typical style. Totally intimidated, I fumbled through his probing. Afterwards, on my way out the door,

Bo tapped me on my shoulder and said, "Report on Thursday, and we will give you a small salary for six months."

When I reported to work on Thursday morning, Bo ushered me into a room with an easel that had a 24" x 18" pad of poster paper in the corner. He picked up a large marker, put a number one on the first sheet, and wrote beside it a task that needed to be accomplished. Then he said, "This is what I expect you to do in the next half year." Four sheets and thirteen assignments later, he turned to me and asked, "Think you can do that?"

By faith, I just nodded. He didn't know that I had not yet learned to turn on a computer! But with Danny McAllister's helpful coaching and encouragement, I was able over the next six months to write countless letters to lapsed donors. By the end of the six-month period, I had miraculously accomplished all the assignments Bo had written on those sheets of poster paper, including writing a brochure.

A New Challenge

I had received no indication that I would be kept on the ANM staff after this trial period, so when Bo called me into the leadership office, I smiled and took a seat, fully expecting to be thanked and let go. I was surprised to learn that he had been reading everything that had been going in and out of my office. Then he shocked me by holding up one of my letters and saying, "This is well written. Victor Morris, our director of publications, is leaving in three days, and we want you to take his position."

Wow! How could I be expected to write ministry updates and do desktop publishing with only a few hours of training? By this time, I could write letters, turn the computer on and off, and compose an occasional email, but I had one big limitation Bo didn't know about: a crippling fear of writing reports and papers. During college, I begged my professors to let me do anything other than write a final paper. Instead of writing a paper for one class, I even chose to make a dulcimer!

Nevertheless, I accepted the challenge, and Bo moved me into Cris Paurillo's office. Between answering phones and welcoming guests, Cris played praise music and sang along. Can you imagine trying to write all day in that kind of environment! It was challenging, but Cris took me under her wing and taught me the basics. I am so grateful for that time of growth. It truly taught me to concentrate!

When ANM moved its office to Crozet, Marlou Barredo became my officemate. We shared working spaces for years in Crozet and then in ANM's next office in Afton. A more beautiful woman, both inside and out, would be hard to find. Just being in her presence has made me a better person. I saw firsthand how Bo and Marlou worked together. Their love for God, one another, family, and all people is genuine.

Twenty-six years ago, God opened a "door" for me, and I walked through that door into the arms of a discerning Filipino man who believed that I had potential. Thank you, Jesus!

God Prepares Us

When God by his grace showered ANM with 2,500 gold coins on the very day that Marlou resigned from her job at the HMO, I believe he was showing her and all of us how much he loved his precious daughter. He seemed to be saying, "Marlou, I have seen your faithfulness to your family and to me. I have seen your sacrifices and your exhaustion as you have worked to support your family, and I want to more than make it up to you."

But one question plagued me: Why did God provide this gift in the form of gold coins? I received what I think was the answer to that question about three weeks later. As I have said, we received this gift at the end of August 2001. On September 11, 2001, the World Trade Center in New York City was struck by planes flown by terrorists. The entire American economy went into a tailspin, and the banking system was in disarray. Across the nation and even around the world, charitable giving slowed to a trickle as donors sat back in shock. During this crisis, we were doubly blessed as the value of gold increased relative to the value of ordinary currency.

God had graciously prepared ANM for this difficult time by sending us gold coins. While other ministries were curtailing their support to missionaries, we were providing financial aid, vehicles, and other support to our missions partners out of our abundance. We could not have planned for this emergency, but God mercifully prepared us for it!

Swapon and Rachel Bose of Bangladesh

In 2000, Jay Temple and I went to Bangladesh to visit missionaries Swapon and Rachel Bose. Their ministry, Faith Bible Center, is located four hundred miles from the Himalayas. An ANM field researcher had identified it as one of the best potential ministry partners for ANM. Our goal was to encourage Faith Bible Center's leaders and provide equipment that would help them reach the unreached. Jay and I each carried close to $10,000 that had been provided by two churches. This was the maximum amount a person could bring into the country without confiscation.

Swapon was born in Bangladesh in 1950. His father was a pastor, and at the age of seventeen, Swapon accepted Jesus as his personal Savior and Lord. He felt God pulling him toward full-time ministry, but he was determined to be a rich man, so he instead trained to be a civil engineer. God's call continued to burn in his heart, however, and at the age of twenty-four, after a year of prayer, Swapon decided to devote all his time to planting churches. His wife, Rachel, a teacher by training, also felt called to this ministry. But the couple didn't know how to go about it, so they went to study at the Discipleship Training Centre in Singapore.

After graduation, Swapon and Rachel returned to Bangladesh, and Swapon became the national leader of a Swedish mission. As a foreign missions executive, he had an office with a big desk and his own vehicle. But in 1996, he felt God leading him to give up these comforts and return to his original calling of grassroots evangelism and church planting among Muslims.

Meeting Swapon and Rachel

When Jay and I met Swapon and Rachel and heard their story, my heart broke. At this time, Bangladesh was practically the poorest country in the world. Only Haiti had a lower per capita income. At this time, fewer than one percent of the people in Bangladesh are Christians, and there were very few Christian missionaries on the mission field. The government allowed mainly Christian medical professionals into the country, but no other American missionaries were allowed. Even the Christian medical professionals had to be very careful, so it was tough ground for evangelism.

Swapon and Rachel felt called to take the Gospel to Muslims, but nobody wanted to help them because of fear of persecution. The couple even had trouble finding native Christians willing to sit on their ministry's board of directors. "Why don't you preach to the easier tribes?" they were asked time and again. "If you try to witness to Muslims, they're going to kill you." But Swapon and Rachel said, "No, this is the burden we have from the Lord."

When we met with Swapon and Rachel, we asked, "What do you need?"

"We need five motorcycles," Swapon answered. Motorcycles in Bangladesh at that time cost more than $1,000 each.

"We'll buy them," I said. "What else?"

"Bicycles," he answered.

"We'll buy them. What else?"

"We need Bibles in Bengali."

"We'll buy them. What else?"

"Petrol lamps," he said. "When our evangelists go from village to village at night, they can be bitten by cobras. We need about twenty lamps so they can see."

"We'll buy you twenty Petromax lamps. What else?"

"An immediate need we have is for three simple village church buildings costing $1,200 each," said Swapon.

"We'll provide you the funds. What else?"

Swapon went on to add mosquito nets, blankets, and flashlights to the list, and we told him that we would buy them all. He was so amazed and humbled that he could hardly speak. I handed him the money. "Go and buy these things today. We will come back tomorrow to see them."

A Joyous Day

What a joy it was the next day to see the missionaries and senior elders with their bicycles, motorcycles, lamps, Bibles, and the other things. They couldn't believe what had happened. It was like a dream to them.

After more conversation, I learned that Faith Bible Center also needed a building for the Bible school they had opened. And they needed several modest-size church buildings for their small congregations in remote villages. When I returned to the US, I connected Swapon with International Cooperating Ministries (often called ICM) in Hampton, Virginia. This wonderful partner of ANM specializes in constructing church buildings around the world. They told Swapon, "We will provide you with church buildings for $5,000 each. Smaller ones we can build for $3,000 each."

We thank God for International Cooperating Ministries. They have helped our ANM partners construct more than seven hundred church buildings around the globe. The construction of over three hundred of these church buildings was facilitated and coordinated for ANM by P. R. and Anju Misra. P. R. serves as ANM's president for international operations, while Anju is the regional director for half of Southeast Asia, which includes Vietnam, Indonesia, Singapore, Malaysia, and Myanmar. (Marlou is the regional director for the other half.)

"Can You Match $10,000?"

When I asked Swapon and Rachel how much money they needed to construct their new Bible school building, they gave me a figure of $100,000. I knew they didn't have this kind of money, so I said, "Come to the US, and I will be your personal driver and take you to churches and introduce you to our friends. We will pray that God will give you the money you need through their offerings." They were so encouraged by this invitation.

A short time later, Swapon and Rachel came to America, and I enjoyed driving them to various churches and flying with them to Nevada and Oregon. Perhaps the most interesting church we visited was Bay Ridge Christian Church in Annapolis, Maryland. The pastor was a retired Marine captain with a compassionate heart by the name of Brett Hicks. His wife's name is Linda.

The day that Swapon, Rachel, Marlou, and I visited the church, many of the regular worshippers were absent. As I looked at all the empty seats, I felt I needed to do something to boost the giving. When it came time for me to introduce Swapon, I said, "I'd like to make a challenge to the church today. After Brother Swapon shares, Marlou and I will match the amount of the offering given by the church from our missionary allowances." Based on the small size of the crowd and the church's Spartan furnishings, I estimated that the offering would be about $1,250, which I figured Marlou and I would be able to match.

After Swapon shared his testimony, an offering was collected. Later that day, Pastor Brett called me. "Bo, tell me again about your challenge this morning."

"Marlou and I promised to match the amount collected," I said. "All the money will be used to help Swapon and Rachel construct a new building for their Bible school."

"Are you sure?" asked Pastor Brett.

"Yes, sir," I answered.

"Can you match ten thousand dollars?"

"What! The offering was ten thousand dollars? Brothers, please forgive me for my lack of faith. Lord, please forgive me. My faith is too small."

"Don't worry about matching the amount," Pastor Brett reassured me. "Just give whatever you have. The Lord really blessed all of us today. I was amazed, because at least a third of our congregation is vacationing. Most are in Florida."

God taught me a lesson that day. The need was met, and the Bible school building was constructed. As we read in Ephesians 3:20, he can do far more than we can ask or imagine. Largely because of financial help through ANM, the ministry of Faith Bible Center in Bangladesh expanded from 17 pastors and missionaries to 175. What's more, 70 percent of these new pastors and missionaries were former Muslims!

MARLOU

A Test of Faith

In July 2002, a month after Bo and I had celebrated our thirtieth anniversary, a routine mammogram revealed something concerning in my left breast. A subsequent biopsy confirmed the presence of high-grade carcinoma cells. When we told our children that I was scheduled for surgery on July 24, they were shaken. Felisa and Jim especially were anxious and sad. With tears flowing down their cheeks, they lifted their faces toward heaven and pleaded, "Lord, why is this happening to Mama, of all people?"

Bo appeared calm until a few days before my surgery. One afternoon while we were driving, he slowed down and turned to look at me. "Marlou," he pleaded, "please don't leave me."

At first, I was very composed. God's grace was upon me, and I accepted this news as God's will for my life. But one evening, after our nightly devotions, I felt a great inner yearning for healing. I strongly desired more years to spend with my precious family and more years of fruitful service to God. Sobs erupted from the depth of my being, the power of which surprised both Bo and me. He wiped my tears and tried to comfort me, but I couldn't stop crying.

After allowing me some time to calm down, Bo gently asked me what was causing me to cry in such a way. I burst out, "I want the Lord to heal me! I want the Lord to heal me! Lord, please heal me!"

I felt that my Heavenly Father had assured me of his love and care. I am his child, and he will never leave me nor forsake me.

I felt like a little girl crying out to her father and asking him for something she desperately wanted. That night, I cried myself to sleep.

Around noon on July 24, before leaving for the hospital, Bo and I decided to have a devotional time. Prior to opening Charles Spurgeon's book for that day's reading, he prayed, "Dear Lord, in Christ's name, please show your hand to my precious wife in such an obvious way today that she will know that you truly care for her much, much more than any one of us could, and please give her the assurance that all will be well for her." After this prayer, Bo read the Scripture verse for that day. It was Exodus 14:13: "Do not be afraid. Stand still, and see the salvation of the LORD, which He will accomplish for you today."

A surge of hope and joy swept over me. I felt that my Heavenly Father had assured me of his love and care. I am his child, and he will never leave me nor forsake me. As we walked together to our car, my heart was peaceful, and my steps were steady. Without a doubt, God had touched me.

While in the preparation room prior to going into the operating room, I stood on tiptoes to kiss Bo. He remarked that my face was glowing like that of a little girl. Then he teared up. "I will wait for you," he whispered. Bo has always been very strong for me and for our children, and he has been strong for our missionary partners, some of God's poorest servants. Bo's strength is derived from his love for God. But this time, I knew I needed to be strong for him.

"God Has Already Healed Me"

The surgery seemed to go well, but we wouldn't know the results for a few days. Bo and I were out of town when my primary care physician, Dr. Theresa Rupp, called later that week. Theresa is a dear friend who loves the Lord and has lovingly ministered to the very poor in Haiti, so she felt comfortable leaving a message on our answering machine. When Bo and I returned and listened to it, we were thrilled to hear her say with excitement, "The results of your surgery and the pathology findings were excellent!"

A second recording was from Dr. Linda Sommers, my breast surgeon. She happily reported that the ball of tissue excised from the area where the cancer had been detected did not have a single carcinoma cell! Nevertheless, she recommended that I see an oncologist as soon as possible.

In obedience to Dr. Sommers, I went to see the oncologist. She suggested several options, including hormone replacement therapy and radiation. I said to her, "Thank you for sharing these options with me, but I know for a fact that God has already healed me. I don't need to do anything further." That was the end of it.

As I write this, it has now been twenty years since God graciously honored my prayers and the prayers of my family and friends with this amazing healing. To this day, there have been no signs of cancer. We rejoiced with the words of Psalm 118:23, 28–29: "This was the LORD's doing; It is marvelous in our eyes. You are my God, and I will praise You; You are my God, I will exalt You. Oh, give thanks to the LORD, for He is good! For His mercy endures forever."

A Trip to Nevada

Shortly after this health challenge, Bo and I embarked on an extended trip to visit churches and donors in the western United States. After flying to Los Angeles and renting a car, we drove first to Utah, then to Colorado, then to Arizona, and finally to Nevada. Knowing that I was not a fan of such road trips, he placated me with two privileges. The first was that I could sleep whenever I wished; the second was that we would stop whenever I told him I was hungry.

This was my first trip to Nevada, a state that holds a special place in Bo's heart and mine. Before we left the Philippines to come to the United States, the Lord had reassured Bo with the following words from Isaiah 43:18–19:

"Do not remember the former things,
Nor consider the things of old.
Behold, I will do a new thing,
Now it shall spring forth;
Shall you not know it?
I will even make a road in the wilderness
And rivers in the desert."

Our destination in Nevada was a tiny town by the name of Winnemucca. From this small desert community over the past thirty years, generous brothers and sisters in Christ have shared with ANM much-needed resources in support of native missionaries. Winnemucca truly has been a "river in the desert" flowing with abundant provisions to help hasten the Gospel work around the world.

The True Value of Wristwatches

My husband has a strange habit of giving away his wristwatches. It's his way of rendering honor and encouragement to those pastors and missionaries whom God has placed on his heart. In the early days, most of these watches were gifts that the children and I had given to him for Father's Day, Christmas, or his birthday.

In any setting, at any given moment, Bo might quietly take off his wristwatch and secretly hand it to one of the most reticent, least-esteemed persons in his presence. Then he would put his forefinger to his lips indicating to the much-surprised recipient, "Shhh, don't say a word." Invariably, a puzzled look would transform into a bright smile when the recipient realized what had happened.

While Bo was ministering to the Myanmar Young Crusaders (MYC) in Southeast Asia, he noticed that one of the local ministry leaders, Pastor Howard, held back and seemed hesitant to participate with the group. One day, as Bo and Pastor Howard shook hands, the pastor's eyes grew wide as he felt a heavy watch deposited in his palm.

Pastor Howard proudly wore that watch until he passed away. His son, Pastor Simon, the assistant pastor of the ministry's church in a leper colony, inherited it. He now proudly wears this watch and tells his friends how the Lord honored his father with it. Danny, the Myanmar Young Crusaders worker who drives Bo around Myanmar during each of his visits, proudly shows everyone his oversized watch hanging on his small arm, also a gift from Bo.

Ronnie Uy

Whenever Bo visited Negros Island, the area of the Philippines where he grew up, he would search for his childhood best friend, Ronnie Uy. When he finally located him, Ronnie was emaciated and suicidal. His family's grocery store was gone, and he was selling dumplings in a basket as a poor street vendor. Deep in debt and hounded by creditors, he was at his wit's end. He shared with Bo that he could not even afford to send their only child to college.

Bo hugged Ronnie and led him to the Lord. Then he gave him a love gift sufficient to pay off his debts (a little over $500). Next, Bo unbuckled the black silicon strap of the diving watch he was wearing, a gift the family had given him, and strapped it on the startled Ronnie's wrist.

By the grace of God, Ronnie turned his life around. He and his wife, Bening, became faithful believers and regular tithers to their church. Bo and I were able to help them send their daughter, Robbie, to college. She is now a full-time missionary to poor children.

The last time Bo saw Ronnie, he was still wearing that watch. The black plastic strap had been crudely sewn in several places, but years of wear and tear had not diminished the watch's value in Ronnie's eyes. Bening told us that Ronnie even keeps it on when he sleeps.

A Eulogy for Tim

When Bo's fourth brother, Tim, died in 2011, Bo was invited to give a eulogy at the memorial service. He began by praising his brother's generosity, which was well known to his fellow pastors. But suddenly, in the middle of his remarks he stopped and asked, "Who is the poorest pastor in the crowd?" Everyone pointed to a shy pastor sitting in the corner named Alarcon.

"I'm only going to do what Tim would do," Bo said. I winced as Bo gave away the watch he was wearing, which was my thirty-fifth wedding anniversary gift to him. In a moment, the deed was done. I rejoiced in this random act of kindness because I am of one heart with my husband.

For his birthdays, the kids and I now give Bo cash, so he can buy his own watches. He scouts for weeks and months, like Sherlock Holmes, for places where watches are on sale. He always wants to have some on hand so he can encourage more of God's hard-working servants, who too often are overlooked by all but God and his angels.

An Unusual Missions Project

One of the greatest blessings of ministry is the relationship we have with our donors. When donors are deeply invested in the ministry, they are loyal until God calls them home. Quite frequently, they may even leave some of their material legacies to the ministry. ANM is blessed to have thousands of donors. All are equally loved, respected, admired, and valued. We are grateful for each one. But there are certain donors that stand out, not because of the amounts they give, but because their stories are so unique and inspiring.

I would like to share a bit more here about Terry McKinley. As I have mentioned, when I first met Terry, he asked me how much support ANM needed for our staff. As I named the eleven people on our staff who needed financial assistance, he immediately wrote checks for $3,000 each. That amounted to a total donation of $33,000 on the spot. He then sent a team of five of his workers who finished in five days a construction project that our unskilled team would have taken three months to complete.

After this, Terry became interested in a ministry in the Philippines led by Wilson and Cora Ladringan. Called the Aetas Bible

Study Center, it ministers to the Aeta aboriginals on Luzon Island. The Aetas are a very poor, dark-skinned, marginalized people who are considered outcasts in the Philippines. When they get sick, some medical people will not treat them because nobody wants to touch them. They are considered dirty, even though they are not dirty.

At Terry's request, I took him with me on a trip to the Philippines so he could personally visit this ministry, which in addition to planting churches among the Aeta, operates Aeta Children's Home, which provides care and education for many Aeta children and some non-Aeta children as well. One day while we were there, the Aeta schoolchildren went on a field trip to a certain resort that had an attractive swimming pool. The children wanted so much to swim in this pool, but the owners of the resort refused to let them. They said they did not want these children polluting the water.

A Bigger God

This rankled Terry McKinley's spirit. When we returned from our trip, he said, "Bo, I want your permission to do something that may be against your ministry's value system. I want you to let me give these children a swimming pool. I don't care how much it costs; I'd like to build them a swimming pool of their own. I'd like to show them there's a God bigger than the people who rejected them."

At first, I was hesitant, because when we are helping native missionaries, we normally don't give them things that could be considered luxuries. But Terry begged me with all earnestness, and I could sense that God had put this desire on his heart. Today, these Aeta children have a lovely swimming pool. How wonderful it is to see them frolicking and laughing with joy in the shimmering water of their pool. In their wildest dreams, they could not have imagined that the God of Missions would provide them with such gift. For them, such a thing is nothing less than a miracle of miracles!

A while later, Terry paid a visit to ANM in Charlottesville. After I had showed him the warehouse his team had built for us, he said, "Bo, what more can I do for you?"

I hesitated to answer because he had already done so much for ANM. But when he insisted, I said, "Well, our ministry is expanding, and we have run out of office space. Could you build us an extension on our building that might give us five hundred or one thousand additional square feet to use as a leadership conference room?" With the help of John Bucchi, Terry built ANM a five thousand-square-foot conference center. What a blessing it has been to us!

In May 2013, three months before Terry Lee McKinley at age sixty-four went home to be with his Maker, he sent the following email to Lucille, Oliver, Marlou, and me:

> Greetings to all . . . Please pray for Pastor Gene Ferrell in the face of his health that is failing due to a nerve issue that cannot be solved as of yet. We both have had a long battle, but as I tell him, two halves make a whole. Me one half and him one half, you get a whole person. We rejoice on our good days and pray harder on our better days. I thank the Lord for cancer and what it has done for me in my relationship with my work, family, wife, and most important . . . God. We pray for you daily . . . love each and every one of you.
>
> —Terry and Nancy

What an amazing man to ask first for prayers for his pastor and friend, Gene Ferrell, and then to thank the Lord for his cancer. This was the last thing he wrote to us, and it showed his character and faith. Below is an excerpt from Terry's obituary:

> *Terry's love for family was equaled only by his passion for spreading the Gospel of Jesus Christ. This was evident by his selfless support of numerous groups and ministries. His legacy will live on through the work of these organizations as they continue to win souls for the Lord in all corners of the world.*

Terry was the son of Dr. Kenneth F. McKinley, a graduate of Wheaton College and Dallas Theological Seminary. Dr. McKinley served as a professor of biblical studies for LeTourneau University until he retired. He also was popularly known for his radio Bible study, *I*

Found a Friend, which aired in Texas. Both father and son were very close. They went home to the Lord in the same year.

It was a time of great sadness when the Lord took Brother Terry McKinley home. I was honored to be one of three speakers at his memorial service at Calvary Baptist Church in Longview, Texas. Terry loved his Heavenly Father, his family, and native missionaries. Perhaps the loveliest legacy Terry left us at ANM is the love story of Alex and Madison. Alex is the oldest son of ANM's president, Oliver Asher. Madison is Terry's youngest child. Alex and Madison met at an ANM retreat in Wintergreen in 2017, and they fell in love and married. Today, they reside in Dallas, Texas.

While in the process of writing this chapter on April 24, 2022, I had the pleasure of seeing Alex and Madison at a family wedding. With them was Baby Aria. Hallelujah!

"We'll Take Them All!"

I would like to tell another donor story, but I will start this one by talking about the missionary leader whose need the donor met. The name of this missionary leader is Shi Sho Tun, and his ministry is in Myanmar (formerly Burma). When I first met Brother Shi Sho in 1994, I was instantly impressed by his humble simplicity. He had eleven missionaries working with him, and they were the poorest of the servants. To support themselves and their ministry, they got up at dawn each day and waded in the cold swamps to gather water vegetables to sell in the local market. Because of these harsh conditions, several of the missionaries had contracted respiratory ailments.

To supplement the money that they earned from selling vegetables, Shi Sho Tun carved flutes from pieces of bamboo and sold them in the market. An expert flute player as well as a master flute maker, he would go to various churches and say, "Could I play Christian music for you with my flute?" They would give him offerings that he would use to promote the Gospel. Shi Sho's ministry especially targeted the Mon people of Myanmar. They are largely unreached with the Gospel because their strong tribal pride makes them resistant to outside ideas. Most of the monks in Myanmar come from this tribe.

I said to Brother Shi Sho, "How much support do you need every month?"

"Our needs are simple," he answered. "It would be a blessing if each of our missionaries could have additional support of $10 to $15 a month." I made a mental note of this need.

A Trip to the Nevada Desert

After I returned to the United States, I was invited to the home of Tim and Virginia Prest. They lived in a ramshackle mobile home in the middle of the Nevada desert. Tim worked as a truck driver for a gold mining company. When he greeted me at the door, he was shirtless. "Sit down," he barked. He had a very gruff temperament, but I think it was more for appearances. He was obviously one of those to whom God has given a marshmallow heart.

After we had talked for a while, Tim said, "Bo, you might think I'm not well-versed in the Bible, but I want to show you something." He led me to his bedroom and pulled a blanket off a folding cot. The entire space down in the cot was filled with tapes by John MacArthur. There were hundreds of them! He had studied enough Scripture to have a PhD in theology.

Tim's wife was named Virginia, but he called her Virgie. "Hey, Virgie, come here," he bellowed. "I want you to listen with me to Brother Bo. Now, Brother Bo, tell us, where is the need?"

I said, "Eleven people led by a leader named Shi Sho Tun are witnessing to the Mon people in Myanmar. This is one of the hardest people groups to reach with the Gospel. Many of these missionaries are sick with tuberculosis, and the money Brother Shi Sho earns by playing his flute in the churches is not enough to support the ministry. Each of these missionaries needs at least fifteen dollars per month of support."

Tim looked at his wife. "Virgie, did you hear that? Fifteen dollars each per month for eleven missionaries."

"Yes," she answered.

The next words out of Tim's mouth have reverberated in my mind ever since that day. I am confident that they prompted rejoicing in the whole realm of heaven. My prayer is that they would be heard by every believer in the world who has some stewardship responsibility over God's resources. Tim said, "Fifteen dollars? Eleven of them? We'll take them all!"

If only we could hear these words from other lips: "We'll take them all!" Oh, how this would help hasten world evangelization!

"We'll take them all!" A simple truck driver and his wife living in a run-down mobile home said they would take them all. If only we could hear these words from other lips: "We'll take them all!" Oh, how this would help hasten world evangelization!

For many years, Tim and Virginia faithfully supported these eleven missionaries. Largely because of their support, the work of the ministry prospered.

Speaking in Myanmar

In 2016, I was invited to be the main speaker at the graduation ceremony of the Bible school run by the ministry of Myanmar Young Crusaders. In my message, I emphasized the brevity of life. To bring home the point, I asked Brother Shi Sho to come up on the stage. He was now eighty-two years old, and we had been friends for twenty-two years. I asked him to play his flute for me one last time. As he played "This World Is Not My Home," I teared up thinking about how he had dedicated his life to reaching one of the hardest-to-reach people groups in Myanmar.

> *This world is not my home, I'm just a-passing through,*
> *My treasures are laid up somewhere beyond the blue.*
> *The angels beckon me from heaven's open door,*
> *And I can't feel at home in this world anymore.*
> *Oh Lord, you know I have no friend like you,*

If heaven's not my home, then Lord, what will I do?
The angels beckon me from heaven's open door,
And I can't feel at home in this world anymore.

When Brother Shi Sho grew too old to continue working, he wrote me and said, "Brother Bo, please stop our support. I can no longer do the work."

Though poor in the eyes of the world, Brother Shi Sho was an honorable man. Around this time, Tim Prest passed away. The two men never met this side of heaven, but I imagine they will be rejoicing together someday with "a great multitude which no one could number, of all nations, tribes, peoples, and tongues, standing before the throne and before the Lamb, clothed with white robes, with palm branches in their hands" (Revelation 7:9).

When God Held Up a Plane

In 2007, I joined an Operation Barnabas International team traveling to Sumatra Island in Indonesia. Our mission was to encourage many pastors and missionaries in the face of an upsurge in the persecution and harassment of believers in the area. Many churches had been razed to the ground by radical elements.

From Sumatra Island, I flew with Paulus Wibowo to Malang on Java Island. Our ultimate destination was his home and ministry base in Yogyakarta. After he and I had boarded the plane and settled into our seats for the next leg of our flight, from Malang to Yogyakarta, the pilot told all passengers to disembark "because there is no power."

After two hours of waiting, I started to feel uneasy about our continuing on this flight, even if the big plane was repaired. I began to pray, "Why, Lord, did you hold back the plane? Many important things are waiting for us. What is the reason?"

I asked Brother Paulus if it would be possible to rent a car or hire a taxi to get us across the heart of Java Island. After expending considerable effort, he was able to find only one taxi driver willing to take us on the nine-hour trip. This driver was a dignified looking man, but I was nervous. There are many fatal head-on collisions on Java's narrow, two-lane highways, where "playing chicken" is part of the culture.

An Interesting Lunch

We decided to talk about the matter over lunch, and we invited the taxi driver to join us. We learned that his name was Yohannas Sugianto. As Paulus was conversing with him, I was startled and disturbed to see his hand and arm freeze suddenly as he was about to take a bite. His eyes welled up with tears, and his nostrils flared in deep-seated emotion. "What is the matter with him?" I asked Paulus.

"I don't know," said Paulus. "I was just asking him about his family. My last question to him was about his eldest child."

With Paulus's translation help, I began a conversation with Yohannas. He told us that his eldest child had just called him that morning, while he had been waiting for passengers at the airport.

"My son's name is Paulus Pujianto," said Yohannas. He paused to blow his nose on his napkin. Then he continued in a soft voice. "It means 'the son who brings praise.' He is quitting college because he does not want to be a burden anymore to our family. He could not take the exams because we don't have money to pay the school. I wept inside my cab when he told me this. My wife was up all last night crying aloud with raised hands to the Lord for him to show his greatness to our children and especially to our Muslim neighbors. She was a former Muslim, and they have been mocking her and her God. I did not have any passenger this morning. I earn about 30,000 rupiahs ($3.00) on a good day. In my desperation, I agreed to drive you."

I said to Paulus, "Please ask Yohannas if he is a Christian." When Paulus posed the question, I knew by the sparkle in Yohannas's eyes what his answer was even before Paulus translated it. I then said to Paulus, "Slowly translate to Yohannas what I am going to say."

Paulus nodded, and I began, "Brother Yohannas, the Lord has held back our plane today because he saw your tears and your wife's tears. He heard your cries. Brother Paulus and I will drop by your house this very moment. Otherwise, the stones would cry!"

Yohannas blinked away his tears. The three of us quickly finished our meal and hopped into his taxi. On the way to his house, doubts began to gnaw at my heart. Is this man genuine? Is he really a believer? Then God put my doubts to rest when Yohannas, like a little boy, began singing a very lovely, familiar tune. Paulus happily joined him as they sang, *"Tak tersembangi kuasa Allah kalan lain ditto lang saya juga. . ."* I sang with them the English version: "It is no secret what God can do. . . . What He's done for others, He will do for you. . ."

I am at a loss for words as I attempt to describe what happened in that little hut that day! We met Yohannas's young son, Paulus Pujianto. He was a sweet young man and very active in his church. He was grateful to receive the gifts we gave him for his school needs. As to the young man's mother, I feel that all the while we were there, angels were kept busy scooping up her fragrant tears of praise for God's golden bowl in heaven. She was rejoicing over the vindication God had given her before the eyes of her mocking neighbors. God held up our flight that day on her behalf.

After Brother Yohannas had driven us to our destination, we gave him his taxi fee plus a very generous tip. He drove back home rejoicing just before midnight. The date was November 19. Christmas came early for this poor and very precious and faithful family of Yohannas Sugianto.

ENCOURAGING AND EQUIPPING HEROES IN THE MISSION FIELD— PART I

As I have shared in the previous chapters, during our October 1992 trip to a church in San Antonio, Texas, the God of Missions gave Carl and me the vision statement for ANM. It is based on Matthew 24:14:

> *And this gospel of the kingdom will be preached in all the world as a witness to all the nations, and then the end will come.*

God also placed in our hearts the following mission statement for ANM:

> *To encourage, equip, and advocate for native missionaries*
> *to help hasten world evangelization.*

This and the following chapter contain brief stories of some selected missionaries among the hundreds that the Lord has allowed Marlou and me to serve.[19] What a blessing and joy it is to personally encourage, equip, and advocate for these leaders and their ministries by God's grace and for his glory. These are the true heroes of this book!

But before proceeding to their stories, let us again ask ourselves the crucial question: "Why native missionaries?"

---

[19] Portions of some of the stories are from *ANM World Missions* magazine.

In response, I would like to share some thoughts offered by our long-time and very close friend and supporter, Andy Ludlum, a former pastor and a recently retired Southwest Airlines pilot. His sentiments are now supported by many missions-loving believers in the West.

INDIGENOUS MISSIONS:
The Wiser Model for Kingdom Extension

On a brisk day in early 1993, my wife and I attended a missions conference at a large church in Charlottesville, VA. During the conference, while helping with the chair arrangement, I bumped into another man who was also assisting. He was beaming ear to ear and bubbling over with energy and excitement. When we grabbed each other's hands for the usual handshake, we instantly connected. Soon we realized that we shared much more than similar personalities. The strongest bond was our love for our Savior, Jesus the Christ, and our desire to serve him.

This man was Bo Barredo, and when the meeting began, he explained his life purpose: to build a missions organization that has as its primary purpose the support of indigenous missionaries around the world. He meant not just financial support, but prayer, visitation, encouragement, and material and personal advocacy for their respective ministries. Having attended Columbia Bible College and Seminary (now Columbia International University), which focuses largely on missions, I had always thought that indigenous missions was the wiser model for effective evangelism, church planting, and kingdom extension. However, the "normal" way of doing missions at that time was to send Western missionaries.

The movement toward a global economy and advances in technology, communications, and travel now called for a paradigm shift in operations. This "new reality" of missions was about to launch with Bo and Marlou as its advocates. They were pioneers of relational missions work globally. Bo related much of this in the early years of our relationship. The vision matured in the ensuing years and blossomed into the current ANM.

As my wife and I got to know Bo and Marlou, observe the formative years of ANM, and track its historical direction, we could not help but notice God's leading on the whole enterprise. The ANM leadership sparked a different direction for God's Kingdom and the preaching of the Gospel to the nations. Their personal integrity, self-sacrifice, prayer, wise decisions, unwavering commitment, and dedication to speaking the Gospel of Jesus to people individually and publicly, were catalysts for ANM's success.

As Bo and I have continued to develop our friendship over the many years, we have cherished our conversations and mutual encouragements, along with life's constant changes. We rejoice together for a relationship akin to David and Jonathan in the Bible. It has been a distinct privilege to continue my close relationship with Bo Barredo as we journey into the future looking to the coming of Our Savior Jesus. Even so, come Lord Jesus!

"I Am Praying That You Will Join Me" *—Paulus Wibowo of Indonesia*

When we started ANM in 1992, one of our first missionary partners was Paulus Trimanto Wibowo, director and founder of Yogyakarta Missionary Training Center in Yogyakarta, Indonesia. Yogyakarta is the royal capital of Indonesia, while Jakarta is the official capital.

Growing up, Paulus was a very naughty boy. One of his favorite pranks was to run with his friends through the mosque and cause much disturbance while the Muslim men were prostrate worshipping. Other days, he would chase the water buffalo through the fields so the farmers would have to round them up. His father was one of the Islamic leaders in the community, and the behavior of his only son greatly shamed him. Out of desperation, he took Paulus to a witch doctor who blew on the top of his head and commanded the evil spirits to leave, but Paulus's behavior only got

"I am praying that you will join me in my vision to serve the Lord." This was a way of saying, "Would you marry me?"

worse. Enraged, his father had another witch doctor come to the house and put a paste made from yellow rice on Paulus's head, but that did nothing to help.

By the time Paulus reached the age of eleven, his father had run out of patience. He said to his incorrigible son, "You are now able to read. Read this and sign it." He handed Paulus a document that said, "I, Trimanto Wibowo, commit that I will become a good boy. If I do not, I wish that I become lame." (Trimanto was the name Paulus was given at birth; Paulus became his name when he came to faith in Christ.)

Paulus signed the document, in essence putting a curse on himself. Then he ran away from home. While on the run, he encountered a missionary who shared the Gospel with him and led him to Christ. A very bright young man, Paulus ended up going to seminary and becoming a missionary.

While Paulus was visiting a Christian school, he noticed a lovely teacher by the name of Sri. They began courting, and as a way of expressing his affection, Paulus gave her gifts. One of her favorites was laundry soap. After they had courted for a while, Paulus said to Sri, "I am praying that you will join me in my vision to serve the Lord." This was a way of saying, "Would you marry me?" After Sri had prayed for a time, she said yes.

A Visit from Carl

In 1989, Carl Gordon came to the Philippines, where I was working for Christian Aid. We joined more than three thousand other missionaries from all over the world at the Lausanne Congress, which was held that year in Manila. While there, we met Paulus. As I mentioned in an earlier chapter, my life was in danger during this time from communist guerrilla groups. Carl tried to convince me to move to the United States with my family, but I refused.

Before Carl left me to return to the US, he asked me to follow up with Paulus, so after the Congress, I called him and promised to visit him in Indonesia. When I got to Yogyakarta a few months later, I looked up Paulus, and we immediately bonded as brothers in Christ. At the time, he was working as a native missionary for an American ministry, but he was experiencing little growth, so we invited him to become a missionary partner of Christian Aid. His partnership with Christian Aid was cut short, however, when Carl and I started ANM in October 1992. Paulus and his wife, Sri, after praying, communicated with us that they would like to join the new work we had started.

In 1993, I invited Paulus to come to the United States and accompany me to some missions events where I was a speaker. At an event in Chattanooga, two couples committed to support him. From there, I took Paulus to visit churches in Texas and other places. I wanted him to say a few words at each event, and because he had a heavy accent, I served as his translator. Quite humorously, I translated his Indonesian English into my Filipino English!

Preparing the Presentation

I have such a great love for brothers in Christ like Paulus. They may have heavy accents, and they may not be as polished as some speakers that American audiences are accustomed to hearing, but many of them have studied the Bible enough to have two PhDs in theology. Paulus, in fact, does have two PhDs. However, because he speaks with such a heavy accent, and American audiences have short attention spans, after Paulus has spoken for two or three minutes, the minds of the listeners stray. I attempted to overcome this handicap by introducing him, as I would others I am privileged to champion, in the way God would want him represented.

In the five minutes allotted for my introduction of Paulus, I related his powerful testimony about what he had done and how he had sacrificed for the Lord. When audiences heard these things, they saw him as fifteen feet tall. He gained many, many friends while in the US. Their support helped him and his team plant almost a thousand churches in Indonesia. His sweet personality and apparent humility earned him loving favor among his American hosts.

Witnesses to God's Work in the World

In 2013, I again invited Paulus to visit us in the US, along with about eight other missions partners of ANM from all over the world. These nine missions leaders were our featured guests at a missions conference ANM sponsored for our donors at Wintergreen Resort in Virginia. Following the retreat, six of these missions partners and I participated in the two Sunday morning services at Covenant Presbyterian Church in Harrisonburg, Virginia.

There were almost one thousand worshippers in attendance in the first service on this Sunday. As I was delivering the sermon, I interrupted my message and said, "By the way, you know that I was an attorney before I joined the Lord's service. As a lawyer, I try to use witnesses, just as the Bible says the Lord Jesus used witnesses. Today, I brought six witnesses to tell you how God is working around the world in terms of the Gospel. I will call them up now."

I had all six ministry leaders come up to the front. They were Jonathan Cortes from Singapore, Roger and Sylvia Elosendo from the Philippines, John Biak from Myanmar, George Johnson (an alias) from Malaysia, Damir Spoljaric from Croatia, and Paulus Wibowo from Indonesia. I asked them to line up on the stage so I could interview them one by one.

For example, to Roger and Sylvia Elosendo I said, "Where are you from?"

"The Philippines," they answered.

"What tribe?"

"The Ati aboriginal group."

"How many languages do you speak?"

"Only five."

"What are the languages?"

"Inati, Cebuano, Hiligaynon, Kinaray-a, and English."

"How many churches have you planted?"

"Only four, plus outreaches, but we're planning for more."

"When you started this work, were you poor? What kind of food do you eat?"

"Yes. We are still poor. We work among the Ati. We eat root crops, snails, frogs, lizards, and snakes."

Introducing John Biak

At this point, because of shortage of time, I had to bring this introduction to a close. I would have loved to have told the audience more of Sylvia and Roger's remarkable story, some of which is included later in this chapter. But in the worship service on this Sunday morning, I barely had time to scratch the surface. So I thanked this remarkable couple and turned to the next missionary.

"What is your name?"

"My name is John Biak."

"From where do you come?"

"From Myanmar, which used to be called Burma."

"How many millions of people live there?"

"Seventy million."

"How many tribes?"

"Around 120."

"How many languages?"

"A hundred and thirty languages?"

"How many do you speak?"

"Seven."

"What is your education?"

"I have a master's in theology."

"What is your work?"

"I plant churches."

"How many churches have you planted?"

"Eleven."

"If God would provide resources for you, would you be able to plant more?"

"Yes, because then I would be able to invite more church planters and pastors to join me. Also, if we had a vehicle and bicycles and motorcycles, we could cover more areas."

I moved on like this from one missionary to another. After I had interviewed all the missionary partners except Paulus, I thanked them and asked them to take their seats.

"I Will Never Do Retreat!" ### *—More about Paulus Wibowo of Indonesia*

I then asked Paulus to come stand with me beside the pulpit.

"Paulus, where are you from?

"Indonesia."

"What's the population of Indonesia?"

"More than two hundred million."

"How many islands does Indonesia have?"

"Seventeen thousand islands."

"How many tribes and languages?"

"There are over 1,200 tribes and over seven hundred languages. It is the most populous Muslim country in the world."

"How long have we known each other?"

"Since 1989."

"That's a long time. How many churches have you planted?"

"Around a thousand churches."

"How many are you now responsible for?"

"Around three hundred."

"Why only three hundred?"

"I gave away all the rest to other denominations because we lack pastors and workers to staff them."

"Why don't you have enough pastors?"

"We don't have resources to help pay their salaries."

"Once when I was visiting you, Paulus, radical Muslims were burning churches and parsonages. Many pastors and their wives and children were burned to death in those fires. Have you considered moving to the United States where it is safer?"

"No, sir. I am staying in Indonesia because this is my mission field. These are my people."

"Paulus, you taught me a song. You told me that this song reminds you to have the courage to stay where you are. You have a beautiful voice. Could you sing this song today to our friends here in this church?"

Paulus, a nightingale of the Gospel of the Lord Jesus in Indonesia, proceeded to sing a heart-stirring song, first in his native Indonesian Bahasa language. Even though the worshippers in the service could not understand what he was singing, they listened attentively. Then Paulus sang the song in English, his voice reverberating inside the church. The song went like this:

> *When I remember the love of God, I will never do retreat.*
> *When I remember the love of God, I will never do retreat.*
> *Oh, yeah, never do, never, never do retreat.*
> *Oh, yeah, never do, never, never do retreat.*

I continued, "Paulus, you have never retreated despite the persecution. Will you ever retreat?"

"No, sir."

"Will you ever surrender?"

"No, sir."

"Paulus, you have hundreds of missionaries working with you, and they have a need. When you came here, what need was in your heart?"

"I wanted to raise money to purchase at least five motorbikes so my senior pastors can supervise more churches."

"How much in Indonesia does a motorbike cost in US dollars?"

"About fifteen hundred dollars."

"You have been here for almost two months. How many more weeks do you have before you fly back to Indonesia?"

"This is my last week."

"Have you received money even just for one motorbike from your brothers and sisters in America?"

Moisture clouded Paulus's eyes. He bowed his head and tried to blink away the tears. Then, quickly, he raised his head. His patented grin flashed across his face. "No, sir," he said.

The room filled with almost one thousand people was so still that the drop of a pin could have been heard.

I said, "Paulus, thank you. You may take a seat."

As Paulus returned to his seat, I said to the congregation, "I'm done with the sermon. Thank you."

No One Stirred

For a few seconds, no one stirred. There was an almost deafening silence. Then, suddenly, people began to rise from their seats. The room erupted in applause. These were Presbyterians, and they were giving Paulus and the other missionaries a long, thunderous, standing ovation! They had experienced a generous taste of God's heartbeat—missions.

After the service, worshippers went over to Paulus and stuffed cash and checks into his hands and pockets. He went home with enough money to buy about seven motorbikes. What's more, the church adopted him and another missionary for ongoing support. A member of the church's missions committee told me later, "The church has never had a time like this. This morning, the missions conference went through the roof!"

Two years later, Covenant Presbyterian Church invited Paulus to come back and give a report at a Wednesday evening service. He would have only eight minutes to speak, and I knew that with his heavy accent, he would have difficulty getting his message across. At my request, Marlou prepared a powerful five-minute PowerPoint presentation, which included photos of the seven motorbikes that Covenant had enabled Paulus to buy. After the PowerPoint, I interviewed him for the remaining three minutes.

When Paulus completed his presentation, people rushed up to put money in his hands and pockets. One person said, "The last time you were here, I was convicted by the Lord to buy you one motorbike on behalf of my family, but I didn't do it. Tonight, I want to obey the Lord. Here is fifteen hundred dollars." Many other people did similarly. Paulus received enough funds that night to purchase five more motorbikes. He visited some other churches in the US as well, and when he got home to Indonesia, he was able to purchase more motorbikes. What a boost this was to his work for the Lord!

In this year, 2022, Paulus's health has not been good, and his eldest son, Daniel, has ably taken his place in the ministry.

"My Heavenly Father Will Pay for Everything."
—Roger and Sylvia Elosendo of the Philippines

At one time, mainstream Filipinos thought the Ati people had no souls. But God brought together a Filipina lowlander and an Ati tribesman to reach them. It's a unique love story.

Sylvia's mother died when she was seven. A year later, her father remarried and left Sylvia and her five brothers and one sister with a grandmother who lived in a city on Mindanao Island. The grandmother was unable to properly care for them, and the children went different directions to survive. Sylvia ended up fending for herself as a housemaid in Ozamiz City.

When Sylvia was sixteen and in her senior year of high school, her employer tried to rape her. To escape from his grasp, she fled on a boat bound for Negros Island. She contemplated ending her life, but a couple on the boat who discovered her hiding in their cabin dissuaded her.

When the boat docked, Sylvia was alone with no place to go. Noticing a "Help Wanted" sign at a hospital, she applied and got the job as a custodian. One day, a hospital technical assistant, who observed that Sylvia was constantly crying, gave her a Bible. In it, Sylvia read, "When my father and my mother forsake me, the Lord will care of me" (Psalm 27:4). When her friend asked her to come with her to church, Sylvia accepted the invitation. In January 1979, she gave her heart to Christ, and in May of that year, she was baptized.

A Life Committed to God

From that moment on, Sylvia committed her life to God's service. Bubbling with joy, she declared to everyone she met, "Now I have a Father to whom I can turn and share all my tears and needs!" Her dream was to marry a pastor, and she enrolled at Doane Baptist Seminary on Panay Island. Her church collected an offering to pay for her travel expenses.

"God is faithful and willing to help me, and he hears my prayers."

When she arrived, Sylvia had only two pesos (four US cents), but her heart abounded in faith. She earned a small amount of money by cleaning rooms around the campus; a sympathetic teacher paid for her food. One day, the school president asked her, "Who is going to pay for your education?" With childlike trust in God's promises in Psalm 27:10 and Philippians 4:19, Sylvia answered, "My Heavenly Father will pay for everything."

For many days, Sylvia was on her knees beseeching her Father to send a signed check from heaven to pay for her tuition. During this period, two American businessmen visiting the school learned of her plight and committed to pay for her entire schooling. "God is faithful and willing to help me, and he hears my prayers," she exclaimed.

After graduating in 1985, Sylvia ministered on Luzon Island for a time. Then she returned to Mindanao Island, where she served as a "Bible woman" for a church in Padada, Davao del Sur. She was still praying to marry a pastor when the church called a young Bible school graduate to be its pastor.

The New Pastor

The new pastor was Rogelio "Roger" Elosendo, a member of the Ati tribe, the aborigines of the Philippines. These nomadic people live in the mountains of northern Luzon and Panay Islands. Diminutive in stature with dark skin and curly hair, they typically are disadvantaged economically, educationally, and socially. Most are illiterate.

Roger's uncle Severo had been the head of an Ati village in Iloilo when an American missionary, William Hopper, vowed to evangelize them. *Why bother? Those people don't even have souls* was the prevailing sentiment, but Hopper was determined. He had to overcome much resistance because the Ati had heard that the Americans would capture them and use them as fuel in the sugar mill.

Hopper was able to lead Severo to faith in Christ, and Severo in turn introduced so many more to Jesus that he became known as Tatay Vero (Father Vero). One of his converts was his nephew, Roger. Roger promised his uncle that he would become a missionary to his own people, and he enrolled at Doane, where he did janitorial work to pay his expenses. When he graduated in 1988, the church in Padada called him to be their pastor.

Not long after he arrived, Roger stood up during a meeting of the elders of the church and announced, "I want to marry the Bible woman, but I have one problem. The Bible woman doesn't like me." Stunned when she learned of Roger's declaration, Sylvia said in her heart, "Yes, Lord, I do want to marry a pastor, but an Ati is not what I had in mind. Besides, I find Pastor Roger's ill-fitting shoes, shabby clothes, and unkempt hair very unattractive."

On behalf of Roger, the church elders said to Sylvia, "Roger is good in music. He is intelligent, a good preacher, and a godly man." They even bought Roger new clothes and a new pair of shoes. After much thought and prayer, Sylvia agreed to marry the Ati pastor.

Starting Out as a Married Couple

After their marriage, Roger honored his promise to Tatay Vero. In 1990, he and his young wife left Mindanao Island and returned to Panay Island and his uncle's church. His uncle was overjoyed!

Roger and Sylvia only had a few pesos when they arrived, and their life did not get easier. The Sunday offering of the Ati church was miniscule, and the ministry work was replete with unfamiliar, daunting

The couple's dream was to lift the Ati people out of their miserable conditions and show them a better life.

challenges. The young couple subsisted on Ati food, such as snails, frogs, snakes, lizards, and cassava. Sylvia, a lowlander, had never eaten such food, but she was determined to live the Ati way. Through these trials, God taught her to be a humble and effective servant.

In 1993, Roger and Sylvia founded Ati Tribes Mission for the purpose of pointing Ati people to Christ. The couple's dream was to lift the Ati people out of their miserable conditions and show them a better life.

I was privileged to meet Roger and Sylvia during the early days of their ministry. It's been my honor to serve them since they commissioned me by the laying on of hands in 1994 in the Ati village on Panay Island.

In the ensuing years, they slowly began teaching the Ati people hygiene and social responsibility, and they introduced simple livelihood projects, such as gardening and handicrafts. Sylvia's heart especially ached for the Ati children who could not obtain medical care when they got sick, simply because they were considered untouchables. She and Roger rectified this situation by starting a children's home. Even more importantly, they taught from the Bible and conducted worship services.

One day in 2010, as Roger was walking through an area of Iloilo City on Panay Island, he saw an old, disheveled Ati woman sprawled on a dirty sidewalk. People indifferently passed by her. Roger stooped to wake her up, and when he saw her face, he burst into tears. She was one of his distant, older Ati cousins! *"Manang"* (older sister), he whispered to her, "I'm soon leaving for America. Bo Barredo has invited me to come. I will ask God's people there to help us buy some land near here. Then we will try our best to gather all of you together."

Roger and Sylvia did visit the US, and what a difference that visit has made! In partnership with ANM, they were able to realize their dream of revitalizing the Ati community. With generous support from American donors, they purchased a thirty-two-thousand-square-foot property near Iloilo City, and on this land, they have built a church, an orphanage, and simple dwellings for several Ati families, many of whom had been street beggars. Roger and Sylvia planted seven churches in the twenty-one areas they targeted for Ati outreach in Antique Province and trained several Ati pastors.

Dedication Day

Seven years later, I again visited Roger and Sylvia at their Ati village near Iloilo City. On February 3, 2017, the dedication day of their new Ati community in Lanit, Iloilo City, seven wondrous events took place. The mayor of Iloilo City and an entourage of his officials arrived with a platoon of press and TV people, along with members of community social organizations. The mayor was especially excited to be there because during one of their visits to city hall, Roger and Sylvia had led him to the Lord.

The first event of the day was the groundbreaking for the proposed government-sponsored concrete road that would connect the Ati community with the nearby public school. Henceforth, Ati children would not have to wade through mud puddles and rice fields to obtain an education. During the proceedings, the mayor delivered a strong Gospel message that caused some people to think he was an evangelist as well as a politician!

Second on the agenda was the dedication of twenty-four new Ati houses that had been financed by a partnership between the city and a foreign charity foundation. Several civic organizations had brought electric fans, blankets, kitchen utensils, and other essential home gadgets as gifts for the poor and homeless Ati families.

The third big event was the dedication of a new, sparkling white Ati church building, with a children's center on the first floor and a worship hall on the second. The jewel of the day, this community center lent dignity and legitimacy to this once-despised people group.

The fourth big event of the day was the baptism of fifty new Ati believers. Fifth was a mass wedding celebration in which many Ati men and women, including some who had been living together, bonded in Christian marriage. The city mayor officiated the mass wedding. Sixth, more than a dozen Ati mothers brought their babies forward to dedicate them to the Lord. And as the seventh big event of this wonderful, jam-packed day, the crowd gathered for a celebratory banquet on the church's ground floor. What a testimony this occasion was to the grace of God and the faithfulness of his precious servants, Roger and Sylvia!

"Jesus Alone Can Save."
—Youssef and Hee Tee Ourahmane of Algeria

One of the missionary leaders we serve around the world who most fascinates me and has gained my deepest admiration is Brother Youssef Ourahmane from the very difficult mission field of Algeria. It was my joy to invite him and his wife, Hee Tee, to come to the US to be one of the major missionary speakers at a missions conference at one of our sending churches, International Christian Church, the biggest Filipino American church in Virginia.

The people loved Youssef and Hee Tee, and they were captivated by Brother Youssef's personal testimonies about God's work in Algeria. Afterwards, the missions committee chairman jubilantly shared with me that the church had their biggest missions offering ever! The following is Brother Youssef's powerful story:[20]

In 2006, the government of Muslim-dominated Algeria passed a law prohibiting the promotion of any religion other than Islam. Article 11 of this statute specifically states that if anyone "shakes the faith" of a Muslim, he would be liable to a prison term. "Shaking the faith" can be something as overt as Christian evangelism or as

---

[20] This is a lightly edited version of the account originally written by Victor Morris. At the time of the writing, Victor was the executive vice president of ANM overseeing the mission's US operations. He is currently the ministry's chaplain.

subtle as helping a sick Muslim friend. If the actions of a Christian were deemed to have caused a Muslim to question his beliefs in any way, the Christian was automatically guilty of the crime. "Guilty" Christians could be imprisoned for one to five years and be required to pay a fine of about $13,000 US.

In 2008, indigenous missionary Youssef Ourahmane was facing such charges. At the same time, many Algerian churches were under intense pressure from the government. Twenty-six churches were ordered to close. But the tiny body of Christ in Algeria, numbering around 100,000, stood its ground and refused. Believers emphatically declared, "We will not close. We will continue to worship and do the work God has called us to do." One Christian leader boldly told a government official, "If you are thinking of putting us in prison, you had better enlarge your prisons because what you have today will not be enough for us."

Youssef was thankful for Article 11 because it allowed him and other Algerian Christians to witness to authorities when they were questioned for possible violations of the law. And because of the persecution, God was delivering the Algerian church from a spirit of fear. Youssef had become a man without fear, and the Algerian Christians were a people without fear. As Youssef put it, "When you overcome fear, the enemy does not have much to frighten or threaten you with."

As a native Algerian, Youssef was raised in a conservative Muslim family. He first encountered the Gospel while traveling in Europe in 1977. In 1980, on another European trip, a group who focused on reaching foreign students led Youssef to the Lord. A short time later, while training for Christian ministry service, he met his future wife, Hee Tee, an ethnic Chinese from Malaysia.

God Blesses the Ministry

God blessed the ministry of the Ourahmane family from the beginning. Through persecution and struggles, they have witnessed the church exploding across the land. It is now the norm for an average size church to baptize 50 to 60 new converts a year. Many other congregations are seeing 100, 120, or even 150 baptisms each year, and the largest local church in the country has more than 1,000 believers. The senior pastor of this large church reports that in the past two years they baptized about 370 new believers!

Youssef and Hee Tee minister through TV and radio, literature printing and distribution, sports ministry, and relief projects. Their Timothy Training School trains workers for the Algerian churches. Youssef's message is quite simple: "Jesus alone can save." His ministry is not about attacking Islam. It's not even about defending Christianity. It's about simply presenting Jesus.

When he visited ANM, Youssef told us with a smile about how he has often been "invited" to visit the local police station. In fact, he has "visited" so often that he is known to some of the local police officials. One official recently said to him, "Tell me, why did you become a Christian?"

"Ah," said Youssef with a grin, "I love that question!" Youssef spent forty-five minutes telling this policeman about Jesus. He said to the policeman, "Show me someone who came either before or after Jesus who is better!"

After thinking, the policeman answered, "There is no one. Mohammed came after, yet I cannot say he was better than Jesus."

"If you cannot tell me someone who is better than Jesus, then why not give your life to Jesus today?" asked Youssef.

"Well, not today. Maybe the next time you come to visit," said the policeman. This caused Youssef to chuckle.

An Algerian Man Meets Jesus

The church in Algeria today may be compared with the early Christian church described in the book of Acts. The truth of the Gospel is being confirmed with signs, miracles, and wonders. Youssef finds that his simple presentations of the Gospel are empowered by the Spirit of God. Here is one such story in Youssef's own words:

There was an Algerian man who had never heard about Jesus. He had never watched any Christian programs; he had never met any Christians; nothing! His wife became sick, and he tried everything to get her healed. He took her to doctors, specialists, and even to a sorcerer, but nothing worked.

One night, this man had a dream. He didn't know who spoke to him in the dream at the time, but much later, he realized it was Jesus. Jesus said to him, "You have tried everything you can, but nothing has helped. I will give you a phone number, and this person can help your wife." The cell phone number that the man received in the dream belonged to one of our team leaders who is a friend of mine.

When the man woke up in the morning, he was filled with amazement. He called the number and told the man who answered the phone about the dream. He asked him, "Can you help me? Can you help my wife?"

The man, who was one of our team leaders, said to the man, "I cannot help you, but the one who helped me, he can help you!" They got together, my friend shared with him about Jesus, and Jesus healed his wife. Hallelujah! Can you believe it? God is working!

Youssef's vision is to reach all of Algeria with the simple message of Jesus Christ and his love. With a multitude of testimonies as to the miraculous power of God at work, and a boldness of witness that comes with being delivered from all fear, it is easy to believe that Youssef will see his vision fulfilled.

"Never Say Die"
—David Yone Mo of Myanmar (formerly Burma)[21]

"Who do you think you are?" the young ruffian challenged his presumed gang leader. "Take a machete, and we'll see who's really tops."

Unfazed, David Yone Mo pulled a razor from his back pocket, snapped it in two, and held out one piece toward his challenger.

---

[21] Much of this information is taken from an article by John Lindner that appeared in the Spring 2010 issue of *ANM World Missions* magazine.

"Jesus, I'm sorry. I've made a terrible mess of my life. Please forgive me. Please remember me when you come into your kingdom."

"Take it," David jeered. "We'll both get in that barrel over there, and the one who comes out alive will be the leader."

The other fellow backed down.

It was an evening in the early 1960s in Yangon, then named Rangoon, capital of Myanmar, traditionally known as Burma. David had grown up the son of devout Christian parents, but the faith never "took" on him. His quest for adventure led him to the dark life of the streets where he soon became the undisputed leader of Myanmar's most notorious motorcycle gang, the Road Devils.

They smoked, drank freely, and indulged in drugs. After all, Myanmar was part of the Golden Triangle of the drug trade. They got their funding by demanding "protection money" from taverns and gambling dens.

In the course of his adventures, David fell in love with a young Filipina named Kathy, a Catholic primary school teacher. She was two years older than he, and both sets of parents strongly objected. When they eloped anyway, Kathy's parents publicly disowned her. Only after they were married did Kathy learn of David's drug use.

A Downward Spiral

David's life of lawlessness and abandon continued its downward spiral. He became hopelessly addicted to heroin, and he sold his services as a hit man, breaking the legs of his victims with a bamboo pole. He set up gambling dens, sold heroin to rich university students, and even stole from his mother and his wife's grocery money to support his habit.

Kathy badly needed the money David spent on drugs. By the mid-1970s, they had five children: Mark (1964), Kevin (1966), Sharon (1968), David Jr. (1970), and Timothy (1970). During these days of severe trial, David's mother, Elizabeth, frequently visited Kathy as if she were her own daughter. Having come to solid faith in Christ through the witness of a Burmese evangelist, Elizabeth shared her faith quietly with Kathy, who hung on her every word. Soon Kathy, too, trusted in Christ.

This further enraged David, but around this time, he lost forty-five pounds, became jaundiced, and was admitted to a hospital. "Hepatitis!" said the doctor, shaking his head. "If you had brought him in earlier, we might have been able to help him. But I'm afraid there isn't anything we can do for him now."

David lay motionless on the hospital bed, too pained to even roll over. Elizabeth left the hospital that August night to order a casket, a necessary procedure in hot and humid Myanmar, where embalming processes were not available. But before she left, she slipped a Burmese Bible under David's pillow.

Remember Me

After his mother left, David begrudgingly pulled the Bible out from under his pillow. It fell open to Luke 23. There he read how the two thieves exchanged words with Christ on the cross, and how Jesus said to the one who begged forgiveness, "Today you will be with Me in Paradise" (v. 43). These words touched David's heart deeply. He prayed, "Jesus, I'm sorry. I've made a terrible mess of my life. Please forgive me. Please remember me when you come into your kingdom."

A tremendous peace flooded David's heart. "Praise the Lord! Jesus Christ just saved me!" he shouted to the other patients in the ward, jumping out of bed. The nurse heard the commotion and rushed to the room. "Are you alright? You'd better lie down."

"No, I'm fine!" David replied. "Let me walk around a bit."

A week later David walked out of the hospital a new man—spiritually and physically. His mother sold the casket.

David entered his new life with the same courage and abandon that had characterized his old life. Soon the members of his Road Devil gang, seeing his astounding turnaround, and unable to resist his witness, committed their lives to Christ. There was only one problem: none of the existing churches would baptize them or welcome them into their fellowship. So, David began his own church.

Launching MYC

At first, they met under a tamarind tree at his house. Soon, they numbered fifty. As they studied the Bible and roamed the streets together preaching God's Word, their numbers grew. David called them the Myanmar Young Crusaders (MYC). Eventually, with the Lord's provision, he was able to construct a large facility where they could meet.

The Lord brought drug addicts, rock stars, and a wide range of others to the MYC gatherings. They got saved, transformed their lives, and many joined the ministry. The MYC conducted crusades featuring new Christian rock music, which drew thousands. One of the many CDs the ministry produced became a bestseller in the secular market.

During the next thirty years, the influence of MYC grew at an astounding pace. With some help from America, David expanded the ministry. He began trucking (or "elephanting") to the outlying regions of Myanmar. Even in the most remote areas, crowds of up to one hundred thousand flocked to his meetings, and thousands came to Christ.

My Visit with Brother David

When I first visited David about twenty-five years ago, he took me to a leper village. While I was interviewing poor children and their leper parents, soldiers led by a captain confronted us. Myanmar had one of the most repressive regimes in the world. Going to the rural areas without registering with the authorities was illegal.

"Come with us!" the captain demanded.

I feared that we were going to jail, but David bravely told the captain that he first would like to speak in the small church that his ministry had built in that village. Surprisingly, the captain granted his request, and David began speaking in his own language to the small group of trembling leper believers who had assembled in that modest structure. Nonbelieving Buddhist lepers peered in through the glassless windows. No doubt, they were eager for the preaching to be over, so they could see us bound and hauled off to jail.

As David's clear, unwavering voice filled the building, a calm descended over the assembled audience. I happened to notice that the captain was writing something in a small notebook. Perhaps he was documenting additional charges to bring against us. When David finished preaching, the captain and his men marched us out of the church to our vehicle. But instead of bringing additional charges, the captain simply said, "Go back to the capital."

We drove all night, passing through numerous military checkpoints. When I at last entered my hotel room, I heaved a sigh of relief.

Several weeks later, I received a letter from David with exciting news. The captain who had spoken to us—the head of the arresting team—had received Christ! In addition, he had granted David a permit to preach not only in the leper villages, but also in the areas that adjoined them. And to top it off, David wrote that many of the unbelieving lepers who had crowded outside the windows had received Christ as well. This is the power of the Gospel and the effectiveness of indigenous missionaries! I have seen it many times.

A Change in Leadership

The life of David Yone Mo, the founder of Myanmar Young Crusaders, came to a sudden end in 2003 when he died of cancer at age fifty-nine. He had once prayed, "Lord, please give me those ministries no one else wants." God answered his plea by trusting him to minister to lepers and other outcasts. He shared God's love with them in tangible ways, even staying in the homes of lepers and partaking of their food. As a result of his sincerity, many came to Christ.

His beloved Kathy had preceded him in death in 1999, so David's daughter, Sharon, assumed the leadership responsibilities, with the assistance of her brothers.

In 2015, Sharon came to the US to visit friends of the ministry. Before leaving Myanmar, the children cared for by the ministry gathered around her and prayed. At this time, the ministry was caring for 135 orphans, children of leper parents, and other disadvantaged children. They fed and clothed them and gave them loving Christian nurture. They also transported them each day on the ministry's bus back and forth to the government school.

After years of service, the seats on the bus were torn, the body of the bus had holes in it, and the engine frequently stalled. On several occasions, the children had to get off the bus and help push it with their little hands until it would start again. On one especially rainy day, the bus's roof began to leak, and a child shouted, "Open your umbrellas!" These circumstances had made the children the butt of jokes in their school and neighborhood. They looked up at Sharon before she left for the US and asked, "Mama, will you bring us back a new school bus?"

Believers in the US, many of them our generous friends, rallied around Sharon and the Myanmar Young Crusaders. Because they responded generously to the needs of the children, MYC was able to buy a brand-new bus. When Marlou and I visited the ministry again in 2016, our hearts sang when we saw and touched that shiny new vehicle. Sharon told us that when it first arrived, the children did not want to get off!

Children have a cherished place in God's heart. This is especially true of children the world has neglected or rejected.

"Lord, How Do I Grow the Ministry?"
—Williams Yindi of Tanzania

In 2000, a missionary from Tanzania by the name of Williams Yindi showed up at the office of ANM. Some years before, while praying on what is known in Tanzania as Prayer Mountain, he had cried out to God, "Lord, how do I grow the ministry you have called me to? I have planted fourteen churches, but the work is stopped because I have no money. You know that we do not even have strings for our guitars, so we burn used tires to get the wires. The few Bibles we have are torn, and many pages are missing. Besides, our thatched buildings are so old that they disintegrate when the rains come. Plus, Lord, the orphans are hungry, and I don't know how to feed them. And how do I take care of the widows and my pastors? When I was a chemistry teacher, I had a good salary, and everyone respected me. Now, even my own family does not respect me."

Williams heard the Lord say to him, "Go to the United States." While he was at a conference for missionaries in Amsterdam, he inquired about America, and someone told him about a ministry in Virginia that might be able to help him. He borrowed some money and traveled to see this ministry. However, the missionary representative he talked to turned him away.

Another person who worked for the ministry overheard the conversation and suggested that Williams go across the city and see another ministry called Advancing Native Missions. Brother Williams hitched a ride to ANM and knocked on our door. "My name is Williams Yindi," he said. "I come from Tanzania. My ministry is in need. Will you help me?"

"Please Interview This Man"

We typically vet ministries in advance, so we were not inclined to respond to this type of cold call. However, Lucille Lebeau was impressed by the young man. She came to me and pleaded, "Bo, please interview this man. Please, Bo, give him a chance to talk to you."

I said, "Okay, I will talk with him. Gather our team in the conference room."

After we had assembled in the conference room and prayed, I said, "Mr. Yindi, my name is Bo. You said that your background is what?"

"I was formerly a chemistry teacher."

"Oh, you say that before you became a missionary you were a chemistry teacher. Here is some chalk. Please write on that board the formula for sodium chloride."

Mr. Yindi went to the board and wrote a formula. I didn't know if what he wrote was correct. I only knew from my school days that sodium chloride is table salt. But I said, "Very good!" We all

They successfully planted ten churches, but he explained that the ministry's work had recently stalled because one of their children had died and the ministry had run out of money.

applauded him. Then I said, "Please tell us about your needs."

Brother Williams told us how he was born into a Christian family in Tanzania, but he didn't know Jesus Christ as his personal savior until an American lady missionary shared the Gospel with him. After he committed his life to Christ, Williams resigned his job as a chemistry teacher and became a local worker for World Vision. One day, God put it in his heart to start a ministry preaching the Gospel to people in remote parts of Tanzania. He resigned from World Vision and started a ministry that he called Unreached Peoples Mission. Its primary goal was to reach tribes in the bush.

Some years after launching Unreached Peoples Mission, Brother Williams met a woman named Naomi. He married her after paying her father a dowry of five cows, and the couple began planting churches. They successfully planted ten churches, but he explained that the ministry's work had recently stalled because one of their children had died and the ministry had run out of money.

"We Are Going to Help You"

As Mr. Yindi shared his story, the Lord made my heart tender toward him. After he had finished, I said, "We are going to help you." One of the first things we did was send a container of goods from ANM's Warehouse for the Nations. As I mentioned in an earlier chapter, this enabled them to start Saint Augustine School, which today has 250 students. Subsequently, we sent additional containers and helped in other ways.

In 2018, Marlou and I visited Brother Williams, who today is respectfully called Bishop Yindi. I preached at his church, and when we knelt to pray, I noticed that our knees were on rough concrete.

The members of the church had wanted to finish the floor, but they could not afford tiles. I also learned that due to lack of funds, the engine in the truck they used to bring corn and other products to market during harvest season and the sunflower press they used to make oil from sunflower seeds were both broken.

When we returned to the US, I requested help for Bishop Yindi from several friends. Thanks to their generosity, we were able to send him sufficient funds to buy a new engine for his truck and fix his sunflower oil press, plus $6,000 to tile his church. Bishop Yindi is a dynamic brother in Christ. By the grace of God, and with containers and other help from ANM, Unreached Peoples Mission has planted more than 250 churches!

"How Did You Know We Needed $25,000?"
—Indah, Wira, and Seti's Radio Ministry in Indonesia

In the early years of ANM, Marlou and I learned about a Christian radio ministry that operated out of a home on the island of Java in Indonesia. One of the densest populations in the world, approximately 90 percent of the island's 150 million inhabitants are Muslim. The ministry had been started many years before when Indah, a nurse who had converted from Islam to Christianity, married a Christian pastor who taught at a local Bible school. The pastor had a burden to broadcast the Gospel to the people of Indonesia, so the couple set up a makeshift radio studio in a garage they rented from a neighbor.

God gave Indah and her husband a son, whom they named Wira. Years later, when the husband unexpectedly died, Indah and Wira decided to carry on the ministry together. Wira married a Christian woman named Seti, and she also pitched in. Radical Muslims in the community tried to get the government to close the station, but grandfathering regulations protected it.

When Marlou and I visited this radio ministry, our hearts were broken by what we saw. The station's antiquated equipment was stuffed into one room of the house. The station's power was so low that its broadcasts reached only a few thousand people. Termites had eaten

"We are all rejoicing!" she said. "How did you know we needed $25,000? We only asked for $12,000." I replied that God knew the amount she needed.

away at the house so that half of it was crumbling. Meanwhile, Indah was very ill, and she slept on a folding cot in the hallway. I cried out, "Lord, these are your servants, and they need help. Please help them, Lord!" At this moment, I felt God impress on my heart, "That is why I led you here."

When we got back to the US, I found friends who had compassion for Indah. They began supporting her, and she was able to better maintain the radio station. She also was able to buy medicines and got well. When we visited her again a few years later, she looked like a different person.

Increased Impact and Conflict

As the ministry's impact increased, radical Muslims sent groups to destroy the house and the radio studio. But a group of Muslims in the community gathered around the house to protect it. Even though they were not Christians, they loved the station's music, the practical information its programs provided, and the talk about the goodness of God. In fact, the station was so popular that listeners, most of whom are Muslim, would come together every year to celebrate the anniversary of its first broadcast.

Around the end of 2021, I received an urgent email from Indah:

The government will close our station in two months if we do not update our transmitter! Would you please help us?

I wrote and asked her how much she needed. She replied that a new transmitter would cost $12,000. She didn't tell me about their total need because she felt that would be too much to ask.

I was able to raise $25,000 and send it to Indah in time to save the station. She immediately sent an email that said, "We are all rejoicing! But how did you know we needed $25,000? We only asked for $12,000." I replied that God knew the amount she needed.

Indah, Wira, and Seti used the money to purchase a new transmitter and antenna, modernize the station's streaming system, and make other improvements that increased the station's broadcasting radius from twenty to thirty kilometers to more than one hundred kilometers. The station now reaches approximately forty-seven million prospective listeners, about 90 percent of whom are Muslim.

"Lord, Give Me the Hardest Mission Field."
—Narayan Paul of India

When Narayan Paul became a Christian as a young man in India, even his own family persecuted him. He left his parents' home and went to Calcutta to live with his brother. When he arrived, he learned that his brother was sick. Hindu rituals had been unable to heal him, but when Narayan prayed for him, he recovered. Narayan's brother became his first convert.

After gaining an education in business, Narayan went to work for Hindustan Motors, a large automobile company based in Calcutta. With a successful career and a wonderful marriage to a Christian woman named Gracie, he seemed to have everything a young man could want. But God had something more fulfilling planned for him. He put in Narayan's heart a strong desire to preach the Gospel.

Narayan prayed, "Lord, if I am going to serve you, I ask that you give me the hardest mission field." God granted Narayan's request by directing him to the primitive Saura tribe in the mountainous border states of Odisha and Andhra Pradesh. The Saura were illiterate, animistic people, many of whom practiced animal sacrifice and were addicted to alcohol.

To reach the various villages, Narayan and Gracie had to traverse rugged mountain ranges with peaks four thousand feet high. They had four children, so they hired a man to carry their two youngest children in a basket. Diarrhea and other maladies constantly plagued them, and more than once, they had to flee for their lives when tribesmen chased them with machetes or shot at them with arrows. Narayan twice broke both hands in hillside falls.

Twelve Years without One Convert

For twelve years, Narayan and Gracie labored without one convert. Finally, after hearing the Gospel numerous times, the man who carried their children put his trust in Jesus. However, Narayan and Gracie still had little success in the villages because the inhabitants distrusted strangers.

One day, as he watched how a mother cow protected her calf by following it, Narayan said to Gracie, "Maybe if I minister to the children in the villages, the parents will follow the children and listen to me." He made some crude castanets by stringing flattened bottle caps together with wire. Then he stood at the edge of a village and jingled his castanets while singing Christian songs and dancing. This attracted the children in the villages, and just as he had hoped, the parents followed their children. Some of these parents invited him inside their huts, and he was able to share the Gospel.

Over time, hundreds of members of this tribe became Christians, and Brother Narayan became known as the Gospel man. In this tribe's language, the word for "Gospel man" is "Paul." That is how he came to be known as Narayan Paul.

Narayan and Gracie noticed that many children became orphans when their parents died of malaria, HIV/AIDS, and other diseases, so they built Mercy Children's Home to house and nurture twenty-two little ones. ANM later furnished boundary walls and cots for this home to protect the children from snakes and other animals. Today, when preachers of the Gospel visit any of these villages, the believers in the village honor them by asking them to take off their shoes. Then they wash their feet. Because of the evangelizing work of Narayan Paul and the esteem with which they regard him, this is the way they welcome ministers of the Gospel.

A Deadly Disease

The big danger on this mission field today is cerebral malaria. When a mosquito carrying this disease bites a person, deadly parasites are transmitted straight to the brain. Death is virtually certain if the disease is not properly treated within seventy-two hours. Out of necessity, Narayan began practicing medicine. He bought syringes and penicillin, and he inoculated children to protect them from malaria. His only son, Timothy, and Timothy's wife, Lydia, helped with the ministry.

Tragedy struck when the first daughter of Narayan and Gracie, Mercy, died from this disease only twenty days after her wedding. Next, Timothy and Lydia's two-year-old daughter, Dawn, was bitten. She died in Narayan's arms. Narayan pleaded, "Brother Bo, I know this would be a big project, but would you please, please build me a hospital? Please, just a small one."

Marlou and I spearheaded a drive to raise money for a fifteen-bed hospital. Brother Narayan came to the US and stayed in our home. I drove him around to churches to gain support. His favorite lunch was a fish sandwich at Burger King. He loved those fish sandwiches, and I loved this man! He was like an uncle to me. I called him Uncle Paul, and he called me Brother Bo.

With perseverance, we raised enough money for the construction of the hospital. Narayan went back to India and had it built. Bethany Hospital opened in 2003. It was equipped for surgeries, X-ray, ECG, QBC (for early diagnosis of malaria), and ambulance service. Narayan's next oldest daughter, Sharon, who was a nurse, became the hospital administrator. But in 2006, she also died of cerebral malaria, and the hospital was converted to a clinic for minor illnesses and cataract surgeries.

In 2008, Narayan also died of cerebral malaria. Realizing that one day someone might sell the hospital, the family buried Narayan on the hospital grounds so the land would be preserved. Sometime before his father died, Timothy started his own ministry. By this time, his ministry had grown to more than three hundred churches. Timothy took care of his father's sixty churches by assimilating them into his ministry.

"Let Me Tell You How You Can Find Jesus."
—Prem Pradhan of Nepal

The guard opened the cell door and waved his flashlight around. "I don't see any Jesus in here," he said.

Between 1960 and 1975, Prem Pradhan spent ten years in fourteen different prisons. His crime? He was guilty of sharing the Gospel in his native land of Nepal, which at that time was the world's only Hindu kingdom.

In one of the first prisons, when Prem began telling other prisoners about Jesus, guards threw him into a cubicle where the bodies of dead prisoners were kept until relatives came to claim them. Prem's hands and feet were in chains, and lice ate away his underwear. Undeterred, Prem closed his eyes and prayed aloud. In his mind, he could see the pages of the Nepali New Testament, which he had read fourteen times.

"Who are you talking to?" the guard asked.

"Jesus," Prem answered.

The guard opened the cell door and waved his flashlight around. "I don't see any Jesus in here," he said.

"You won't find him that way," Prem said. "Let me tell you how you can find Jesus." Prem led the guard to faith in Christ, and the guard used his influence to have Prem returned to normal dungeon confinement. But when the authorities noticed that Prem was again witnessing to the other inmates in his cell, they transferred him to a different prison. Prem kept right on witnessing, and the authorities kept right on transferring him. This is how he passed through fourteen different prisons. When the prisoners who came to faith in Christ through Prem's ministry were released from prison, they carried the Gospel to the far corners of this Himalayan country faster than Prem ever could have done as a free man.

After his release, realizing the need to educate Nepali mountain children, Prem began a school in Lazimpar, a section of Kathmandu. The three-story building that he constructed happened to be on land next to the backyard of the king's palace. In 1972, police raided the school and beat the teachers, killing one. Prem was given a sentence of twenty thousand days (about fifty-four years).

A Tribute to Prem

In one of his articles, John Lindner wrote the following tribute to Prem:

Prem's sentence was for 20,000 days—54 years. Bob Finley, the president of Christian Aid, learned about it and visited him in prison in 1973. Later, Prem learned that he could be released if he paid a ransom of 20,000 rupees (one rupee for each day of his sentence). This was at the time the equivalent in U.S. currency of about $2,000. He wrote a letter to Bob Finley asking for help. To get it past the guards, he pinned it to the inside of the dress of a tiny tot who was visiting her mother, who was confined in the same prison.

The girl was small enough to slip between the bars, and the message was relayed to Bob Finley. Bob shared it with a group of believers in Harrisburg, Pennsylvania, and they raised the required ransom. The $2,000 was smuggled into Nepal by two teenage girls and brought to the prison. After the ransom was paid, Prem was released.

In 1980, Prem began another school—this time on his farm in Sarlahi District, a day's journey by bus from Kathmandu. Christian Aid backed the enterprise, and he reserved for me the honor of laying the first brick. By 1984, one thousand pupils were enrolled in New Life School. Most walk miles from the surrounding areas and stay in boys' and girls' hostels built by funds provided by Christian Aid.

In 1986, the king of Nepal awarded Prem the Social Service Medal of Honor for his humanitarian and educational work—perhaps as an act of atonement for the 1972 persecution. Today, Prem's body lies in a grave at the entrance to New Life School, a silent witness to the resurrection in this Hindu kingdom. His spirit, however, is with the Savior he loved and served.

Five years after ANM was launched, we had the honor of hosting Prem Pradhan in the United States. He needed to visit his friends and supporters, so in January 1998, despite a painful left knee, I drove him to meetings in Louisiana, Tennessee, and Alabama. His supporters respected and adored him.

But the harshness of life had taken a toll. After a meeting at one of the places we visited, Prem complained of chest pains, and I had to take him to the hospital. The doctors prescribed bed rest, and I held his hand throughout the night while he slept. The following day, we were able to drive back to ANM in Charlottesville. After more US travel and meetings, Prem went back to Nepal. In November of that year, he went home to glory.

"I Heard from the Lord!"
—Alex and Eunice Malanday of the Philippines

By the second year of ANM's ministry, numerous people had begun giving to Marlou and me for our family support. Carl Gordon came to me one day and said, "Approximately $5,000 that has been given to your family is just sitting in the bank. You should withdraw it and use it for your family's needs."

"No, just let it stay there," I told him. I didn't tell this to Carl, but I was keeping that money in reserve. It was my plan B safety valve. If ANM didn't survive, I planned to use it to buy plane tickets to fly our family back to the Philippines.

Not long after that, God gently woke me at 3:00 a.m. and reminded me about that $5,000. I got out of bed and sat on the stairway of the second floor of our small apartment. "Lord, is this you? Do you really want me to give this $5,000 away?"

I clearly felt the Lord answer yes, so I sat down at our kitchen table in the early morning hours and wrote down the names of about eight ministries around the world where fifty dollars a month for one year would be a good investment. One of these eight ministries was Reaching Parents Through Children Ministry, or RPCM. (Today it is called Church Builders Ministries.) It was operated by Alex and Eunice Malanday in the Philippines.

Alex had invited Jesus into his heart when he was eleven years old. In high school, he had vowed to serve God full time. His wife, Eunice, had grown up in a Christian family that walked approximately three miles to church every Sunday. After an eleven-year courtship, Alex and Eunice married in 1984.

Alex and Eunice lived and worked on the small island of Guimaras, which lies between the larger islands of Panay and Negros. It can be reached only by boat and is very poor, yet it is home to one of the world's sweetest varieties of mango. The couple embarked on an ambitious vision of operating kindergarten schools to teach God's Word to children and their parents. They taught children under the trees and at bus stops.

Alex and Eunice received only modest contributions from the parents of the children they served. To provide extra funds for the operation of the ministry, they sold plastic sachets of cocoa powder door to door. This did not provide sufficient income, however, so Alex decided to take a full time job with a company that sold coffins. Knowing that this could bring an end to their ministry, Eunice said to him, "Before you accept that job, why don't you ask your boss upstairs?" Alex agreed to wait and pray for two weeks for God's guidance.

During this two-week period of prayer, Alex received a letter from me. It contained a check for fifty dollars. "Eunice, I heard from the

Lord!" he shouted, jumping up and down. "I heard from the Lord! I will continue to work with our ministry."

Alex forgot about the job selling coffins, and the couple continued their ministry work. Today, they have seven kindergarten schools, six of which function as churches on Sundays. Through Church Builders Ministries, many families have come to faith in Christ. The entire community has benefited.

"Jacob Was a Missionary!"
 —Jacob Hall of Iowa

In Ottumwa, Iowa, on Friday, July 23, 1999, eleven-year-old Jacob Hall tragically lost his life in a go-cart accident. Local citizens knew Jacob as a dedicated Christian who had a heart for the less fortunate and cared about where people would spend eternity. A paper he had written for a school English class included the following notation:

> *Jacob Andrew Hall . . . wants to make the world better . . . plans to be a missionary . . . final destination is Heaven.*

The church that the Halls attended, Ottumwa Community Church, had adopted me as their first missionary in 1989. As a supporter of ANM since 1992, the congregation had hosted missions conferences, gone on mission trips, and opened their homes to ANM staff members and missionaries.

Richard and Debbie suggested that people donate to missions instead of buying flowers, and after the service, the couple asked me for advice about where the money should go. Oliver Asher and I sensed after prayer that the money should go to Church Builders Ministries. The Malandays were deeply moved by this generous gift, which they used to build the Jacob Hall Training Center.

As additional gifts poured in, the Halls established Jacob's Gift. ANM helped by suggesting international children's ministries run by native missionaries that could benefit from the foundation's gifts. Richard said, "These dedicated men and women of God were now partners with our son. Jacob was a missionary!"

Years later, the Halls were able to visit Church Builders Ministries and see the schools that Jacob's Gift had helped to start and maintain in the Philippines. They were thrilled to see how parents were hearing the Word of God with their children and accepting Jesus as Savior, just as they had done with Jacob as a child.

Over the past twenty years, Jacob's Gift has been used by God to help bless thousands around the world. In rural Kenya, for example, funds from the foundation have been used by an African ministry to build a library and a birth center. They also have enabled this ministry to hire a university graduate who teaches Bible classes at five elementary schools every week. Often on Saturdays, more than 150 children show up to sit in the fifty available seats.

"If Jacob *saw someone without shoes, he wanted to make sure they got some. At a young age, he seemed concerned for others' welfare and where they would spend eternity."*

The leader of this Kenyan ministry told the Halls, "One of the boys who came to the library was the first in the community to qualify for college. He grew up in poverty, and at age fifteen, his father and mother died. He raised his three younger siblings, regularly walking with them to the library to study. Because of the tutoring and support he received at the school, he not only qualified to go to college, but he was also trained in children's ministry."

Jacob is truly one of ANM's heroes. His picture hangs with the photographs of other outstanding missionaries on the walls of the ministry's headquarters.

From Bricks to Living Stones
—Bako and Nelelum of Chad[22]

Bako was born in Chad, a very poor country in the heart of Africa. When he was two, his father was poisoned because he would not comply with the pagan tribal practices. Then his mother died, and his grandmother took custody of the child and raised him. Christianity had come to their country only a few generations earlier, and she was one of the first Christians in her village. Bako embraced Christ in a village Sunday school class. As a believer, this sickly orphaned boy in the neglected country of Chad trusted in the promise of Psalm 27:10: "When my father and my mother forsake me, Then the LORD will take care of me."

That was more than forty years ago. Bako not only survived the harsh climate and desperate conditions of his country, he has gone on to become a beloved pastor and a leader in mobilizing the churches of his country to reach their nation with the Good News of Christ. Wheaton College honored Bako's efforts in December 2000 by awarding him a Billy Graham Scholarship, which enabled him to earn a Master of Missions degree. He also has earned a Master of Theology degree from Bangui Evangelical Graduate School of Theology in the Central African Republic, and in June 2021, he earned a PhD from UNISA, the largest university in South Africa.

After returning to Africa from Wheaton, Illinois, Bako extended the Macedonian call to Christians in the US to "come over and help us." So, in 2004, Advancing Native Missions began to partner with this gifted pastor in his multi-faceted ministry in Chad. ANM realizes the strategic nature of Bako's ministry. If Islam permeates Chad, it has a base from which to penetrate sub-Saharan Africa.

---

[22] This article was a combined effort of Jackie Howard, ANM advocate for Bako's ministry; Gary Darcus, former ANM Desk Director for Africa; and John Lindner, editor.

Caring for Orphans

Pastor Bako is deeply burdened by the plight of the half-million orphans in his country. One in twenty children in Chad are orphans. Bako passionately desires to pass on to some of them the same Good News that gave him hope as an orphan. He wants to raise them up to be warriors for the Lord and reach Chad for Christ.

Bako and his lovely wife, Nelelum, rejoiced when their first child was born. They named her Altonodji, which means "the orphan needs your love." Her name represented their life's calling to care for the orphans in their land. One night after an evangelistic meeting, Bako arrived home to find his six-year-old daughter very sick. He had no means of transportation, not even a bicycle, and because it was already late in the night, he put his precious Altonodji on his back and ran all the way to the hospital, which was very far from their home. Altonodji didn't make it, which broke Bako and Nelelum's hearts.

Nevertheless, Pastor Bako's vision remained steadfast. It became a reality in 2006 when ANM and some other organizations partnered with him to build an orphan village in his home area of Moundou in southern Chad. This partnership helped turn a pile of bricks on a scrubby, forsaken piece of donated land into a home for 123 orphan children, cared for by ten godly widows and other support staff.

The property also boasts a chapel, a health clinic, and a Christian school for the orphans and children from the surrounding area. The computer-equipped school offers an excellent education to children from various tribal backgrounds. It teaches them the ways of Christ and how to live in harmony with one another. Pastor Bako knows that some of these children may well become the future leaders of Chad. What a blessing it will be if Chad's future leaders love Jesus!

Bako and Nelelum named this facility Village Altonodji, in honor of their daughter. It is a wonderful place for children to be loved and cared for and has caught the attention of people throughout Chad. Government officials and others consider it a national treasure because it welcomes children from all tribes. God has even granted

Pastor Bako favor in the eyes of Muslim leaders who have observed his sacrificial love and care for orphans caught in Chad's orphan crisis.

One of the most recent newcomers to Village Altonodji is a precious Muslim girl who was found on the streets by government officials. When her parents died, extended family members gained custody of her. They severely abused her and even bound her in chains. She managed to escape, and after authorities investigated her background, they asked Pastor Bako to care for her. This little girl is now recovering from her trauma as she drinks in the love and care that the village workers offer to her in the name of Christ.

Producing Its Own Income

ANM has found a number of friends for Bako, especially through the fervent advocacy of Dr. Wes and Jackie Howard, ANM volunteers who are former missionaries to Africa. But while Pastor Bako needs and appreciates help from Western partners, he also has instituted measures to help Village Altonodji produce some of its own income. A bakery supplies bread for the orphans, and the surplus is sold to the villagers. A fund for microloans for projects, such as sewing and carpentry, has been established, and agricultural projects are being launched as funding is provided.

When Brother Bako came to the US, I recommended he be the main speaker at a big church missions banquet. He is one of the brightest minds to come out of Chad, and he's also one of the gentlest and humblest persons one could meet. This gentle humility tends to cause him to speak softly. The pastor of the church, a close friend of mine, interviewed Bako, and he counseled me to help him enliven his presentation. I spent several hours with Bako giving him pointers on public speaking. I even suggested to him an opening for his talks.

It is wonderful to see how audiences sit up with attention when Bako fervently opens his talks by saying, "My name is Bako. I am an orphan coming from an orphan country with a ministry of helping and loving orphans." As anyone who knows him can attest, these words come from his heart.

Mobilizing Churches

In addition to overseeing the orphan village and pastoring a large church in Mondou, Bako actively seeks to mobilize churches to bring the message of Christ to their countrymen. Islam controls the government, businesses, and military. Poverty, disease, political instability, and corruption abound, leaving a devastated and oppressed population with high unemployment and a disproportionate number of orphaned children and widows. Islam gains allegiances by providing food and education funded by Middle Eastern oil production. Mosques are being erected everywhere to make Islam appear more dominant than it is.

Proclaiming Christ in that environment is challenging. To spread the light and hope of Christ, Bako encourages churches to share the Gospel house to house in the surrounding villages during the Christmas season. He also utilizes the chapel at the village to train Chadians to reach their own people for Christ. When they are trained, Bako sends these ambassadors for Christ out into the field as funds are provided.

Pastor Bako is another committed indigenous missionary who is obeying the injunction of Proverbs 31:8–9:

> *Open your mouth for the speechless,*
> *In the cause of all who are appointed to die.*
> *Open your mouth, judge righteously,*
> *And plead the cause of the poor and needy.*

PHILIPPIANS 3:10-11

I want to know Christ—yes, to know the power
of his resurrection and participation in his sufferings,
becoming like him in his death, and so, somehow,
attaining to the resurrection from the dead.

ENCOURAGING AND EQUIPPING HEROES IN THE MISSION FIELD— PART II

ANM formed new and lasting relationships with many mission partners around the globe. As of this writing, we have almost 300 native ministry partners comprising more than 13,500 missionaries. They are engaging with almost 1,500 unreached people groups in 112 countries, and they have planted or helped to plant more than forty thousand churches.

No one book would be large enough to contain all the remarkable stories of these missionaries. These mission partners who are so successfully advancing Christ's kingdom under difficult circumstances are the real heroes of this book. For this reason, I consider this chapter and the previous one to be the most important parts of my story. In the remaining pages of this chapter, I will share just a few more stories about some of the missionaries I have interacted with personally, with sincere apologies to those I am unable to include.

"Thank You for Having Believed in Us!"
—Helman and Rosalba Ocampo of Colombia

Missionaries Helman and Rosalba Ocampo are especially dear to Marlou and me. The fruitfulness of their ministry among the indigenous tribes in the jungles and remote places in Colombia has come at great cost. In the face of severe difficulties, danger, and even loss of life, they have persevered with courage. ANM has partnered with the Ocampos since 1994. We have had them as

"I see you are very religious, but you are missing one thing—Jesus Christ himself."

the guests of ANM in the US numerous times, and the many ANM friends to whom we have introduced them have been deeply touched by their powerful testimonies.

Helman Ocampo was one of twelve children born to poor parents in a rural region of Colombia. Half his siblings died at young ages due to poverty, and Helman was sent at age five to live with his aunt. Each day, he would trek barefoot for an hour into town to beg for food for the household. When he began attending school at age seven, the other kids made fun of his dirty, patched clothes and the brown sugar-water he brought for lunch.

At age eleven, Helman quit school and began working as a lumberjack. Later, he became a laborer for meager wages in the rice fields, where the water so saturated his hands and feet that for the rest of his life he had fungus under the nails of his fingers and toes.

When Helman was eighteen, he met a missionary who said, "I see you are very religious, but you are missing one thing—Jesus Christ himself." Helman fell on his knees and accepted Jesus. For the first time in his life, he felt loved.

An American offered to send Helman to seminary, but he had only completed one year of primary school. Determined to be a preacher of the Word, Helman completed his primary schooling in just three months. He then began studying at the seminary during the day, while earning his high school degree in the evenings. Helman had no spending money, so he washed and re-washed the same three shirts and trousers. His ragged shoes were tied together with wire. For school materials, he retrieved pencil stubs and used paper from the trash.

Upon receiving his high school diploma and seminary degree at age twenty-four, Helman began pastoring a church. In 1980, when he was twenty-six, he met and married a young woman named Rosalba. For the next eight years, they ministered to the indigenous tribes of Colombia, which were almost totally neglected by other Christian missions. They also founded a school to train missionaries to reach them. They called their ministry Crisalinco, an acronym of the Spanish for Christ to the unreached tribes.

Called by God

In 1990, Helman felt God calling him to also take Bibles and the Good News to the drug barons, armed guerrillas, and right-wing paramilitary forces. The work was dangerous, and some of his co-workers were kidnapped and held as hostages for ransom. A few were even brutally murdered. Helman himself was taken captive several times. To date, he has buried more than forty pastors.

The national churches of Colombia had no interest in supporting Crisalinco's work, so in 1993, the couple began working part-time jobs in Bogotá to support their ministry. With what they saved, they ventured into the rainforest for two or three months at a time with few supplies, traveling down dangerous rivers without lifejackets for themselves or their two small daughters. Often, they didn't have proper clothing to protect them from the heat and cold, and the rains came in at night through the holes in their tent.

The love God had placed in their hearts for the unreached gave them strength to carry on, and Christ's power was made perfect in their weakness. "We saw that the need was great in every place, and our hearts clung to this," Helman says. "We felt that we couldn't give up, but sometimes, that was exactly what we felt like doing."

But dividing their time between earning a living in Bogotá and ministering in the remote regions stretched them to the breaking point. They earnestly laid before the throne of grace a petition that had been on their hearts since the beginning of their ministry: "Lord, could you please send someone to come beside us in this ministry, someone who will partner with us in prayer and finances to help us accomplish the work you have called us to do?"

Around this time, I happened to read an article about Helman in *Charisma* magazine, and I asked Graham Stewart and Danny McAllister to travel to Colombia and check him out. They went and were impressed with what they saw; a new and lasting relationship was quickly formed. With financial and prayer support from ANM, the ministry of Crisalinco began to expand and thrive.

Persevering Through Trials

One day, we received a distress call at the ANM office from Rosalba. "Helman is not at home," she explained, "and I just discovered a note. I will read it to you. It says, 'Our commandos are following your steps. You must bring us ten thousand US dollars—alone. If you do not do exactly as we say, your wife, family, home, and workplace will be subject to punishment.'"

Before the guerrillas could capture Helman, we were able to evacuate the Ocampo family to South Florida, where Helman ministered among Hispanics for a while. But after a few months of praying and fasting, he responded to the Lord's call to return to the same dangerous regions of Colombia.

Despite the dangers, Helman, Rosalba, and their daring missionary co-workers have been used by God to plant 150 churches among thirteen of Colombia's eighty tribes. The training school they operate has commissioned twenty-seven missionaries and eighty-two tribal pastors. Their workers have translated the Bible into twenty-seven of the estimated seventy languages spoken in Colombia, and a refugee center they operate keeps approximately one hundred children safe from guerrilla kidnappings, while providing comfort and aid to widows and their children.

In the midst of ongoing trials, Helman, Rosalba, and their co-workers are continuing to work among the tribes and distribute Bibles to all people, including drug producers, drug traffickers, armed guerillas, and paramilitary forces. "God has sustained us," Helman testifies. "With ANM's help, the ministry has grown. Our brothers and sisters at ANM continue to help us. Their commitment is real: spiritually, emotionally, and financially."

A Visit to Colombia

In 2015, I was able to visit Helman and Rosalba in Villavicencio, Colombia. On December 13, 2021, Marlou and I were honored to receive the email below from Rosalba on behalf of Helman and the family[23]:

Pastor Bo, good morning and blessings from the Lord,

I just want to tell you "Thank you!" for having believed in us, an unknown ministry. Helman, my daughters, and I always remember you with deep sentiment and gratitude. Be sure that [what] you have sown together with your wife and your team have borne fruit in this beautiful country, that in the jungles and mountains of Colombia there are men and women that praise the Lord through your sowing it. No doubt that there will be a reward for your wife and you, it is great in the Kingdom of God.

Receive a big hug and may the Lord continue to be your refuge and your strength each day.

Rosalba

Faithful Servants in a Closed Country
—"Renaldo" and "Anita"

In the thirty-six years that my family and I have been privileged to serve the Lord as missionaries, there have been many rejoicings. There also have been many pains, such as when we left Marlou's widowed mother in the Philippines and came to the United States with few possessions. It was very painful, especially for Marlou, when her mother died while we were ten thousand miles away.

But there are other pains that we also suffer. As we pray for and help provide for missionaries who make severe sacrifices, endure torture, and even lay down their lives for the Gospel, we suffer with them. In this way, all believers participate in the sufferings of Christ (Philippians 3:10).

---

[23] The original Spanish was translated by our Latin America department.

I will now tell you a story about the sufferings endured by one missionary and his wife. We will call the man Renaldo, and we will call his wife Anita. I am not going to share their real names because this is a communist country and closed to the Gospel. Most Christian work must be done underground.

This young man was very bright, one of the brightest in his nation. The government made him a scholar and sent him to another communist country to be educated for government service. But when he came back home, he somehow heard the Gospel and received Jesus Christ into his heart. Instead of using his mind for communist purposes, he proclaimed the Gospel of the Lord Jesus. He was highly effective at bringing people to faith in the Lord Jesus because he was much respected and loved in his region. In due time, he planted twenty churches.

The authorities warned him to stop his activities, but when somebody knows God, he has no fear. This man continued telling people about Christ, until one day, he did not return home. Witnesses reported that a truckload of people had been following him while he was driving his motorcycle.

After several days, the body of this evangelist was found. He had been stabbed several times in the chest and back. A rock with blood on it that had been used to bash his head was found nearby. His head had been turned totally around, and a message had been hung on his neck that read, "This is what will happen to anyone else who would believe."

"I Will Take His Place"

The people in the region were so scared that they trembled. But his wife, Anita, did not tremble. Instead of cowering in fear, she said, "I will take his place. I will take my husband's place."

Other family members questioned her. "You will take your husband's place? You have young children to care for. What will happen to them if you are killed? You are crazy!"

"No, I will take his place," she insisted.

Sister Anita was an educated teacher. She went to the Christian leaders in her area and said, "Train me. Disciple me." They complied, and after she was trained, she worked day and night sharing the Gospel. Hostile elements threatened her, but she said, "Kill me anytime you want. I'm going to continue."

This faithful widow taught the women in the surrounding villages how to prepare delicious food they could sell in the streets or at fairs. The wives who came to her classes would bring their children, and many members of the families would become Christians.

ANM was already helping the larger ministry with which Sister Anita served, and in 2019, Marlou and I had an opportunity to personally visit with this courageous widow. When we asked her how we could help, she said, "Brother Bo and Sister Marlou, could you build for me a simple structure near my house? It just needs a roof. The sides can be open. But make it large so we can have our ladies' cooking seminars under it."

By God's grace, some of our friends were able to provide the finances she needed to build the shelter. Hundreds have come to faith in Christ through the cooking lessons and seminars Sister Anita has given in it. Since she began proclaiming the Good News, she and her courageous team have planted more than sixty churches.

"Brother Bo, Please Pray for Me!" *—A Brave Missionary in a Hostile Field*

Pratam was a professor in a big university in a country dominated by a very oppressive religion. When he was told one day to study the Scriptures so he could show others they were untrue, he embarked on this assignment with gusto. But when he came to John 14:6, which records Jesus as saying, "I am the way, the truth, and the life," he asked himself, "Why does Jesus say he is the only way to God?" He could not get these words out of his mind.

One day as dawn was breaking, the truth broke through to Pratam's heart. He realized that Jesus is the only way to eternal life. He immediately asked Jesus to come into his heart. Thrilled with excitement, he longed to share this Good News with everyone on the streets, but he knew this would be too dangerous, so he went to the home of his best friend.

When Pratam told his best friend that he had become a Christian, his friend said, "You what? You changed your religion? Go away! I won't even touch you, and I won't let you touch me. You are unclean!"

He knocked on the door, excitedly thinking about how the person was going to enjoy reading about Jesus. But when the door opened, instead of being welcomed, he was ambushed by an angry mob.

Pratam was surprised and hurt. But that was only the beginning of the harassment and persecution. His best friend was a popular radio commentator in their area, and he announced on the air that his professor friend had become an infidel. People began hunting for him to kill him. Pratam said to his wife, "We need to protect our five children. We will escape to a city in another part of the country and hide among the millions of people."

His wife agreed, and they retreated to a certain large city. But because they had no money, they had to live in the squatter area that had a high mortality rate because of diarrhea, cholera, and other diseases. Cholera attacked his family, and two of their children died. During this time, however, his wife also became a serious believer in the Lord Jesus.

Cholera Strikes Again

One day, Pratam went on an errand to another part of the city, and his wife, full of the love of the Lord, ventured out into the community to witness to people about Christ. The authorities arrested her for sharing an illegal religion and put her in prison. Pratam ultimately succeeded in getting her released, but while in prison, she had contracted cholera. Soon after her release, she also died, and Pratam was left to raise the remaining three children alone.

A few years later, another child died of cholera, and Pratam was left with only one son and one daughter. When the daughter reached the age of fourteen, she also became a believer. A few years later, with her father's permission, she enrolled in a missionary training center. Upon completion of her studies, she said to her Christian leaders, "Send me to an island to reach the most fanatical people entrapped by the oppressive religion." They allowed her to go to a remote island that was very dangerous.

Meanwhile, as Pratam continued to minister in the large city, he heard about an underground Bible translation project. He joined the translation team, and after he had finished translating several chapters of the Bible, he had copies printed and began giving them away. The people who received his printed Scriptures said to him, "Thank you! Thank you! Thank you!"

Martyred for Christ

One day, Pratam received news that while his daughter was witnessing for Jesus Christ on that remote island, five young men had ganged up on her and stabbed her dozens of times, killing her. Pratam was so distraught that he almost went crazy. He didn't even have the strength to go to the island to retrieve his daughter's body. Day after day, he wailed and cried out to God, "What have I done? What have I done? What have I done?" He felt so helpless and remorseful about not being there for his daughter.

After two or three weeks, a family took pity on Pratam and gave him money. He immediately went to the island by boat and was relieved to find that some people had buried his daughter. He went to his knees and cried, "Please forgive me, Lord! Please forgive me!"

After Pratam returned home, he resumed his ministry of delivering printed translations of chapters of the Bible. One day, this faithful servant of God went to a home to deliver a copy of his translation to a person he didn't know. He knocked on the door, excitedly thinking about how the person was going to enjoy reading about Jesus. But when the door opened, instead of being welcomed, he was ambushed by an angry mob. They rushed at him and began to maul him.

While he was being pummeled, Pratam prayed, "Lord Jesus, to you I commit my spirit!" At that moment, some concerned people intervened. They called the police, and Pratam was taken to the hospital. Thankfully, God spared his life, but he was still in danger because these fanatics would be looking for him.

Pratam moved to another place that was extremely remote. He rented a house for the equivalent of twenty dollars a month, and he continued serving the Lord by witnessing to the people who worked on the surrounding plantations. God blessed his ministry, and many people, including the owner of the house he rented, received Christ. This country is divided into hundreds of people groups, and the tribe he was ministering to was composed of the most unreached people in the nation. Many of these converts felt they needed to keep their new faith secret, so he started an underground church.

When I heard Pratam's life story, I was deeply touched, and I suggested to Marlou that we should go and visit this hero of the faith. "Visit Pratam?" she said. "That would put us and him in danger."

"I'll talk to him first," I promised. When I contacted Pratam, he recommended a safe place to meet, and Marlou and I traveled there. From a safety standpoint, it was helpful that travelers wear masks as a precautionary measure against catching air-borne diseases.

A Meeting with Pratam

When we met Pratam, Marlou and I were brokenhearted. His teeth had all rotted from years of extreme poverty; one would have never imagined that he was once a dignified professor. I said, "Brother, we will take you to the mall so you can pick out what you need." We took Pratam to a department store, and he chose two pairs of trousers, a few shirts, and a pair of shoes. What an honor it was to buy a pair of shoes for this man of God!

After we had purchased these things, I said to Pratam, "Why don't you pick out a watch?"

"A watch?" he asked.

"Yes, pick out a watch."

Pratam was so happy to get that watch! Then he told us he had one special request. He wanted a smartphone. We were delighted to purchase this for him, also.

Back at the hotel, Pratam became overtaken with emotion. He couldn't get over how Marlou and I had come all the way from America to see him. He hugged me, and while doing so, he took my right hand and put it on top of his head. In his own language (which Marlou and I understood through an interpreter), he said, "Brother Bo, please pray for me."

I had the privilege of praying for this great man. Afterwards, we also sent him about $1,500 so he could buy the small house he was renting. This allowed Pratam more freedom to use the house for ministry. It also was a blessing to the new believers who owned the house because they needed the money. Today, this faithful servant of the Lord Jesus is persevering to the end, as he brings disciples to his home for underground training.

Learning English through the Bible
—Khan Khon of Cambodia

Between 2014 and 2018, I took several trips to Southeast Asia, almost always accompanied by Marlou. On one trip, we went to Cambodia, where we had the pleasure of meeting for the first time a bright and dynamic missionary leader by the name of Khan Khon, or Sokhon for short.

Sokhon was born into a Buddhist home in 1980, the sixth of eleven children. His parents lived through Cambodia's Khmer Rouge Killing Fields era, but when Sokhon was eleven, they lost their profitable business exporting rubber to Vietnam. As the debts mounted, the debt collectors converged, and the family split up. Sokhon's mother began to drink heavily, and eventually, she committed suicide.

An older sister tried to care for Sokhon, but she had no schooling or skills, so she sold her body each night while Sokhon pretended to sleep. He cried in deep compassion for his sister every time this happened, and finally, he ran away. His life went downhill fast as he began drinking, smoking, gambling, and fighting. Life seemed so hopeless that he contemplated suicide.

Sokhon felt that money would solve his problems, and to earn money as a successful business man in Cambodia, knowledge of English was essential. Even though he hated Christianity, Sokhon enrolled in an English class that used the Bible as the textbook, run by a small church started by Filipino missionaries. As Sokhon read the creation story, he was reminded of his boyhood days when he would care for the family cow. Alone in the fields, he used to wonder about who created the plants and trees. He believed in God, but he didn't know God's name.

As he studied Genesis, Sokhon learned about the one true God who created everything. In the Gospel of John and Paul's letter to the Romans, he learned that God loved him, a sinner, and that Christ died on the cross for him. He began going to church, and five months after he had enrolled in the English/Bible class, he welcomed Jesus into his life.

Called to Serve the Lord

Feeling a strong call to serve the Lord, Sokhon attended a Bible school for four years. During this time, he drew closer to a young lady named Esther who had been his classmate in the English class. After she became a believer, they married, and in succeeding years, God blessed them with three daughters.

After graduation, Sokhon started a ministry that he called Evangelical Mission Association. Putting his strategic thinking abilities to work, he developed various approaches for reaching the people of Cambodia with the Gospel. His goal was to establish churches in all twenty-five of the nation's provinces. When Marlou and I met

Sokhon, assisted by fewer than fifteen workers, he had planted a total of about twenty churches in seven provinces.

Over the next seven years, ANM advocated for Evangelical Mission Association's work and found friends for Sokhon. Today, the ministry has 115 workers and has planted almost 150 churches in numerous provinces. In addition, it operates several homes for underprivileged and destitute children. The ministry feeds and clothes them, nurtures them spiritually and in other ways, and gives them access to education.

It's a win-win for the people of the village. They get clean drinking water, and they are offered the true living water.

Sokhon's severe childhood endowed him with compassion to help vulnerable children. He and his co-workers feed no fewer than one thousand hungry children every week.

Evangelical Mission Association also initiated the Living Water Project, which installs water wells in the remote villages of Cambodia. Most of these villages have no access to clean water, so the people must collect their water from canals and ponds that are infested with waterborne diseases. This causes many deaths, especially among young children. The ministry so far has installed more than a hundred water wells in many remote villages in different provinces.

When a well is completed, the ministry holds a dedication ceremony where Sokhon shares the Gospel. The whole village turns out, and many put their faith in Christ. It's a win-win for the people of the village. They get clean drinking water, and they are offered the true living water.

In 2017, we brought Sokhon to the US as one of the missionaries for the ANM annual retreat at Wintergreen Resort. While he was here, we took him around to several churches. His youthful and transparent ways, coupled with his powerful testimony, endeared him to everyone he met.

Upholding God's Work in a Closed Country —A Missionary Called "Kham"

On our trip to Asia in 2014, Marlou and I also visited a dedicated missionary in a closed communist country. To protect his identity, we will call this man Kham. In his native country, openly sharing the Gospel is regulated, and believers can be harassed and persecuted. Kham had the good fortune to grow up in a Christian home. His father, who worked with the government while also serving as a pastor, was imprisoned more than once for sharing his faith.

Kham has a wonderful sense of humor. He told us about how his mother, when she was pregnant with Kham, suddenly needed to use the toilet. While doing so, she unexpectedly gave birth. He laughingly says, "Mother used the toilet to do number two, and I came out!"

While Kham was in high school, the communists took over. He became attracted to the ideology of communism, and when he completed high school, the government gave him an academic scholarship to study agriculture in another communist country. He became so indoctrinated while there that he wrote to his mother, "Stop believing in Jesus because the true religion is socialism." This broke his mother's heart. She and his father prayed for him every day.

Kham was in that country when a great social, cultural, and political upheaval took place. Disillusioned and confused, he didn't know what to do or even how to get home. He thought back to the faith of his childhood and prayed, "God of my father and my mother, if you are really the true God, help me go back home. If you allow me to go home, I will serve you for the rest of my life."

Coming Home

Due to a series of miraculous circumstances, Kham made it back to his home country. But instead of returning to government service as he was supposed to do as a government scholar, he went to a neighboring country and trained to be a missionary. After completing his education, he returned to his native land with the intention of finding a wife. He would say to the women he met, "I am looking for someone who will share my vision of spreading the Gospel in all the villages of our country. If you join me, this work will be difficult, our family life will be disturbed, we will be responsible for many people, and there will be much suffering. But if you are interested and not afraid, you can be my wife."

A lady named Anida, who went to the same church as Kham, told him that she shared his vision. They married, and she joined him in the ministry. As one of their first initiatives, the couple took in about twenty young people from approximately ten different tribes. They nurtured them spiritually and materially, trained them in the Gospel, and provided them with access to education. When the students were ready, Kham and Anida sent them back to their villages to become missionaries. They repeated this process a couple of times to hasten the spread of the Gospel.

When Marlou and I first met Kham and Anida, we were impressed by the size of the farm they owned. Kham shared that his dream was to have an agricultural research center on the farm to train farmers in agricultural skills. Marlou and I committed to help them. When we returned to the States, by the grace of God and through the generosity of God's people, we were able to raise enough funds for Kham to build the agricultural research and training center he had envisioned.

Visiting Kham and Anida Again

In 2019, Marlou and I had the pleasure of returning to Kham and Anida's country for the dedication of this new facility. It was wonderful to see them again and meet their own natural children, all of whom were involved in the ministry. The two-story Agricultural Research and Training Center contains a dorm room, workshop, classrooms, meeting room, dining room, and library. It can house up to fifty students. Because more than half the people in the region are farmers, agricultural education enables the school's students to provide for their families and teach farming skills to others. Students also learn other vocational skills such as construction and motorcycle repair. Most importantly, they learn the Bible.

While there, we heard about how a missionary couple who worked with Kham's ministry needed a vehicle but couldn't find one that fit within their budget. Without consulting Kham, Anida gave this couple their own four-wheel-drive vehicle. When Kham learned about what she had done, he exclaimed, "Why have you given away our only means of getting around?"

"The Lord will provide," Anida answered. When we heard the story, we advocated for Kham and Anida with Christians in the United States. Friends of ANM, especially one church in Toledo, Ohio, were generous, and we were able to send them money to buy a brand new four-wheel-drive vehicle. They can now cover more areas for the Gospel.

Kham is a marvelous leader who is making a significant impact in his country. He is a bright, strategic thinker and a very dedicated worker who is full of ideas. In early 2021, he shared with me that there was a farm for sale in the north of his country, where there was very good land for planting all kinds of crops. The property also had a water source and an existing structure. Marlou and I advocated on Kham's behalf, and the Lord blessed our efforts. The farm is now producing a bountiful harvest of agricultural crops and fish that is helpful to their work.

"Why Only Five?"
—Jeph and Apple Garcia of Thailand

While in Asia, Marlou and I also visited Jeph and Apple Garcia in Chiang Mai, in the north of Thailand. Both Jeph and Apple are from the Philippines, but they met in Thailand when they were doing missions work there. Apple is a nurse by profession. She trained herself to be a missionary, as did Jeph. After they married, they started House of Hope Thailand, which today is called Destiny Children's Home. Their ministry rescues at-risk children who are highly vulnerable to sex trafficking. Some of these children are orphaned, distressed, and abandoned. Many have parents who have been imprisoned for helping drug traffickers. Others are from poor families of the seven hill tribes who live in the surrounding mountain area.

"Please take my child with you! Please take my child with you!" Their cries have haunted Jeph ever since.

Jeph told us about how in a certain remote village he made a discreet announcement one day that Hope House was able to take in a few needy tribal children. The next morning, the place where Jeph had spent the night was over-flowing with tired parents and crying children. When told that the home could only accept five more children, the villagers wailed, "Why only five? Why only five?" As Jeph drove away with the five fortunate children, other parents ran after his vehicle pleading with tears in their eyes, "Please take my child with you! Please take my child with you!" Their cries have haunted Jeph ever since.

When Jeph and Apple first started their ministry, they rented a facility because they didn't have enough money to buy a building. But time after time, the owners of the properties they rented asked them to leave after they had been in the building for only a short while. It was impossible for the children under their care to make friends and have stability in their lives when they were being constantly moved from one place to another. Jeph and Apple began praying fervently for a permanent facility.

Meeting Jeph and Apple

When Marlou and I first met Jeph and Apple in 2014, we learned that they had found a property with several buildings on it in Doi Saket, Thailand. It seemed ideal for housing boys and girls sepa-rately, which was a requirement for their ministry. The problem was that they couldn't meet the $90,000 purchase price.

Marlou and I, along with Carl Gordon's wife, Minda, set to work to raise the needed funds. Jeph and Apple also approached their own friends, especially in Singapore. Together, we were able to raise the needed $90,000, and the couple purchased the property. Later, Marlou and I helped raise $40,000 that Jeph and Apple used to erect a dorm for girls. The seed money for this project was provided by our kindhearted and generous friends, Anne and Jonas Beiler, the original owners of Auntie Anne's Pretzels, the delicious and fragrant-smelling pretzels found in malls and airports. Jeph and Apple named the building Angela's Dorm in honor of the Beilers' daughter, Angela.

Twist of Faith

I want to depart for a moment from the story about Jeph and Apple to say a bit about Angela. When she was about nineteen months old, a tragic accident occurred. The Beilers lived on a farm in Pennsylvania, and while one of the family members was backing up a tractor, Angela was accidently run over. Anne Beiler has documented this story in a best-selling book, *Twist of Faith*. Marlou and I were so touched to be with Jeph and Apple on September 8, 2018, when Angela's Dorm was dedicated. That was the calendar date that little Angela went home to be with the Lord.

Sometime after Angela's Dorm opened, Jeph and Apple shared with us their vision to have a dorm for boys, and we committed to help them raise funds for it. In the meantime, because the number of boys they were ministering to was increasing so rapidly, the couple moved the girls into a temporary facility and allowed the boys to occupy Angela's Dorm. Of course, the name Angela wouldn't do, so they modified the sign to read Angelo's Dorm. With the help of Anne and Jonas Beiler and other friends, we raised $40,000 for the boys' dorm. It has now been completed, and the girls have moved back to their original home. Once again, the girl's facility is called Angela's Dorm.

Over the years, many children cared for by Jeph and Apple Garcia have entered professions and become valuable members of society. Most of them have witnessed on behalf of Christ to their families and tribes, and some have chosen to work with Jeph and Apple's ministry to help other children. If Destiny Children's Home did not exist, many of these kids would be homeless, vulnerable to slave traders, addicted to drugs, or engaged in prostitution.

In one of our visits to Hope House, prior to the Lord's provision of the new property, I spoke on a Sunday morning in Jeph and Apple's church. My message was about the "new thing" mentioned in Isaiah 43:18–19. Below is a thank-you letter we received from Jeph and Apple after they purchased the property:

Dear Brother Bo and Sister Marlou,

Thank you so much for having the heartbeat of our Father in reaching out to the fatherless and abandoned. Your partnership with us makes us more effective as we reach out for more children here in the north of Thailand. God made all things beautiful in His time. It is HE who ordained from our first meeting in 2014 in Bangkok this partnership. Brother Bo's message in our church about "new things to come" indeed was so powerful. His tremendous work of advocacy for Hope House [now Destiny Home] helped us in acquiring the land and buildings that we dreamed of many years back from our humble beginning at the foot of the mountain. God knows how grateful we are to ANM and your supporters who helped us in this endeavor.

Jeph and Apple Garcia, Thailand

"Christ Died for Me!"
—Mabud Chowdhury of Bangladesh[24]

"These Christians are confused. And they are violent—just look at the Crusades! They are also perverse and immoral. You can tell that from their movies. What's more, they worship three gods—Father, Son, and Mary—instead of the one true God, Allah. And they have

---

[24] Much of the information is taken from an article by Dee Brookshire that appeared in the Fall 2014 issue of *ANM World Missions* magazine.

many Bible translations that are full of errors, and they have many different denominations with different beliefs. Yes, Christians are a confused people!"

As Abdul Mabud Chowdhury listened to this discussion by some of his Muslim college friends, he felt sorry for Christians. A devout Muslim himself, he longed to tell the unenlightened Christians about Islam and how they could work their way to Paradise. He decided to study the Bible so he could show them its weaknesses.

But as Mabud began reading the Bible, his interest and excitement grew. When he came to Romans 5:8, he eyes became riveted on the words, "But God demonstrates his own love toward us, in that while we were still sinners, Christ died for us."

Mabud pondered what he had read: "God loves me? Christ died for me? Could this really be true?" As he read on, he learned about the free gift of salvation that would be his if he simply asked for it. On January 12, 1985, he did ask Jesus to be his Lord and Savior. His father, who was a Muslim priest, immediately kicked him out of the house, and his brothers, who were radical Muslims, even discussed killing him. Mabud's friends also deserted him. In his loneliness, he cried out to God for help.

Studying God's Word

A pastor God had put into Mabud's life suggested that the Young Christian Workers Program of Operation Mobilization would be a good place for him to get grounded in his faith. Mabud joined the training program and joyfully participated in it for two and a half years. Afterwards, he diligently studied at a Christian discipleship center for three years to build his capability for sharing the Gospel. The whole time, he had so little money that he wore the same shirt and trousers every day.

One day, a fellow student introduced Mabud to a young Christian lady named Sandhya. They became friends, and Sandhya even bought Mabud some new clothes. After their graduation, Mabud married Sandhya in a coat and tie he borrowed for the occasion, and the couple moved into a rented tin shed.

In Bangladesh, 90 percent of the people are Muslim. Now that Mabud had the training and a passion to serve as an evangelist, he was determined to reach them. He sent out numerous resumes to churches, but he received no offers of employment. No churches wanted to hire him because they feared persecution from Muslims who killed MBBs (Muslim background believers). But Mabud didn't give up. He began distributing Gospel tracts, while working part-time as a typist.

But the income from this job didn't support the family the couple now had, so in 1992, with Sandhya's agreement, Mabud moved to Saudi Arabia and began working for Saudi Arabian Airlines. For four years, he lived alone and sent the money he earned back to his family. This arrangement worked out better economically, but it was not fulfilling the burden God had placed on Mabud's heart of reaching Muslims for Christ in his own country. Against his family's wishes, Mabud returned home and secured a job as an accountant. For Christian fellowship, he would meet with a few Muslim converts on Friday evenings for prayer.

One day, while Mabud was at his accounting job, the telephone rang. When he answered, the voice on the other end said, "I'm sorry! I think I have the wrong number." There was a pause, and then the voice said, "Wait! Who is this? I think I know you."

The voice on the telephone belonged to an old friend, who ended up hiring Mabud to work with his overseas generator company. This gave Mabud some financial stability so he could devote time to ministry. After prayer, he decided to start MBB churches by reaching out to MBBs who were scattered throughout Bangladesh.

"God, I Trust You"

The Rev. Asish Muhuri, who had become a mentor to Mabud, offered to give Mabud some of the proceeds of a land sale he had just consummated, but the wives of both men objected. Still wanting to help, Asish offered to write a letter of recommendation for Mabud, so he could raise financial support. But the very next day, Asish died. Still, Mabud's faith did not falter. He prayed, "God, I trust you to guide me and provide for me."

"We praise and thank God Almighty that he uses us for his ministry," Mabud says. *"May he continue to guide and sustain us for the expansion of his kingdom."*

In 1999, Mabud gathered thirty MBBs to begin a ministry he called, "Isa-e Jamat" ("Followers of Jesus Fellowship"). The ministry's goals were to glorify God, evangelize Muslims, and plant churches in Bangladesh. Mabud's wife and two daughters said, "Papa, this is God's will for you. We will help."

By 2013, Mabud and his co-workers had started 112 churches, whose six thousand adherents were active in thirty of Bangladesh's sixty-four districts. The ministry became so large that it formed a government-registered denomination, Isa-e Church Bangladesh.

To provide financial support for the ministry, Mabud founded several businesses, including a rental car agency, a printing press company, and a generator repair shop. To gain acceptance into Muslim communities, he started literacy programs and Christian preschools in Muslim areas. His preschool teachers were "dropouts" who had been forced to discontinue their education due to lack of money. The money they earned as teachers enabled them to finish their schooling. Some became doctors, operated rural medical clinics, and ran camps for children.

Mabud's next challenge was to figure out how to train believers to become leaders. He hit on the idea of developing a Bible correspondence course for unreached people. As a first step, he built a residential training institute where he offered four terms of seminars and workshops per year to all genders and age groups in the society. Mabud also wrote ten books and published a bi-weekly magazine, *Somoyer Bibortan* (*Time of Change*), that promoted Christian values. Today, this magazine reaches thousands of people in seventy countries via the Internet.

Isa-e Church uses the media of song and drama to present the Gospel throughout the year. It also conducts special worship training sessions for other churches. "We praise and thank God Almighty that he uses us for his ministry," Mabud says. "May he continue to guide and sustain us for the expansion of his kingdom."

Mabud Comes to America

Mabud was able to come to America, I accompanied him on a trip to Lynchburg, Virginia, where he spoke to a group of church and community leaders. I was fascinated and blessed to watch how he interacted with brothers in the Lord. He is one of the brightest missionary minds in Bangladesh—or in any mission field in the world. I have the greatest admiration for Mabud Chowdhury, not only because of his knowledge of the Bible and his expertise at running businesses, but because of the joy that emanates from him.

Later, I invited Mabud to be one of the major speakers at an ANM Wintergreen Fall Retreat, so our donors and friends from all over the US could meet him and hear his testimony. His talk brought tears to the eyes of many, including his own daughter, Rachel, and her husband, Simon. People were deeply touched as he described how he was mocked and beaten for preaching the Gospel of Jesus Christ in the public market. I love this brother and greatly admire his courage.

Ministering to the Aeta People
—Wilson and Cora Ladringan of the Philippines

In 1986, the Ford Fiera that Wilson Ladringan was driving hit a deep pothole and crashed head-on into another van. Wilson's daughter, Tootsie, and two other passengers were killed. Wilson was airlifted to a nearby US Navy hospital, where doctors saved his shattered leg and his life.

At the time, Wilson's wife, Cora, was working abroad as a nurse to help support the fledgling church Wilson pastored. Devastated, she resigned her job and flew home. The couple received no assistance from their parents and siblings because they all opposed the Christian faith. To cover their medical expenses, Wilson and Cora sold all their material belongings. The one bright spot during the next two years was the birth of another daughter, whom they named Praise.

In July 1988, as Wilson was leading a Bible study under a mango tree, an Aeta man accepted Christ as his savior. The Aeta are a marginalized Negrito tribe, despised and maltreated by many Filipinos. This new believer invited Wilson and Cora to come to his home, and while visiting with the man and his family, the Ladringans noticed the dirty and malnourished Aeta children roaming about the village.

Nurturing Five Children

In an instant, the Lord revealed to Wilson how he could reach the children's parents and relatives for Christ. He and Cora went to the poverty-stricken parents of these street children and offered to provide nurture and schooling for five children ranging in age from seven to ten years. This appealed to some of the parents, and the Ladringans took five children home. They bathed, clothed, and fed them, and they enrolled them at a nearby public elementary school. The children responded to Wilson and Cora's evening Bible teaching because the couple shared the Gospel in action as well as in words.

After several months, Wilson and Cora returned the five children to their parents. Everyone was impressed to see how respectful and obedient the children had become and how delightfully they sang worship songs. More Aeta parents wanted the same benefit, so these initial five children multiplied to ten, and the ten soon multiplied to twenty. The Ladringan's ministry, Aetas Bible Study Center, was growing in favor with God and man, but the meager support Wilson and Cora received from friends was insufficient to support the budding work.

A Gigantic Eruption

In June 1991, life got even more difficult for Wilson and Cora. Nearby Mount Pinatubo erupted in the world's largest volcanic eruption since Novarupta erupted in Alaska in 1912. Lava flowed down the mountain and filled the valleys up to 660 feet deep. Hundreds of Aeta people living on the slopes of the mountain had no way to escape and were buried alive. The ground within a twenty-four-mile radius around Mount Pinatubo was covered with ash one to ten feet deep.

Shortly after this volcanic eruption, the region was hit by Tropical Storm Yunya. Volcanic ash is light when dry, like wood ash, but when soaked with water, it becomes lahar, which is like concrete. The rain caused the ash that had accumulated on the roofs of homes and other buildings to harden into lahar, and thousands of structures collapsed under the weight. One of the casualties was the building where Pastor Wilson's church met.

I met Wilson and Cora Ladringan in 1993, just two years after this volcanic eruption. My heart broke when I saw how their personal home and the Aeta Children's Home had been flattened under the weight of a solidified lahar. Wilson and Cora, nevertheless, were still dedicated to continuing their work with the Aetas Bible Study Center, and I assured them that I would try to find help for them.

When I returned to the States, Philip and Kathie Zodhiates and their close friends and co-workers spearheaded a fund drive for this wonderful couple. Wilson and Cora have wisely used this support to plant seventeen churches. They also have built a medical clinic and a vocational school to train welders, teachers, and workers with other skills. Aeta people who graduate from the ministry's vocational school lead better lives and become more useful citizens.

Today, more than eighty-five children live in the Aeta Children's Home and attend the ministry's school, which is called To God Be the Glory Academy. Some are orphans who saw their parents die from crime or starvation. Others are orphans because their parents dropped them off and never came back.

I Was Amazed!

In 2015, Jonathan Constant visited the ministry as a staff representative of ANM. The moving report that he wrote after he returned
to America was published in *ANM World Missions* in the summer of
2015. Below is a slightly edited version:

*I have been all around the world: the great cities of Western Europe,
the hills of Jamaica, the bush of Ethiopia, the tribes of India. But
never in all my travels had I met such a respectful, disciplined,
talented, and God-honoring group of children. All of them were
extremely skillful and well-trained by their teachers and leaders in
both knowledge and righteousness. I was amazed!*

*During dinner on our second night at the school, we unexpect-
edly heard singing. We had no idea where it was coming from; there
was no special program planned. We decided to investigate.*

*Rounding the corner and entering the gym, we saw a line of
flip-flops neatly arranged along the wall. Then we saw a guitarist
leading all 85 students and most of the teachers and staff members
in song. The students sat on the floor in rows according to grade,
with twelfth-grade students sitting in front of each row. We had
no idea what they were singing as they worshiped the Lord in their
language, but it was the most beautiful singing that any of us had
ever heard.*

*We sat down in the back with the teachers and worshipped with
them. After a few more songs, including a glorious rendition of
"How Great Is Our God," a teacher got up and led a devotional, followed by a prayer. Then all eyes turned to us.*

*Suddenly, a stampede of 85 Aetas came running toward us, grab-
bing our arms and gleefully dragging us across the gym floor. They
giggled at our confused looks. The group that grabbed me was the
kindergarten girls, and they seemed to be the giddiest of them all.*

*We sat in a circle, and our twelfth-grade leader, Evelyn, started
to talk about the devotional. She had the most contagious smile
I have ever seen. After we finished talking, we went around and*

shared requests for prayer. I was used to this—we did it all the time at my church in the States—but I was not at all prepared for what happened next. After I gave my request, one of the young girls looked me in the eyes and said that she wanted to pray for me. She dragged me into the middle of the circle.

All at once, a dozen pairs of tiny hands were laid on me, and the children all began praying out loud, petitioning the Father on my behalf. My emotions broke loose, and I wept. Looking up, I saw that every group was doing this. This was not just special treatment for me as a guest; this was simply how they prayed. I was in awe at the faith of such little ones.

She had never gotten love from her father, but she knew the love of Jesus inside and out, and she could recognize it when she saw it.

After the meeting, I went out to the courtyard with my new best friends and sat there, trying to communicate with children who were just starting to learn English. They tried to get me to say certain words, and I tried to get them to say English tongue twisters. We laughed for what seemed like forever. In one of these silly moments, a girl named Edeline said to me, "You are my father."

Am I her father? Not at all—I had only met her two days before. It took me a while, but I think now, after a few months, I have finally figured out what she meant. This orphaned and abandoned girl, who had never experienced love until coming to Aetas Bible Study Center, was telling me that she saw the Father's love in me. She had never gotten love from her father, but she knew the love of Jesus inside and out, and she could recognize it when she saw it. This was the fruit of Aetas Bible Study Center's loving care.

More Than Three Decades of Ministry

On July 18, 2021, Aetas Bible Study Center marked thirty-three years of ministry. After the celebration, Wilson and Cora sent us the following letter:

Dear Brother Bo and Sister Marlou, Brother Oliver,
and all our brethren at ANM,

Warmest Christian love and greetings!

Attached are pictures taken during the 33rd Founding Anniversary of ABSC last Sunday, July 18, 2021. Praise God for the faithful partnership of ANM in this ministry.

Through ANM faithful prayers and support throughout the years, the Lord has amazingly blessed this ministry which began under a mango tree way back in 1988.

From our hearts to yours, thank you so very much. Words could not fully express the joy and gratitude in our hearts as we ponder God's faithfulness to us and His work here throughout the years!

To God be the glory, great things He has done (and will continue to do).

Sincerely in Christ,

Wilson and Cora
ABSC Philippines

"They Want Me Dead!"
—Niranjan Bardhan of India

In 1994, I received a call at ANM from an Indian missionary by the name of Niranjan Bardhan. He informed me that he was attending a missions camp in Ashland, Virginia, with many missionaries from different parts of the world. I was eager to meet him, so I drove an hour and a half to Ashland. Immediately, God gave me a special love for this man. His seriousness about God was accented by an endearing wit and humility.

Niranjan told me that when he was nineteen, he was struck by the words of John 3:16: "Whoever believes in Him should not perish." He surrendered his life to Christ, and immediately afterwards went to work for an international Christian organization. He served with this organization for twelve years, until the Lord spoke to him at a Billy Graham conference, "Evangelize your own unreached people."

In 1983, in obedience to this word from the Lord, Niranjan resigned from his ministry position and began a ministry that he named India Gospel Outreach and Social Action.

With this new ministry as his platform, Niranjan successfully spread the Gospel among the sixty-two tribal groups and ninety-three oppressed classes living in Odisha and, to a lesser degree, in Andhra Pradesh. He focused on the most neglected people who knew nothing about Jesus. Traveling to remote villages and sleeping outdoors or in people's homes, he shared about the one true God who could save souls and forgive sins. Gradually, house churches formed, and Niranjan trained new leaders for them.

Thirty-Eight Years of Showing Compassion

For the next thirty-eight years, Niranjan faithfully ministered. God blessed his work, and thousands were added to God's kingdom. Churches, pastors, and evangelists were raised up by the hundreds. The ministry started four daycare centers and a children's home, which a visiting ANM team member praised as "some of the best-run centers I have seen in India." As the years passed, the children who graduated from these centers became nurses, computer programmers, business administrators, and successful workers in other occupations. Their grateful parents, many of whom were from lower-class communities, became interested in the Gospel and in improving their own education.

The ministry's door-to-door distribution of Christian literature and other outreaches always are covered with prayer. Healings in response to prayer have brought entire families to the Lord. In one report, Niranjan shared about how two extremists gave up violence and accepted Jesus. This was soon followed by eighteen more commitments to Christ. Approximately six months after a witch doctor came to the Lord, ten more souls joined the church. And after a young bedridden boy was delivered from an evil spirit, twenty people were added to the local fellowship.

Niranjan's hardships have fueled his compassion. He was born into a lower class and endured constant humiliation. Socializing with his higher-class schoolmates was forbidden. His water came from a different well, and he had to drink from a clay cup. Today, providing freshwater wells for the lower classes of India is one of his priorities. His ministry also provides educational programs, childcare, and health camps for the poor and disabled. To help people better support themselves, the ministry offers instruction in the making of mats, the raising of goats, and other income-producing activities.

Niranjan has received national and state awards for his social work. He was elected national secretary of the National Christian Council, a human rights network in India that serves minorities and the disadvantaged and promotes unity among Christian leaders. These activities have made him a popular speaker at worldwide missions conferences.

In September 2006, I hosted Niranjan in my home. Despite my exhaustion from a recent trip, I felt led in my heart to take him with me and advocate for him in meetings in Indiana, Illinois, and Ohio. I asked a very close friend and neighbor, Chuck Cole, if he could help with the driving. God gave the three of us such a wonderful, blessed, and fruitful time together. Below is a write-up from Chuck about the trip:

A Trip with Bo and Niranjan Bardhan
by Chuck Cole

I met my dear friend, Bo Barredo, in December 2004, within a day or two after we moved to his neighborhood in Crozet, Virginia. Little did I know how that our friendship would enrich my life and walk with Jesus Christ.

In September of 2006, I accompanied Bo and Niranjan Bardhan, a missionary leader from India, on a trip to visit churches and friends of Bo in Illinois, Indiana, and Ohio. We had a great time together, and I enjoyed the opportunity to participate in a domestic "mission" trip.

During our travels, Bo was moved to pray during heavy fog through the mountains of Virginia and West Virginia. I was reading my journal of that trip, and I could not find the details of his prayer. However, I do recall that many of the things for which he prayed were answered during our five-day journey. Bo felt the Holy Spirit was asking him to stretch my faith.

Bo asked me if the Lord brought $100,000 of business to me in the next sixty days, would I use a portion of it to help brother Niranjan purchase a new van for his ministry. If I brought in that amount in the next sixty days, he told me that might be evidence that it was of the Lord. I had no problems saying yes, because I had never seen a sixty-day revenue of $100,000 like that in my executive recruitment or "headhunting" business.

Our trip was very fruitful, and we saw the Lord answer specific things that Bo prayed during our five-day trip. After we returned to Virginia, the Lord brought $100,000 of new revenue to my business within sixty days! I was grateful to give a portion to Brother Niranjan's ministry to assist him with the purchase of a new van for his ministry. Those five days together also formed a wonderful friendship through the years with Brother Niranjan. I was saddened to learn of his passing in 2021.

When I look back on that trip, I am grateful for the vision the Lord gave Bo during our travel through heavy fog. I still remember that Bo was recovering from an illness brought on by fatigue. As we got on the interstate, he encouraged Pastor Bardhan and me to talk while he napped. In no time, he was awake to see the fog that was slowing our travels. He decided that we should pray, but he encouraged me to keep my eyes open while driving. It may have been an hour that he prayed and sought God's guidance and help. It was a truly blessed time.

In 2019, I had the privilege of traveling to Kenya and Tanzania with Bo and his wife, Marlou. As we visited the ministries of brother Timothy Kinyua and Williams Yindi, I was overwhelmed by the self-sacrifice of both brothers. As we heard their testimonies and bore witness to the fruit of their ministries, I still think of the dedicated pastors and church planters we met who live and minister to the lost tribes. Their testimonies of joy in the midst of great difficulty are a beautiful reminder of God's power to save the lost in the uttermost parts of the earth.

When I think of my friend Bo, I think of his natural way of praying. When we lived in the same neighborhood, we would walk through the community and storm heaven with prayers. He has taught me to pray as naturally as if I was conversing with a good friend. It simply flows out of him.

My Last Visit with Brother Niranjan

In 2008, Brother Niranjan visited the offices of ANM in Virginia. "I am a wanted man; they want me dead!" he told us. Niranjan's success in evangelizing the outcasts of Indian society had made him a target of various extremist elements. During the peak of the violence in Odisha, India, that year, his name was at the top of the list of those to be killed. The riots had started when a Hindu leader was murdered by some Hindu extremists. Christians were falsely blamed, and the Hindus began killing Christians and destroying their property.

"People who lost loved ones are still traumatized," Niranjan informed us. "Many are living as refugees because they are too afraid to return to their ancestral villages. Evildoers poured gasoline on my Jeep and set it ablaze one night. Then they entered my office building intending to burn me alive. They thought I was asleep in the office, but by God's grace, I escaped. I am now proclaiming Jesus among Hindu fanatics and people who are blinded by Satan."

To the end of his life, Niranjan never backed down. "I want to live with the love and power of God operating inside me because no one can destroy my soul."

SOME RECOLLECTIONS

The pivotal Scripture in our family's decision to pull up stakes in our native land and come to the United States was Isaiah 43:18–19:

> *Do not remember the former things,*
> *Nor consider the things of old.*
> *Behold, I will do a new thing,*
> *Now it shall spring forth;*
> *Shall you not know it?*
> *I will even make a road in the wilderness*
> *And rivers in the desert.*

It has now been thirty-one years since we bade goodbye to the Philippines, our country of birth, and the Scripture that is stirring in my heart today is Isaiah 46:9:

> *Remember the former things of old,*
> *For I am God, and there is no other;*
> *I am God, and there is none like Me.*

Ecclesiastes says that for everything there is a season, and for Marlou and me, this is a time for recollections. As we look back over the past three decades, so many special people, events, travels, and God-stories warm our hearts and reverberate in our minds. Marlou will begin this chapter with some of her recollections, and I will conclude it with a few of mine.

PART I
RECOLLECTIONS BY MARLOU

"The Sound Was Brilliant!"

A few weeks after we arrived in the US and settled into our rented townhouse, Bo and the children noticed that I was beginning to miss my piano that we had left in Manila. After scouring newspaper ads for affordable used pianos, we noticed one that was being offered in a silent auction by a local country club at a Saturday yard sale. We all went to see it, and it turned out to be a well-used piano with cigarette burns on some keys. But the price was right, and most of all, when I tried it, the sound was brilliant.

We bid on it, but we were nervous about whether we would get it because other buyers were also interested. That evening, we got a call from the yard-sale coordinator. "Our manager saw your young family this morning," she said, "and he would like you to have that piano. Just add five dollars more to your offer, and you'll outbid the others."

We love that piano! It has now been with our family for thirty-one years, and as it ages, its sound gets increasingly brilliant.

"I Despaired for Life"

Just as I had my cancer scare, Bo also has had his share of health challenges, perhaps because of his stressful schedule. He typically goes to bed around midnight and wakes up each day before 4:00 a.m. to pray over a long list of concerns that he takes to heart. In addition to working hard, he is constantly thinking. He keeps a stack of used envelopes at hand for recording ideas, initial sermon outlines, things to do, and—most of all—what he feels are clear instructions from the Lord.

Bo's hectic pace has led to burnout twice. When it first happened, in 1997, the ANM board insisted that he take a three-month rest. A more serious burnout that occurred at the end of 2004 totally sidelined him. It spiraled down into depression.

For almost six months, he "despaired of life." During this trial, Bo held on to the divine promise in 1 Peter 5:10:

> *May the God of all grace, who called us*
> *to His eternal glory by Christ Jesus,*
> *after you have suffered a while,*
> *perfect, establish, strengthen, and settle you.*

God honored his Word, and Bo recovered. He regarded this harrowing, painful, and dark period of his life as a season of cleansing and pruning, preparing him for a deeper commitment to serve and love God and God's people.

In a letter we sent to our friends in October 2005, I wrote about this painful and challenging season in our lives:

Again, we thank our beloved Lord Jesus, the Brightness of God's glory, for each one of you who cared for us and prayed and cried with us during the first half of this year. We were given by ANM a six-month sabbatical leave as Bo underwent an "Elijah experience." It was a season of total physical, emotional and spiritual exhaustion of a hard-working servant of the Lord. A much-needed, long-overdue rest was mandatory.

Thank you, too, for the provisions you sent us for our Philippine trip. We did not stay there as long as we had planned because Bo could not help but continue to minister to God's needy servants. He was running on fumes. His heart drove him. For instance, when Bo came to know that our taxicab driver Anthony was a church planter in a slum area of Manila, leaving the ministry to his wife Thelma so as to earn a living to pay off debts incurred in the treatment of their two-year-old daughter's heart ailment, he wept. Despite his weakened condition, he made arrangements to visit and help Anthony's family and their work. That night, he prayed for God to extend his life on behalf of many more "Anthonys" and "Thelmas" in many mission fields.

When we came back to the US it was still winter. For us, it seemed to be all nights. It was very difficult for us. We were almost isolated at home. But God had a word for Bo—"Be still and know that I am God" (Psalm 46:10). The Lord made Bo a virtual prisoner of His.

As it was a season of "spiritual hibernation" for Bo, it was also a season of testing of my own faith. Many nights I would awake gazing at the pained look on the face of my sleeping husband. I would cry in the darkness. His pain was my pain—but much more. Indeed, "the earthquakes that happen in the lives of our loved ones register a higher intensity on the Richter scale of our own hearts." We needed friends. And you were there. Your cards and words of hope and counsel mean so much to Bo and me—far more than you would ever realize. We also came to know that many servants of the Lord have undergone this same experience. Many encouraged us that an experience like this prepares God's servants for greater blessings and responsibilities.

Indeed, the Lord makes things beautiful in his time! He brought "mornings" into Bo's life and mine, too, right in the middle of spring! The exhaustion, confusion, cold, and pain were replaced by more vigor, steadfastness, sunshine, and joy! The wonderful transition was so immediate that it almost caught us by surprise—"weeping may endure for the night but joy cometh in the morning" (Psalm 30:5)!

Two Humorous Stories

Bo loves pranks, and sometimes he can be like a kid. I love his sense of humor. Allow me to give two examples.

In their early days together at Christian Aid, sometime in 1989, Bo and P. R. Misra were guests for a night in the home of Steve and Linda Lanning near Hagerstown, Maryland. They slept in a very large basement room that had a bathroom at the far end. Bo occupied the lower bunk, and P. R. took the upper. At midnight, Bo was awakened by a movement of the bed. He opened his eyes and watched as P. R. slowly climbed down the ladder and made his way in the dark across the room to the bathroom. While P. R. was in the bathroom, Bo got up, detached the ladder, and quietly hid it behind a door. Then he crawled back into bed.

When P. R. came back to the bunkbed and started fumbling around in the dark looking for the ladder, Bo had a hard time suppressing his laughter. After a while, P. R. realized what had happened, and he let out a few Hindi expressions Bo had not heard before. "It was probably a good thing I didn't understand the Hindi language!" he told me later. The prank ended well, however, because in the next instant, P. R. burst out laughing.

A second humorous incident occurred early one morning in 1998, when ANM had a tiny office in the Pantops area of Charlottesville. As the entire staff assembled in a hallway and participated in prayers with their eyes closed, Bo happened to open his eyes and see that one of Dee Brookshire's shoes had slipped off her foot. He quietly stooped down, grabbed the shoe, and put it on top of a refrigerator that was behind him. When the prayers were over, Dee looked everywhere for her shoe. When she and the others realized what had happened, there was much hearty laughter.

Crime Does Pay!

Dee Brookshire is one of our closest friends in the world. She had always dreamed of having a nice boombox so she and her family could listen to music in their home. One day, Dee's car was stolen by some joy-riding young men. A few days later, the young men abruptly abandoned the car when they saw a police car approaching. The police returned the car to Dee and allowed her to keep the contents that the thieves had left in it. One of the contents was a nice boombox!

Bo's Travels to the Churches

Below is part of a report I wrote for ANM donors about how a few churches and individuals graciously responded to Bo's message as he traveled during a particular period of several weeks:

*In **Wickenburg, Arizona**, God gave Bo favor in the hearts of the people of the church he visited. The pastor's children gave money for bicycles in India. A dentist and his wife were led of the Lord to* sponsor a Gospel team of Hiligaynon missionaries on Panay Island, Philippines. Bo's hosts, a retired cowboy and his wife, committed to sponsor a Gospel team of Mandaya-Mansaka missionaries on Mindanao Island, Philippines. The church itself committed to pray about sponsoring five missionaries, and the missions committee tendered a dinner for Bo.

At a church in **Winnemucca, Nevada**, Bo was so overwhelmed by God's obvious display of favor that he was moved to tears. In addition to reaffirming their love for him as their own missionary, the congregation decided to begin supporting an indigenous Bible school in the hills of San Rafael, Philippines. On top of this, they sent Bo home with a love offering of $14,200 for God's work.

In the city of **Chicago**, Bo was invited to speak at a three-day church missions conference in lieu of the original speaker, who was not able to come. Prior to the conference, the church's senior pastor, a medical doctor, had challenged the congregation to pledge support for at least fifteen native missionaries. After the missions pledges were counted on the last day, the pledges were sufficient to support fifty missionaries. One couple gave a generous gift for the purchase of a "house church" in Indonesia. Thanks be to God!

At the end of his three-day stay in a camp for girls in **St. Anne, Illinois**, Bo received a bundle of candies and notes from the precious children, promising him that they "will be there in heaven" someday.

Here in our own small city of **Charlottesville, Virginia**, a Mennonite pastor (now a chaplain at the University of Virginia) and his wife are personally supporting our ministry. The local Presbyterian church sent generous provisions for street children in Manila, and it is supporting Filipino Bible translators. Another local church is helping Indonesian and African missionaries, and still another is supporting some of the ANM staff. The acting chaplain of the local Salvation Army and his wife are also active supporters of ANM's missionaries and administrative needs, and recently the church where Bo and I are members raised funds to provide 100,000 Gospel tracts in Thailand.

In **Tenstrike, Minnesota**, the regular Wednesday night prayer meeting turned into a three-hour worship service as many responded to the altar calls. The generous offering gathered that night was designated for the purchase of fifteen bicycles for rural evangelism in India!

In **Blackduck, Minnesota**, the host pastor of a small church was reluctant to have Bo come because he feared their church was too small. The ANM Deputation Director, Lucille Lebeau, assured the pastor that the Lord had placed it upon Bo's heart to visit his church, and that no church is too small for the blessings of the Lord. This was again proven true. With the funds raised by the congregation, a group of native missionaries was able to buy a power generator they had been praying about for seven years!

In five messages at a three-day family camp hosted by a church in **Park Rapids, Minnesota**, Bo highlighted the issues of holiness, righteousness, cleansing, and purification. The spirit of love and meekness among these people of God brought about a revival. Bo was touched when the pastor exclaimed, "Thank you, Lord! Our church has just turned the corner." The church committed to sponsor five native missionaries in Bangladesh, and the children in the church provided funds for the purchase of several hurricane lamps for Manobo missionaries working along riverbanks.

These are just some of the "incidental blessings" of the Lord. In all his travels, Bo saw many adults and children come to faith in the Lord Jesus. Numerous other hearts were brought back to their "first love"—the Lord Jesus Christ—by the proclamation of God's Word.

Letters from the Hearts of Saints

For the glory of God, may I share with you excerpts from two letters I received from loving Christians in places where Bo ministered as an advocate for native missionaries:

Dear Sister in Christ, I want to tell you thank you for your service to Jesus. You give your husband freedom to obey Christ as he is led. . . . Because my husband is a police chief, I too know how it is to send your husband out, wondering if he will come back physically whole. . . . Bo has brought great blessing, conviction, repentance, and revival through the Holy Spirit. Because you place God first, he is able to serve with more complete joy knowing you are beside him in his walk with Jesus."

—from a wife and mother of two

. . . thank you, sister, for releasing your husband to come to us. . . . His messages brought conviction, as well as insight into some of the issues I've been struggling with and healing for wounds in my spirit. . . . Thanks again for your husband's being used of God to touch my life this week, and his being a missionary to America.

—from an American lady missionary

Indonesian Haunted Houses Become House Churches

During Bo's mission trip to Indonesia in 1989, he had the privilege of meeting Sister Rina, a missionary much loved by the people in the town where she ministered on Java. When Rina's husband, a pastor, left her for a Sunday school teacher, a great uproar took place in the community. Because no one had been trained to replace him, the church elders elected Rina, and God blessed her. Her eldest son became her co-pastor, and by the end of twenty-seven years, they had planted twenty-seven village churches. The main church had five hundred adults and two hundred children.

Three things especially impressed Bo about Sister Rina. First, he was touched by how she volunteered to personally wash the broken dead bodies of accident victims. The grieving Muslim families were touched, and God used this to bring many to faith.

Second, in villages where Muslim priests prohibited the building of Christian churches, she converted abandoned houses that the villagers felt were haunted into places of worship. ANM was privileged to provide funds for this purpose.

Third, her church provided free caskets for the poor who could not afford decent burials for their loved ones. This was the only church Bo has visited in Asia or the US where wooden caskets were stored on church premises!

One Van after Another

In 1995, the Barredo family's only vehicle was an old station wagon with close to two hundred thousand miles on it. It was not suitable for long-distance trips, and with two full-grown children and two younger, growing children, our family could not fit comfortably into it.

When God provided our family with some financial gifts through generous supporters, many friends encouraged us to use these funds to purchase a bigger and better vehicle. However, Bo, true to character, could not overlook the "more pressing" needs of native missionaries, so the better vehicle had to wait.

In November of that year, a deer collided with our old station wagon, causing serious damage. At least three very close friends told Bo that maybe this was God's way of saying it was time for another vehicle. Bo agreed, and again some generous provisions were given to us for the purpose of buying a van.

Before we had time to buy a van, however, we received a heart-breaking letter from the wife of a missionary leader in India. This woman's husband had just been killed in a terrible traffic accident, which also had destroyed their old "Gospel van" containing all their ministry equipment. The ministry had just elected this widow interim leader, and she did not know what to do about the many missionaries in the ministry who were serving without having even the minimal necessary support of thirty dollars per month.

Bo gently pleaded with me, "Marlou, this poor widow has no one to turn to. This provision for our van could be used by the Lord to provide her and her co-workers a ray of hope."

There was no need for him to plead on her behalf because I whole-heartedly wanted to respond to the needs of this dear and precious sister in Christ across the seas. Advancing Native Missions sent the

She was not won by doctrinal arguments; rather, she was drawn by God's love manifested in and through us. Many tears of joy were shed that night. It was an answer to many prayers!

money to her, and this enabled the mission she now led to buy a new van and replace the equipment that had been destroyed. How overjoyed our family was to be a channel of this special and timely blessing to Sister Manjula and her ministry in their time of mourning and need!

God gave us peace about it, and life went on. Little did we know that the story was not yet over. Our Jehovah Jireh—the God who provides—once more touched his people's hearts concerning our need for a vehicle, and a generous gift came from a family in Indiana. With it, we were able to purchase a moderately used, very dependable family van. We gave away the old station wagon, and in the months and years ahead, our family had many long trips in this new vehicle the Lord had provided!

"It Was as Though Morgan Went to Those Places"

A close family friend, Mrs. Marion Bond West Acuff, is a writer for *Guideposts* and the author of several inspiring books, including *The Nevertheless Principle, Overwhelmed,* and *Look Out Fear, Here Comes Faith.* Her husband, Gene, is a retired pastor. When she read our family's Christmas newsletter that I wrote in December 1995, she responded as follows:

Thank you for your Christmas letter. It is powerful. I need to reread it. I'm enclosing a small check for your friends in Leyte and Samar islands (the ones with the enormous smiles and hungry stomachs). They seemed to jump off the page at me.

Our dear brother's [Morgan Malcom] homegoing service was yesterday. [Morgan supported Bo with gifts and prayers. During his wedding preparations, he made known his request that whatever cash gifts would be given to them should go to the ministry of Bo Barredo. However, a few months *before his wedding, he was found to have terminal bone cancer. It spread so fast that he never made it to his wedding day. He died not having met or heard his missionary Bo Barredo personally. However, we are consoled in our grief in that this sweet brother is waiting for us in heaven.]*

I am enclosing a program we handed out at the service. . . . Gene's message was so simple. . . . So many people came to the funeral. It certainly was a witness. . . . Gene shared in his remarks about you, Bo, and the suit that Morgan so carefully selected for you and how you wore it in many places, including to other countries, and in a way, it was as though Morgan went to those places. . . . He was an only child and his father died five years ago.

Know that we love and appreciate you and your ministry of spreading His love wherever He leads you. We appreciate the way your family so willingly share you with those who need to hear.

Just What the Doctor Needed

In November 1995, my single, younger, and only sister, Dr. Maria Belen Carisma, a practicing cardiologist in the Philippines, attended the American Heart Association's congress in Anaheim, California. After the congress, she came to Charlottesville and stayed with our family for almost a month.

Belen is brilliant, extremely capable, and highly principled, with an excellent work ethic. She is loved and respected by her staff and fellow doctors. One evening, the Lord opened the way for Bo to witness to Belen and lead her to the Lord in the presence of our whole family. She was not won by doctrinal arguments; rather, she was drawn by God's love manifested in and through us. Many tears of joy were shed that night. It was an answer to many prayers!

Belen returned to the Philippines as a different person. Always tenderhearted and generous, God gave her even more love and compassion for the poor, especially for her heart patients. Several years later, she was elected president of the Philippine Heart Association. In 2009, Bo and I had the joy of witnessing her induction into the

"Search me, O God, and ransack my heart!"

American College of Cardiology at a conference in Orlando, Florida. After a very successful career, she recently retired from her position of deputy executive director at the Philippine Heart Center.

Belen is like a second mother to our children. They love her very much, and so do we. She hosts us every time we are in the Philippines. She devours God's Word and quotes Scripture in her addresses at professional gatherings. Bo tells her that she has become the de facto pastor of her high school class because her classmates so often ask her for counsel and prayers.

The Ministry of Peacemaking

As Bo travels overseas to visit ANM's ministry partners, a number of times he is requested to arbitrate or settle disputes among members of the body of Christ. One of the most difficult situations was the long-standing dispute that took place between two missionary leaders who were former close friends and partners in the Gospel on Mindanao Island, Philippines. These two seemingly irreconcilable, warring leaders and their followers didn't see each other face to face for almost fifteen years! And it affected the testimony of the Lord in their area.

In 2002, the Lord laid it strongly on Bo's heart to intervene and use the platform God has graciously provided—he was loved and respected by both men who were much older than he. Bo brought a team of speakers, with Pastor Bubba Rose as the main speaker, to a missions revival and conference that Bo had requested Pastor Claro Loquias, one of the two leaders, to organize. Bo then invited the other leader, Pastor Galo Tellano, together with his wife, to join us and sit close to Bo and me. Almost four hundred of their followers came to the event. There was tension in the air in the midst of the music and prayers. Then Pastor Rose started a fiery message on Psalm 139:23–24, and instead of using the phrase "Search me, O God, and know my heart," he used the phrase "search me, O God, and ransack my heart!" Pastor Galo jumped out of his seat crying, ran up and tightly hugged

Pastor Claro! The two men publicly asked for forgiveness from each other. The chilly atmosphere was suddenly electrified by the reconciliation and love shown by the two leaders. Their followers began hugging each other and expressing love for one another!

Bright and Joyful

Shortly after returning home to the US, Bo received a long, handwritten letter from Pastor Galo. It brought such joy to Bo's heart. The letter is reproduced below:

> Thank you, Bro. Bo, for your invitation extended to me and my wife Elvira to come to the revival meeting last April 15. It was a meeting I will not forget for the rest of my life. I cry only before God, not before people. But in that meeting I could not help it. I had to cry—tears dropped from my eyes and my life [was] ransacked by the Holy Spirit through the messages preached. I was turned upside down, and I made some genuine confessions before my great God. Then joy, peace and genuine love came into my heart.
>
> For the last 14 years I confessed I have no good dealings with Rev. Claro M. Loquias, my co-laborer in the ministry. We parted ways 14 years ago. . . . However, I have found life dry. And then we were genuinely reconciled! Today life is bright and joyful with a bright prospect to work together with Claro in winning the lost for Christ. . . . Last April 26 our churches and Rev. Loquias' churches had a very special fellowship. . . . Our pastors and people hugged Rev. Claro Loquias and Pastor Loquias' pastors and people hugged me with joy. What a genuine reconciliation indeed!

One Sunday morning, a few years after the reconciliation, Pastor Tellano was killed outside his church by a suspected communist guerilla assassination team. He was very courageous in being open about his stand against the communist ideology.

Conducting Meetings in Public Parks in Vietnam

During Bo's trip to Vietnam in 1996, he was able to meet with some of the seventeen Vietnamese missionaries being helped through

ANM. Although their testimonies were heartbreaking, their numbers were multiplying.

- Pastor Quang told Bo that he had been imprisoned three times. The last incarceration was for smuggling Bibles into Vietnam through the Cambodian border.

- Pastor Den showed Bo his arrest warrants given to him by the police who almost weekly summoned him to their station for interrogation.

- Pastor Trung sheepishly confessed that he does not bring his Bible to his outreaches. Instead, he writes his lessons on a piece of paper, which he folds so it can be easily swallowed when the police come. That way, there will be no evidence that can be used against him or those he teaches.

- Fang, a white-haired grandfather, tearfully admitted that he does not pastor a church anymore because of the risk. His old body can no longer take the beatings. Instead, he disciples groups of four or five young men to train them to become missionaries.

When Vietnam opened its doors to Western trade, it clamped down doubly hard on groups doing evangelism, especially by foreigners. Just before Bo arrived, an American missionary who was caught visiting underground churches had been jailed; two newly arrived Korean missionaries had been deported for telling people about Jesus; and several American teenagers had been placed on a plane and sent home for distributing tracts on the streets.

But these penalties for foreigners were only half the story. Local believers and pastors caught fraternizing with visiting missionaries got the brunt of the oppression. They would suffer imprisonment, beatings, and public humiliation. Christian visitors must exercise wisdom so as not to jeopardize their Vietnamese brethren. To protect local Christians, Bo conducted his meetings in public parks or restaurants.

Rebecca's Birthday—Colombia

On his birthday in 2012, Bo traveled to Colombia to encourage Helman and Rosalba Ocampo. Their ministry had trained and sent out ninety-two indigenous workers representing thirty-two tribes and languages or dialects, mostly in communities along the Amazon River. The Lord provided through ANM a motorized boat, resources for the completion of a missionary couple's house, and a one-year budget for the couple's travels to remote communities.

During this trip, Bo met a missionary named Rebecca, a widow of forty years who helped the Ocampos. When he told her that he had left the United States on his birthday, January 23, and that this was an answer to his prayer that "the Lord find me in his work during my birthday," she said that January 24 was her birthday, and that she was sixty years old. Following Bo's visit, she wrote the encouraging letter below:

> Dear Brother Bo,
>
> You will ever be part of my heart, Brother Bo—you ministered deeply to me just by being who you are—gentle, warm, accepting, tender, REAL. You and your three companions have so much reason to think much of yourselves and lift yourselves up. You didn't. You lifted up JESUS. And in the process, Jesus was so vividly seen in and through you. If you knew the desert that I have traveled through these past 40 years, you would know how important it was for me to meet men like you. The need was profound. I do hope people made your birthday a happy one as you did for me. In spite of ourselves, we really do have a wish that somebody notice it is one's birthday. You did that and took it a HUGE jump further. Your prayer for me that evening was the best part. Thank you too for the gift.
>
> The Lord you serve continue with you, Rebecca

From Law to Grace—A Taxi Conversation

The weather was rainy and windy on February 13, 2018, as our plane landed at Manila International Airport. Bo and I had just flown in from Bacolod, where we had visited his dad in the hospital. Bo hailed a taxi to take us to our next destination. As was his usual custom, he sat up front so he could talk with the driver, and I sat in the back.

We introduced ourselves to the driver, and the driver introduced himself to us as Mang Dante. ("Mang" is the respectful Filipino equivalent to "Mr.") Once underway, Bo said, "We are former lawyers, and we are now serving the Lord."

My husband looks for every opportunity to tell people about Jesus, and by mentioning the Lord, he had just set the stage for the conversation he hoped to have. In the practice of law, this is called "laying the predicate."

A few minutes into our drive, Bo gently asked Mang Dante in Tagalog, his native language, "May I pray aloud while you drive us?"

Mang Dante seemed pleasantly surprised that a lawyer would ask him for permission to pray. "*Aba'y opo, opo!*" he responded. ("My gosh, of course! Yes, sir, yes, sir!")

In a long, fervent prayer, Bo brought before God, among other things, the proposed sale of my parents' property in my hometown on Leyte Island. He specifically asked the Lord to let the transaction take place smoothly and remove whatever impediments might arise. He also prayed for God to bless Mang Dante and his family.

After Bo finished praying, there was silence for a while. Then Mang Dante said, "Boss, *puwede po bang magtanong?*" ("Boss, may I ask you a question?")

"Certainly," said Bo. "I would be happy to hear your question. And please, it is not necessary to call me 'boss.'"

"Thank you," said Mang Dante. "My question is about my father. He recently died, and I need advice about what to do."

As Bo learned more about the matter, it was amusing to watch him struggle to resurrect some of the course material he had learned in his "Land Titles and Deeds" and "Testate and Intestate Succession" classes in law school four decades earlier. After collecting sufficient background information, he gave Mang Dante a brief discourse on the relevant legal issues, followed by two bits of practical legal advice.

"*Maraming, maraming salamat po!*" Mang Dante exclaimed. ("Thank you, thank you so much, sir!") He was obviously pleased to get helpful legal advice for free. Mang Dante turned to Bo again, while continuing to skillfully maneuver his cab through Manila's notorious traffic, and said, "*Puwede po bang magtanong ulit?*" ("Sir, could I ask you another question?")

God providentially arranged for Mang Dante to have as his passengers that day two believing lawyers who gave him free legal advice, and best of all, introduced him to a relationship with Jesus Christ.

When Bo nodded affirmatively, Mang Dante asked him for advice about a valuable piece of property that his father had given to his brother. After Bo had provided an overview of the pertinent laws on conveyance of real property and offered some helpful legal advice, Mang Dante was so thankful that he almost cheered.

Bo then said to Mang Dante, "*Puwede po bang ako naman ang magtanong?*" ("May I be the one to now ask you a question?")

Mang Dante said that would be fine, and Bo politely asked, "*Mang Dante, kung kayo po ay mamamatay ngayong gabi, alam po ba ninyo kung saan kayo patutungo?*" ("Mr. Dante, if you die tonight, would you know where you are going?")

With knitted eyebrows, Mang Dante pondered the question for several seconds. Then he replied, "*Naku po, hindi po.*" ("Oh my, I'm not sure, sir!")

Bo then shared with him God's plan of salvation through the Lord Jesus. Up to this point, I had been silently praying, but able to contain my excitement no longer, I exclaimed, "Jesus said, 'I am the way, the truth and the life. No one comes to the Father except through Me.'" Suddenly realizing that I had spoken in English, I repeated what I had said in Tagalog: "*Ako ang daan, at ang katotohanan, at ang buhay: sinoman ay di makaparoroon sa Ama, kundi sa pamamagitan ko.*"

Bo then asked Mang Dante if he wanted to be saved. Without hesitation, he said, "*Opo! Opo!*" ("Yes, sir! Yes, sir!")

When we reached our destination, Bo directed Mang Dante to a corner where he could park his taxi. With all heads bowed, he led our driver in a prayer of repentance, and Mang Dante invited Jesus into his heart.

What started as a stormy, dark, and dreary day in the Philippines had now turned into a bright, calm, and glorious day in the heavenly realm. God providentially arranged for Mang Dante to have as his passengers that day two believing lawyers who gave him free legal advice, and best of all, introduced him to a relationship with Jesus Christ. I am certain the angels were singing glorious choruses, rejoicing over one soul that once was lost and now was found.

Not a Cent More!

In a meeting with several ministries in the lovely town of Boyolali, Indonesia, Bo's heart was filled with compassion when he saw Brother Siswo P., leader of Gema Kalvari Ministries (GKM), sitting with his young team across the room. Bo remembered that these faithful servants of the Lord had been praying for almost ten years for God to give them their own missionary training center on the island of Java.

Everyone present was caught by surprise when Bo in a loud, clear voice suddenly challenged Siswo and his team to find a property (land with a building) within one week that would be suitable for use as a training center. He declared that the cost should be not a cent more than $15,000!

The missionaries were bewildered. Why was he saying this? And why not one cent more?

Over the next week, however, they displayed a beautiful illustration of the interplay of obedience and faith. The awesome results of this unique adventure can be gleaned from the following remarkable report, which I have excerpted from a four-page letter of appreciation that Brother Siswo wrote to the donors in the US who contributed to the project:

I would like to share the information that we have formally concluded the acquisition of the property before a public notary on Wednesday, February 25, 2015. . . . We could not believe that we finally obtained our own training center. . . . We have been praying for this since almost a decade ago, when we realized that we need a facility in which our native missionaries could be equipped with proper training in contextual ministry as well as with basic living skills before they are sent back to their own people to proclaim the message of salvation in Jesus Christ. . . .

We met Pastor Bo and the ANM team in Boyolali, Central Java. . . . I also brought my beloved 76-year-old mother [Mrs. Yosef] with us, since she is an active member of GKM's senior fellowship. . . . At one point in the meeting, Pastor Bo [in a surprise move] challenged us in front of other ministries to pray and find a building and land for our training centre for only $15,000!. . . [and to find it while they were still here. It meant just a week!]

We had mixed feelings hearing Pastor Bo's challenge at that time. Except for my mother, we all had puzzled looks in our faces. At that time, I would say in embarrassment that our team doubted that a property with such a low price even existed. But then what Pastor Bo said about the importance of having faith in God made us accept his challenge as a test of faith. . . .

We still remember that Pastor Bo and Sister Marlou added that the $15,000 fund was not yet [even] available at that time, and then Pastor Bo asked us to join in a prayer so that God would provide the training centre. . . . Pastor Bo and his ANM team have strengthened our faith to believe that at the right time God will wisely answer our prayers. . . .

We started to try to quickly find a property right after [the meeting]. . . . We visited some places. . . . Then on [a] Sunday . . . God led us to a village . . . some 4.5 kilometers south of our ministry homebase. . . . We learned that [the property]—the land, the building and the environment—are just what we imagined as an ideal spot to have a training centre. . . . It is easily accessible due to the good road network around the site. Electricity and clean water installations have also been well provided. . . . Unfortunately, the land and the attached building was [being] sold as a package at 200

We could hardly believe that there was a property with such a cheap price, and we thank and praise God for His guidance in finding this property!

million rupiahs . . . equal to USD 15,905, which is actually a very good deal but beyond the budget and the owner required that the payment should be in spot cash. . . .

Something Unusual Happened

Pastor Bo asked us to negotiate the price lower, at exactly [and] no more than $15,000. By faith we kept visiting the owner to negotiate for a lower price. . . . One day we visited the owner again . . . but then something unusual happened and this was what made us strongly believe that God Himself had been involved in what we were doing. Although he insisted the payment had to be spot cash, the owner finally agreed to lower the price down to 190 million rupiahs which at that time was equal to $14,960! We could hardly believe that there was a property with such a cheap price, and we thank and praise God for His guidance in finding this property!

A few days later, Advancing Native Missions informed us that they sent $15,000 to us. We immediately met the owner of the property and closed the deal in spot cash. . . . We have shared the good news with all members of our ministry. We all burst with great joy knowing that GKM has now its own ministry training centre, after almost a decade. Praise be to the Lord! . . .

We would like to share two important things that we learned from God's grace. Firstly, Pastor Bo and ANM have encouraged us to have faith in God and to take steps based on that firm faith. . . . We also didn't have any slightest idea about where we should find a property with such a cheap price. . . . We [now] understand better what is written in Hebrews 11:1 that "faith is the confidence that what we hope for will actually happen; it gives us assurance about things we cannot see."

Secondly, we also learned that Pastor Bo shared our need with selected ANM supporters and that only in [a] short period generous brothers and sisters—who did not know our ministry personally—came forward and *sincerely provide[d] the needed funds. . . . This convinces us more that God is at the centre of events leading to the acquisition of the property. He is capable of connecting people, and He places them in particular position in His whole plan. . . .*

We thank God for connecting us with such wonderful people like you. . . . It is our great hope that one day you would have the opportunity to visit us in Indonesia to see how your donation has brought such important impact to what we do in reaching the unreached in Indonesia."

—*Siswo*

Six dear friends in the US, in obedience and in faith, had responded to this need. One of them, Josh Barrett, a young husband, father, and businessman, wrote us the following very moving letter about how Brother Siswo's letter of appreciation had affected him:

Bo and Marlou,

We both love you. Thank you for sending us this email [Siswo's thank you letter]. I am going to take it home to Melody.

Bo, I believe that God keeps bringing the movie Schindler's List back to my mind recently. At the end of the movie, Liam Neeson's character (Oscar Schindler) has to flee Germany to escape the allies. He looks around at the Jewish people that he has saved (around 200) from the [Nazis], and he talks to his foreman about how he should have sold his gold ring and his car, just to save one more. I don't know what Jesus wants from me and my family, but I can't wait to see.

I cried at my desk after reading this. Thank you for introducing me and Mel to Brother Siswo. I hope I get to hug him this side of heaven.

—*Josh*

Like a Duck into a Pond

Bo has mentioned Roger and Sylvia Elosendo earlier in this book. They are the very poor leaders of Ati Tribes Mission in the Philippines. ANM has been supporting this ministry since 1993. Prior to that, while planting churches in the hills of Panay Island among the pygmy-like, nomadic Ati aborigines, they subsisted on snails, snakes, lizards, and root crops.

In 2010, by faith, I suggested to Bo that he ask ANM's itinerary department to invite Roger and Sylvia to come to the US. The US embassy in Manila at this time rarely approved visas to Philippine citizens who lacked financial resources because of the risk that they would not return to their native country. When Roger and Sylvia received the invitation from ANM and went to the US embassy for a visa, they were disheartened to see ahead of them even some apparently rich Filipinos being turned down by the interviewing consuls.

When their turn came, the consul did not ask them the usual questions, such as "Do you own land?" and "How much money do you have in the bank?" Instead, having noted Roger's occupation as a pastor, he asked three questions in rapid-fire succession: "What was your sermon last Sunday? What was your text? Can you please explain it?"

This was like throwing a duck into a pond. Like Paul might have responded when he was grilled in Agrippa's court, the diminutive Roger—the first seminary-trained Philippine aborigine pastor—rose to his full height and in a loud voice gave a brief but eloquent discourse on Romans 1:11. Even people in the halls were listening. When we asked him what happened, Roger excitedly told us, "I was not only able to preach Christ, but they issued us visas!" Roger is the first Ati (Sylvia is a "lowlander") to ever set foot in the US.

When people in America hear the testimony of the Elosendos, they are moved to tears.

Roger and Sylvia also shed many tears when they left the US for home. Their tears were tears of joy and deep gratitude to God for their brothers and sisters in Christ who had shown compassion to them.

They flew home on November 16, 2010, with provisions for a church lot, a small used vehicle, simple Christmas gifts for their co-workers and the Ati orphans, and a small amount of start-up capital for a self-help livelihood project that would support the ministry's work. Roger also carried a brand-new laptop, another first for the Ati aborigines. Christmas came early for the poor Ati workers and orphans that year!

"Haiyan"—Super Typhoon of the Century

On Friday, November 8, Typhoon Haiyan (called Yolanda in the Philippines) swept across Leyte Island. It seemed demonically targeted for Tacloban, Leyte's provincial capital of two hundred thousand.

Winds exceeding two hundred miles per hour stripped and uprooted approximately fifteen million coconut trees, robbing thousands of natives of their livelihood. The storm tossed cars and jeepneys like toys and left several large ships marooned inland.

The fierce and merciless winds also ripped corrugated metal sheets off roofs and sent them flying at bullet speed. Woe to anyone who got hit. One family watched in horror as a flying metal sheet cut off a man's head.

The largest storm ever to make landfall sent a swell of water sixteen feet deep rushing nearly a mile inland. As the brackish water rose, one family went to the second floor of their house and stood on a bed. As water rose up to their knees, they feared they would drown. Through the window they could see their neighbors being swept away.

The storm left disaster, devastation, destruction, death, and discouragement in its wake. Government statistics as of December 31, a little more than a month later, were 6,155 dead, 1,785 still missing, 1.14 million houses destroyed (plus churches and businesses), and 4 million people displaced. Most of the deaths occurred in Tacloban, where on Christmas Day, 1,400 cadavers still lay unburied awaiting identification.

When news of the tragedy unfolded and emails started arriving at Advancing Native Missions, I was smitten to tears. Because I was born in Tacloban, Bo urged me to speak out as an Esther on behalf of my Waray-Waray people. I told a local TV reporter:

*I am
heartsick
and have been
in tears even
in my sleep.
Please help
my people!*

My father was a widower with seven children, and my mother a widow with two children. I was the first-born of the four children they had together.

My father served in the guerrilla army during World War II and was among those who met General Douglas MacArthur in 1944, when he landed on the shores of Palo, Leyte, in fulfillment of his promise, "I shall return."

I have beautiful memories of my birthplace: the school I attended, the high school where my mother taught, the provincial capitol building where my father had his office, the streets I walked on. . .

All of these are now gone. Looking at the photos of devastation, I am heartsick and have been in tears even in my sleep. Please help my people!

My plea was placed on the Internet and sent via email to the ANM community. Immediately, donations targeted for typhoon relief started pouring in. Bo immediately began wiring financial aid to Philippine missions leaders. With funds in hand, they rushed out and purchased supplies while they were still available.

Living Rock Ministries

Living Rock Ministries is headquartered in Calbayog City, which is on the western edge of Samar Island immediately north of Leyte. This area escaped the worst of the storm, and two days after it had passed, Danny Montes, leader of Living Rock Ministries, drove from Calbayog City to Tacloban to check on the branch of Living Rock Ministries there. It took him ten hours to traverse the fifty miles of debris-filled roads.

"I could not believe what I saw!" he told ANM on November 14. "Dead bodies were everywhere. There was no public transport. People were wandering like zombies—hungry and thirsty, looking for food and water. I could not hold my emotions."

Danny found his sister, Ruth, and her husband, Pastor Eugene Ramirez, alive. He also learned that my brother had survived the storm. However, five of my relatives had perished, and several had lost their homes.

Danny found Pastor Ronald Impang and his wife, Marlyn, managing, but Living Rock Center was damaged and covered with tarps to protect it from the continually falling rain. Even so, the pastor and his congregation had taken on the care of two hundred additional homeless families.

Danny left to get provisions, and two days later, he returned with water, rice, noodles, canned goods, salt, sugar, straw mats, medicines, and cooking kettles. "ANM was the first to respond in our hour of need," said Pastor Impang. "The funds sent by ANM were like a can opener. When ANM trusted us with this great responsibility, so did other relief agencies. They saw there were no blockages in our channel." As a result, Living Rock Center became a distribution hub for relief goods from several sources.

Meanwhile, Dr. Linda Balugo, of Philippine Gospel Association (PGA) on Cebu Island, also sprang into action. After receiving funds from ANM, she took the first medical team since the typhoon to Medellin in northern Cebu and to Bantayan Island. The team had planned to stay three days, but after seeing one thousand patients in two days, their medical supplies ran out.

At that time, Dr. Joy Tica of Health Education Medical Ministry joined them for a trip to Palawan, where they treated seven hundred patients, forty-six of whom yielded their lives to Christ. Later, after receiving additional funds from ANM, Dr. Linda took two vehicles containing medical supplies and a team of ten doctors, nurses, and pharmacists to conduct a medical clinic in Tacloban.

In addition to participating in the medical trips with PGA, Dr. Tica also made several trips to Panay Island, where she treated hundreds of patients and distributed over one thousand bags of food,

"We have come with no agenda but to love you and to remind you that you have not been forgotten. We are here to tell you that your tears have been our tears and the tears of your brothers and sisters in America."

clothing, and hygienic supplies. "They told us we were the first medical team to reach them," Dr. Joy said. The team also distributed 1,500 Gospel tracts, and about two hundred people raised their hands to indicate they made a profession of faith in Jesus Christ.

Meanwhile, on nearby Guimaras Island, Alex and Eunice Malanday, leaders of Church Builders Ministries, sprang into action. With aid sent by ANM, Alex purchased supplies and took relief goods to people living on the smaller, nearby island of Salvacion. In one village of 157 homes, only 8 remained. He thanked God that he had brought wire and nails to help the people construct temporary shelters out of the debris.

It was highly significant that as government and NGO aid gravitated to the major cities, ANM teams targeted the small and remote places that were missed. Because our people were native to the land, we knew where to go.

A Christmas Celebration

After six weeks of sending financial aid, Bo decided, "We must go there and give them the Christmas they otherwise will miss." Bo, staff members Jay Temple and Jerry Harding, and ANM donor Michael Riley took flight toward the Philippines and landed in Tacloban early Christmas morning. Buildings lay in ruins, and piles of debris lined the streets. A stench rose from pools of black water left by the storm surge. Families were living under tarps.

The next day, fifty-eight pastors, most with their wives, gathered at Living Rock Center for an ANM-sponsored Christmas celebration. "Tacloban is the hometown of my wife," Bo told them, choking back tears. "We have come with no agenda but to love you and to remind you that you have not been forgotten. We are here to tell you that your tears have been our tears and the tears of your brothers and sisters in America."

At the celebration, the pastors and their families first feasted for four hours on the Word of God. Jerry Harding reminded them that the heroes of the faith mentioned in Hebrews 11 did not always have things go their way. He challenged those present, "Don't run! Don't quit! Don't hide!" Jay Temple reminded everyone that David did not hesitate to bring his complaints before God. "In so doing, he was affirming God's justice, love, and power."

How different these messages were from what some other Christians were saying, such as, "You didn't pray enough; you weren't spiritual enough; that's why this tragedy came upon you."

After the spiritual feast, these servants of the Lord joyfully helped themselves to a sumptuous traditional holiday feast of two whole roasted pigs with ample rice and all the trimmings. It was the best food they had eaten in weeks, and the most! With the meal, each family received one sack of rice and a Christmas card with cash inside.

The next day, the team traveled to Calbayog to host a similar pastor's conference at Danny Montes's church. Dante Lingo, pastor of Hope in Christ Fellowship in Tacloban, spoke for all when he handed Bo a handwritten letter that said:

> Thank you for this opportunity to gather all the pastors and wives in this ministry on behalf of LRM church with Pastor Impang. Even though we lost three of our four kids to Typhoon Yolanda, the Word of God remains in our hearts. Help us to pray that God will continue to give us strength so we can continue serving Him.
>
> Thank you for this blessing that you have given to us. It will help us start a second life. May God bless you always.

Through these combined efforts, at least 10,000 families received packs of relief goods; more than 6,000 patients were treated, and 1,553 people received Christ. A rainbow of hope transcended the city of Tacloban.

After "Haiyan"—Visiting My People

A few months after the horrific disaster, I visited my loved ones and my beloved Waray-Waray people in the super-typhoon-devastated islands of Leyte and Samar. My heart was broken into a thousand pieces when I beheld the remains of the destruction in my birthplace and the condition of my people. Many of them still lived in tarp-covered tents.

But my heart leaped with joy when my loved ones came to a family reunion. I was so blessed to see almost forty of them—some with their children, all survivors—coming from different areas of the hardest-hit area, my hometown and birthplace, Tacloban City. It was very touching to have a heart-tugging, face-to-face encounter with each of them. My loved ones and I had lots of tears and tight hugs. Some of the women peppered me with wet kisses. My older brother, Carlo, did not attempt to hug me because he was afraid of breaking down. One of my widow cousins, Aida, came as a representative of five of my relatives who had perished in the huge storm surge, and whose bodies have never been found. Bo and I hosted them in the cleanest restaurant available, which joyfully served them with an abundance of available food. (At this time, the city was burying the last of 1,200 decomposing bodies.)

As they ate, I tearfully surveyed the touching scene. They had all come in their best shirts and dresses to honor me. Joy and hope were on their faces. One would not suspect that they were survivors of a terrible storm that had killed almost seven thousand people and destroyed over a million homes. Bo commented that almost all the young ladies looked like me. The women had a photo taken with me, and one of them was even named after me!

It further touched the hearts of Bo and me when some of them shyly asked if they could take the leftovers home. We gave each one—from the youngest to the oldest—a cash gift for their encouragement and their special small needs. Before we adjourned, each head of family stood up to express thanks for the large boxes of food and other relief goods that had been sent through ANM days after the storm. The loving care of ANM donors was conveyed through my reminder of the gift of eternal life through our Lord Jesus, our words of personal encouragement, and the practical gifts we shared. It was hard to say our goodbyes when the moment came.

The next day, we had a gathering of almost fifty missionary pastors and their wives, as well as some children. They came from different towns and villages in my island of Leyte. I felt pangs of deep nostalgia when I learned that some had come from my father's hometown of Carigara and my mom's hometown of Dagami. It caused me to miss my parents, both of whom are deceased.

In addition to serving them the best food available, our team had the joy of encouraging them with God's Word. There was much excitement and thanksgiving when I handed each couple an envelope with cash assistance for their family needs. These precious servants of the Lord were also provided with help for repairing their homes, especially for the roofs. In addition, each person received a conference T-shirt, and each family received a very large box of goods.

During the program, I was given time to speak to everyone in our Waray-Waray language. They cried with me when I told them that we came because I really loved them and cared about what had happened to them and their loved ones. But they also broke into big smiles when I told them that our friends in the US (or valued ANM friends) had sent with us some help for them.

This celebration was repeated that same week in Calbayog, Samar, and this time we distributed sacks of rice to almost 100 native missionaries and their families. After anointed messages from several ANM team speakers, Bo concluded our time together with a strong and convicting message about the urgent need to preach the Gospel, make disciples, and plant churches—at all costs, storms or no storms. It so convicted the missionaries and their wives that they were on their knees crying. Some said revival and hope took place that day.

Dying Is Gain—Iran

During our mission trip to London in 1997, Bo spoke at an Iranian men's breakfast meeting. The Lord gave him a very challenging message that broke the hearts of the men. One of them who wept openly said, "How I wish there were a thousand of us who heard this message!"

Bo was also invited to share the pulpit in the Iranian church on Sunday morning. It was such a moving experience to hear his message being translated into Farsi, the Persian language that was spoken in the times of Daniel, Esther, and Nehemiah. Again, the Lord greatly anointed the message that morning, and God instantly knitted our hearts with the hearts of these wonderful Iranian brethren.

Our hearts melt when we remember the story of one Muslim in Iran who recently became a Christian. When the authorities arrested him for being an apostate, they said to him, "Renounce your faith, or your family and friends and the community will disown you."

"I will still love Jesus," the new believer replied.

"Your children will be expelled from school!" they threatened.

"I will still love Jesus," he replied.

"We will throw you into jail, and you may be subjected to torture."

"I will still love Jesus."

"We may kill you!"

"Sirs, you have just handed me the Good News," the man responded, tears running down his cheeks.

One night as Bo and I prepared to go to sleep in our guest room in the headquarters of Elam Ministries, we found ourselves weeping over our seeming unworthiness, insignificance, and helplessness. God had called us to advocate for his native workers laboring among the world's unreached and unevangelized. How we longed to have more personal resources so we could provide for the urgent needs of missionary groups and their committed, sacrificing, and courageous trainees! We fell on our knees and consecrated our lives anew to the

Lord's service. We promised to be obedient as he opens doors for us in the churches and in the hearts of men.

PART II
RECOLLECTIONS BY BO

In 1994, a full three weeks after returning from my trip to the mission fields of the Philippines, Thailand, Myanmar, Cambodia, Hong Kong, and China, tears continued to come to my eyes as I recalled my experiences. Here are some snippets:

Burning His Bridges Behind Him—Myanmar

Lepers today are violently rejected by men, just as they were in the days of Jesus of Nazareth. Brother Aung Myint is not a leper himself, but he ministers to three thousand lepers who live in a malaria-infested village in Myanmar. To burn his bridges behind him when he accepted God's call to this mission field, he married a leper girl from the village. He has faithfully and joyfully ministered to lepers in this village for nine years, and he pastors a church composed of several leper families.

I asked Pastor Myint what his reaction would be if one morning he woke up and discovered that he had caught the dreadful disease. The answer he gave still haunts me on some sleepless nights. He softly replied, "Brother Bo, when that day comes, it would be a day of triumph for me, for then I could truly say, 'I have come to know the suffering of Christ.'"

Another image from this leper village keeps flashing before my eyes. It is of a sad-eyed little boy of three. With his tiny hands, he is holding to his face in a tender caress the decayed, sore-laden, leprous hands of his young mother. As I gazed upon this scene, I thought: "Many would recoil with revulsion from a single touch of those fingerless hands. But this little child does not recoil, nor would all the other little children of the world recoil. Little ones know that a mother's touch is the nearest thing to the touch of a loving God."

This incident stirred a deep ache in my heart for my own lovely young mother, who died of cancer when she was only forty-five, leaving eight children.

Good Overcoming Evil—The Philippines

A lump appears in my throat each time I remember the smiling faces of Danilo and Emelyn Milan, Filipino missionaries to the Maguindanao Muslims in the southern Philippines, one of the most difficult-to-evangelize mission fields in the world. When I visited them, Emelyn was swollen, soon to give birth to their first child.

"One day, I saw one of them stealing my chicken. I wanted to chase after him, but the Lord distinctly spoke to my heart to let good overcome evil.

As I surveyed their circumstances, I was barely able to hold back my tears. The couple's income for that month had been fifteen pesos, or the equivalent of fifty US cents. Their little thatched-roof church was furnished with just two benches. It also served as their home, and it was full of holes. Their outhouse was a hole in the ground, surrounded by torn jute sacks that were propped up by sticks. The curtain was only two feet high. I knew in my heart that no lady who used it would be considered worthy of dignity before the eyes of her neighbors. The Muslim unbelievers would never believe that she had a great God who truly cared for her. I had to look away, as I thought about my own sacrificing wife.

I asked Danilo how the Lord opened the door for him to share the Gospel on Mindanao Island among neighbors highly hostile to Christians. He said, "One day, I saw one of them stealing my chicken. I wanted to chase after him, but the Lord distinctly spoke to my heart to let good overcome evil. The next day, my wife and I took three of my four pairs of pants and went to the house of my neighbor thief.

When we gave him the pants, he was open-mouthed with surprise, and he invited us inside. That was our first open door to Muslims."

The Highest Number of Amputees Per Capita—Cambodia

When twilight comes, I recall the sobering darkness that creeps over Cambodia, a nation still filled with hate, bitterness, and pain. During our time of fellowship, Paulerk Sar, the chairman of the Cambodian Council of Christian Churches, said to me through soft sobs, "Our country remains so poor. Most of the fields remain unplowed because land mines have been strewn all over the countryside. Ten million of them! There is no joy among our nine million people. Per capita, our nation has the highest number of amputees in the entire world."

During the 1970s, the xenophobic and genocidal regime of Pol Pot and his Khmer Rouge hordes declared a terrible cleansing war against the nation's own people. More than two million Khmers died in the Killing Fields of Cambodia. Intellectuals were targeted, and anyone who wore glasses was considered suspect. To survive, people tried to play dumb, because anyone who seemed scholarly was herded off to an extermination camp. I visited one such camp, and I wish I hadn't!

Missionary Setan Lee was a medical student in Cambodia in 1975. He survived the killings by pretending to be an illiterate farmer in a labor camp. In his fourth year of enduring hard labor from 3:00 a.m. to 10:00 p.m. every day, his educational credentials were discovered. The authorities buried him alive up to his chest and left him to die. At night, Setan would raise his eyes toward the dark skies littered with sparkling stars and cry out, "God of the Universe! If you are real, please rescue me! Please save me!"

Setan Lee miraculously was able to escape, and he headed through the jungles toward Thailand. On the way, a stranger witnessed to him about Jesus, and he accepted Christ as his Lord and Savior. That very first day of his own salvation, he led thirty-four other escapees to faith in Jesus!

At night Setan would raise his eyes toward the dark skies littered with sparkling stars and cry out, "God of the Universe! If you are real, please rescue me! Please save me!"

In 1992, Setan Lee founded the only Bible school in Cambodia. The school has planted fifteen churches.

On this trip, I also met Paulerk Sar, another Cambodian Christian with a remarkable story. During Pol Pot's regime, the three hundred families in his town were ordered to move to another place, which they were told would be better. On the day of the move, Paulerk's family arrived late at the boarding area. They were disappointed to find that the trucks loaded with their friends had left without them. "But this was God's hand," Paulerk told me. "We later learned that the three hundred families were taken to a killing field outside town and slaughtered."

Paulerk dreams of starting a training center for Cambodian pastors and lay leaders. He has planted five churches.

A Missions Book-a-Thon—The Philippines

In an earlier chapter, I shared the story of Wilson and Cora Ladringan, missionaries to the Aeta people in the Philippines. My heart was broken when I climbed the hills of Zambales with Wilson in 1993. The eruption of the volcano Mount Pinatubo in June 1991 had destroyed thousands of houses, flattened towns, and laid to waste thousands of acres of fertile land around it.

Many native missionaries also suffered, but the Ladringans suffered more. The churches they had planted among the Aeta people were destroyed, along with their home and the orphanage they had built for Aeta children. Everything was now covered with ash and stone. But instead of giving up, they wiped away their tears and started over, serving the Aeta who survived. Wilson and Cora humbly named their ministry the Aetas Bible Study Center.

When I was with Wilson and Cora, I shared the provisions sent by our friends, including the money raised in a missions book-a-thon by then seven-year-old Ashley Davidson, daughter of the chief of police of Winnemucca, Nevada. These gifts were used by the Ladringans to buy food and medicine for the hungry and sick Aeta children.

ANM stands behind these sacrificing servants of God. I felt so undeserving of the following kind words that Brother Wilson wrote after my visit:

Praise the Lord for the short yet fruitful visit of Brother Bo Barredo here in Zambales. Though we just met for the first time, [it is] as if we are long time brothers. He was so humble, kind, and an accommodating man of God. We are so blessed and encouraged by his coming. How much we wish we can have a longer time together, fellowshipping and praising the Lord. And our Aeta people also like him. He was so gentle in his ways that he has captivated the hearts of the Aeta people even if it was also their first time to meet or see him. He did not mind the dirt, the dust and ashes from Mt. Pinatubo. He came to share the love of Christ to all of us. How much we appreciate him. How much we appreciate you for sending him. And above all, how much we praise the Lord for touching his heart to come and visit us here in the Philippines.

Falling in Love with Jesus and the Lady Who Shared Him—Indonesia

Missionary S. A. Soejitno of Batu Radio Ministry initially struck me as a tottering old man. But the moment he put on his headphones and began preaching the Gospel of Christ in his makeshift studio, he was half his age!

Brother Soejitno operated a homemade radio station inside his home, which was located in the middle of a Muslim community in Indonesia. A retired policeman, he fell in love with Jesus when a lady shared the Gospel with him. In the process, he also fell in love with the lady. He accepted Jesus as his Lord, and he married the lady!

Brother Soejitno started the radio station with his retirement money. He bought his first speakers and put the antenna on a tall bamboo pole. Initially, his station could reach only fifty homes. Later, a new antenna enabled him to reach all of Indonesia. At midnight, with his daughter Ester's help, he would broadcast Scriptures in Arabic. He timed his broadcast to coincide with the Muslims' prayer time. More than a hundred letters came in each month from listeners, some of them professing Jesus Christ. A few Muslim listeners would even enclose some money to support the ministry.

After ANM sent Brother Soejitno money for a new transmitter, headphones, and electron tubes, he sent the following touching letter:

> *Thank you very much for helping BRM finish renovating the studio and for supporting the ministry monthly. Thanks so much for helping Ester (my daughter) go to Bible school to study broadcasting. Thank you for providing not only for the tuition but also for the pocket money and books. May the Lord bless wonderfully and once again please accept our great thanks for all of your love, concern and help.*

When Brother Soejitno died, his son took over the ministry. It brought those of us at ANM deep sadness when his son later was killed in a tragic motorcycle accident.

The Story of Two Bus Drivers—Honduras

In 1998, I was invited by Brother Roberto Ventura, leader of Asociación de Ministerios Cristianos, a ministry in Honduras, to speak at the ministry's annual National Pastors Conference. Brother Roberto also invited me to be the keynote speaker at the fourteenth anniversary of Mount Gerizim Church, the main church of the ministry.

At the conference, I addressed the approximately three hundred pastors and lay missionaries with all my heart. My love and esteem for them overflowed in my messages because they represented the very reason and purpose of my calling from God. What a blessing it was when most of those in attendance came forward to reconsecrate their hearts in service to the Lord!

On the morning of the anniversary celebration at Mount Gerizim Church, the sanctuary was jam-packed. More than 1,500 joyful Christians sang Gospel songs to a Latin beat and waved colored flags. It was marvelous! After I spoke, several people came forward to receive Christ.

Among them were two burly, mean-looking men dressed in dirty clothes. They had grease on their arms, and they looked so different from all those who were dressed in their Sunday best. Tears were running down their faces. They seemed to be the most broken and repentant worshippers in the assembly.

The message struck their hearts so hard that they found themselves running toward the inside of the church. When the altar call was made, they rushed forward.

Later, Roberto Ventura shared this story with me. It seems that these two men had been creating a disturbance during the middle of the four-hour worship service. They were the drivers of the two church buses, and they didn't like waiting around so long. They had said to a member of the church staff, "If this meeting doesn't end soon, we are going to leave with or without our passengers!"

When the staff member reported this to Brother Roberto, Brother Roberto figured that he would have to fire these two drivers the following day. He had been aware that they were not Christians when he hired them, but he had hoped that constant exposure to Christians would draw them to Christ. After this incident, however, it seemed that he would have to give up this hope.

It turned out that the two men heard the words I preached through the loudspeakers on the outside of the building. The message struck their hearts so hard that they found themselves running toward the inside of the church. When the altar call was made, they rushed forward. To Brother Roberto's delight, they became Christians that day!

So shall My word be that goes forth from My mouth;
It shall not return to Me void,
But it shall accomplish what I please,
And it shall prosper in the thing for which I sent it.

ISAIAH 55:11

"Cuba para Cristo, Cristo para Cuba!"

In 1999, Graham Stewart, then ANM's Latin America Director, and I went on a mission trip to Cuba. The Cuban government issued us religious visas at the last moment, and the US Treasury granted us travel permits. These documents allowed us to preach in churches. We also had the freedom to encourage pastors and believers in fourteen towns and villages scattered throughout the central and eastern parts of the island.

Fires of evangelism and revival were taking place all over the island. Cuban pastors and evangelists were boldly preaching the Gospel, and churches were baptizing new converts by the hundreds each month. Churches did not observe denominational lines, and house churches were everywhere. Joy was written on the faces of Cuban believers. The rallying cry was, *"Cuba para Cristo, Cristo para Cuba!"* ("Cuba for Christ, Christ for Cuba!")

The Methodists, who were very evangelistic and fast growing at this time in Cuba, were celebrating their hundredth anniversary in the country during that year. I was extremely honored to deliver the anniversary message in the biggest Methodist church in Marianao, Havana, per the invitation of Bishop Ricardo Pereira. God blessed the proclamation of his Word, and twelve people gave their hearts to Jesus at the end of the service.

The country's economy was in very bad shape. Food supplies and other basic commodities were rationed, and everyone had to use a certified government card when shopping. Government-owned stores monopolized the sale of basic goods, which had to be imported from other countries, and prices of basic commodities were expensive. The typical Cuban family earned an average of only ten to twenty dollars per month, so life was extremely hard. Graham and I found it hard to eat the bread that was offered to us by one of our host families because it represented their entire bread ration for the month.

Families of Cuban pastors and missionaries suffered doubly because churches or congregations could barely support them. A Cuban pastor received an average of five dollars a month. A bar of bath soap cost almost a dollar, and a pound of ground beef cost a little over two dollars. A gallon of gas was sold for two dollars and fifty cents, and an ordinary pair of shoes commanded a price of fifteen dollars. A Cuban pastor who wished to buy a pair of shoes for himself or a nice Sunday dress for his wife would have to give up buying food for his entire family for three months!

One missions leader I met was on the verge of leaving the ministry. He felt so helpless and shamed by his inability to pay debts, which he had incurred to feed the hungry families of his co-workers in the ministry. His total debt: fifty dollars!

Christians had to be resourceful to survive. One pastor served us boiled grapefruit rinds with syrup for lunch! A very big church with one thousand members bought two gowns to lend to brides and their maids of honor from the congregations. One Christian leader put together a mission vehicle with worn-out parts bought from junkyards. The body was Japanese, the transmission was American, the engine was Russian, and the rest of the vehicle was Chinese!

Impacted by a Missions Trip— A Letter from Pastor Bare

Earlier in this book, I mentioned how Pastor Harold Bare ministered in important ways to my family and me over the years. He has been like a loving big brother to me. Growing up, I regretted that I did not have an older brother, but God graciously gave me Pastor Harold Bare, just as he gave me Carl Gordon. Over many years as my pastor, friend, brother, and counselor, he has been there for our family during seasons of joys and tears.

In 1996, Pastor Harold's godly and lovely wife, Laila, asked me to please bring him with me on one of my overseas trips. So I took him with me one year to the islands of Java and Sumatra in Indonesia. What a great blessing he was! He is a missionary-pastor, both by calling and by gifting.

After we returned from our trip, this born leader and dynamic pastor wrote the following thank-you letter to the leadership and staff of ANM:

> . . . Please know how grateful I am for your love and support. Thank you for facilitating my missions venture with Brother Bo. It was a trip of a lifetime, and Bo was more than gracious as a host. His incredible knowledge of peoples and their culture is astounding, a gift which God is using to touch unknown thousands of ministries and lives. . . . Now I must pray for a larger heart in which to carry many new friends.
>
> This trip cannot become history. There are precious names and faces which are written in my heart, dear ones with whom I feel a sense of desire and responsibility to stay in touch. Thank you for your belief and support in me. I am deeply grateful, especially to Bo for taking me under his "wings," and to all of you for your prayerful and loving support.

From Cage to Mission Field

When Pete Wong and I traveled to one Asian country in 2014, we met with a group of missionaries who were reaching the most remote villages of the country. One of them was a former witch doctor who became a Christian when he heard the Gospel from a missionary that ANM supports. He and his team shared a story that is remarkably like the account in Mark 5:1–20 about Jesus' encounter with the man in the country of the Gadarenes who walked among the tombs naked. Andrew Needham, an ANM editor, wrote the story below:

Amkaen was thirty-five when it descended upon him. His behavior became erratic, sometimes uncontrollable and violent. The villagers said an evil spirit had taken over. His family wore themselves out trying to help him with traditional methods, with no success. In this rural village, there was little else to do but confine him.

The family built a raised wooden cage, just a few feet across, with no room to stand, and put Amkaen inside. They passed food and water through an opening. Amkaen lived inside the cage with no relief from his inner torment for five years.

Last fall, a pastoral team from a church in another part of the province visited a new Christian family in the next village. They intended to encourage and disciple the new believers. Hearing about these spiritual men in the next village, Amkaen's mother thought, perhaps they and their God could do something. She walked there and asked, "Can you please help my son?"

The people witnessed Amkaen's mind return to wholeness, and then something more. Amkaen said lucidly to the missionaries, "I would like to follow Jesus."

The pastors visited Amkaen's village and preached to those who gathered near the man's small wooden prison. "Jesus Christ is the center of power and healing!" they proclaimed. Then they had Amkaen brought out, laid hands on him, and prayed for him. Villagers invited them to stay the night, so they did, praying and praising God.

The following day, the people noticed the beginning of a transformation: Amkaen was responding to the missionaries' attempts to converse with him. Through the day, the people witnessed Amkaen's mind return to wholeness, and then something more. Amkaen said lucidly to the missionaries, "I would like to follow Jesus."

Like the Gadarene demoniac, he began to share the story of his healing. His own village became home to a church of thirty-five people. One day, Amkaen crossed the river to share his story in a nearby village. Fifteen people committed their lives to Christ, and they now gather in a house church. The testimony of Jesus is going across the land.

Unchained

A similar account in another remote part of the same mission field resulted in the formation of a home church in the village. Sue Morris, an ANM writer, recounts the story on our behalf.

As they began to pray, Souk growled and barked like an animal. They continued praying, and the evil spirit could not withstand the power of God.

Souk [not his real name], who was demon possessed, was chained by his father to protect himself and others. His foul language, stench, and behavior caused the village to call him "The Crazy Man." A team led by a pastor from an ANM ministry partner in Southeast Asia entered Souk's village to distribute gifts and share the Christmas story. The animist villagers believed that all things in nature contain spirits that need to be worshiped and appeased.

The gift-giving strangers said, "The gifts are from our God who loves you. He offers grace and hope and exercises power over everything. Nothing escapes his notice, and all things are possible with him."

"If He is so powerful, can he heal the sick?" asked a villager. When the team replied affirmatively, the villagers took them to the house of a woman suffering with an incurable disease. Other curious villagers, including Souk's father, followed to see what would happen next.

When the pastor prayed, the woman was healed! Witnessing the miracle, Souk's father implored the team to pray for his son. As they approached his home, they were shocked at the sight of the filthy, unkempt young man shackled to posts. As they began to pray, Souk growled and barked like an animal. They continued praying, and the evil spirit could not withstand the power of God. It left Souk silent and crumpled on the ground.

The team approached Souk, and it was apparent to all that the young man was now transformed. The amazed villagers, now with softened hearts, wanted to hear more about God. When the pastor shared the Gospel, the woman who had been healed and her entire family, along with Souk and his father, all received Jesus as their Savior. Subsequently, five families totaling more than twenty people became followers of the one true God. Today, a home fellowship meets in Souk's house!

"Thank You for Changing Our Story!"—Liberia

Marlou and I were blessed to be able to support the work of Michael Holder in Liberia. One of our provisions was a large water well for the ministry's school and community, which Michael believes has greatly impacted lives. Below is the note of thanks that he sent to us:

Our profound thanks and appreciation for your timely and meaningful giving, which will enable us to dig a well that will provide safe drinking water for our 175 students and faculty members. Your action and giving have saved us from TONS of water-borne related diseases and sicknesses. [Diarrhea is a major killer in Africa.]

Having a well has been a major prayer request on our prayer list. We have lifted our voices to the Lord for many years asking him to bring us a breakthrough in this great need. Today, our prayer has become a testimony; the Lord has provided the well through you.

We had faith that the Lord would do it, but we didn't know HOW or WHEN. As we are now in the dry season in Liberia, it is very terrible to drink from a stream because of dead frogs and rotten leaves that pollute the water, making it unfit for drinking. We are glad that your loving intervention has brought this ugly nightmare to a close.

Thank you for changing our STORY!

"I Have Your Second Motorcycle!"—Togo

When Emmanuel Guidi, a poor missionary from Togo, arrived at the ANM offices in 2017, he was dismayed to learn that not a single meeting had been lined up for him. He was very downhearted, but he shouldn't have been surprised. Although he had been our ministry partner for twelve years, he came without an invitation, and everyone at ANM was busy attending to the needs and schedules of more than twenty missionaries who had been invited.

The only speaking slot we could give Emmanuel was at our regular Thursday morning Bible study. Since there were already three speakers scheduled for that day, we could only allot him ten minutes. When it was Emmanuel's time to speak, he shared about five rather modest but very urgent needs: (1) a fence to protect the 150 orphans in his school from wild animals, (2) six simple church structures consisting of a roof and four posts, (3) two motorcycles, (4) food for the children, and (5) a video projector for village evangelism.

When Emmanuel finished, he was on the verge of tears, and our hearts were broken. I stood up and gently wrapped my arms around his shoulders. Then I spoke on his behalf about the needs of this precious missionary from Togo. In that Bible study group composed mainly of missionaries, most of whom were struggling to raise their own support, provisions for six church structures at $500 each were given! As for the two motorcycles, a widow among the group committed to buy one. That was a gift of $1,200!

Emmanuel still needed one more motorcycle, so prior to the closing prayer, I said to him in a clear voice, "As soon as the prayers are said, go and shake the hands of everyone in the room. In one of those hands is your second motorcycle."

After the prayer, Emmanuel heartily began shaking hands. After he had shaken just about all the hands in the room without receiving any money, he began to get a little discouraged. There was only one person remaining whose hand he had not shaken. The man was standing across the room, and Emmanuel was reluctant to walk over to him, so he simply waved. The man was Dr. Zapanta, then director of ANM's International Medical Ministries. Dr. Zapanta walked briskly across the room to Emmanuel, stuck out his hand, and said with a smile, "Here, please shake my hand. I have your second motorcycle!"

"As soon as the prayers are said, go and shake the hands of everyone in the room. In one of those hands is your second motorcycle."

The next day, Marlou and I went to a doctor's office for flu shots. The lady doctor, who is a very beloved friend, inquired about our work. We told her the interesting story about Emmanuel Guidi, and she was deeply touched. She said, "The Lord recently blessed me. If I put up a gift of $5,000 for Emmanuel, would you match it?" We told her with delight that we already had $5,400 in matching funds for him!

When Emmanuel Guidi flew back home to Togo on Thanksgiving Day, he was overflowing with praise and thanksgiving to the Lord. We later learned that sixty people greeted him when his plane landed at the airport. The doctor's gift provided a fence for the school and food for the orphans. When we told this story at ANM, the entire staff wanted to get flu shots from the same lady doctor!

A Son's Goodbye to a Loving Father

In April 2018, I learned that my dad was gravely ill, and I hastily flew home to the Philippines and spent a few days with him in my parents' home in Bacolod City. On the last day, before flying back to the US, I went inside his room to say good-bye. I didn't realize that it would be the last time I would see him alive—that this would be our final goodbye in this sad and weary world.

After the visit, I sent the following email to Marlou:

Dear Marlou,

As I shared with you yesterday, I went inside Papa's room the evening before yesterday. He was peacefully asleep. I found myself alone with him. I sat on the bed next to his. For a long time, I was just looking at his face—aged by years. I reminisced with much thanksgiving of our beautiful times together as father and his son. Then, my reverie was broken by his sudden but slow turn, still with closed eyes, to his left on my direction.

After a while, he slowly opened his eyes. His eyes focused on me, and he looked a bit startled and disoriented. But after a few seconds, something very beautiful unfolded. His face, especially his eyes, broke into the sweetest smile I have ever seen of him all these years.

Holding that heavenly smile, like the tinkling of a glass, he distinctly and clearly said, *"Ara ka. . . ?"*

["You are there . . . ?"]

"Yes, father. I've been here a while."

"Gusto ko magpasalamat sang imo pagpalangga gid sa akon halin pa sang bata pa ako."

["I would like to thank you for loving me so much since my younger days."]

As I spoke the words, I felt some warmth crept on my eyes. I felt like a little child.

He smiled some more.

I softly said, *"Balik tulog."*

[Go back to sleep.]

"Ari lang ako diri."

[I will be here.]

With that assurance, he closed his eyes and went back to sleep. This time with a trace of a smile in his mouth.

After some time, a couple of people came into the room. It was to pump a small amount of liquid food into his stomach through the tube running through his nose.

I rose up to leave. I kissed his forehead and stepped toward the door.

Then I turned around.

I saw him slowly raise his arm.

And wave at me . . . a goodbye.

"Good night, Papa."

"Mabalik ako."
[I will come back.]

Your Beau,

Bo

P.S. This Monday, at sunrise, I will fly out of Papa's island to Manila. Then home to you and to our precious children and grandchildren.

"Be There!"
(When the Roll is Called Up Yonder)

My father went to be with the Lord he loved on May 15, 2018. He had planted the love of God in his sons and daughters and in thousands of others. Marlou and I returned to the Philippines together to be present for the memorial service. As the funeral procession traveled through the city on its way to the cemetery, the back of the hearse had a large tarpaulin sign that said, "If you die today, where will you spend eternity?"

More than a week later, as Marlou and I were waiting for our flight back to the US, I wrote our friends the following:

Thank you for your messages of condolences and encouragements while we were traveling and in the midst of days saying our final goodbye to Papa Ben here in the Philippines. Please know your consoling words of comfort and generous help meant a lot to us. They were used by the Lord to help lighten our family's burden and wipe the tears from our eyes.

We apologize for the delay in responding to each one of you. It seems that it takes a little more time for our inner selves to recover from an event like this—where part of you feels such depth of loss, and another part feels a sense of joy because "heaven seems nearer when someone so dear is waiting there for you."

My three precious sisters—Gigi, Joy, and especially our family event leader, Joji (Bong)—asked me to lead three of the four nights of vigil. (We arrived late on the first night straight from Negros Island's airport after over forty hours of travel spanning four flights and four layovers.)

The all-day visitation and the nightly vigil and worship services were held at the small chapel in the basement of the Bacolod Evangelical Church, where my grandparents had taught Sunday school many years ago. It can hold 120 worshippers. People, young and old, filled the place to overflowing each night. Different missionary leaders spoke at the vigil services. Their messages had the same theme: evangelism. Also involved in the programs were other older and younger members of our family who have a calling to the ministry. The spiritual ambience was one of unity, love, joy, peace, and hope.

With help from some family members, I made sure to shake the hands of everyone who came, and I had conversations with many guests, relatives, former classmates, family members, boyhood friends, politicians, pastors, missionaries, and others from all walks of life.

The Lord gave me liberty to humbly share an evangelistic message, "Be There!" It was anchored on a primordial biblical question, "If a man dies, shall he live again?" (Job 14:14). The message is grounded on two questions of scrutiny: "Who was this man?" and "What did he do?"

The last two questions are from an email that our dear friend Ruth Graham sent to me in relation to the recent passing away of her own beloved father, Dr. Billy Graham. Dr. Graham noticed that these two questions were raised by many young people around the world. By God's grace, the message stirred the hearts of many. Many hands were raised when an invitation to receive Christ was issued.

Our father, Benjamin G. Barredo, left us the heritage of those who fear God's name (Psalm 61:5).

ᴀ MOTLEY CREW

In the early days of ANM, our close family friends, Max and Beth Johnson, arrived from Atlanta to be full-time volunteers at ANM. After meeting the others who were there in our office, Max looked around and said, "What a motley crew!"

He was right. In appearances, backgrounds, and skills, we probably were far from the type of people a senior business executive with an MBA degree or somebody with a PhD in missions would want to hire when launching a ministry. But as I have said about myself, and I am confident that my fellow workers at ANM would say the same about themselves, all that any of us has to offer to the God of Heaven, the Creator of the universe, is a willing heart.

Our desire from the beginning has been to allow God to bring the people and guide the decisions. The character trait we most value is humility. When we acknowledge our weaknesses, the Lord is our strength. When we cover every decision in prayer, the Holy Spirit is our faithful guide. When we have the courage to move forward despite our limitations, Christ is our sufficiency.

In earlier chapters, I have talked about some of the remarkable people God brought to ANM over the years. In this chapter, a few more members of our motley crew, including some of the newer members, will tell how the Lord brought them to ANM. I will also include some information about the management style we've adopted since the very start of ANM. Leadership and management are such important topics these days, and I hope some of this information may be helpful to others.

Unfortunately, time and space do not permit me to include the stories of all the wonderful members of ANM's motley crew, even though we know that in God's eyes every single person is precious, and every deed done for his glory is sacred. If we had time and space, I feel certain we could fill many books with marvelous stories about what our gracious God has done in and through each of us.

But before getting into the personal stories, I would like to share some insightful thoughts by Dr. Dan Reichard. After working as a school principal, Dan became ANM's vice president for spiritual development, and today, he serves as regional director for East Asia.

"The Main Thing Is the Main Thing" by Dr. Dan Reichard

We have sometimes been called a motley crew here at ANM. Some might take that as an insult, but not the ANM motley crew. As we look back at church history, I think most people would have called the first disciples a motley crew. They were fishermen, tax collectors, zealots for political change, and so on. They fit no mold, held no credentials, and only knew to do what their master told them to do in the way their master told them to do it.

I remember that when I first came to ANM in 2006, I had never been around "people like this." I remember saying to my wife, after a few weeks of being with ANM, "I can't believe these people are as good as they seem or that they love each other the way they seem to. I'm just waiting for the shoe to drop." Well, after sixteen years, I am still waiting. The shoe hasn't fallen yet. Yeah, they are that genuine.

One of the miracles of ANM is the love and respect that we have for one another. Here are Presbyterians, Southern Baptists, Pentecostals, Non-denominationalists, Calvinists, Arminians, Independent Baptists, etc., all working together for the cause of Christ and the goal of reaching the unreached. Not one time in all these years have I ever heard one word of disagreement or disrespect to another's positions. The key is that denominational differences pale considering the need to tell the world about Jesus Christ, the only hope of salvation for all men. In other words, the main thing is the main thing, and that is the main thing.

One of the things I learned, as part of the motley crew, is that ANM doesn't fit the missiological mold. Many mission agencies do missions the way they learned in school or the way their denomination prescribes. ANM has no actual "missiologists." We have people who, in their past lives, served as engineers, schoolteachers, lawyers, football players, school principals, accountants, businessmen, and in a host of other fields. We go into strategic missions planning with no preconceived ideas as to how it is to be done. We rely on the leading of the Holy Spirit, and he continually leads us to dream and plan outside of the box. He is key to the success of ANM.

In my tenure as a part of the ANM family, and as a Christian for more than fifty years, I have never seen a ministry or an organization that more closely pictures the body of Christ than the motley crew of ANM. Fellowship doesn't begin to explain this phenomenon. It is *koinonia*, that sense of family and community that goes to the very core of being one in Christ and living heart to heart and spirit to spirit. It is that unity that God has honored.

For Christ said of his relationship with the Father, "I in them, and You in Me; that they may be made perfect in one, and that the world may know that You have sent Me, and have loved them as You have loved Me" (John 17:23). What is the result of this kind of unity? That the world would know that the Father sent his Son into the world to save the lost.

"The Best Gift a Mother Could Ever Receive" —The Oliver Asher Story by Bo Barredo

Oliver's story reads like a highly inspiring movie plot, along the lines of *Fireproof*, *Flywheel*, *Facing the Giants*, and other award-winning movies by Christian movie producers and directors Alex and Stephen Kendrick. But this story is for real.

Oliver's father escaped from a chain gang in South Florida and ran across the Everglades toward Tampa, while being pursued by prison guards. His purpose? To see his newborn son, Oliver. After his release from prison, he moved the family to the poverty-stricken hills of southwest Virginia. Oliver's mother, Carol, and his grandmother, Lilly, raised him, his younger brother Danny, and his younger sister Missy in the knowledge and fear of the Lord.

Oliver's first deep sorrow occurred when he was in seventh grade. The trailer in which his family lived burned to the ground. "We'll move to our tool shed for six months until we can build another house," said his father. Six months turned into six years. The small shed that served as the family's home had no plumbing and only one lightbulb in the middle of the room. They washed their clothes in the creek, and on cold winter nights, the harsh breezes blowing through the shed's rough wood slats caused Oliver's teeth to chatter.

Oliver's second deep sorrow occurred when he was sixteen. Missy was thrown from their old truck and died. But life on the farm had to continue. Most days, Oliver would help his father cut and log wood. He grew strong lugging a heavy chainsaw. Occasionally, he would bring classmates home from school. They were surprised to see his family's poverty, but fortunately, Oliver didn't know they were poor.

Winning Games

The high school Oliver attended had posted only four winning football seasons in the past twenty years. "Once we found ourselves cheering for our biggest rival, Chilhowie High," Oliver says with a smile. "They were beating us 91–0, and all the fans wanted them to reach 100!"

Coach Alderman, a man of faith, saw the potential in the curly-haired, boyish-looking fellow who always seemed to be smiling. He loved this 6'1", sturdy-framed woodcutter like his own son. During Oliver's junior and senior years, the coach encouraged him to drink gallons of milk and eat loaves of bread, so he would get bigger and stronger. He also allowed him to take showers at school because of the poor conditions at home.

In his senior year, Oliver was made captain of the team. The coach trusted Oliver, and the whole team admired his gracious and humble leadership style. His sweet and gentle spirit inspired others to follow him. But as a middle linebacker on the football field, Oliver was anything but sweet and gentle. His spectacular tackles mowed down opponents like a bulldozer or chainsaw, causing the crowd to erupt in cheers. During his senior year, the team won the first district championship and playoff game in the school's history.

Coach Alderman, a man of faith, saw the potential in the curly-haired, boyish-looking fellow who always seemed to be smiling.

News about this phenomenal player spread fast around the football circuit. Droves of college football scouts got lost looking for Oliver's small school in this remote part of southwest Virginia. Oliver became the local hero and the toast of the town. When a local dentist watching Oliver being interviewed on TV noticed that he had a broken front tooth (Oliver had lived with this problem since the third grade!), he promptly called Oliver's coach and told him to send the boy to his dental office the next day.

When Oliver finished high school (the first in his family to do so), he visited the University of Virginia as a prized recruiting target of the football program. He was wowed by the elegance of the grounds and immediately accepted a scholarship offer. The prospect of someday making it big as a professional football player prompted him to promise his mother, "I will someday build you a nice house on top of the hill. No more watching the snow fall through the slats on winter days. You will no longer have to use an outhouse and wash laundry in the creek."

The late 1980s were exciting years for Oliver. He loved playing football at the University of Virginia, and he excelled academically. He graduated with a degree in environmental science, went on to earn a master's degree in civil engineering, and married his beautiful sweetheart, Andrea McGuire, the only daughter of the UVA's director of academic advising.

Oliver and Andrea put God first. After graduation in 1988, they went as young missionaries to the Dominican Republic, where they helped build a local church, physically and spiritually. After almost one year, they were blessed with the birth of their first child, Oliver Alexander, and they returned to Charlottesville. During the succeeding years, Oliver became one of the youngest elders in the large church they attended, and he taught the adult Sunday school class. The dynamic pastor of the church loved him as a son.

Staying Close to the Lord

In 1993, Oliver and Andrea were enjoying married life; they loved raising a family, and they had just moved into a lovely new home they had built. But in the early dawn of Christmas Day, they found themselves watching their new home burn to the ground. This brought back painful memories to Oliver of his seventh-grade year, when his parent's house burned. But drawing on his deep faith, he and Andrea stayed close to the Lord and patiently waited for God to show them the next steps.

I happened to be one of the members of Oliver's Sunday school class when his house burned, and I decided to pass the hat at an ANM staff meeting, in hopes that we could offer a modest bit of financial help. After the seven members of our staff were assembled, as I was about to pass the hat, there was a knock on the door. It was Oliver. He looked disheveled, exhausted, and red-eyed.

"I'm sorry that our family's missions offering is late," he said, handing me a small envelope.

While Oliver was giving me his missions offering, I imagined God, our Father, calling out to the angels and saying, "Look at that young man. Do you see him? Look at him . . . that's my boy!" There was not one dry eye in that room.

Two years later, I observed that Oliver was moved to tears as he was praying for the members of the Sunday school class he led. I recognized this as an anointing of the Holy Spirit, but I suspected it might also be something more. It turned out that on the preceding night, Oliver had dreamed that he had lost his job.

I said to Andrea, "If that dream should come true, please have Oliver give me a call. I would like to talk with him about taking a six-month vacation and serving with me at ANM before he starts looking for another high-paying engineering job."

The God who wisely ordains all things made the dream come true. One Sunday night not long after that, Oliver found himself kneeling at the altar of his church asking for God's direction. One friend, Jerry Thomas, who did not know what was going on in Oliver's life, prayed for him, "Brother Oliver, the Lord has already prepared ahead everything for you."

Stepping Out in Faith

That was all Oliver needed to hear. By faith, he answered God's call to missionary service for six months at ANM. But when Carl reminded me that Oliver should raise his support first so his young family could be taken care of, I inquired in our accounting department and learned that our family's remaining support for the year was just over $9,000. I went to Marlou and asked if she would agree with me that, by faith, we would offer whatever support we had at ANM to Oliver and his family so he could start working with us immediately.

"Like you, I also love Oliver," she answered. "Yes, let's give everything we have now and trust God to supply for our family."

With Marlou and Carl's concurrence, Oliver began volunteering at ANM. He was such a blessing! I came alongside him, and together we operationalized about four prospective departments. All during this time, I was thinking about how the six-month agreement would soon come to an end.

At the conclusion of his fourth month, Oliver entered our leadership room and straightway said to Carl, Graham, and me, "Brothers, I know that only two months remain in my commitment to work with you. But Andrea and I have prayed and decided that, by faith,

"Brother Bo, I am the one thanking God for calling my son to serve him. That's the best gift a mother could ever receive."

I will stay with you, as we believe this is God's plan for me."

Noticing that the three of us froze when he said this, he added in a more serious tone, "And if you insist that I should leave, and you decide to drag me out of this place, please remember that I used to be a football player. I know how to tackle, wrestle, kick, and push hard!"

We were tremendously moved by the seriousness of Oliver's faith and dedication for our Heavenly Father's business. At the time of this writing, those six months have turned into twenty-six years, and he's not done yet! The journey has been filled with joy and tears, sacrifices and miracles, disappointments and loving favor. But most of all, the Lord has granted Oliver spiritual growth and exponential ministry increase.

What gave Oliver the courage to commit to serve God by faith? I believe it was his true love for his Savior. True love can be measured by the willingness to give and the capacity for sacrifice. Oliver has always had both, and God has mightily blessed him.

Oliver succeeded me as president of ANM on January 1, 2018. On that date, he became the new captain of the ANM missionary team serving more than thirteen thousand native missionaries in 112 countries. These dedicated servants are sharing the Gospel with some of the remaining seven thousand people groups, language groups, and tribes that have not heard about Christ.

Some years ago, I asked Oliver to take me to southwestern Virginia to visit his mom. We drove to a remote, mountainous area and went inside a ramshackle, one-story building with a rusted tin roof. It was a sock factory, the ambience of which reminded me of the sweatshops I had seen in Asia. But there was one difference: the workers in this factory had gray hair.

A plain-looking, elderly lady scurried toward us, brushing the lint and fiber out of her hair and off her apron as she approached. With a smile beaming across her tired face, she wrapped her arms around her son. Her baby boy hugged her back, lifting his mom off her feet as if she were a little doll. This beautiful scene brought tears to the eyes of this veteran lawyer-missionary.

"Ma'am," I said, choking back tears, "I'm here to personally thank you on behalf of thousands of native missionaries around the world for giving away your beloved son to serve them." I had to pause to clear my throat before continuing. "Please forgive us, because as a missionary-servant your son may not be able to keep his promise to build you that nice house on the hill with all the conveniences in it."

Oliver's mom blinked away the tears and smiled at me. "Brother Bo, I am the one thanking God for calling my son to serve him. That's the best gift a mother could ever receive."

"God Is Calling Me to ANM"
by Victor Morris, ANM Chaplain

In the fall of 1994, I was working as an associate pastor at Covenant Church in Charlottesville, Virginia. During that season, I began to feel God was stirring my heart to do something new and different in my life. As I prayed about this, I felt a pull in my heart toward Advancing Native Missions. The more I prayed, the stronger the impression became. In fact, this impression became so strong that when I would pray, I would see the letters "A-N-M" flash through my brain like a neon sign.

After several weeks, I told Bo that I felt God might be calling me to ANM. He was a parishioner at Covenant Church, and he did not want to see me leave the pastoral staff, so he tried to dissuade me. However, the sense that God was directing me to ANM only increased, so I called Bo and asked him if I could come in for a talk.

On the day of my visit, after Bo had shown me around the new ANM office suite, I asked him if we could go for a ride. We got into my car, and I began to drive without any destination in mind. We found ourselves riding far out into the country past sites that were very familiar to me because of my family history. Finally, we stopped in the parking lot of Evergreen Church of the Brethren, a small rural church at the very foot of the Blue Ridge Mountains. Members of my family had attended this church for many years. We got out of the car, walked across the road to the church cemetery, where generations of the Morris family are buried. Instinctively, I walked to my grandparents' graves.

Bo and I stood there in the shadow of a large cedar tree chatting for a few moments. Then I asked the question that was burning in my heart: "Bo, do you think there could ever be a place for me at ANM?" A strange expression came over Bo's face. After hesitating for a moment, he said, "Brother Victor, I think that possibly there might be a place for you at ANM." This was all I needed to hear for my hopes to soar.

A short time later, Bo invited me to accompany Carl Gordon, Graham Stewart, and him on a day-long business trip to Lynchburg. They picked me up early the next morning. All day, I enjoyed watching them interact, tell jokes, and talk about the ministry of ANM, and I observed them as they conducted some business with a friend of ANM. At the end of the day, as Bo dropped me off at my home, he explained that he had just wanted me to spend time with the leadership of ANM. "We are just ordinary guys," he said. "In fact, we are really just little boys."

As he said this, tears welled up in my eyes. "Bo, that makes me want to work at ANM even more. What a joy it is to work with people who are genuine and real!" I think this was not what Bo had expected me to say. I believe he hoped that I would recognize that my dream of working at ANM was just a passing fancy. He advised me to take three months and think and pray about what God was telling me.

Threatening a Founder

I did this, and on March 13, exactly three months to the day after our conversation, I called Bo to schedule another talk. I think he was a little surprised that I was still pursuing the matter. Nevertheless, he invited me to come in and meet with Carl, Graham, and him.

I still vividly remember our meeting in a small conference room that day. As I sat across an eight-foot table from the three ministry leaders, they all tried to convince me that there was no place for me at ANM. Bo reminded me of my responsibilities at Covenant Church and what it would mean if I left. Carl said, "Victor, we have no place for you here. We do not have a desk; we do not have any space; we do not have a position for you; and we do not have any money to pay you. We have nothing to offer you."

"Brothers," he proclaimed, "this is the work of God! What can we do? We are dealing with a call from God."

When he said this, my heart erupted, and I began to sob. "Brothers, I don't care! I don't care if there's no place for me. I don't care if there's no money. All I know is that God is calling me to ANM!"

At this moment, Graham pushed his chair back from the table. "Brothers," he proclaimed, "this is the work of God! What can we do? We are dealing with a call from God."

The entire atmosphere of the room changed. All three men acknowledged that God was at work. They recognized that the Lord had called me to ANM. After that, Bo talked with the pastor of Covenant Church, and it was arranged that for a month or so I would work several days a week at ANM, and on the other days, I would work at the church.

After this transition period, in April 1995, I began working full-time at ANM as the director of publications. After I had worked at ANM for some months, Bo said to me, "Do you realize what you did to me that day you took me to the cemetery? You must understand that in the culture where I am from in the Philippines, if you want somebody to do something that they are reluctant to do, you take them to a cemetery. There you will make your proposal to them. You are basically saying, 'If you do not agree to do what I want you to do, I will put you here in this cemetery.'

Naturally, I was surprised to hear this. To this day, I think I am the only person who has been hired at ANM by threatening the life of a founder!

Responding to God's Calls

I worked at ANM for three years, and then, in 1998, I answered a call to be the pastor of a church in Pennsylvania. Eight years later, while I was serving at this church, Sue and I received an invitation to speak at a retreat for the ANM staff. At the retreat, we greatly enjoyed seeing everyone and fellowshipping with old friends.

On the drive back to Pennsylvania, we both commented about how spending the day at ANM felt like coming home. As we began to pray, we sensed that the Lord was stirring our hearts for a return to ANM. I wrote about this to Bo and the ANM leadership, and in June 2006, after months of prayer and seeking God's wisdom by all concerned, Sue and I returned to Virginia. I rejoined ANM, and later, Sue joined me.

Since 2006, I have undertaken numerous roles at ANM, but through the years, I have always remained a pastor. When Gordon Shira passed away several years ago, I became the senior chaplain of ANM. It has been my joy to serve in this role for the past sixteen years.

"The Definite Hand of God"
by Kishor Pandagade[25],
Regional Director for South Asia

When I met Brother Bo Barredo and other ANM team members in Calcutta in 2006, I was the principal of Calcutta Bible College. We immediately went to the downtown area, where the team was scheduled to meet with a family who intended to donate property that they owned to ANM for missions work. For some reason, the team included me, and I still recall Brother Bo asking me to end the meeting with a word of prayer. When the meeting was concluded,

---

[25] In 2022, four years after Bo stepped down as president, Kishor left ANM.

we toured the city together, and I was given an opportunity to share a bit about my life story and the missions work of our college. This was eye-opening to many team members.

After the tour, we all went to a restaurant and enjoyed a gentle conversation over dinner. Brother Bo and I happened to be seated across the table from each other, and I noticed that he was keenly observing me. At his request, I shared about my life and my missions work for about thirty minutes during the meal, until the team had to leave. We did not meet again while they were in India on that visit.

In 2007, I was surprised to get a call from Brother P. R. Misra, who at this time was the South Asia director for ANM. He had just arrived in Calcutta, and he invited me to meet him at the airport for a cup of coffee. When we got together, he informed me that Brother Bo had enjoyed talking with me, and that he would like me to come to the US as a visiting missionary. I was shocked because Brother Bo and I had met only once for a single day, but I also was thrilled because I knew that this must be from the Lord.

When I told my wife, Sikha, and our daughters, they too were surprised. Without losing any time, I applied for a passport and zipped through the interview at the American consulate in Calcutta. In July 2008, I was on my way to the United States.

A Warm Welcome

Upon my arrival, the ANM staff gave me a very warm welcome. At the conclusion of the regular Thursday morning Bible study, Brother Bo introduced me to the jam-packed audience and asked me to share my life story. I was very nervous and emotional to be speaking to an American audience for the first time with full liberty, but Brother Bo reassured me by placing his hands gently on my shoulders and smiling. In what I have learned is his usual manner, he interviewed me to extract more of my life story. I was surprised at how well he articulated my story because he had met me only once for a short time. It was so encouraging to see how clearly he had understood my struggles, pains, and sufferings. This is one of his amazing God-given gifts.

From that moment, I saw Brother Bo as a father figure, an excellent mentor, a man who loves missions and missionaries, and a gifted leader. These qualities were confirmed even more when he and Sister Marlou took Sikha and me to churches in the US to allow us to speak and raise support for missions in India. Since then, he has become my role model, whom I will always admire.

I know today that it was not a coincidence that the team from ANM came to Calcutta. During this process, I saw the definite hand of God. His plan became even clearer when Brother Bo graciously offered me a position at ANM in the United States. We are grateful to the Lord for raising up Brother Bo and Sister Marlou and inspiring them to bring us to the US. This is something we would have never thought about in our wildest dreams. Now we are blessed to be part of the ANM family, where in nurturing love and fellowship, I have the opportunity to serve our fellow missionaries as the South Asia regional director.

"OBI Is a God-Idea!"
by Jerry Harding,
Director of Operation Barnabas for ANM

In the fall of 2000, a group from Advancing Native Missions came to the church in Charlottesville, Virginia, where Rachel and I were attending. They spoke about "indigenous missionaries"—people who were native to their country, knew the language and customs, did not require a visa, lived as their people lived, and actively shared the Gospel. I was fifty-seven years old. I had been to Bible college and served as a pastor, evangelist, and conference speaker. But I had never heard about indigenous pastors and missionaries.

After one of the services, I inquired about the possibility of traveling overseas to India. I wanted to follow a leader around to see for myself how these indigenous missionaries operated. On October 9, 2001, a month after 9/11 and one day after the US started bombing

Afghanistan, I flew out of the Charlottesville airport on the first leg of my journey to Delhi, India.

My total excursion took twenty-eight days, during which I boarded sixteen flights and visited thirteen ministries. All aspects were led by Indians who were dedicated, qualified, and effective spiritual leaders who had been called by God to reach the unreached, plant churches, take care of the widows and orphans, and baptize and train disciples. And they were doing all these things without many of the tools and resources that are considered necessary for successful ministry. I came home with a broken heart and shared the stories with family and friends with tears. My eyes had been opened, and I wanted to help.

Refreshing Tired Feet

I talked about my desire with the leadership of ANM, and they felt my gifts best suited a ministry called Operation Barnabas International. Operation Barnabas was initiated in 1996 by Bo Barredo and John Varghese. One of the first ministries of ANM, its purpose was to "refresh the tired feet" of the pastors, evangelists, and missionaries with whom ANM partners. There are more than ten thousand servants of God all over the world, and far too often, they are unknown and unheralded by the American church. In addition to supporting missionaries who otherwise might be faceless and forgotten, Operation Barnabas provides a platform from which American pastors and teachers can participate in indigenous missions. It is an opportunity for these spiritual shepherds and their wives to renew their vision, deepen their spiritual walk, and reaffirm their calling.

Members of Operation Barnabas teams often so heartily catch the vision for indigenous missions that they return to the US not simply as supporters of the missionaries they have met, but as enthusiastic advocates on behalf of them with their families, friends, and churches. For more than twenty-five years, many thousands of dollars have been sent through ANM each year to native missionaries overseas as the result of Operation Barnabas excursions. That is why the ministry in 2008 adopted the theme, "Refreshing tired feet . . . Fitting them with sandals." It captures the ministry's twin goals of encouragement and advocacy.

Since its inception, Operation Barnabas has conducted nearly 250 overseas conferences and excursions that have challenged and encouraged thousands of spiritual leaders. The sound biblical preaching, spirit-filled worship, warm fellowship, and delicious food provided at these conferences refresh the souls of many who are experiencing struggles. These conferences have inspired hundreds of beleaguered and discouraged ministers of the Gospel to renew their commitment to God's call on their lives.

There is a definite intangible element about Operation Barnabas, an anointing of sorts that cannot be quantified. It is not a pep rally or a temporary emotional fix. It is a time of learning from the past and moving with faith and confidence into the future. It is a time of hearing God's Word with more receptive ears, receiving God's guidance with more open hearts, and pursuing God's purposes with clearer vision, renewed commitment, and greater strength.

In April 2007, I was privileged to become the director of Operation Barnabas International, standing on the shoulders of previous US leaders Oliver Asher, Jay Temple, Bubba Rose, and Dan Reichard. What a joy it is to be able to refresh the feet of the shepherds of God's flock through this marvelous ministry. As a friend from Kenya accurately declared, "OBI is a God-idea!"

"My Journey to ANM"
by Krista Darcus,
Vice President, International Operations

My husband, Gary, and I had been attending Covenant Church in Charlottesville with our children for only a short time when a new family arrived. We became fast friends with this family, and our children attended school together. One Sunday, the father of this family, Bo Barredo, was invited to the stage for prayer about a new missions organization that he and his colleague, Carl Gordon, wanted to start.

I joined in the prayer for this venture, and once the mission was established, my husband and I through the church became regular supporters. As I recall, we donated for the staff of the mission, so they could in turn serve the indigenous missionaries.

I would just laugh it off, but now I wonder if I was being like Abraham's wife, Sarah, who laughed when the angel said she would bear a son.

As the years passed, Gary and I continued to support the mission and read its publications. One day, a letter came from Jay Temple saying he was moving to a different position, and ANM needed someone to take over the Africa region. When I read this, I took the newsletter to Gary and asked, "Is this you?" This initiated his journey at ANM.

During these years, I was initially a stay-at-home mom and then a teacher's assistant at the school our children attended. Subsequently, I served on the staff of a local church, and after that, I accepted a position with a noted author while working part-time in retail. But in 2011, the position I held was eliminated, and I found myself unemployed. What was I to do next?

I was familiar with the staff and structure of ANM because of my friendship with several staff members. Also, Gary and I regularly attended staff family events, and we had hosted several missionaries in our home over the years. But when Gary suggested that I explore working at ANM as his administrative assistant, I was hesitant. After receiving some wise counsel from my friend Betty Westmoreland, however, I joined the ANM team in December of 2011.

Looking back, I remember the times when I would visit the mission and Brother Bo would tell me where my picture would go on the wall of the building. I would just laugh it off, but now I wonder if I was being like Abraham's wife, Sarah, who laughed when the angel said she would bear a son. Later, I learned that I was one of those that Bo envisioned being on staff. He said how he wished that I was going to be part of the first group to join ANM. That was never my dream or goal, but God had other—and better—plans.

Four or five job titles later, I am now the vice president of international operations. Each position has offered different experiences and opportunities for growth and development. My work of helping to facilitate needed changes has been most rewarding. I have had the privilege of advocating for and supporting those who deal closely with our missionary partners. I also collaborate with the other vice presidents to align interdepartmental activities for the advancement of the whole organization toward agreed-upon goals. I am so grateful to be here!

"Hooked on Indigenous Missions"
by Renee Lilly, Senior Regional Director

In the middle of my first year in Bible school, the Lord began to draw me together with my future husband, Shane. He was 1,300 miles away ministering in Virginia as a youth pastor, and I was still in Oklahoma, but the Lord made it clear that we were to be together. There was only one problem: he had no missions call. So we each devoted ourselves to a day of fasting and prayer, laying on the altar our relationship and the ministry and everything. That day, the Lord told me very clearly, "Lay down your missions call." I sensed this would be only for a season, but my wait for the mission field lasted twenty years!

After I completed Bible school, Shane and I married, and we began to minister together. Over the next few years, we had two beautiful boys. I worked as a public-school teacher for twelve years, and I also helped at the church by leading worship, counseling, and leading the women's ministry. Everything I needed to know for my missions calling I learned from my husband and through the experiences gained during those twenty years.

When our sons were twelve and seven, I became restless and began to sense that a change was coming. I resigned from my responsibilities at the church and prayed and waited for direction. One day, while at my son's school, I saw a flyer announcing a talk by a visiting missionary from Egypt. I was fascinated and decided to attend. It turned out that this missionary was sponsored by ANM. As I listened to her speak, I was overwhelmed with her humility and love. I had never witnessed such power in any Christian. I was hooked on what I would later learn is indigenous missions.

A modest donation to ANM put me on the ministry's mailing list. A few months later, I received a newsletter from a woman I had never met. Her name was Autumn, and she was starting a new ministry at ANM called International Women's Ministries. She was seeking new team members, and I knew immediately that I had to contact her. When we met, we instantly felt a connection. I began working on the women's ministry team, and soon I was planning a trip for the team to India.

A New Calling

As I was raising funds, I came to ANM for the Bible study and to turn in some funds that had been donated. While there, the ANM president, Bo Barredo, approached me. To my knowledge, I had never met him before, and I was surprised that he knew who I was. He asked me if I would join Sister Autumn and him in a meeting. When we entered Sister Autumn's office, I quizzically looked at her for an indication of what this was about, but she knew nothing.

Brother Bo began by telling me the testimony of how ANM was founded. Then he started asking me questions, and when he found out that I had received my call to missions in the Philippines, he took extra notice. "Sister Renee," he said, "I want you to go home and talk to your husband, Shane, and your boys, Cameron and Christian, about whether the Lord would have you come to work at ANM as the desk director for Southeast Asia!"

I was shocked! I didn't know exactly what a desk director was, but something in my heart told me that this is what I had been waiting for. When I shared with Shane what had happened, he said with tears in his eyes, "This is absolutely God!"

Financially, we would need to step out in faith, and I would have to raise my own support, just as the missionaries in the field must do. We decided to put it before our children, so the next day during breakfast, I explained to the boys the opportunity set before me. After we had discussed the financial and practical changes it would require, our oldest son, Cameron, responded, "Mom, this is God's way of rewarding you for all these years you've taken care of us!" Our youngest son, Christian, who is always the least talkative, simply said, "That's cool!"

A short time later, I took over the management of the Southeast Asia region, while continuing to teach part-time to help with our personal finances. As I served in this role for the next three years, I was continually amazed by the sacrifice, humility, and joy of the missionaries we served.

In 2017, I felt the Lord tell me to quit my teaching job altogether and trust him to take care of our family. I informed the ANM leadership team of this, and about a week later, Brother Bo asked me to develop the Latin America region, which had been leaderless for many years. In 2018, I assumed responsibility for this region, and over the next few years, I was blessed to see it grow, develop, and stabilize.

In 2018, I accepted an invitation to serve as ANM's senior regional director. In this role, I get to troubleshoot challenges and provide help for all the regions. I have now worked at ANM for ten years, and it has been an incredible blessing to rub elbows with the royalty of the kingdom. God took my desires and planted me in the center of his plan for the kingdom of God.

"In Meandering Ways"
by Will Hasley, Chief Financial Officer

When I met Bo Barredo during my sophomore year of college at the University of Virginia (UVA), he told me that he was already recruiting me to ANM. I just smiled. At that point in my life, God had laid a calling on my heart to serve the Lord and others, and I had a deep passion for missions work. I graduated from UVA with a degree in finance and accounting and headed off as a missionary to Costa Rica, where I helped build a children's home and a church and host tons of American mission teams.

Fast forward a few years, and I had my master of divinity degree from Duke University and was serving as a pastor in Raleigh, North Carolina. As God would have it, my family and I moved to central Virginia thirteen years after I had first met Bo Barredo, and my heart was open to finding new work. Bo struck while the iron was hot and let me know that ANM was ready for me. It turned out that I was ready for ANM because my work as a missionary and a pastor had only served to reinforce ANM's model of native missionaries as the best approach for bringing the kingdom to fruition.

God has often worked in my life in "meandering ways," as I like to say. There's clearly a hand of Providence involved, but I do not always see it for what it is. Thankfully, I landed here at ANM, where I am able to serve God in a way that uses the gifts and graces God has bestowed upon me. To God be the glory!

"My Work at ANM Has Given Me Fulfillment" by Stanley Honour, IT Manager

I owe my interest in international cultures to my father, Stanley Beck. He was the international sales director for Diamond Shamrock, a billion-dollar oil and chemicals corporation. As I was growing up, we had many house guests from Asia and South America. I tend to be interested in history and in cultures as a dynamic system. I'm not particularly interested in individuals, except for world-changing individuals like Elon Musk. I've never wanted to be rich, but I have wanted to change the world for the better, to make a lasting difference.

In the ten years following graduation from college, I worked at several different companies as a computer programmer and database analyst. Later, my friend, Tim Henderson, and I discussed with Carl Gordon how we might create a receipting system for missions. Out of this conversation, the ANM information system was born.

From about 1995 to 2004, ANM grew steadily from about eight staff members to twenty. During this time, I was the sole IT guy at ANM. I began by volunteering part-time for several years, and then I transitioned to half-time work. Most of the daily needs and issues involved changes to the hardware and network, so while my background and training were mostly in database programming, my practical experience was as a network administrator.

In 1997, I started full-time at ANM as the IT manager. For the next seven years, I designed and installed five miles of network wiring with 160 nodes, culminating in the building of our new office compound in Afton in 2004. I have stayed at ANM for thirty-plus years because I have enjoyed so much meeting people from all over the world and selecting and installing computer equipment that makes the staff's Gospel work easier and more productive. How satisfying it is to see the direct, positive results of my labor! My work at ANM has given me fulfillment I could never have hoped to enjoy at a typical for-profit company.

"The Lord Has Much More to Give You"
by Amber Parker, Chief Operating Officer

When I graduated from college, even though I was trying hard to hear from God and prepare for his call, I had no idea what should come next. My parents made a major life change by selling their home and moving to Charlottesville to work at Advancing Native Missions. On my frequent trips to visit them, I was introduced to the ministry's partners and staff. It was not uncommon for my parents to host visiting missionaries from other lands, and my interactions with men and women from Ghana, Egypt, India, and many other nations opened my eyes to how God was working around the world. I was amazed at the impressive scope of ANM's work. Like the missionaries they served, I found the staff of ANM to be full of humility, love, and passion.

Each time I visited ANM, I felt challenged to grow in my faith. And almost every time, the president of ANM, Bo Barredo, made a point to talk to me. He would encourage me and invariably say, "Young lady, one day you will work here." I would smile and nod, thinking inside that maybe someday I would like to be a part of ANM or a similar organization, but I didn't plan on doing that anytime soon. I had moved from student worker to associate director in my job at the university, and it seemed to be the right place for me.

But one day, as I was sitting in my office, I felt a release. God seemed to be shifting everything within me and preparing me for a new direction. I mentioned this to my mom, and she said, "They were talking about you today at ANM." I wondered if this could be the new direction. The connection to what was happening on the front lines all over the world through ANM was unmistakable. Maybe, just maybe, God could use me to make an impact there.

At this time, a story in 2 Chronicles 25 challenged my thinking and confirmed my call to ANM. Amaziah, the king of Judah, was preparing for a difficult battle. He had invested financially in a plan for victory, but God had another plan. In a conversation with God's prophet, Amaziah questioned all he would be giving up. The prophet responds, "The LORD has much more to give you than this" (2 Chronicles 25:9 NASB).

The Next Generation of Leadership

I resigned from my job and joined ANM. The verse quoted above summarizes both my time at ANM and my walk with God. God always has much more for us than we have for ourselves. Surprisingly, my time at ANM lasted only two and a half years. Despite my love for the ministry and the people, I somehow felt something was off. In sharing my unsettledness with God, he pointed out an open door. I went through that door, and for four fruitful years, I worked at my local church. These years brought more growth and maturity, as I learned about building teams, loving people, organizing projects, teaching God's Word, and developing a missions program.

I will always remember my church's trip to visit an ANM ministry partner in the Philippines. As we traveled out to remote villages, I saw Filipino pastors share the Gospel with love and practical care. They fed people physically with rice and spiritually with the Word of God. One evening, the ministry leader shared with us the priority of raising up the next generation of leadership for his organization. As I read my Bible the following day, I was burdened to pray for the next generation of leadership for ANM. I had a sense that somehow this impacted me, but I had no idea how.

About one year after I returned from that trip, Bo reached out to me. He shared that it was time for him to move into a new season of ministry by transitioning out of his role as president of ANM and turning the leadership responsibility over to Oliver Asher. Then Bo asked me to prayerfully consider returning to ANM. As I prayed, I saw how God was indeed raising up the next generation of leadership. Despite my initial resistance, I recognized my part in that new movement of God.

In 2018, I returned to ANM to serve as a member of the executive team. I cannot say that every step of the way has been easy, but I *can* say that it has been one of the greatest privileges of my life. I love serving alongside our amazing team, advocating for native missionaries, loving and caring for donors, and seeing God move among the nations. In this season of ANM, we continue to build on the foundation put in place by God's faithful servants.

No Rambos Here—
An Editorial by John Lindner[26]

Someone once said, "If you want to know if you are a leader, turn around and look. If no one is following, you are not a leader." Conversely, if you have followers, you are a leader, whether you intend to be one or not. There is always someone watching us. Therefore, we should give attention to what we do, where we go, and how we get there.

---

[26] This is a slightly edited version of an article that appeared in a 2016 issue of *ANM World Missions* magazine.

At Advancing Native Missions, a leader is not perceived as a heroic crusader, but rather as a member of a team. Sometimes leaders speak to the team; at other times, they listen to the team. There are no Rambos here.

The foundational concept of leadership at ANM is teamwork. Five of the leaders—co-founders Carl Gordon and Bo Barredo, CEO Oliver Asher, SVP of US Operations Dick Prins, and SVP of International Operations John Bucchi—all share the same large office space. A visitor once looked into the leadership room, saw the five desks arranged without cubicles around the perimeter, and remarked, "I never saw anything like it in the corporate world!"

There is always someone watching us. Therefore, we should give attention to what we do, where we go, and how we get there.

I also notice that ANM's leaders follow the pattern exemplified by the Lord Jesus when he washed the disciples' feet. Our leaders are feet washers. Whether it be a staff member or a foreign missionary visitor, if a person has a need, ANM's leaders make sure it is met—often taking care of it themselves. One reason ANM has been successful as a missionary organization is that our leaders know that when one member of the team falters or has a need, the whole team is hindered. Similarly, when one member of the team is blessed, all are encouraged.

At the Evangelical Press Association in California in May [2016], ANM World Missions was twice recognized. We won a second-place award for Tony Weedor's first-person article, "When the Devil Danced on the Water" (Fall 2013 issue), telling how he, his wife, and daughter escaped from rebel terrorists in Liberia.

Considering we were being judged against such major magazines as *Christianity Today*, *World Vision*, *The Banner*, and *Decision*, taking second place was a real honor. Overall, our magazine earned an Award of Merit among the sixteen missionary magazines that were members of the EPA last year.

It's all because our writers, editors, designers, proofers, printers work as a team. I am so honored to be the head coach of such a wonderful team. Let us rejoice together and give God the glory!

"I Was Finally Home!"
by Eric Vess, Writer

"If I answer God's call to ANM, I'll starve to death!" That was my faithless response to what I knew was a genuine call of God to come to ANM. It was 2005, and I was in a difficult but well-paid position at another missions organization. A traumatic misunderstanding on a recent mission trip had left me discouraged, even depressed.

When I had initially met ANM founders Bo Barredo and Carl Gordon in 1996, I had been immediately attracted to the ministry they led. So in the aftermath of this discouraging experience, I contacted Bo and Carl and asked them to pray for me and for my vocational direction. I think Bo thought I would come to ANM right away, but it was another five years before the time was right.

I have always been attracted to intercultural relationships and media storytelling. As a child, my parents took me to see the film *The Inn of the Sixth Happiness* about the life of missionary Gladys Aylward. Even though Hollywood romanticized the story, the bravery and dedication depicted in the film captivated me. God used that experience to help point my life toward media and missions.

As a teenager, I found my way into an early career in radio announcing. After military service and marriage to my wife, June, I re-entered radio and eventually learned video production. In 1991, I founded a media-production ministry that served Christian and missionary organizations. This led to travel and work in more than thirty-five countries.

Shortly after coming to Christ through the ministry of African American evangelist Tom Skinner in 1972, God placed the following passage of Scripture on my heart as a life calling:

The LORD GOD has given me
the tongue of those who are taught,
that I may know how to sustain with a word
him who is weary.
Morning by morning he awakens;
he awakens the ear
to hear as those who are taught.

ISAIAH 50:4 (ESV)

God reasserted my core calling as a biblical encourager in 2000. Over the next few years, my involvement with media production slowly decreased, and my dedication to Bible teaching increased, both in my local church and on the field as an encourager of frontline missionaries and leaders. In 2009, I left this well-paying job and spent almost two years as a leader of a development ministry.

By 2010, however, I could see clearly that I needed to be part of a larger and more diverse team. ANM offered this team and so much more. In addition to being a highly effective missions organization, the ministry was an intercultural family with staff from multiple countries. In 2011, I chose to follow God's call to ANM. Bo's affirming nature and his Asian cultural approach to leadership provided an inviting context. From day one, I felt at peace within this family. I was finally home!

A Team Approach to Leadership

When I joined ANM, I experienced firsthand a team approach to leadership that models respectful consensus-building and biblical mutual-submission. Bo surrounded himself with other experienced leaders who had freedom to speak their minds from their hearts. He encouraged mutual listening and, even more importantly, keeping an open ear to the voice of God in Scripture.

The executive committee would meet weekly to prayerfully consider a range of ministry issues, challenges, and opportunities facing ANM. Selected emerging leaders were intentionally "fast-tracked" into this circle of leadership for a period of months to accelerate their exposure to the culture of ANM and mentor them in preparation for greater responsibility. This also ensured a constant refreshing of opinions and viewpoints within the executive committee. All members were encouraged to share openly and candidly.

Also included on the executive committee were two members of ANM's board of directors who were welcomed at the proactive invitation of the senior leadership. This is rare in leadership circles today. One of the two board members, Kathy Hassell, attributed this invitation to intentional transparency:

> *The interesting thing is that this request did not come from the board, but rather directly from leadership itself. Here is a ministry intentionally desiring, inviting transparency. Thus, for the last two and a half years, I've joined another board member, Dr. Don Richardson, who has been serving in this capacity for over four years.*

It was encouraging to witness both the goal and the process of healthy leader development at work within the circle of ANM leadership. Again, Kathy Hassell shared her perspective on the spiritual dynamic of prayer building character, calling and competence in the context of Christ and community.

> *Prayer with the leadership at ANM is not something you just open or close the meeting with or hurriedly incorporate into the meeting. Prayer is vital to the entire meeting. Topic by topic on the agenda will be bathed in prayer. And when we pray, we are excited and looking forward to just how God will answer. We expect God will overwhelm us with exactly what is needed—and He does not disappoint!*
>
> *From time to time when I would walk into a meeting, I might see a long agenda to cover for the day. This would assuredly mean a great deal of time would be spent before the Lord inquiring of Him to give us wisdom, direction, and His discerning Spirit.*
>
> *I must also mention how the team takes delight and great joy when God's will is revealed to us. This in turn leads to more time*

praising and thanking Him. Many leaders in ministries today believe that power through prayer is available, yet they don't engage in it. ANM engages in prayer. We have learned that God delights to lead His people, and in response to their trust, He lets them see "great and mighty" things.

Along with Kathy, I had witnessed Brother Bo bring a meeting to a complete stop and lead us into a period of extended sharing and prayer over a particularly difficult issue or new missions opportunity. The agenda can wait; prayer cannot. It was this determined dependence upon the Spirit of God and an intentional desire to bring glory to Jesus Christ that characterized everyday leadership decision-making at ANM. All glory to God alone!

Today, as a writer in ANM's marketing department, I tell stories about what God is doing in the nations and help answer important missions questions for readers of the ANM blog. And as anyone who knows me can see clearly, I have not come close to starving. All glory to God alone!

"Called to ANM"
by Jay Temple, Director,
Comforting the Persecuted Church[27]

Neither the ring of the hammers, the sloshing of cement being mixed, nor even the squeaky wheel of the wheelbarrow I pushed could drown out the still small voice of the Lord.

I was working with a construction team in Ecuador in 1992 when I felt the call to ministry—a call that I knew had missionary bearing. I began to prepare, anticipating that I would leave everything behind to go and serve God in a foreign field. Along the way, however, I encountered Advancing Native Missions and learned of another paradigm for missionary service: serving native missionaries.

---

[27] Jay left ANM in 2018 to answer a call to the pastorate.

He has done it through a team of people chosen by him, not for their talents or abilities, but for their willingness and obedience.

During the more than seventeen years that I served with ANM, my appreciation for *what* was being done steadily grew. But more than that, I became increasingly grateful for the *way* it was being done. While some members of the staff, by virtue of calling and position, were more visible than others, the work of ANM was always a team effort. This teamwork was modeled by the group known as the senior leadership.

This team of seven men was responsible for the day-to-day operations at ANM. Five of the seven shared the same office. Co-founders Bo Barredo and Carl Gordon set the tone for the rest of the senior leadership team by the effective way they jointly lead the mission. Oliver Asher and Jay Temple served as elders and were ordained together in their local church. Two others had served in pastoral ministry.

All had experience in vocations outside of ministry. A lawyer, an accountant, an engineer, a telephone lineman, a coal miner, a businessman, and a teacher made up the leadership team. All had heard that same voice of the Lord calling them to serve him together at ANM.

Operating as a plurality of leaders is not easy, particularly when each one is a strong-willed man of vision and action. Working together, praying together, wrestling with decisions together may not be the *quickest* way to get things done, but it certainly is the most *durable*—and *biblical*. "For by wise counsel you will wage your own war, And in a multitude of counselors there is safety" (Proverbs 24:6).

More than once, outside observers advised that we could get more things accomplished if one leader made all the decisions. I agree that there would have been more activity, but would the will of God have been so powerfully accomplished?

In the six or so years that I was part of senior leadership, much was accomplished by God's grace. It is satisfying to look back and realize that no individual can take credit for any of it. Rather, God has done it. He has done it through a team of people chosen by him, not for their talents or abilities, but for their willingness and obedience. He has done it through a group of people more interested in building the Lord's kingdom than their own.

I am thankful for Bo and Carl, who took me on board and gave me a place to fulfill my calling. I am grateful for the blessing of serving with them and with such an excellent staff.

"Sit-By-Me Leadership"
by Oliver Asher, ANM President and CEO

I thought I knew some things about leadership before I joined ANM. By age thirty, I had earned two degrees at the University of Virginia, one of the finest educational institutions in the world. I was an ordained minister and an intimate part of the leadership team of one of the most dynamic and thriving churches in our community. Yet, little did I realize how much more I still had to learn.

When I came to ANM, Bo introduced me to the "sit-by-me" leadership training model. Yes, it's as simple as it sounds. It was just a matter of sitting (and sometimes traveling around the world) beside Bo, watching him, and mimicking what he did. Besides learning the fundamental elements of how to build and run a missions organization, I learned the deeper and more profound truths of servant leadership from the meekest (defined as power under control) leader for whom I had ever served.

I learned how to deeply love and serve my coworkers (and everybody, for that matter). I learned how to bathe everything in prayer, how to be open and vulnerable with others, especially with my co-workers, and how to be a more loving husband and father. Most of all, I learned how to adore and worship Jesus my Savior more each day. These are lessons that can't be learned from college lectures or best-selling leadership books. They are learned only by living together, hurting together, praying together, and loving together.

I was deeply humbled when in the spring of 2018, Bo recommended me to succeed him as president of ANM. As he explained, Ecclesiastes 3:1 tells us that for everything there is a season, and Bo felt it was the right time for him to step down from the key leadership position and become ANM's global ambassador. I was strongly encouraged to know that I would be surrounded by a great leadership team that Bo and others had cultivated over the years. They included Dick Prins as CEO, George Ainsworth as COO, and P. R. Misra as international president.

By God's grace and for his glory, Bo has discovered and polished many "diamonds in the rough." I was (and in many ways still am) blessed to be one of them. Now, my greatest hope and desire is to follow his example by discovering and polishing some "diamonds in the rough" of my own, by God's grace and for his glory.

LIVING LETTERS

God gives each of us a limited amount of time on this earth. What will we pour our lives into? What kind of legacy will we leave behind?

The world frequently measures success in terms of wealth, titles, power, or fame. It's so easy to invest our time and energy in things that don't last. In the following passage of Scripture, the Apostle Paul gives us a different and better perspective:

> *Do we begin again to commend ourselves? Or do we need, as some others, epistles of commendation to you or letters of commendation from you? You are our epistle written in our hearts, known and read by all men; clearly you are an epistle of Christ, ministered by us, written not with ink but by the Spirit of the living God, not on tablets of stone but on tablets of flesh, that is, of the heart.*
>
> 2 CORINTHIANS 3:1–3

It has been my lifelong desire to emulate Paul. Paul invested himself in people. His letters of recommendation were written on human hearts. His measure of success was transformed lives.

> *A good name is to be chosen rather than great riches,*
> *Loving favor rather than silver and gold.*
>
> PROVERBS 22:1

God has called each of us to love well. By God's mercy and grace, I want my story, to the extent that I have one, to be written on the hearts of those whom God has graciously allowed me to love and serve. I want my life to count.

In his farewell address to the Ephesian elders, as recorded in Acts 20:18–21, we get a glimpse of how Paul's commitment to living with eternity in view worked itself out in his everyday life:

> *And when they had come to him, he said to them:*
> *"You know, from the first day that I came to Asia, in what manner*
> *I always lived among you, serving the Lord with all humility,*
> *with many tears and trials which happened to me by the plotting of the*
> *Jews; how I kept back nothing that was helpful, but proclaimed it to*
> *you, and taught you publicly and from house to house,*
> *testifying to Jews, and also to Greeks, repentance toward*
> *God and faith toward our Lord Jesus Christ."*
>
> ACTS 20:18–21

The love of Jesus empowered Paul to love people. If I had been present with these elders when Paul bid them farewell, I am sure that tears would have been flowing down my cheeks.

In the moving 1998 film *Saving Private Ryan,* the desire to have one's life count was poignantly illustrated by the final words of the dying Captain John Miller. He said to Private James Ryan, "James, earn this . . . earn it." He was telling Ryan to be worthy of the sacrifice he and his other soldiers had made to save him.

We can never be worthy of God's sacrifice, of course. We can never "earn it." But we can seek to be obedient to the call that God has on our life.

> *And He died for all, that those who live should live no longer*
> *for themselves, but for Him who died for them and rose again.*
>
> 2 CORINTHIANS 5:15

As a missionary with a global ministry, I find myself falling in love with my family, my co-workers, my friends, the supporters of the ministry, and the native missionaries we serve. And as a former practicing lawyer, I am accustomed to calling witnesses. In this final chapter, I am going to ask some dear friends and family members to offer some evidence. My purpose is not to try to demonstrate whether I have loved well—only God can judge that—but to use their testimonies as a starting point for talking about the fruit of love. Jesus said that the fruits of our actions reveal much about the condition of our heart.

Love begets love. When God enables us to love people, those we love will be inclined to love others. And even more importantly, when we love them with godly love, they will be inclined to love the Lord Jesus more. "We love Him because He first loved us" (1 John 4:19).

With that introduction, let's call some witnesses. These are just a few of the people who have enriched my life, and for whom I am thankful to God. I would like to have mentioned so many more, but space does not permit it. Perhaps we will see in the actions and words of even these few people how receiving love stirred them to greater love for God and others.

> *Love begets love. When God enables us to love people, those we love will be inclined to love others. ... When we love them with godly love, they will be inclined to love the Lord Jesus more.*

The First Set of Witnesses— Three Co-workers I Love: Lucille, Virginia, and Pete

One of the sweet blessings of ANM is the privilege of working with people who love and respect each other, and who have enthusiasm for their work. Three of those co-workers are Lucille Lebeau, Virginia Tobias, and Pete Wong. We build one another up.

A smile comes to my lips as I remember my younger days when our children's Sunday school class would sing a certain song. While singing, we would all go around and shake the hands of the others. At the end of the song, we would give someone a hug! Here is what we sang:

> *Ang Dios gugma, ang Dios gugma,*
> *Maghigugma-anay kita.*
>
> *God is love, God is love;*
> *Love one another, God is love.*

A new commandment I give to you, that you love one another;
as I have loved you, that you also love one another.
By this all will know that you are My disciples,
if you have love for one another.

JOHN 13:34–35

An Edifice of People—A Tribute to Lucille Lebeau

On October 26, 1997, days after our ANM board meeting in which I had spoken about my physical and emotional exhaustion due to my very busy ministry schedule since the inception of ANM, Lucille Lebeau, the board secretary and Director for International Communications, wrote me a wonderfully honoring letter. I felt undeserving of it and filed it away. As this book was in progress, however, Marlou insisted that I should share it with readers as a way of honoring Lucille's intention. Our family deeply loves Lucille, and God has mightily used her to impact my spiritual life. Her faithfulness and God-honoring prayer life could be a model for all believers. She is now eighty-seven years old and living in a retirement community. Marlou and our ANM co-workers know that I am a favorite of Lucille. Below is her beautiful letter:

Dear Mr. Vice President, Missions Development

Dear and Precious Brother Bo,

The following thoughts evolved from some of the notes I recorded as secretary from your own report on Saturday morning at the ANM Board Meeting. Many sentiments were expressed in loving concern toward you as you shared about the issue of a finished task as Vice President of Missions Development.

My own heart, though remaining silent, was also bursting forth with loving concern, and also with loving pride for your accomplishments in the beautiful architecture [at ANM]. It seemed to me you were saying, during a moment of great fatigue, that the accomplishment of a beautiful vision given to you by the Lord was a "fait-accompli," and you were wondering "what to do next."

"Oh! No!" my heart was crying out! Can Bo not see that the infrastructure so lovingly and beautifully built up by him is not of stone and mortar, but rather an edifice of people? They are "your children"—"diamonds that need to be polished"—"jewels in your crown as unto the Lord."

I was thinking again of what the Lord had put on my heart to share with you the afternoon just before the ANM [Elam] Missions Banquet (this event was another one of the "children" that you birthed). I said to you that you are as a "Father" among us. You graciously smiled at that remark and soon walked away. I felt a bit "foolish," perhaps, but I still believe that it is so!

The discussion that ensued among the board members upon your declaration of "having finished" a task brought the implication of what I had said that day, and the epithet "Father," again to my heart. And my thoughts seemed all mixed up—and, yes, deeply saddened in a selfish moment—at the possibility of an ending "sometime."

I was resting later in the afternoon, from my study on the book of Isaiah. Again, the wondrous idea of God as a Father is revealed by the prophet, especially in Chapter 40. Please receive these words not as 'foolish' but rather from loving thoughts instilled by Our Father's heart as a gift of encouragement to your own heart.

God has created the world—"fathered it." But He has not abandoned it. All the created universe is in His hands and under His control. He "holds it together." He makes the stars to shine for His purposes and enjoyment. The entire universe is under His management, His guidance. It is His pride and joy! Father means somebody who is able to regulate the life of his children, from a centre outside themselves—to pull them towards wholeness; to offer them warmth, joy, gentleness, security; to be an 'integrating factor' also shaping the whole to produce balance, interaction in diversity and unity.

On Saturday morning, did you perhaps feel as a "nothing"—having emptied yourself, emptying your very heart of every vestige of energy? The Lord Himself will surely build you up and edify you in some wondrous and surprising way soon.

Dear Gentle Brother, you are honored and respected and greatly esteemed and affectionately loved in our midst—"your ANM family." Your *presence brings "yes! yes!" It brings great joy and warmth and sunshine. How we love you! You "treat" each one of us as "your own." The special sharing you give to each is a gift of yourself. In it each feels greatly encouraged and loved and appreciated and exalted. You have built warm relationships!*

In many of your prayers for us and with us you have declared and wished for and promoted an "atmosphere of home and respect"—a family circle within our prayer circle. How can we ever thank you enough for your sharing of yourself, in material and spiritual gifts again and again.

You know, Dear Bo, that the beauty that you admire in each of "your children" as "Directors of this and that department" reflects the qualities and loveliness of your own heart. You "saw" it all in the marvelous "vision" that the Lord gave you so long ago perhaps—to be settled and put into place.

—Lucille Lebeau

Gratitude Starts with a Good Memory—
A Tribute to Virginia Tobias

What a great, great joy it was when the pastor's widow from Rensselaer, Indiana, by the name of Virginia Tobias, finally joined ANM! She became our donor relations director, and friends of the ministry were nurtured by the prayerful notes she wrote on the receipts for their contributions. She loved carrying on a correspondence with many of them. As of this writing, Virginia is eighty-seven years old, and she still works for ANM from home. I remember her in many wonderful ways. She has been such a blessing to me!

One fond memory is how she would always hand me two hundred dollars each time I was about to travel overseas, with the instruction that I should give it to a needy pastor's wife or a pastor's widow. That's how she became friends with a number of these ladies, and these friendships have lasted for years.

The other fond memory is even more unforgettable. During my six months of depression, when I despaired even of life, Virginia would send me cards and letters of encouragement *every other day*! She served as one of the Lord's lifelines for me on those days of seeming hopelessness. A line that she wrote on one card was so highly honoring that I felt unworthy of it. I hid the card for a long time, but Marlou encouraged me to share a line from it in this book as a way of honoring Virginia. Here is what she wrote:

> *Bo, you are often God's arms embracing us; you are His voice speaking to us; you are His eyes seeing over our needs; and you are His heart, loving us.*

I will be forever grateful to Virginia.

On the twentieth anniversary of the founding of ANM, our Scripture theme was Psalm 126, with emphasis on the verses that read, "Then they said among the nations, 'The LORD has done great things for them!' The LORD has done great things for us, And we are glad." (v. 2–3).

Indeed, the Lord had graciously brought ANM thus far, for his glory and for the sake of thousands of native missionaries we served, who are declaring the glorious Gospel among the nations.

Looking Back

Virginia was among the dozen or so church leaders and pastors we consulted at the founding of this humble ministry, and she was one of the seven co-workers we had during the first two years of ANM's operations. In response to my request on the occasion of ANM's anniversary, here is a brief "look-back" article she wrote:

> It is with fondness that I recall one special day twenty years ago in August. I was honored to sit around the table in Ron and Pam Tillett's lovely home, and to meet Bo Barredo and Carl Gordon, who had driven thirteen hours to Indiana. We spent the day visiting and praying as our brothers sought wisdom regarding "digging another well." I fondly remember the sweet spirit that enveloped those hours. I sensed a loving Christlikeness in Bo and Carl as they shared their hearts. The

Lord that day tucked a longing in my heart to someday be a part of their vision.

It was two years later, in 1994, following many confirmations from the Lord, that I found myself headed for Charlottesville with my belongings in a U-Haul. Leaving Indiana was a painful parting, for these dear friends had walked with me through times of grief following the death of my pastor husband. The sweetest confirmation was from my 86-year-old mother (who lived to be 101) when she granted me her blessing to move nine hours away from her!

I soon realized that I had a "new" family of seven/eight in the little office of ANM. Oh, the happy memories I cherish of that first year! Our office was a place of prayer—and a place of joyous laughter. One by one, new members joined the family, and leadership soon realized it was time to find larger quarters. So, we moved—not once, not twice, but three times—as we outgrew each location!

Finally, in 2005, we built a new office in the midst of the beautiful Blue Ridge Mountains. This special place I see as that "city set on a hill" that sheds the light of Jesus Christ on all who enter—and on those we serve around the world. This building sufficed for eight years. Then more construction was required to give us a wonderful auditorium and more area for staff. Numbering now over fifty, we continue to be that "motley crew" that only the Lord could bring together.

As I walk the halls of ANM, there is a "story" associated with each missionary photo—memories of their visits and their servant hearts, each serving as a reminder to pray. I have often thought that we surely already had the "cream of the crop," but then, lo, a new missionary would arrive, and the rest must "scoot over" to make room for another precious one.

I recently saw a note I had written in the margin of my Bible the month before I came to ANM: "My desire at ANM – 8/10/94." I didn't know then that I would be writing encouragements on many donor receipts, but the verse turned out to be remarkably appropriate. It was Isaiah 50:4: "The Sovereign Lord has given me a well-instructed tongue, to know the word that sustains the weary" (NIV). To this day, our leaders continue to manifest that quiet confidence as they guide us into greater and richer growth in his kingdom.

Our ANM president, Bo Barredo, frequently reminds the staff that "gratitude begins with a good memory." The Apostle Paul's memory of his churches allowed him to greet them in his letters with words, such as "I thank my God every time I remember you." He wrote that to the Philippians from prison. May this attitude of gratitude become our standard!

He Dared to Believe— A Tribute to Pete Wong

Sometime in mid-January 2013, as Marlou and I were busy preparing for a trip to the countries of Nepal, Sikkim, North Bengal, Bhutan, and the Philippines, I saw an email from a pastor by the name of Pete Wong, who said he was looking for a place in a church or ministry. I could not shake the email off my mind, so I turned to Marlou and said, "Sweetheart, this brother's email is a job application, but somehow it strikes me as a cry for help, if not a cry of despair. Do you think I should contact him?"

Marlou stopped what she was doing and told me, "God gave you a spirit of obedience. Why don't you act on it by emailing him back, or by texting or calling him?"

I emailed this pastor, but there was no response. I texted him, and still there was no response. Then I called him on the phone, but there was no answer. Feeling relieved, I told Marlou, "I think God took this off my hands."

But the next day, Pete Wong called back. This is how my "love story" with this precious brother and his wife began. Below is a brief recollection from Pete:

PETE

Pete and Melody's Story

Our Father God Almighty, the all-knowing master orchestrator, took great delight in intertwining my life and Melody's with Bo and Marlou's. We had been in transition since September 2012, when I concluded my pastoral ministry in Pembroke Pines, Florida. Our longtime missionary friends, Rev. Bernard Beverly (now with the Lord) and his dear wife, Carole, had opened their home in Winston-Salem, North Carolina, to us. In their words, they wanted to provide a "soft landing" for us while we sought what our Lord Jesus had for us to do next.

During the next four months, we emailed my resume all over the US attempting to find a ministry opening. We explored every lead, but all our exhausting efforts proved futile. Little did we know that God was working to bring us back to his call to global missions, after having served as Filipino missionaries to Thailand from 1986 to 1996. We would learn later that in early January 2013, as Bo and Marlou were making extensive preparations for a mission trip, God providentially directed one of my emails to show up in their inbox. Don't ask me how Bo's email address got included on the list for my mass emailing!

The night of January 15, despite his very busy schedule, Bo called and emailed me. That happened to be the same night that our gracious hosts informed us that we needed to find another place to stay. My phone was turned off, so I didn't get Bo's voicemail message until the following morning. When I heard his message, my utter dejection turned into an adrenaline surge. I called Bo back, but my low morning voice sounded so incoherent that Bo asked to talk to Melody instead. By the end of the call, Bo had arranged for us to visit the office of Advancing Native Missions in Afton, Virginia, which was a four-hour drive from Winston-Salem.

What a God-ordained visit that was! The greeting they lavished on us would have befitted dignitaries! It was a godly testimony to Bo and Marlou's generous hearts and their selfless love for God's servants. We were given a tour of the ANM offices and introduced to members of the missionary staff. They gave us a $150 cash gift to pay for our gas, treated us to a sumptuous dinner at Red Lobster, and put us up for the night at a very comfortable Hampton Inn.

At the Thursday morning Bible study the following day, I was given an on-the-spot interview by Bo. Afterward, we had a great lunch at the New Ming Garden Buffet and Grill. To top it off, Bo asked us after lunch to enumerate our immediate needs. They totaled over $800, and later, to our pleasant surprise, our kind-hearted host produced a white envelope containing over $1,400 in cash. That was the total offering from the ANM missionary staff taken at the Bible study. We were simply incredulous!

Joining the Team

Melody and I joined the ANM team on January 22, 2013. From that time until now, God has been using Bo's mentoring skills and brotherly love to shape and mold us to become staunch advocates for the more than thirteen thousand native missionaries that ANM partners with, and liaisons to the more than four thousand individuals, couples, families, churches, and organizations in the ANM donor database. Bo has patiently and selflessly poured his life into our lives, multiplying himself through our own missionary and advocacy efforts.

Bo consistently has been a godly mentor to Melody and me, teaching us by example how we should be desperate for God in prayer and worship. His diligent discipleship has paid off. By God's grace, our passionate appeals on behalf of native missionaries have reaped an abundance of prayers and financial support from congregation after congregation and home after home.

A year after coming on board, God used Bo's mentoring in a very specific way. Between 2014 and 2018, we held our biggest assignment yet: director and administrator of the Southeast Asia region. In those five challenging years, we trusted the Lord for the wisdom and strength to structure a supportive system for the 1,700 native missionaries in nine countries under our care. Often we visited missionaries in their own mission fields, sometimes traveling with Bo and Marlou. Our travels have taken us to the Philippines, Thailand, Laos, Cambodia, Indonesia, Myanmar, and Malaysia.

"Let's Search for a House"

God stretched our faith numerous times (and he still does), but on one unforgettable occasion, the Lord involved Bo profoundly. Bo came to our office at ANM one fateful day in 2015, and after greeting both of us, he said to Melody, "Melody, open a web browser on your computer, and let's search for a house of your own to buy!"

When we heard these words, we were in disbelief. If our faces had displayed our thoughts, the word would have been "incredulous"!

Melody and I had served the Lord for thirty-four years. Because of the nature of our vocation as missionaries, we had never dreamed of owning a house. When we heard these words, we were in disbelief. If our faces had displayed our thoughts, the word would have been "incredulous"! But God chose to honor the faith of this man on our behalf. One miracle led to another, and despite having no fixed income and no credit standing, both of us surprisingly qualified for a rural development housing loan. By December of that year, Melody and I, still incredulous, had moved into our very own 930-square-foot, three-bedroom, one-bath, single-family, single-level house on a 5,000-square-foot corner property in the city of Waynesboro, Virginia, population twenty-two thousand, with no down payment! The mortgage company didn't even ask us to start paying the monthly payments until February of the following year!

Seven years later, Melody and I are still pinching ourselves to see if we're awake from an ongoing dream of homeownership! And it's all because Bo dared to believe what we ourselves could not believe. That is, he believed the impossible!

Our Father in heaven indeed took great delight in bringing Bo into our lives. This man's love for the God of Missions is truly evident to all who know him. We are among the many beneficiaries of his devotion and faith. We are doing what we do today because God chose to reflect his glory in the obedient life of his faithful servant Benjamin Mijares Barredo Jr.

The Second Set of Witnesses— Three Dear Friends: George Bokorney, Pastor Otis Spellman, and Pastor Gerald Ripley

You are the salt of the earth; but if the salt loses its flavor,
how shall it be seasoned? It is then good for nothing but to be thrown
out and trampled underfoot by men. You are the light of the world.
A city that is set on a hill cannot be hidden.
Nor do they light a lamp and put it under a basket,
but on a lampstand, and it gives light to all who are in the house.
MATTHEW 5:13–15

When someone receives love, he becomes more motivated to give love to others. In scriptural terms, when we give love to others, we are helping them fulfill their God-given purpose of being salt and light in the world. But giving godly love to another person does something more: it also shapes the recipient of the love. It opens the person's heart to the love of God, the source of all love. "We love Him because He first loved us" (1 John 4:19). If the one receiving godly love is already in love with the God of Missions and is already being salt and light in the world, receiving more love will enhance the savor of his salt and the brightness of his lamp.

I witnessed this dynamic with three of my closest friends in the world. These friends, who are precious among the many friends with whom God has blessed me, are George Bokorney, the late Pastor Otis Spellman, and the late Pastor Gerald Ripley. I'll talk about each below, starting with George:

He Nicknamed Him "Fitter"— A Tribute to George Bokorney

During the time of the year when many men like to go hunting, George Bokorney longed to go duck hunting in his native state of Texas, but he had no dog. One day, a fellow hunter called him up and said, "George, my Labrador retriever just had puppies. Would you like one?"

"I sure would," George replied.

"OK. Just send me a check for one thousand dollars, and you'll be number three in line."

George and his wife, Cindy, agreed early in their marriage to discuss in advance any expenditure over twenty-five dollars. "I learned this from reading about how Pontius Pilate didn't listen to his wife," George told me. "This arrangement may not work for every couple, but it has served us well."

The very next morning, George learned from ANM about a native missionary who had a desperate need that required $1,000. "I knew what I had to do," George told me. "I told my friend to take my name off the puppy list, and I sent Advancing Native Missions a check for one thousand dollars."

At this time, dogs were being trained at Lackland Air Force Base to sniff out explosives, and George and Cindy were part of a squad of volunteers who walked the young pups until they were mature enough to be trained. A few days after George sent the check to ANM, the director of the puppy-walker program called and said, "We know you love dogs, and we have one that lacks the motivation to be a bomb detector. He's a sweet Labrador retriever, and he would make a great family pet. Would you be willing to give him a forever home?"

George about fell through the floor. "Yes!" he answered, straining to keep from shouting.

Like all the dogs in the program, this pup was named for one of the victims of the 9/11 attack: a forty-year-old man by the name of Michael A. Uliano. George nicknamed the pup "Fitter," which was an old family name. "Fitter wasn't much for fetching balls or sticks," George told me, "but when I took him duck hunting, he charged into the water and fetched ducks as he was born to do. He was a natural."

My relationship with George goes back to the founding of ANM. Thirty years ago, Carl and I drove to San Antonio at the invitation of Abundant Life Church to speak about the vision of ANM. George and Cindy heard me preach a sermon based on Luke 11:5–8 that I titled "Midnight Advocate." As I stood before the congregation, I said, "Native missionaries are knocking at our door, and we need to give them some bread. We need to help them reach the unreached."

The message moved the congregation, and it stuck in the ears and hearts of George and Cindy. "Spreading the Gospel through native missionaries was a concept we had never heard anyone talk about before," George said. "It ignited a fire in us, and we've been with it ever since."

In fact, George and Cindy became midnight advocates themselves by subsequently hosting numerous visiting native missionaries in their home. Their list of guests included Alex and Eunice Malanday from Guimaras Island in the Philippines; Paulus and Sri Wibowo from Indonesia; Swapon and Rachel Bose from Bangladesh; Dr. Linda Balugo from the Philippines; as well as Marlou and me. Even their neighbors have gotten into the act. Many are professionals, and they have freely offered free medical, optical, and dental services to missionaries.

"Our young sons learned more from visiting missionaries in our home than they would ever pick up in any geography class," George told me. "Our association with ANM has increased our faith and trust in God in ways we otherwise would never have experienced. We have especially learned the joy of giving. We are glad to support the ministry through prayer, financial support, advocacy, and hosting traveling missionaries or staff."

Chocolate Birthday Cakes

A while back, George put his side of the story in writing. Below is what he wrote:

GEORGE

I vividly remember when Brother Bo and I met. It was on a Sunday morning at Abundant Life Church in San Antonio. He and Carl Gordon had come to share about their vision for identifying and supporting native missionaries. In his message, Bo introduced himself as "The Midnight Advocate." It was "Love-In-Christ" at first sight! He touched my heart for missionaries as none had before.

Over the next three decades, our friendship deepened, and Bo and Marlou, through Advancing Native Missions, brought a whole new world into our home. We were introduced to beloved brothers and sisters in Christ who stayed in our home on their travels. Our sons have grown up hearing first-hand accounts of the miraculous mission works from around the globe. All our hearts have been touched.

More importantly, through the influence and encouragement of my precious Brother Bo, I have become a "Junior Midnight Advocate," sharing the needs of native missionaries and raising support for their activities. I've been especially motivated to help them respond in the love of Christ to the needs of their neighbors following tsunamis, volcanic eruptions, droughts, typhoons, and medical emergencies. As they have responded to the temporary, yet immediate, physical needs of their neighbors, they have been able to open the door of salvation to meet their neighbors' eternal needs. Their dedicated service has been an inspiration to my family and me.

Even though we are normally many miles apart from Bo on his birthday, our family has embraced an annual tradition of baking a chocolate cake in his honor. Each year, we text him a picture of the cake and tell him how delicious it is, even though he can't personally taste it. That may be a little sadistic because he loves chocolate cakes, but we do it every year with much love!

My precious Brother Bo has introduced me to the joy of cheerfully giving to support the work of expanding God's kingdom. Oh, what immeasurable joy lies ahead of us in the kingdom of Jesus Christ as we meet face to face with saints from around the world who came to salvation through the work of these treasured native missionaries. Bless God!

"That Ship Will Not Sail!"— *A Tribute to Pastor Otis Spellman*

In the very early days of ANM, Otis Spellman's beloved wife, Hazel, worked in the same building where we rented our tiny office. Otis came to the building from time to time to pick up his wife, and occasionally, he would drop by our office. Unbeknownst to us, he later said to Hazel, "That ship will not sail." But by God's grace, ANM did sail, and years later, Otis became our missionary-at-large. The following is his story:

OTIS

I was born in Norfolk, Virginia, and educated in the public schools. Life was comfortable because my father owned or operated several businesses. After graduating from high school at age seventeen, I served six years in the Air Force. Then I went to work for the federal government in northern Virginia as a computer analyst/operator.

I met Hazel at a friend's house in 1962. She was a student at Norfolk State College, and after two years of long-distance courtship, we were married in 1964. We started attending Star of Bethlehem Church in Woodbridge, Virginia, and after much soul-searching and inquiring, I embraced the Lord Jesus Christ as my Savior on October 10, 1967.

I was active in the church, but I had never considered being a pastor. One September day in 1976, God spoke to my heart that I should

Now, I was doubly scared! Not only was my car skidding; I was hearing the voice of God.

preach. I was stunned and didn't know how to answer. Several days later, as I was driving home from work in a rainstorm on Interstate 95, my car began to skid. Instinctively, I looked for a place to pull over, but a voice that I knew was the Lord's said to me, "Don't touch those brakes!"

Now, I was doubly scared! Not only was my car skidding; I was hearing the voice of God. In a flash, God gave me a vision. It was the first vision I had ever seen, and it clearly showed that if I touched the brakes, the car would flip over and over and burst into flames! Through this same vision, God then told me that if I did not agree to preach, I would not leave that highway alive. "I'll preach!" I shouted. Immediately, the car stopped skidding and straightened itself out. I drove home safe but shaken.

On October 16, 1976, I preached my first sermon. It was based on 1 Corinthians 13:13: "And now abide faith, hope, love, these three; but the greatest of these is love." And in 1979, I accepted a call to pastor the Galilee Baptist Church in Louisa, Virginia, a small town outside Charlottesville. My wife and I and our three young girls moved by faith to Charlottesville, and the next thirty years were the most rewarding of my life. People came to Christ, believers were discipled, and the church grew. I plunged into the study and the preaching of God's Word, and the wonderful people helped me to grow and mature as a pastor.

In late 1992, Hazel was working in the same building in Charlottesville where Bo Barredo and Carl Gordon had just opened a tiny office to begin Advancing Native Missions. I would occasionally drop by their office for a chat, and I was struck by their sincerity. But I was more amused than impressed by their vision: world evangelization through native missions to hasten the Lord's second coming according to Matthew 24:14. That was certainly a noble purpose, but I felt it was beyond their capacity. I told Hazel, "That ship will not sail."

Years later, after attending an ANM missions conference at a church in Charlottesville, I met Gary Darcus, ANM's Africa director. He re-introduced me to ANM, and I began inviting visiting native missionaries to our church. ANM even held a Building the Kingdom Together missions conference at our church. This stirred our church to give generous missions offerings, and many of our members hosted native missionaries in their homes.

"Come to Africa."

At one such missions conference in October 2005, two African couples were our guests. During a question-and-answer period, I asked each one how we could help them. Hellen Malande of Kenya looked me straight in the eye and said, "Come to Africa."

I had always reasoned that it was better for the church to send the money than to send me. Yet on Easter weekend of 2006, I found myself on a plane with Gary Darcus bound for Nairobi, Kenya. Our mission was to conduct one of ANM's pastor-encouragement conferences called Operation Barnabas International. I was relaxed because eight others would be joining us, and my role would be minimal. Then, at thirty-seven thousand feet over the Sahara Desert, Gary informed me that the other eight people couldn't make it. He and I would have to do the entire conference alone! High in the sky, the Spirit ministered to me as never before.

The next two weeks marked a turning point in my life. The sights, sounds, preaching, people, and reality of God's presence mightily impacted me. The people were poor and often hungry for food, but they were even more hungry for the Word of God! Their rich praise, zeal for Christ, and unbounded joy overwhelmed me. It was I who was humbled when the humble pastors looked to us for encouragement. God had blessed me with so much, while they had so little in material things. Yet they were rich in faith, and I was encouraged by them. I determined that I would from that moment on try to be a help to millions, for as long as God enabled me.

I prayed that the Lord would place people in my path whose hearts he had prepared, just as he had prepared my heart before I got hooked on missions.

The next two years brought drastic changes in my life. In 2008, Hazel, the love of my life, lost her battle to illness and went home to glory. Her quiet charm, affection for children, teaching skills, and love for all people had endeared her to many and left lasting impressions on their lives. I cherished my memories of her as a lonely widower and waited on the Lord.

Eventually, the Lord brought Janice into my life, and in September 2010, our lives were joined. At the same time, my wondrous season as pastor of Galilee Church ended, and I waited patiently for the Lord's direction.

During this period, Bo sent me two gracious cards telling of his concern and love for me. I started attending ANM's Thursday morning Bible studies, where I enjoyed meeting visiting overseas missionaries. One day, ANM leadership asked me if I would like to be one of the ministry's missionaries-at-large. It would require serving by faith on whatever support I could raise. Janice would be my missions partner as I conducted revival meetings to advance the cause of missions.

I accepted that call, and I prayed that the Lord would place people in my path whose hearts he had prepared, just as he had prepared my heart before I got hooked on missions. My challenge came from Romans 10:14–15:

> *How then shall they call on Him in whom they have not believed?*
> *And how shall they believe in Him of whom they have not heard?*
> *And how shall they hear without a preacher?*
> *And how shall they preach unless they are sent?*

The four questions posed in this passage of Scripture motivate me day by day. We are commissioned to go and be a light in darkness and a hope for tomorrow. Come alongside us and let us harvest more souls for his coming.

Today, ANM has grown from two people to sixty-five people serving no less than three thousand native pastors and missionaries in seventy-eight countries around the world. Yes, that ship sails!

"I thank God for every remembrance of you."
Otis was one of the best preachers I'd ever met and heard. He had almost everything a preacher could desire. He was eloquent with a winsome personality. He was a bear of a man with the charm of a little boy. Most of all, he was much loved by the community, and I loved, respected, and admired him, too!

In the fall of 2010, when I learned that Otis's season as pastor of Galilee Baptist Church was over, I sent him a Thanksgiving Day card expressing my love. I later learned that he tossed it in the trash. "I'm just one of the many he writes to," he said to himself.

About a month later, the Lord put Brother Otis so strongly on my heart that, even though I was extremely busy, I sent him another card with a longer, loving message. That prompted him to visit ANM, and he stayed around until he went home to the Lord on March 29, 2022.

As a missionary-at-large for ANM, Otis went to revival meetings, where his sweet presence ministered to people and brought honor to ANM. Along the way, he answered a call to be the pastor of a church in Meherrin, Virginia, and several years after that, he became the pastor of Union Baptist Church in Waynesboro. He was successful in all these pastorates, while continuing to serve as a volunteer missionary-at-large with ANM. ANM became a ministry base for him as well as a personal oasis. In 2017, Otis and I had a most joyous time together on a trip to Israel.

A Celebration

I was privileged to be one of the speakers at the memorial service of Pastor Otis at the large and jam-packed Mt. Zion First African Baptist Church in Charlottesville on April 9, 2022. It was a celebration of his life, with tributes fit for a beloved servant of the King of Kings. He was truly adored in the African American community.

In my talk, I related my love story with Otis. I concluded by reading a handwritten letter he had written to me on December 26, 2019, about two years before he went home to be with the Lord. In this letter, which is reproduced below, he finally acknowledged my deep love for him:

> Dear Bo,
>
> I am reminded of your quote from your father that "gratitude unexpressed is ingratitude implied." I want to profoundly thank you for the love, care, and concern that you have shown me over the years. Many times, your prayers and encouraging words have sustained me in crisis and trials. The kindness you have shown in the "little" things in my life has meant so much. Although I can't name them all, be assured that your love for me affected me more deeply than I realized.
>
> I thank God for the opportunities you created for me to minister and to be ministered to. Please accept my heartfelt appreciation and thanks for the way you have ministered to me and my family. To have been at ANM was a constant beacon of what has been and what could be. My growth here has helped me be a better husband, father, pastor, preacher, and person. Thanks be to our Lord for his guidance on this journey through life with my friend, Brother Bo! I thank God for every remembrance of you.
>
> Love you,
>
> Otis R. Spellman

A few months before he died, Otis wrote me another letter. It was just one line. I didn't share this letter at the memorial service. I told the church that I planned to take this treasure to my grave. But with the joyful approval of his widow, Janice, I am sharing it below:

> To one who has impacted my life like none other! Thanks Bo!
>
> —Otis

"You See the Latent Good . . ."— A Tribute to Pastor Gerald Ripley

Pastor Gerald Ripley and his wife, Sharon, are very close friends of Marlou and me. When Carl and I launched ANM, he asked me if I could recommend a church where we could introduce our ministry. After days of prayer, I suggested that we drive to Abundant Life Church in San Antonio, Texas, where Gerald was the pastor.

Pastor Ripley and the church warmly received us. As I have previously shared, on the Sunday that I shared the message about the midnight advocate, they encouraged us and surprised themselves by collecting their largest missions offering ever: $880.87. But the greatest gift that the Lord gave through Abundant Life Church was a deep friendship with Pastor Ripley. He was a combination of father, pastor, and brother to me, besides being a dear friend. Pastor Ripley honored me one day by telling me that our relationship was like that of David and Jonathan.

Pastor Ripley was one of those rare men who could pass the test of one of the most scrutinizing questions in the Bible. This question is found in Proverbs 20:6: "Most men will proclaim each his own goodness, But who can find a faithful man?" Pastor Ripley was that faithful man. At ANM's twentieth anniversary celebration at our fall retreat at Wintergreen in 2012, we honored Pastor and Mrs. Ripley with a plaque expressing our appreciation. The Lord has since multiplied the $880.87 offering of their church many times over to assist thousands of native missionaries around the world, who are reaching unreached tribes and people groups with the Gospel.

Pastor Ripley went home to glory on May 25, 2021, and I miss him. Prior to his passing, he sent me a letter and called me to make sure I had received it. I have kept that letter as one of my treasures. With Marlou's encouragement and Mrs. Ripley's permission, I am sharing it below:

January 8, 2020

It's been on my mind to write a letter of tribute and deep gratitude to you. Perhaps it will reach you by your birthday.

I am amazed and grateful to be counted among your close friends. I realize it is a gift from God. It certainly is one of the greatest blessings in my richly blessed life.

You have encouraged me numerous times throughout the years. That's not surprising since your middle name could aptly be Barnabas. You and he must be two peas in a pod. Encouragement flows through your veins. I do hope God is using some others to minister encouragement to you.

You are an astute discerner of people. You see the latent good even in those with lots of rough edges. Authors Jack and Jerry Schreur wrote, "One of the deepest needs we have as men is the need to be respected, to have someone believe in our abilities and us." That's what the servants of the Lord in all the nations experience when they spend time in your company. I am among them.

I usually have a healthy self-image. God has gifted me with good qualities and abilities. Yet you accord me with still more, more than I think is warranted. My high regard for your ability to evaluate people nudges me towards thinking more highly of myself. I don't want to overdo that.

I appreciate your validation. I fully realize it was God who gave Abundant Life the opportunity to encourage you and Carl to launch ANM. We were blessed to be His instrument. All the glory goes to Him!

I did appreciate and I want to thank you for that validation when you gave it at our Golden Wedding Anniversary celebration. Two of my brothers and their wives heard it. So did a number of my colleagues who are engaged with me in ministry in San Antonio. They saw a worship center that could seat maybe 100. They heard about a ministry that reaches 62 countries! Something good has come out of Abundant Life Church.

I appreciate you and Marlou so much. I rejoice when I read your combined reports of mission trips you have completed. My heart is warmed when I look at pictures and read reports of your children and grandchildren. I am grateful each time your itinerary comes through San Antonio.

You are always welcome to preach at Abundant Life. But if your schedule doesn't permit that, it is a special blessing to spend some time together.

Brother Bo—I love you. Thank you for your friendship, your encouragement, your validation!

Your Brother in Christ.

Gerald A. Ripley, Jr.

The Third Set of Witnesses— Beloved Missionaries Timothy Kinyua and Chandra and Uria Tobing

And so it was, when Moses held up his hand, that Israel prevailed; and when he let down his hand, Amalek prevailed. But Moses' hands became heavy; so they took a stone and put it under him, and he sat on it. And Aaron and Hur supported his hands, one on one side, and the other on the other side; and his hands were steady until the going down of the sun. So Joshua defeated Amalek and his people with the edge of the sword.

EXODUS 17:11-13

Native missionaries are on the frontlines and in the trenches of the world's mission fields, battling for the hearts and souls of men against the forces of darkness. God calls us to encourage and equip them. We are called to help raise their arms so they can prevail against the enemy and push further into the frontiers of the whitening harvest fields. We must work while it is still day, bringing in the bountiful harvest, before the night comes.

"God Provided More Than Twice!"— Timothy Kinyua of Kenya

Pastor John Kirema founded Cornerstone Evangelistic Ministries in Kenya, Africa, in 1976. In conjunction with several other pastors, he served more than twenty churches. The older of his two sons,

Timothy, had an interest in the ministry, and he often accompanied his father when he preached at various churches.

In September 1997, one month after completing a course in Bible studies, Timothy dreamed that he should join the ministry full-time. He thought this was just like any other dream, and he dismissed it. A month later, he heard a voice that he knew was the Lord's. The voice said, "Timothy, I am sending you to do my work." After prayer and by faith, with his dad's encouragement, Timothy began preaching full-time alongside his dad and the other pastors. But in March 1999, Timothy's father died, leaving a ministry with twenty-four churches.

Cornerstone's board agreed that Timothy should take his father's place. This represented a huge challenge. The ministry encompassed nearly one-third of the country and required many workers and considerable resources. Many of the churches met under trees because they had no buildings, and temperatures often soar to over one hundred degrees Fahrenheit. Illiteracy is high in Kenya, and much of the water is unclean and infested with malaria-carrying mosquitos. Out of a population of 44 million people, Kenya has about 1.1 million AIDS orphans. They often roam the streets and get involved in drugs or prostitution. Unrest in the neighboring countries of Somalia, Ethiopia, and Sudan brings refugees and criminal gangs into the country.

God has given me a strong interest in helping younger ministry leaders like Timothy. I love these young leaders as I love my own sons. My desire is to help polish these diamonds in the rough for greater use in ministry. Timothy Kinyua soon proved himself to be a "son after a father's heart." God honored his faith and hard work, and by 2014, with perseverance and help from ANM, the ministry had grown to 212 full-time pastors, and it had planted more than four hundred churches and outreaches.

Timothy's First Visit to the US

In 2016, we invited Timothy to come to the US to be one of ten missionaries featured at an ANM fundraising retreat at Wintergreen

Resort in the Blue Ridge Mountains west of Charlottesville. We usually schedule the missionaries who are good speakers to present on Friday and Saturday, and before we adjourn on Saturday night, we invite people to contribute. On Sunday, we have a worship service, during which each of the remaining missionaries speaks for five minutes. We then dismiss at noon on Sunday without taking an offering. The missionaries who speak on Sunday are provided for from Saturday night's offering.

On this occasion, I had to schedule young Timothy for Sunday morning because he was one of the newer speakers. But I love this young leader and his wife, Yvonne. I said to Marlou, "I will be the emcee on Sunday, and Timothy will speak, but he will have only five minutes to present. I would like him to bring home some additional funds, but we will finish our offerings on Saturday night. Can you please prepare a three-minute PowerPoint presentation for his ministry with the theme music from the *Lion King* movie in the background?"

Marlou made one of the best PowerPoint presentations I ever saw of any ministry. On Sunday morning, I called Timothy up to the podium and said, "Let's show your PowerPoint presentation." We showed it, and all the people were blown away. Then I began interviewing him.

"Timothy, what are your primary needs?"

"I have three top needs," he answered. "First, we need water wells because my people are dying from water-borne illnesses. Second, we need church buildings—even just simple ones that cost around two thousand dollars. My people are worshipping under the trees in the hot sun and the rain. When the lions, jackals, and other wild animals come, they must scamper for their lives. My third need is for a vehicle because the one I inherited from my father sometimes breaks down at night. If I am in the mission field and I get out of the vehicle to try to fix it, the lions and other beasts will tear me to pieces. But if I stay in the vehicle, I must wait for several days until a mechanic comes. In my absence, my wife, Yvonne, worries."

"Brother Bo, please forgive me. I'm a poor missionary like Brother Timothy, but my wife and I by faith are going to give $1,000 for half a well."

I said, "Okay, let's do something about this." I then said to the congregation, "Brother Timothy needs water wells. Is there anybody here who would like to donate half a well?"

The first one who raised his hand to donate half a well was a missionary from China. His name was Daniel Wen, and his wife's name was Maggie. He had been deeply moved by Timothy's testimony. He said in between his tears, "Brother Bo, please forgive me. I'm a poor missionary like Brother Timothy, but my wife and I by faith are going to give $1,000 for half a well."

People were electrified. Then Karen Thomas, Papa Tom's widow from Arizona who was sitting far in the back, raised her hand and said, "I'll complete that well." Just like that, we had funded one well. Others started raising their hands. That morning we raised $35,000 for Timothy!

When the giving had stopped, Timothy said, "Brother Bo, could I speak?"

I smiled at him and said, "No more. If you speak, they might change their minds." People laughed, and Timothy went home rejoicing with $35,000 for water wells, a couple of church buildings, motorbikes for his senior pastors, and dozens of bicycles for his workers.

Marlou and I Go to Kenya

Marlou and I went to Kenya in 2018 to visit Timothy and Yvonne and learn about their needs. Timothy drove us around, and it was obvious that he needed more water wells. He also needed more church buildings, motorbikes, and bicycles, and we saw that he really could use a Toyota Land Cruiser. That seemed beyond reach, however, because a slightly used Land Cruiser costs about $65,000.

While there, we visited City of Refuge Church, which is pastored by Pastor Richard Mwenda, one of the men on Timothy's team. Pastor Richard's wife is Sister Pauline. We learned that City of Refuge Church had grown from about fifteen worshippers to around five hundred, and all the people could not fit into the small, wooden building that was originally meant to be temporary. The congregation had started building a larger concrete and brick structure around the wooden building, but they didn't have the needed $20,000 to put a roof on it.

Brother Timothy told me that he and Yvonne planned to come to the US a few months later, and I promised to be waiting for them. After Marlou and I returned home, we drove to Alabama to see long-time friends Roger and Debbie Cornelius. Roger asked me, "What's the need?"

"Pastor Timothy's co-worker, Pastor Richard Mwenda, needs twenty thousand dollars to put a roof on the church building his congregation is constructing," I replied.

Roger went to another room and came back with a check for $20,000. Debbie said, "That's the remaining balance of my inheritance from my mother."

When Timothy and Yvonne came to the US, Marlou and I took them around, and God blessed our efforts. The following is excerpted from the letter they wrote to us in 2019, after they returned to Kenya:

Before our July-August US travel, Uncle Bo, Auntie Marlou, and their close friend Chuck Cole had come in June to visit us and our ministry in the Samburu and Turkana tribal villages in Kenya. Before they left Kenya, they asked for a list of needs we would be sharing during our US visit. By faith, we listed: ten church buildings, five water wells, and three motorbikes. We have congregations meeting under the trees. We have urgent needs for water wells and motorbikes.

Uncle Bo and Auntie Marlou took the time to set up meetings for us in Virginia and Maryland despite being tired from passionately advocating for us in five other states almost right after their arrival from Africa! This was a demonstration of their compassion for us as our fellow servants. They introduced us to their precious friends. They are also missionaries like us—also in need of their own support, yet they showed us unselfish love by sharing their God-given friends with us.

We especially loved the prayer and fellowship times we would have in their car while driving to our many meetings. Our long prayers while traveling were faithfully answered. During our visit, God manifested Himself beyond what we listed. We asked Him for forgiveness for limiting Him. After all our US meetings, God's people provided more than twice what we had prayed for! Twenty church buildings! Seventeen water wells! Seven motorbikes! We also had an urgent need of a mission truck (our old truck has a broken frame and frequently breaks down in the bush placing us in danger of being attacked by lions). It was Auntie Marlou who felt so heavily burdened on Yvonne's behalf to pray for a new truck. Uncle Bo said it would be very difficult due to the big amount needed. But God is an awesome God full of surprises: More than $40,000 was initially raised for a new or slightly used truck!

Another great surprise was the roof of our large but unfinished City of Refuge Church in Maili Saba. In a miraculous way, friends in Alabama gave $20,000 towards the church roof. We never expected this. It was just a pure blessing out of Ephesians 3:20—'. . . more than all we ask or imagine . . .'

We thank God for the help of our ANM family, Fred and Darby Walls, Bud and Pat Voight, Jerry Harding, Tony Weedor, Lou Mancari, Laverne Castillo, Chuck Cole, and for Uncle Bo and Auntie Marlou and all their friends who were so loving and supportive. They invited us into their homes, cooked meals for us, and treated us to nice restaurants where we had some meetings. We were truly honored. We went home rejoicing! We pray God's exceedingly abundant blessings upon all those who helped and blessed us.

An Email from Timothy in 2022

In early June 2022, Timothy sent the following email to me:

I came to know about Uncle Bo way back in 1999 when I joined Cornerstone Ministries after the passing on of my dad, John Kirema, who was the founder.

Uncle Bo is a great man of God who has a heart for missionaries across the world. In 2004, Uncle Bo sent a team of ANM brothers to come to Kenya to encourage me and our fellow pastors. He had founded Operational Barnabas International, and this great ministry encouraged me as a young minister who had suddenly huge shoes to fill. The working conditions were quite harsh even then, and most pastors were at the verge of quitting the ministry.

After the conference the discouraged pastors were very encouraged, and they actually became the pillars of Cornerstone Ministry Kenya. They went back to the field with renewed strength and a purpose. In 2004 we planted hundreds of churches in Northern Kenya, and as of today, we have more than 500 churches and 382 pastors serving in various places, but with a base in Northern Kenya.

As the ministry grew, Uncle Bo and the leadership thought I should travel to the USA to meet some of the sponsors because they wanted people to hear my story. I tried securing an American visa for six years, and every time I got denied because the Embassy thought I didn't have strong ties here in Kenya. (I was a bachelor . . ..)

In 2010 God blessed me with a beautiful, loving and godly wife. In 2014 God made a way, and I was able to travel to the United States. This trip was quite the highlight because I could finally put faces to the people who had been praying and supporting us. Auntie Marlou helped a great deal by making a PowerPoint presentation with a soundtrack from the *Lion King* movie. ANM had organized a conference at Wintergreen for donors and partners to meet the missionaries from different parts of the world. During that time God used Uncle Bo on the last day of the conference to advocate for our ministry, and we were able to raise $35,000 to go towards church buildings and digging of wells. The trip was such a blessing!

In 2016 I was again blessed to travel to the United States, but this time with my wife. The whole trip was glorious! Uncle Bo went an extra mile to advocate for us to some of his good friends, and they were such a blessing to our ministry.

The highlight of this trip was the fellowships that we would have in the car while traveling to meet his friends. He would give us a brief intro on who we were to meet, and in the car (Uncle Bo would personally drive us to all these meetings) he would ask Auntie Marlou to tell us a story . . . the most interesting was the story of how they met and their lives in the university where they both studied law. Auntie Marlou would crack us up with stories of how it was hard for Uncle Bo to win her heart, but he finally did!

After these beautiful stories we would pray for the meeting ahead and the friends we were about to meet, sing and tell stories. It was always a beautiful fellowship. Needless to say, all these prayers were answered, and God continued to surprise us.

We visited the United States again in 2019, just when Uncle Bo had left the leadership to become a Global Ambassador so that he could advocate for more missionaries. During this trip we had bigger needs (from a human perspective, but very small from God's). Some of the needs were a church roof for Pastor Richard and funds for a new truck (our old truck would break quite often and sometimes we would have to spend nights in the wild). We were also appealing for more church buildings, water wells, and motorcycles for our pastors. To us this was quite a bigger mountain. BUT WHO IS GOD?!!!!!!

Even before we traveled back home to Kenya, we had already met the target of the funds needed! God worked through Uncle Bo and Auntie Marlou and their friends, and they really surprised us. During this time our relationship with Auntie Marlou and Uncle Bo also continued to grow. When they made their first trip to Africa, they visited us in Kenya, and it was such an honor to host them and take them to meet the missionaries who help in the spreading of good news. They were really impressed with the work we are doing here.

During Uncle Bo's leadership, we have witnessed such growth to our ministry. From people worshipping under trees to having structures that could offer a shelter to protect them from the scorching sun and the wildlife. To digging wells for so many homesteads and providing them with clean water for their personal use and for their animals. We have seen such growth and how God has worked through them and the ANM family to uplift the lives of the nomadic people. Traveling has really become safer and easier for us. With the new truck we don't have to worry about our vehicle breaking down in the middle of nowhere and exposing us to wild animals. We give God all the glory!

"You Care More for Us the Person . . ."
—Chandra and Uria Tobing on Bali Island

Chandra Tobing grew up as a member of the Batak tribe in North Sumatra. In the early 1800s, two Christian foreign missionaries came to witness to this tribe, but they were killed and eaten by the natives. Forty years later, a German missionary by the name of Nomensen courageously brought the Good News to the region. The king didn't appreciate this intrusion, however, so he had Nomensen tied to a tree and prepared to sacrifice him to the tribe's idol. During the night, a large storm with intense thunder and lightning frightened the natives so much that they freed Nomensen and allowed him to freely share his faith. As a result, about 90 percent of the Batak people today are Christians. This is how Chandra happened to grow up in a Christian home.

Chandra wanted to be a minister of the Gospel, and he labored for a time in Bali, but the work was difficult and the fruit minimal. Turning his back on Bali, he enrolled at Bethany International University in Singapore with the dream of becoming a pastor of a large, prestigious church. One night, while reading about Moses and the burning bush, he felt God telling him to take off his sandals and walk on holy ground. He understood this to mean that he should let go of his pride and go to the island of Bali.

Initially, Chandra tried to bargain with God by complaining that he had no financial support. But God gave him a vision of the cross. A voice in Chandra's heart said in essence, "Even if you were the only person in the world, I would have gone to the cross

"Even if you were the only person in the world, I would have gone to the cross for you because I love you so much. Are you willing to go back to Bali for me?"

for you because I love you so much. Are you willing to go back to Bali for me?"

Chandra was scheduled the next day to share his testimony before numerous missionaries and other students at the university. When he said that he planned to resign from his studies and go to Bali, they were shocked. He stated that he would do this even if he had no money, and even if no girl would marry him. One girl who was present approached him afterwards and said, "Your testimony made my heart rejoice and feel afire."

The next day, feeling led by the Lord, Chandra proposed to her. The young lady, Uria, asked for seven days to pray. At the end of this time, she accepted Chandra's proposal. They began a two-year engagement that consummated in marriage in 2005.

To Bali with Love

During their engagement period, Chandra and Uria moved to Bali and started a house church. Although Indonesia is the largest Muslim country in the world, Bali and the surrounding islands have retained a Hindu heritage that dates to the second century AD. About 85 percent of Bali's five million people are Hindu. The beautiful tropical island, often called the "island of the gods," is covered with shrines, temples, and holy sites.

In Bali, it is acceptable for someone to be a Christian if he or she also worships all the Hindu gods. But life is difficult for Christians who are devoted to Christ alone. This is especially true for men, because when a man inherits the property of his family in Bali, he also inherits all the idols and ancestors that need offerings three times every day. If the son neglects the idols, it is believed that the idols will become angry and cause trouble for the family and the community. Diseases, crop failures, and conflicts among neighbors and even between villages will be blamed on the son's neglect. Committed Christians can lose their homes, their jobs, and their standing in the community.

These traditions and superstitions made evangelistic work very difficult for Chandra and Uria. They had no money and little to eat. Many times, they and their team members would go to the dump and catch cats to cook and eat for dinner. More than once, they wanted to give up, but they remembered their promise to God and labored on.

By 2006, quite a large number of people were attending the church Chandra pastored, and ten students were enrolled in the Bible school affiliated with the church. But when a new leader was appointed over the church, he forced Chandra and Uria to leave. Uria was three months pregnant with their first child, and the couple departed with only their luggage and one thin mattress. They had no money. Chandra was understandably bitter about this maltreatment. When God convicted him sometime later, he wrote and asked this leader to forgive him.

A Buddhist businessman allowed the Tobings to sleep on the floor of his house, and he fixed up his store for them to use as a place of Christian worship. Chandra marveled at the kindness of this non-Christian. The church grew, and one day, Chandra invited the leader of his former church to come and preach. Touched by this act of kindness and Chandra's humility, this former leader accepted the invitation. When he saw the sizable church that Chandra now led and what God had done through him, he was so overcome that he asked with tears for Chandra's forgiveness.

Over the next few years, Uria had three miscarriages. "Sometimes we will wonder if God is even there," Chandra says, "but God uses these circumstances to refine us and build our faith. If we can pass these tests, we will grow in spiritual maturity."

By faith, Chandra started a residential Bible school as part of the church he pastored. This required more money, and he sought ways to supplement his income. After prayer, God led him to start a micro-business producing coconut milk, which is a basic ingredient in Indonesian cooking. Using six dollars from his son's piggy bank as startup capital, Chandra bought coconuts and began selling their milk in the city market.

Our First Meeting

When Marlou and I first met Chandra and Uria in 2014, we were immediately impressed with their dedication. Their ministry, Promised Land Training Center, was ministering in two villages and educating seven Bible school students who lived with them. We noticed, however, that they had only one small machine for extracting milk from coconuts, and their income was meager. At my request, Chandra took us to the company that sells the coconut extracting machines, and I bought him the biggest machine available. The vendor even accepted my credit card!

After Marlou and I returned to the US, we were able to raise more money for Promised Land Training Center. Chandra and Uria used these funds to upgrade their equipment to at least three large coconut-milk extractors, five coconut graters, and one coconut-husking machine. This suddenly boosted their income by more than 600 percent and allowed them to significantly expand their ministry. Today, eight workers operate the coconut business. Most of their employees are either graduates of their Bible school, or they end up as students attending it. At the time of this writing, the ministry has almost one hundred churches and outreaches.

How Chandra and Uria treat their workers and live their lives is a strong witness in Bali for Christ. Because they buy coconuts from Hindus and sell the coconut milk to Muslims, they are ideally positioned to minister to both groups. They have good relationships with their suppliers and customers, and they often visit them and pray for their sick. Chandra challenged one supplier saying, "If you continue gambling, we will stop ordering coconuts from you. We are Christians, and we don't agree with your using profits you earn from us for gambling." The man quit the gambling.

Marlou and I were heartbroken as we thought about Uria's three miscarriages. The doctor had strongly advised Chandra to cease taking Uria on his motorbike drives to the villages. When we heard about this, we advocated on their behalf for a ministry vehicle. God graciously inspired donors to give for this cause, and Chandra was able to get a new van just as the COVID crisis was in full swing in Bali. The car salesman who delivered the van told him that because of the virus, his van was the only vehicle sold on the whole island! Chandra saw it as God's hand, as it was also his birthday. In addition to safeguarding Uria's health, the vehicle has helped Promised Land Training Center expand its ministry faster and farther!

Two Updates from Chandra

On April 9, 2020, Chandra wrote us the following report:

Dear Pak Bo and Ibu Marlou.

Something very miraculous happened to me in this pandemic. Even my friend, the sales manager of the car dealership, says no one bought a vehicle for a month now, and I am the only one in the whole island of Bali to have bought one! God blessed me with a new van exactly on my thirty-eighth birthday in the middle of the pandemic. We have been praying for a van for three years already, as there are five of us riding on our tiny motorbike, and it is not safe. This blessing of a new van gave me a new lesson in my life—Pak Bo and Ibu Marlou came to visit in January 2020, and in April 2020 the van came! I only need a visitation of a great man of God and my problem is solved. How much more if the visitation is by our Almighty God, not only to me but to the world, to the heart of each and every one of us?

Later, Chandra wrote me a lengthy, informative email. The entire letter was meaningful, but one section meant so much to me that I am reprinting a lightly edited version below:

I and my wife do remember the first time we met you, Pak Bo and Ibu Marlou. We have a very strong impression that you are totally different from other friends that we had. Most of the time when people come, they are concerned about your work and the fruit of your ministry, your success story of ministry. The other hand, we are a normal people and not superhero. We need love and care, and we do also have struggles and problems. We know God is caring; we need someone sent by God to understand and care about us.

We need love and care, and we do also have struggles and problems. We know God is caring, we need someone sent by God to understand and care about us.

We find the difference in you. You care more for us the person, not the work we are doing. We as a missionary are the most important in your eyes, not just our work. You appreciate us and care for our relationship as husband and wife. You value the family.

In you, I found the real love of the Father. My wife, Uria, told me that your coming brings us understanding about the heart of the father in the story of the prodigal son. When the father sees the son, the father hugs him, no time for the son to confess his failure or to discuss what the son is doing out there. Out of his joy, the father plans a big party, a celebration, and when he saw the clothing of his son, he took the new one, the best garment, and put it on his son.

We see this kind of fatherly love through you. That makes us not afraid and discouraged any more, as we receive the Father's love through you. Thanks for loving us.

Chandra Writing in 2022

On June 2, 2022, Chandra wrote to me the following email (lightly edited):

Praise God, my wife is doing wonderful, she is so blessed by God with so many new talents during covid, not just helping our family but also other pastors' wives. She is very talented baking cakes and teaching other women also that become their new source of income.

She learned how to do sewing and help some of the dancers in our church with their costumes.

Recently she attended a course for makeup artist, to make woman face beautiful. She attended course with another 20 pastors' wives and missionaries that after four months they could be professional and that can be the way of reaching out and also helping family income.

Our three boys are also doing wonderful. The oldest, Isaac, is now 15 years old and going to senior high school. He is helping play the keyboard in our worship service and got a chance two weeks ago to give testimony by zoom with participants from six different countries.

Number 2, Shalom, is eight years old now, he is the top in the class and he loves to read, two to three books he will read for a week.

The youngest Ivan is six years old and he is already playing keyboard at our kids church. He is willing to be an artist in future.

Before I joined ANM, there were only two of us as pastor or missionary, myself and another brother Ronal, and we only have one church in Denpasar, with attendance of about 30 people.

After joining ANM, in Bali itself we now have seven churches and 45 pastors/missionaries, and all over Indonesia we now have about 140 missionaries and pastors. Churches and house churches all over Indonesia now about 96 and our vision for 1000 churches. Our main church in Denpasar about 500 plus attendance now.

Beside churches we have Mission school in Denpasar, Bali. We do have children ministry that serve about 300 children at 12 different villages. We also have Mobile clinic ministry, providing health help to those in need. We will plan doing outreach by open formal school.

The Fourth Set of Witnesses—
Five Members of My Dear Family

Leadership starts at home. Who we are as a leader at home reflects who we are as a leader in the workplace. For each of us, our family is our "Jerusalem." For this reason, I considered calling my family members as my first set of witnesses, but I decided to save the best for last!

As a young boy growing up in a Christian family, one of the children's songs we sang in our island language had these lyrics that we repeated again and again in a spirit of gladness:

> *Si Hesus sa panimalay*
> *Masadyang balay, masadyang balay,*
> *masadyang balay.*

> With Jesus in the family, happy, happy home;
> Happy, happy home
> Happy, happy home.

Indeed, with Jesus in the family, the home is happy. Despite my significant shortcomings, God at least to some extent has allowed me to be a leader with my family. The Bible cautions us, "Let another man praise you, and not your own mouth; a stranger, and not your own lips" (Proverbs 27:2). I want to reiterate that my purpose is not to bring praise to me, but rather to show how love given to others is multiplied and ultimately brings glory to God. With that caveat, and with gratefulness to God, allow me to share the following excerpts of letters and cards I have received from my own beloved wife and children:

From Marlou, on our 25th wedding anniversary, June 17, 1997:

Bo, my beloved husband, you're a jewel of a father to our children and a treasure of a husband to me. How wonderfully blessed I am to have you not only as my husband, my best friend, my love, but also as the father and best friend of our children. When you walked into my life and into my heart, I never imagined the enormity of the blessing the Lord had heaped upon me.

Through the years to this very day, I've realized, grasped, and acknowledged the priceless gift God has given me some 29 years ago. Daily, I thank God for you. You're indeed the best thing that ever happened to me. Forever I'll cherish, love, and esteem you. You're the perfect man for me, and I deeply thank God for you. What a privilege, a joy, a blessing, to face each day with you by my side. What a great honor to have you as the perfect father for Benjie, David, Felisa, and Jim. I truly love you and treasure your love.

From Benjie Barredo, our oldest son
(excerpted from a 2019 interview by a book writer):

My father, Bo Barredo, is an amazing father and one whom I am proud to call my Papa, my friend, my confidant and my role model. He is encouraging, loving, generous, and humble. Growing up, my life has been impacted by him in so many ways. He is as close to the definition of what a true and real father is. He made sure we were provided for and encouraged us to do our best and taught us to love God's people. He has a special heart for what he calls the underdog—the poor and marginalized. Growing up modestly, we were never rich, but there was a lot of love in our home. He also emphasized to us to be grateful and always to say thank you for everything and anything . . . These things resonate with me to this day, and I will try to pass these on to my own children as I try to emulate a lot of his qualities. I can only hope and pray that I am even just half the man that he is.

Thoughts shared by Judge David C. Barredo,
our second oldest son:

Papa, God has really loved us for giving you to us as our father and best friend. Thank you so much for touching our lives and mentoring us all these years. Thank you for being the best example of how a Christian father, man, and friend should be. I love you, Papa. . . . It is a special blessing to have had all these years, a front row seat to witness a special servant of the Lord living out his faith, fully trusting God, loving his family and God's servants all over the world. You have lived a life lived for others. Thank you for choosing the theme for our family—". . . As for me and my house, we will serve the Lord." Our prayer is for the Lord to grant you your desire to continue many, many more years of serving Him. You have impacted us and many people around the world. God the Father's love flows through you and blesses us and many others. We are very blessed to have you as father and as grandfather of our children.

Thoughts shared in cards that Felisa, our only daughter, sent in 1997 and 2003:

Dearest Papa, you're a wonderful father. You are an amazing person. Your generosity towards other people is humbling. Your great love for God, your family, and your friends can be seen. Your humility surprises even the meekest of God's people. Your words of wisdom are a treasure. Understanding is another trait which you possess. We can come to you for help on our mistakes knowing that you will have a listening ear. You know when to laugh and smile and when to have a shoulder one can cry on. I just wanted to tell you that I love you very much and I am grateful to have a wonderful idea of what true, godly love is like. Your and Mama's relationship is one I desire to emulate when the right man comes in God's appointed time.

Thoughts shared by Jim, our youngest son, in a Father's Day card:

Dear Papa, Happy Father's Day!

Other terms that have come to mind are: love, time, encouragement, patience, and, above all—an example of what it means to be a God-fearing father and husband. Your impact on my life cannot be quantified or adequately captured by words, but I am eternally grateful for you, Papa. I will always cherish our times of reflection, laughter, joy, prayer, and bonding, and I hope that my son and I can have the same loving relationship you and I have. . . . Thank you for living your life in such a way that inspires others, including me, to seek after God and to put others first. I was so touched when you brought up La Salle College and the opportunity to express gratitude for the school and what it represents. I hope our gift can serve as our expression of gratitude since we are also *direct by-products of the school. Praise the Lord for using your time there to bring you and Mama together! . . . I'm looking forward to more time with you in the years to come!*

Love, Jim

These and other thoughts that my wife and children have shared over the years are more precious to me than thousands of pieces of silver and gold. I hope they would say the same about things that I have said or written about them.

Concluding Remarks

After a lawyer has presented his case, he gives his concluding remarks, and then he rests his case. I hope the evidence I have brought has sufficiently testified to the power of love. When we fall in love with the God of Missions—the God who commands us, "Declare his glory among the nations. His wonders among all people"—we are motivated and empowered by the Spirit to love others. And best of all, we are motivated and empowered to love God more.

This love story never ends. It continues as a big celebration in heaven. Can you imagine the joy we will experience standing in the presence of the Lord Jesus, surrounded by others we have loved well? Some may be there strictly *because* we loved them well. Perhaps we loved them personally, or maybe we loved them by giving sacrificially to a native missionary on a remote island who told them about Jesus. Isn't this the kind of legacy we all want?

We know how much God loves us, and we have put our trust in his love.
God is love, and all who live in love live in God, and God lives in them.
And as we live in God, our love grows more perfect.
So we will not be afraid on the day of judgment, but we can face him
with confidence because we live like Jesus here in this world.
1 JOHN 4:16–17 NLT

1 JOHN
3:1

*See what great love the Father
has lavished on us,
that we should be called children of God!
And that is what we are! (NIV)*

THE ONE WHO WILL MORE THAN MAKE IT UP TO US

One of my favorite songs that I often sing from my heart is "O Jesus, I Have Promised," which relates to my love and service for the God of Missions. It starts with the following lyrics:

O Jesus, I have promised
To serve thee to the end;
Be thou forever near me,
My Master and my friend;
I shall not fear the battle
If thou art by my side,
Nor wander from the pathway
If thou wilt be my guide . . .

During my tenure as president of ANM, I asked the Lord to guide me in preparing a succession plan. I believe that every Christian leader should prepare for the future by raising up a Joshua, Solomon, Joseph, or Timothy. There is much truth in the saying, "There is no success without a successor." Ideally, such a successor should be complemented by a team of godly leaders. Leaders are needed, not just managers.

I had already begun sharing these views with Oliver Asher, who had worked by my side for twenty-one years. On my twelfth anniversary as the ministry's primary leader, I began to pray about the transition more earnestly. Then, on a sunny day during the last week of October 2017, while driving on scenic Virginia Route 151 towards the ANM office, I felt strongly in my heart that it was time to discuss this with Oliver and the leadership team.

We had these discussions, and on the following Saturday, I announced at the ANM board meeting my decision to step down as president. When queried by the surprised board about my reason, I simply said, "It's about time." I then recommended a leadership team with Oliver as president. After long hours of prayerful deliberation, the board gave its approval. I had prepared Marlou for this a year in advance, but it still caught her off guard. Because of the exciting move of the Lord upon our lives and the ministry, the years had flown by.

Announcing the Leadership Change

In the spring 2018 issue of *ANM World Missions* magazine, I wrote the following about the transition:

> The growth of the work of the Lord at Advancing Native Missions, even with its share of seasons of plateaus, has always been on the upward trajectory. From a few indigenous ministry partners overseas in 1992, we now have over 250 partners in more than 80 countries. From the few hundred native missionaries we served in the initial years, we now have the honor and blessing of serving more than 8,000. Together they are bringing the Gospel to hundreds of unreached people groups.
>
> There is also growth from within. Starting with four workers in its first two years, ANM now has around 50 full-time staff workers and more than 20 volunteers on site and on call. The Lord has also trusted us with His resources. We started with $55,000 in contributions during our first year of operation, and in 2016 we received the highest cash offerings for missions in our history: over $8 million cash and over $4 million in gifts-in-kind.
>
> Most recently, an NGO watchdog, MinistryVoice, gave us the distinct recognition of being one of the "92 Most Trusted U. S. Non-Profits." Also, TheologyDegrees.org classed ANM among

the "Top Ten Most Amazing Christian Charities." Another non-profit watchdog, GuideStar, gave us their highest recognition for integrity—the "Platinum Seal of Transparency." And Ministry Watch gave us their highest rating—five stars.[28]

So, why the sudden decision on my part to step down now from the top post of president to become ANM's global ambassador? The answer is clear and simple: I believe it's the Lord's timing and purpose. The Bible reminds me, "To everything there is a season, A time for every purpose under heaven" (Ecclesiastes 3:1).

One expert and author on leadership, Mike Myatt, who many consider to be the top CEO coach, has pointed out, "Great leaders discover pivot points and transitions that create a certain rhythm and balance . . .." I don't claim to be a great leader, but I pray to be sensitive to the Lord's ways, changes, and transitions, and I strive to take commensurate actions in humble obedience.

My first awareness that we were entering a major pivot point, when I might transition into something else, was during an evaluation of ANM by an excellent professional consultant last year. He identified the following three major strengths the Lord has given us:

1. "A compelling core mission and clear biblical vision."

2. "A widespread passion for the mission of the organization among its team members, and a sincere, deep-rooted love for one another and for the missionaries we serve."

3. "The blessing of a diversely gifted, passionate, and much-loved leader, who is inspiring, articulate, and caring.

He finished by saying, "These core and compelling strengths provide a major foundation to build upon, and they are not universally found in all non-profit ministries."

---

[28] A copy of the report is in Appendix C.

I took the above as a loving commendation from the Lord, who called me in 1986 to his service. I also took it as a signal of the end of my term as president. I spent days in prayer thinking of the answers to an interesting query raised in the report: What would be the profile of the next leader? Would he be operational? Inspirational? Strategic?

The Next Generation of Leadership

To my delight, the Lord has given us several co-leaders, all of whom fit these three profiles in varying degrees. Oliver Asher's strong suit is inspirational; George Ainsworth's gifts are primarily operational; and Dick Prins is blessed with strategic skills. And P. R. Misra from India represents so well the heart, passion, and "color and accent" of most native missionaries we serve.

My transition creates rhythm and balance on the issue of succession. The Lord, by his grace, has allowed us to prepare an excellent leadership team to succeed me, with Oliver as president, Dick Prins as CEO, George Ainsworth continuing as COO, and P. R. Misra as international president (still under Oliver).

Last November 4, the ANM board approved my strong recommendation for this divinely supplied and balanced leadership team, composed of godly, highly competent, and trustworthy brothers I love. I thank God for leading us together all these years to create a culture of teamwork, loving relationships, and self-sacrifice.

My years as ANM's primary leader were strengthened by the precious members of our staff, our beloved donors and friends, and all the faithful and fruitful native missionaries God has accorded us the honor of serving.

Encouraging feedback on the change prompted Oliver to email me, "Brother Bo, I believe we are receiving these positive responses because you are a gracious and magnanimous leader who properly prepared the groundwork for the transition of leadership. Thank you for your proactive preparation."

Regarding my subsequent appointment as ANM's global ambassador, a much-respected missionary partner reaching unreached Aeta aborigines in the Philippines says it for all the brothers we serve: "Indeed, Brother Bo's new title and responsibility is a great blessing to us in the field because he has more time now to come and visit and encourage us. He is now free to pray with us, laugh with us, cry with us, and fellowship with us in the field. He can now give more attention and focus to advocating for the needs of ANM as well as the needs of ANM missionaries all over the world."

As my season of developing ANM's culture of leadership comes to an end, please pray with us. We are asking the Lord to trust ANM with additional resources to recruit more young leaders and acquire technology that will help us strategically improve how we work together and serve the Lord's people. We believe this growth will enable those we serve to declare God's glory among all the nations, tribes, and language groups—'til all hear!

"Father God, Will You Remember Me?"

In the early days after I stepped down as leader of ANM, I felt a sense of peace. I had obeyed what I believed were God's instructions and timing. However, as more days passed, a deep sense of loss crept over me. With some amount of grieving, I began asking the Lord, "Father God, will you remember me?" I thought about how some prominent figures in the Bible—Nehemiah, Jeremiah, Hezekiah, and King David to name a few—had asked God this question. And I recalled how the second thief on the cross had made this request of the Lord Jesus.

The matter of being remembered became a little more poignant when I realized that once I returned the Honda CRV that ANM had assigned to us, we would be without a vehicle of our own. (I was charged a certain amount per mile if I used the car for personal use, but there was no charge when I used it for ministry purposes.

I've noticed that the Lord seems to delight in surprising the givers of gifts with much greater gifts than they gave.

Marlou would sometimes say, "But you are doing ministry almost all the time, even in your sleep!" I would just respond with a smile.)

At the fateful ANM board meeting when I announced that I was stepping down, without being asked, I shared with the board my financial status as a matter of accountability. Marlou was present when I explained that we still had a remaining balance of about $100,000 on our home mortgage, an outstanding home equity loan of about $30,000, and credit card debt of almost $5,000. We had no savings and no retirement funds, except for social security. I humbly requested that the board help us pay off our credit card balances, which they kindly agreed to do.

In the weeks that followed, I continued to seek from my Heavenly Father an answer to my question, "Will you remember me?" I felt confident that the Lord would answer my prayer in a way that I would recognize as coming from him. In the "Wristwatch Story" of Chapter 10, I related how the pastor who had almost no material possessions was so surprised to receive the blessing of a nice watch. I've noticed that the Lord seems to delight in surprising the givers of gifts with much greater gifts than they gave. God is love, and he gives access to those who love him. Not long after that, a clear answer came from the God who never disappoints.

The Highlander Story

One day, as Marlou and I were discussing our need for our very own car to take us around, we came face-to-face with the realization that we were old enough to retire (although our view is that the Lord's servants never retire). I shared with her that I had already inspected a good used vehicle at Madison Motors, which was owned by my close friend Dwight Foster. "It's a five-year-old Toyota Highlander with 115,000 miles on it," I informed her. "The price is $15,000, and I am praying that a down payment of $4,000 will be acceptable."

"And where will you get your down payment?" Marlou asked with a smile.

"I'll borrow $1,000 from each of our four children in the form of a soft loan," I answered.

"Well, you will have to do that by yourself," she replied. "I feel awkward borrowing money from our children, especially from Felisa and Andrew, who are missionaries as we are."

In a prayerful attitude, I approached our three sons: Benjie, David, and Jim. Our daughters-in-law were the ones who happily handed us their checks, adding that we didn't have to pay them back. I decided not to approach Felisa and Andrew, but when they heard of our need, they pleaded with me to accept their $1,000 check.

A week prior to my planned visit to Madison Motors to buy the used Highlander, Marlou and I attended a memorial service for the beloved wife of a much-loved friend. After the service, as I was walking to our Honda CRV that belonged to ANM, I heard a familiar voice calling from behind, "Bo, wait for me!" It was one of my closest friends. He sidled up to me, and as we continued walking, he said, "Brother, why do you look so sad?"

"Who would not look sad, coming from that memorial service?" I replied with a forced smile.

"No, no, your sadness seems different," he said. "What is it, Bo?"

Surprised by his perceptiveness and knowing that I was in the presence of a trusted friend, I shared openly about our car situation. To my surprise, I even took out my wallet and showed him the checks our children had given us. As he listened, I felt like a little boy pouring out my heart.

When I had finished, he said with a glint in his eyes, "Please come and visit us, and bring Marlou with you." We set a time, and he went on his way.

When the day of our appointment arrived, my friend and his beloved wife, a woman of great character, met Marlou and me in a Bob Evans restaurant near their place. After we had eaten, the husband shared that they would like to give us something to help with our transportation need. Marlou and I looked at each other, surprised. The wife added, "But we have two conditions: First, you must not divulge our names to anyone. Second, you must not give it away."

When she said this last sentence, Marlou gave me a poke. "Did you hear that?"

"Yes, yes!" I promised.

The husband immediately took Marlou and me to a nearby Toyota dealership and bought us a spanking new Toyota Highlander—for cash! The whole affair was almost surreal. We were speechless. We couldn't believe we had a brand-new SUV. Gratitude to the God Almighty flooded our hearts. We profusely thanked our friend for his generosity, which had caught us completely by surprise. This was our first new car—ever!

Father, Is This Really from You?

A few days later, while I was driving the new Highlander from the dealership to our home, I felt like I was in a dream. The SUV and I were floating along the highway. It was so comfortable, so very comfortable. But then I found myself asking the Lord, "Father, is this new car really a gift from you? O Father, you are so wonderful, but is this really from you? Do you really care that much for us?"

Upon arriving home, Marlou and I laid hands on the new vehicle and in thanksgiving solemnly prayed a blessing over it. We also prayed a blessing over the family of the donors of the car. The Highlander became our "feel-good" place. When we are inside it, we are reminded of our Father's love. When we drive it, we almost always pray blessings over the couple who gave it to us and their family. But the question still lurked in my mind, "Father, do you truly love me this much? Is this car really a gift from you?"

Around eight months later, after we had enjoyed driving the Highlander several thousand miles, I received a call from the friend who had given it to us. "Bo, I have to apologize," he said, "but my wife would like me to take back your Highlander."

My mind went blank for a moment. The thought flashed through my mind, "The Lord giveth and the Lord taketh away. This is like Job!" I took a deep breath. "Oh, yes, my brother, by all means you can." As I said these words, I pretended I was glad that he called. But inside, my heart was starting to break.

"Bo, I have to apologize," he said, "but my wife would like me to take back your Highlander."

Before I could say anything else, my friend added, "I really could not understand it, Bo. My wife is doing something that is out of character for her. She is very careful with our money, and normally, she would not even buy herself a new dress. But now, she wants me to return your Highlander to the Toyota dealership and buy you another new one with leather seats."

I was speechless. Under my breath I muttered, "Father, it's you! That's lavish love! *Amay, kapalangga-palangga ko gid sa imo!*" (Father, I really love, love you so much!)

My friend then proceeded to fill me in on the whole story. When he and his wife had recently visited the same Toyota dealership to check out cars for their family's use, one vehicle they looked at was a Highlander. After the test drive, the wife said, "I don't like the cloth seats on this car. I'm glad you bought Bo and Marlou one with the leather seats."

Taken aback, my friend replied to his wife, "Honey, the Barredos are already very happy with their new Highlander that has cloth seats."

"No! They should have one with leather seats," she insisted. "You need to return their car and get them a new one with leather seats."

On Thanksgiving Day of 2017, we were again at a Toyota dealership, where the Lord gave us a new Highlander with leather seats. It was costly, but our Lord owns the cattle on a thousand hills. I believe this manifestation of my Father's presence was his way of telling me, "I will remember you."

God never disappoints:

"God is not man, that he should lie, or a son of man,
that he should change his mind.
Has he said, and he will not do it?
Or has he spoken, and he will not fulfill it?" ESV

NUMBERS 23:19 ESV

God's love is lavish:

See what great love the Father has lavished on us, that we should be
called children of God! And that is what we are!

1 JOHN 3:1 NIV

He who did not spare His own Son, but delivered Him up for us all,
how shall He not with Him also freely give us all things?

ROMANS 8:32

God remembers:

Remember these, O Jacob, and Israel, for you are My servant;
I have formed you, you are My servant;
O Israel, you will not be forgotten by Me!

ISAIAH 44:21

I remember you, The kindness of your youth,
The love of your betrothal, When you went after Me
in the wilderness, In a land not sown.

JEREMIAH 2:2

He will not leave you nor forsake you.

DEUTERONOMY 31:6

Marlou's Letter to the Family

While Marlou and I were having breakfast on February 27, 2021, she suddenly stopped eating and started typing on her iPhone. As her fingers flicked, the tears flowed. Twice, I asked her why she was crying, but she didn't answer. When she finished typing, she showed me the letter she had written. After I read it, we raised her phone towards heaven and offered a prayer of thanksgiving to God. Then we sent the letter as an email to our four children and their families.[29] The following is what she wrote:

To all the members of our family,

Today, February 27, thirty years ago, we landed close to midnight at Dulles International Airport, Washington, DC. We walked out of the terminal to a freezing 27F in our Philippine summer cotton wear! The Lord brought our young family to this country for the first time. By faith, we had pulled up our stakes from the land of our birth to obey God's call in our lives. We did not know what awaited us, but compelled by God's love and the desire to obey His will and please Him pursuant to Isaiah 43:18-19, we bade goodbye to dear family and beloved friends to embark on a journey of faith.

It was not an easy journey. It was marked by deep sadness because we were leaving behind dearly loved ones (the deepest pain was leaving behind my elderly widowed mother) to go to a foreign land. Yet, at the same time, we were filled with hopeful anticipation about what God had in store for us. It was a journey of trials and triumphs, of disappointments and victories, of seeming obstacles and break-throughs. All throughout this thirty-year journey of ours, God has never left us nor forsaken us, JUST AS HE PROMISED. He has always been there for us—faithful, loving, providing, protecting, strengthening, encouraging, affirming, leading, guiding, upholding, prospering.

You all have played such a significant and invaluable part in our family's faith journey. Your Papa and I thank you all so much. We never heard any complaints nor murmurings from anyone of you. YOU HAVE INSPIRED US BEYOND WORDS. God has proved Himself faithful and strong on our behalf these past thirty years. He has

---

[29] Before the day was over, we also sent the letter to several friends, many of whom sent kind responses. Their thoughtful comments can be found in Appendix D.

brought all of us thus far, and for this we are deeply grateful. He has granted us the very beautiful blessing of touching and influencing many lives, for His glory. On this day let us also remember and thank God for all those dear ones WHO HAVE IN TURN BLESSED AND LOVINGLY TOUCHED OUR LIVES.

Happy thirtieth anniversary, Benjie, David, Inday Felisa, and Jim! Papa and I are so proud of every one of you. We love you all so much! And we thank God for blessing us with wonderful, loving, and godly children-in-law, Tanya, Jenn, Andrew, and Kris, and beautiful, lovable, and delightful grandchildren, Luke, Halle, Jessica, David, Eric, Georgia, Darcy, Jude, and Isaiah, whom we all love so very much!

Indeed, the Lord our God has always honored your father's consistent encouragement to all of us during this journey—"The God whom we love and serve is One who will more than make it up to us . . ."

Much love and thanks,

Mama and Papa

Let's Finish the Task

A remarkable story of perseverance occurred at the 1968 Olympics in Mexico City. That year, Tanzania formed its first Olympic committee and, among other athletes, sent John Stephen Akhwari to compete in the marathon. He had not trained at such a high altitude, and nearly halfway through the race his legs began to cramp. When some jockeying for positions occurred, Akhwari stumbled and fell, severely injuring his knees.

Mamo Wolde of Ethiopia finished the race in two hours, twenty minutes, and twenty-six seconds. About an hour later, after the sun had set and the crowd had thinned, as the officials were preparing to award the medals, John Stephen Akhwari came stumbling through the entrance to the stadium and hobbled across the finish line. Eighteen of the seventy-five marathoners had failed to finish, but Akhwari completed the race.

When an interviewer later asked Akhwari why he kept on running in such pain and disability, he answered, "My country did not send me five thousand miles to start the race; they sent me five thousand miles to finish it."

Beloved, the race was started long ago. The question is, will we finish it? ANM partners with 260 indigenous ministries in more than one hundred countries that have at least 13,500 native missionaries on the field. They know the culture and the language. They are often multilingual, and they can communicate the Gospel effectively. Yet so many of them struggle because they lack generators, video projectors, motorcycles, bicycles, vehicles, and many lesser items that they need to reach the furthest outpost and finish the task.

Our Lord promised, "and this gospel of the kingdom will be preached in all the world as a witness to all the nations, and then the end will come" (Matthew 24:14). Will we be partners in helping that last tribe to hear? Are we investing our lives, time, and treasure in this greatest of causes? Are we bidding the Lord to return to claim his own?

Just think of the power that lies in our hands. Our gifts can help indigenous missionaries go up the river farther, climb the mountain higher, walk into the forest deeper, and survey the desert wider to find the last tribe and the last people group to hear the Gospel. These missionaries are already ministering among 1,500 people groups classified as "unreached."

For God's glory and the love of our neighbor, let's finish the task. Till all hear!

REVELATION
7:9-12

*After this I looked, and there before me was a great multitude that no one could count, from every nation, tribe, people and language, standing before the throne and before the Lamb.
They were wearing white robes and were holding palm branches in their hands. And they cried out in a loud voice:*

> *"Salvation belongs to our God,*
> *who sits on the throne,*
> *and to the Lamb."*

All the angels were standing around the throne and around the elders and the four living creatures. They fell down on their faces before the throne and worshiped God, saying:

> *"Amen!*
> *Praise and glory*
> *and wisdom and thanks and honor*
> *and power and strength*
> *be to our God for ever and ever.*
> *Amen!" (NIV)*

EPILOGUE

Bo Barredo, the co-founder and president emeritus of Advancing Native Missions, continues to serve the Lord as ANM's Global Ambassador. He travels on mission trips overseas to visit, encourage, and help equip native missionaries. A dynamic missions speaker, Bo also speaks across the US in church and group meetings and at conferences.

Marlou Barredo continues to serve as Bo's executive assistant and as ANM's regional director for Southeast Asia covering the mission fields of the Philippines, Laos, Thailand, and Cambodia. For the past eighteen years, she and Bo have lived in the same simple townhouse in the community of Crozet, VA, twelve miles from the ANM offices.

On June 18, 2022, Bo and Marlou celebrated their fiftieth wedding anniversary. More than 150 friends and family members gathered for a moving renewal of vows ceremony at International Christian Church in Virginia Beach. This was the church that Bo joined when he first came to America in 1986.

"But as for me and my house, we will serve the LORD" (Joshua 24:15).

Michael Dowling, editor and publisher of this book, provides ghostwriting and editing services to thought leaders through his company, Wool Street Writers. He also is the author of *Frog's Rainy-Day Story and Other Fables*, the award-winning Christian picture book that his wife, Sarah Buell Dowling, illustrated. Through their ministry, Creators for Christ, Michael and Sarah create literature and art that open hearts and minds to the truth, beauty, and love of God as revealed in Scripture and Creation. The couple resides in a log cabin overlooking the Cumberland River in Nashville, TN.

Michael and Sarah Dowling with Bo and Marlou at their anniversary celebration.

APPENDIX A

The Daily Progress Article

As mentioned in Chapter 5, Bo Barredo and Rod Montgomery in August 1988 met with the editors of the Charlottesville, Virginia, newspaper, *The Daily Progress*, to discuss various concerns that had been raised about the operations of Christian Aid. The article below was the result:

Aid Mission Shows More Than Thorns

By Rachel Buchanan
of The Progress Staff

Progress Photo by Chris McKenney

Bo Barredo, Left, And Rod Montgomery
Mission Supports Charities Around The World

Bo Barredo is a "hidden person in a hidden land," the type of missionary the Christian Aid Mission promotes in its brochures and magazines.

But Barredo, a 38-year-old Filipino, is a modest man, reticent until he begins speaking about his travels to nearly 300 rural towns and villages across the 7,187 islands that make up the Philippines.

Barredo oversees the rural churches and community organizations that receive aid from the Charlottesville-based Christian Aid Mission.

Opening a 12-inch by 14-inch cardboard box that he uses as a briefcase, Barredo pulls out the photographs he took of some Christian Aid recipients. Among his 20 or 30 photographs are pictures of a one-armed missionary in front of the church he built by himself, converted "scavengers" and the church they built near their home in the Manila trash dump, a new church to serve the 3,000 residents of a tiny volcanic island and the corpse of a 20-year-old missionary who was shot by communist guerrillas while he was preaching in a rural church.

Barredo tells of another Christian beneficiary, Pastor Romualdo Lindayao, who approached Christian Aid after his rural mountain church was burned by communist guerrillas.

Barredo said Lindayao sold the family horse to buy materials to build the new church but could no longer travel to the remote mountainous area of his parish.

Please See MISSION, Page B2

★ *Mission*

Continued From Page B1

Barredo said Christian Aid provided Lindayao with a horse at a cost of about $100.

"We look for the people no one else will help," Barredo said. "We respond to special needs."

Barredo has been living in Charlottesville for the past two months, reporting to the mission about the Filipino charities it supports. He is scheduled to return to the Philippines in late August with his wife and four children. He said he is not concerned about the "disappointing stories" that have been reported about the mission during his stay here.

In June, the Christian Aid Mission was expelled from the Evangelical Council for Financial Accountability, a Christian watchdog organization in Herndon that offers donors an independent assurance that donations are properly managed.

Clarence Reimer, a spokesman for the ECFA, said the mission was expelled partly due to a fund-raising program that involved mission employees sending monetary "gifts" to a Brooklyn donor, Charles Alsdorf.

Alsdorf matched the employee "gifts" and sent the funds to the mission, who issued him a receipt for the entire contribution.

Robert Finley, director of the mission, said the Alsdorf program was stopped in November 1987, and said he expects to be reinstated with the 500-member Herndon-based group after an ECFA hearing next month.

Barredo, who received his law degree from La Salle College in the Philippines, said he also expects the mission to be reinstated but emphasized that readmittance to the ECFA is not as important as carrying on the mission's work in India, East Asia, Africa and South America.

"We must continue our work," Barredo said. "The feeding centers, orphanages, churches and medical centers are relying on us."

During the 1986-1987 fiscal year, the mission raised $2.99 million for charities it sponsors around the world, according to its annual report.

Rod Montgomery, office manager for the missionary, said he estimates that the 1987-1988 annual report will show a 13 percent increase in donations.

In the past 10 years, donations have increased 29.4 percent, according to the 1986 financial report.

Sponsoring what it calls the "hidden missionaries," Christian Aid helped 230 indigenous church organizations in 1986 to raise funds to build churches, feed the poor, house orphans, set up bible schools and set up medical facilities, Montgomery said.

Christian Aid literature says the mission does not send North American missionaries to other countries, instead foreign ministries approach the mission and ask for help in fund raising.

Barredo said local ministries are investigated and judged according to their spiritual quality, evangelical doctrine, the integrity of their financial system, the love and dynamism of their workers, and the growth potential of their ministry.

Once a ministry is accepted by Christian Aid, the mission will solicit funds for the ministry from the nearly 300 churches across the United States and Canada that regularly donate to Christian Aid.

The funds will then be sent to the foreign ministries, minus any expense such as postage or travel.

To raise funds, Christian Aid also sponsors trips for foreign missionaries to come to the United States and lecture in churches across the country.

"You can't just look at our thorns," Montgomery said Tuesday. "You have to see the petals and smell the fragrance, too."

$\mathcal{A}$PPENDIX $\mathcal{B}$

Excerpts from Letters of Commendation

As mentioned in Chapter 6, the commendations of Bo Barredo below were vital for establishing the credibility of Advancing Native Missions during the early days of the ministry.—Editor

It is an honor to me to commend Bo as a sincere and devoted follower of our Lord Jesus Christ. He has always come among us in humility, with a powerful grace enablement from the Lord, to communicate His heart for the lost. His messages have not only been informative regarding missions but have also stirred our hearts to greater love for and devotion to the Lord.

The Bible says, "Many a man proclaims his own loyalty, but who can find a trustworthy man" (Proverbs 20:6 HCSB). I believe such a man is found in Bo Barredo.

CHUCK TEMPLE
Pastor, Christian Fellowship Church, Bellefontaine, Ohio

Bo is a very humble man. He is courteous and has sensitivity unequalled by most men. His character and integrity are above reproach, and his love for Christ is commendable.

Bo presents well the case for Advancing Native Missions. He and his wife both left substantial positions of employment to work full time to advance the kingdom of God.

I unreservedly commend Bo to you and encourage you to invite him to minister to your congregation. He is totally submissive to the local pastor's authority and God uses him to bless folks wherever he speaks. I'm confident your people would be richly blessed through his ministry in your midst.

GERALD A. RIPLEY JR.
Pastor, Abundant Life Church, San Antonio, Texas

It is a joy and a privilege for me to be able to wholeheartedly and unreservedly commend to you the life and ministry of our dear brother Benjamin Barredo, Jr. His authentic humility toward others and before God makes him a delight to serve with. He never speaks ill of anyone, nor impugns anyone's motives. His goal is always to build up others. I commend Bo Barredo and his ministry to everyone who wants to be used by the Lord to reach this generation for Christ. By the grace of God, you will be challenged, strengthened, and shown a practical path to follow.

GEORGE AINSWORTH
Associate Pastor, Christ Community Church,
Charlottesville, Virginia

Having been ordained as a Lutheran pastor in 1952 and having served four different Lutheran churches; also, having had a Skid Row ministry in Los Angeles, California, for seventeen years, I have come in contact with many people from all walks of life. Few people have so impressed me as Bo Barredo; he is truly one of God's chosen vessels!

I was so blessed to work in close association with Bo for four years. During that time, I observed Bo's integrity, faithfulness, and sincerity. His love for the Lord and commitment to winning souls for the Lord is a top priority for him. He was always a real team player and was encouraging and compassionate with his fellow staff members. He was truly loved by all.

I was so impressed with Bo's Christian character, intelligence, training, leadership and dedicated family that I recommended him twice, by letter, for the position of President for the organization for which he was working.

So it is a privilege for me to give the highest recommendation for Bo Barredo for your support and prayers. To invite him to your church will be a great blessing for you as you see God's mighty power working through him.

GORDON SHIRA

Pastor, Salvation Army, Charlottesville, Virginia

November 23, 1992

Dear Friends of Brother Bo Barredo,

My name is Carl Gordon, and before my resignation (after twenty years) from Christian Aid last September, I was its Overseas Director. My work entailed overseeing indigenous missions work in almost sixty countries and working directly with Christian Aid's field staff missionaries known as Missions Researchers.

The one working with us in the Philippines was Bo Barredo. He travels extensively to survey, evaluate, and encourage native missions in the different islands of his country and sacrificially leaves his family three to four months each year to report in the US churches on behalf of Christian Aid and indigenous missions.

I am writing to give you my personal assessment of the person, work, and ministry of Brother Barredo. It has been my greatest pleasure to have worked directly with this wonderful saintly man for the past six years and to have known his heart and personal integrity. Bo is his brother's keeper. He is a deeply committed team person who will stand with those who are standing for the Lord and his people.

Working with a very low profile and reporting to us under the pen name of "Rey Siervo," our brother Bo was almost killed several times by communist guerrillas known as the New People's Army (NPA) while working in the NPA-controlled villages of the Philippines. Many Christian workers have died violently in their hands.

In July 1989, when Christian Aid's evangelistic work through indigenous workers in the Philippines was "exposed" in the front page of a Filipino daily newspaper as helping fight insurgency, we greatly feared for his life and the safety of his family. We made plans to evacuate him and his family to the US (we could do no less for a very faithful and fruitful servant), but he declined our offer and faithfully continued his dangerous work.

This October, Bo and I, together with other brethren, opened, by faith, a new work—ADVANCING NATIVE MISSIONS—to serve as "another well" from which more native missionaries around the world can drink. He continues to show the same desire to lay his life down for the Lord Jesus and His poor missionaries by stepping out in faith from Christian Aid. He could have conveniently stayed and continued to receive his living allowance, but he has chosen to throw himself and his family at God's mercy.

Please continue to pray for this spiritually sensitive man of God who loves the brethren and only desires to serve and honor the Lord and his poor native missionaries in the un-evangelized countries of the world.

Your brother in Christ,

CARL A. GORDON

APPENDIX C

Below is the report from MinistryWatch mentioned in Chapter 16. ANM received one of the highest ratings.

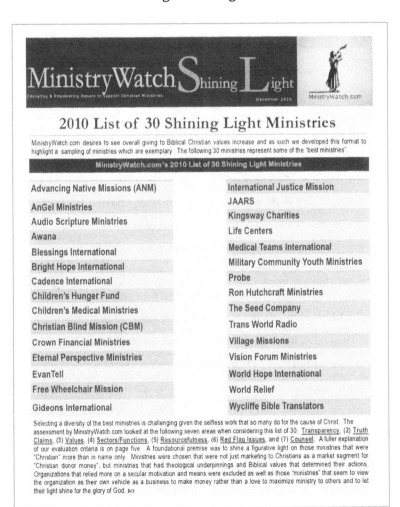

MinistryWatch Shining Light

Educating & Empowering Donors to Support Christian Ministries

December 2010 · MinistryWatch.com

2010 List of 30 Shining Light Ministries

MinistryWatch.com desires to see overall giving to Biblical Christian values increase and as such we developed this format to highlight a sampling of ministries which are exemplary. The following 30 ministries represent some of the "best ministries".

MinistryWatch.com's 2010 List of 30 Shining Light Ministries

Advancing Native Missions (ANM)	International Justice Mission
AnGel Ministries	JAARS
Audio Scripture Ministries	Kingsway Charities
Awana	Life Centers
Blessings International	Medical Teams International
Bright Hope International	Military Community Youth Ministries
Cadence International	Probe
Children's Hunger Fund	Ron Hutchcraft Ministries
Children's Medical Ministries	The Seed Company
Christian Blind Mission (CBM)	Trans World Radio
Crown Financial Ministries	Village Missions
Eternal Perspective Ministries	Vision Forum Ministries
EvanTell	World Hope International
Free Wheelchair Mission	World Relief
Gideons International	Wycliffe Bible Translators

Selecting a diversity of the best ministries is challenging given the selfless work that so many do for the cause of Christ. The assessment by MinistryWatch.com looked at the following seven areas when considering this list of 30: Transparency, (2) Truth Claims, (3) Values, (4) Sectors/Functions, (5) Resourcefulness, (6) Red Flag Issues, and (7) Counsel. A fuller explanation of our evaluation criteria is on page five. A foundational premise was to shine a figurative light on those ministries that were "Christian" more than in name only. Ministries were chosen that were not just marketing to Christians as a market segment for "Christian donor money", but ministries that had theological underpinnings and Biblical values that determined their actions. Organizations that relied more on a secular motivation and means were excluded as well as those "ministries" that seem to view the organization as their own vehicle as a business to make money rather than a love to maximize ministry to others and to let their light shine for the glory of God. ✍

PSALM
103:15-18

The life of mortals is like grass,
they flourish like a flower of the field;
the wind blows over it and it is gone,
and its place remembers it no more.
But from everlasting to everlasting
the LORD's love is with those who fear him,
and his righteousness with their children's children—
with those who keep his covenant
and remember to obey his precepts. (NIV)

$\mathcal{A}$PPENDIX $\mathcal{D}$

Loving Responses to Marlou's Family Letter

Chapter 16 includes a letter that Marlou wrote on February 27, 2021, to all the members of the Barredo family. Before the day was over, Bo and Marlou also emailed the letter to a certain number of close friends and members of the ANM staff. They were immensely blessed by the many kind and encouraging responses they received. A few of them are reproduced below:

"The day your feet hit the ground in this country thirty years ago was an absolute blessing and continues to be a blessing to us all. Thank you for coming to America and for the sacrifices you have made. We love and appreciate all you do."

—**BOB AND LINDA FRANTZ**, *Pennsylvania*

"Bo and Marlou, thank you so much for sharing your family letter. It was touching and your example provokes us in life and service. It has been and continues to be a privilege to know you and your family. We have been blessed beyond description by your presence in our lives. It stirs joy in our hearts and gratitude to our Lord for His kindness. We love you and your family!"

—**AUSTIN AND SUZANNE SPRUILL**, *Virginia*

"Dear ones, you both express yourselves and his love in such marvelous ways. Your words go right to my heart. You have endeared yourselves to us with love I never thought possible. Bo too put words and feelings together in a powerful and yet often gentle way. Two days ago our son Jeremy was yearning to see you, Bo. Know we love you two and your children and grandchildren. You have impacted and changed our lives. In His love and ours."

—**MARION BOND WEST**, *Georgia*

"Just a lovely letter from a lovely family I think to each other. God has been so good to you and made you such a blessing to hundreds of others through your obedience. It's a privilege to know you."

—**MAUREEN TAYLOR**, *United Kingdom*

"Thank you for sharing. What an amazing story of God's gracious favor and excellent gifts! Thank you, Lord! Psalms 85:12"

—**LESTER AND VELINA STRAW**, *Arkansas*

"We did not realize that when I met you in Bemidji, possibly in 1991, you had just recently arrived in America! It was agape at first sight! Thank You Jesus!!! We are especially grateful for the love and grace and faith in our Lord that you all have walked in from your beginnings, as well as the sacrifices, the disciplines in godliness and personal and corporate integrity in carrying out the mission God gave you!!"

—**STEVE AND BECKY RUDE**, *Minnesota*

"It is exciting to be able to 'look back' and see how God was moving and orchestrating His Will. To hear about your faith adventure from thirty years later gives me encouragement to trust Him in my life . . . thirty years into the future! To trust Him in the things of my life I can't yet see! To trust that He is there ahead of me 'orchestrating' His Will for me. Thank you for sharing a slice of life from your journey. Love you all."

—**PASTOR LINDSAY ELLIS**, *Virginia*

"I testify to the good fruit I have witnessed borne by Bo, Marlou, and family's humble examples, prayer-filled petitions, godly actions and servant leadership. The Barredo family has inspired me and many others to better understand our Lord God, His loving redemptive purposes, His compassionate hand, and the ability of Holy Spirit-led faith in action to reach out to His humble native servants through the hearts of supporters, who through prayer, materials and finances, are assisting the completion of His mission vision – an eternal servant people borne of His spirit."

—**RON TILLETT**, *Indiana*

"I will forever be grateful for your presence in and impact upon my life. Thank you and Marlou for obeying God and coming to America. Thank you for joining with Carl to launch ANM. And thank you for drawing me with cords of love into the ANM family."

—**ERIC VESS**, *Virginia*

"Thank you for sharing this touching tribute on the anniversary of your arriving in America. You are leaving a monumental legacy to your family for the glory of God. Our nation along with many other nations of the world have been extremely blessed by your family's decision to leave your homeland and sojourn in a country that was not your own. The kingdom of God has been advanced in many unreached nations of the earth through you pioneering work called Advancing Native Missions. My life and many others have been radically and positively changed by your decision to abandon all to follow Jesus. Somehow, I believe that the God we serve has made it up to you along the way. I am blessed to call you precious friends, co-workers and mentors in the Lord. I pray you will continue to build on your godly legacy. May your children and grandchildren carry that legacy for many generations."

—**OLIVER ASHER**, *Virginia*

"Those thirty years are like the way the Gospel of John describes the works of Jesus. If everything God did in those thirty years was to be written down, I do not believe the whole world could contain the stories. Thank you, Bo, and thank you, dear Barredo family. For being a blessing to SO MANY—and to me."

—**GEORGE AINSWORTH**, *Virginia*